AFRICAN ETHNOGRAPHIC STUDIES OF THE 20TH CENTURY

Volume 53

TOWN AND COUNTRY IN CENTRAL AND EASTERN AFRICA

TOWN AND COUNTRY IN CENTRAL AND EASTERN AFRICA

Studies Presented and Discussed at the Twelfth International African Seminar, Lusaka, September 1972

Edited by
DAVID PARKIN

LONDON AND NEW YORK

First published in 1975 by Oxford University Press for the International African Institute.

This edition first published in 2018
by Routledge
2 Park Square, Milton Park, Abingdon, Oxon OX14 4RN

and by Routledge
711 Third Avenue, New York, NY 10017

Routledge is an imprint of the Taylor & Francis Group, an informa business

© 1975 International African Institute

All rights reserved. No part of this book may be reprinted or reproduced or utilised in any form or by any electronic, mechanical, or other means, now known or hereafter invented, including photocopying and recording, or in any information storage or retrieval system, without permission in writing from the publishers.

Trademark notice: Product or corporate names may be trademarks or registered trademarks, and are used only for identification and explanation without intent to infringe.

British Library Cataloguing in Publication Data
A catalogue record for this book is available from the British Library

ISBN: 978-0-8153-8713-8 (Set)
ISBN: 978-0-429-48813-9 (Set) (ebk)
ISBN: 978-1-138-59130-1 (Volume 53) (hbk)
ISBN: 978-0-429-49045-3 (Volume 53) (ebk)

Publisher's Note
The publisher has gone to great lengths to ensure the quality of this reprint but points out that some imperfections in the original copies may be apparent.

Disclaimer
The publisher has made every effort to trace copyright holders and would welcome correspondence from those they have been unable to trace.

TOWN AND COUNTRY IN CENTRAL AND EASTERN AFRICA

Studies presented and discussed at the Twelfth International African Seminar, Lusaka, September 1972

Edited with an Introduction by
DAVID PARKIN

INTERNATIONAL AFRICAN INSTITUTE
1975

Oxford University Press, Ely House, London W.I

GLASGOW   NEW YORK   TORONTO   MELBOURNE   WELLINGTON
CAPE TOWN   IBADAN   NAIROBI   DAR ES SALAAM   LUSAKA   ADDIS ABABA
DELHI   BOMBAY   CALCUTTA   MADRAS   KARACHI   LAHORE   DACCA
KUALA LUMPUR   SINGAPORE   HONG KONG   TOKYO

ISBN 0 85302 044 2

© International African Institute 1975

*All rights reserved. No part of this publication may be reproduced,
stored in a retrieval system, or transmitted, in any form or by any means,
electronic, mechanical, photocopying, recording or otherwise, without
the prior permission of Oxford University Press*

TO

THE MEMORY OF

MAX GLUCKMAN

*Printed in Great Britain by
Clarke, Doble & Brendon Ltd., Plymouth*

Contents

	Page
FOREWORD	ix

PART I. INTRODUCTION
DAVID PARKIN
French Version

PART I. INTRODUCTION — 3

French Version — 45

PART II. SPECIAL STUDIES

MODELS OF MIGRATION

J. C. MITCHELL. *Nuffield College, Oxford*
Factors in rural male absenteeism in Rhodesia — 93

G. KINGSLEY GARBETT. *University of Aberdeen*
Circulatory migration in Rhodesia: towards a decision model — 113

PATRICK O. OHADIKE. *U.N. Economic Commission for Africa, Addis Ababa*
The evolving phenomena of migration and urbanization in Central Africa: a Zambian case — 126

DAVID PARKIN, *School of Oriental and African Studies, London*
Migration, settlement, and the politics of unemployment: a Nairobi case study — 145

MIGRATION AND RURAL DEVELOPMENT

TIBAMANYA mwene MUSHANGA. *University of Nairobi*
Notes on migration in Uganda — 159

VICTOR C. UCHENDU. *University of Illinois, Urbana*
Inter-rural migration and East African rural development — 165

H. U. E. THODEN VAN VELZEN. *University of Utrecht*
Controllers in rural Tanzania — 178

ELIZABETH COLSON. *University of California, Berkeley* and T. SCUDDER. *California Institute of Technology*
New economic relationships between the Gwembe Valley and the line of rail — 190

vi **Contents**

Page

THE RURAL-URBAN FLOW OF LANGUAGE, BELIEF, AND EDUCATIONAL OPPORTUNITY

PETER RIGBY. *University of Dar-es-Salaam* and FRED. D. LULE. *Makerere University*
Continuity and change in Kiganda religion in urban and peri-urban Kampala 213

MUBANGA E. KASHOKI. *University of Zambia*
Migration and language change: the inter-action of town and country 228

W. T. S. GOULD. *University of Liverpool*
Movements of schoolchildren and provision of secondary schools in Uganda 250

THE RURAL LINKS IN URBAN SETTLEMENT

AIDAN SOUTHALL. *University of Wisconsin*
Forms of ethnic linkage between town and country 265

PHILIP HALPENNY. *Makerere University*
Three styles of ethnic migration in Kisenyi, Kampala 276

CHRISTINE OBBO. *University of Wisconsin*
Migration and language change: the inter-action of town and country 228

J. VAN VELSEN. *University of Aberystwyth*
Urban squatters: problem or solution 294

A. B. CHILIVUMBO. *University of Malawi*
The ecology of social types in Blantyre 308

M. A. HIRST. *University of Western Australia*
The distribution of migrants in Kampala 319

CUMULATIVE BIBLIOGRAPHY 337

INDEX 359

Maps

		Page
I	Location of areas with male absentee rates.	96
II	Gwembe District and the Kariba Lake Basin.	200
III	Distribution of secondary schools in Uganda.	252
IV	Intensity and Density:	325
	Mubende, Acholi.	326
	Groups I, II, III, IV.	332–5

Foreword

The papers in this volume were presented at the 12th International African Seminar, held at the University of Zambia, Lusaka, from 11th to 20th September, 1972, under the chairmanship of Professor Jaap Van Velsen. In the absence of the Vice-Chancellor, the seminar was opened by the Pro-Vice-Chancellor, Professor J. Omer-Cooper.

For various reasons Professor Van Velsen has been unable to prepare the volume for publication and to provide an introduction. These tasks have been performed by Dr David Parkin, to whom the International African Institute is most grateful.

We are happy to express our continued gratitude to the Ford Foundation for its generous financial support which made possible both the holding of the seminar and the publication of these papers. And we thank the staff of the University of Zambia for their efforts and kindness which made the seminar itself so pleasant and memorable an occasion for the participants.

J.M.

PART I
INTRODUCTION

Town and Country in Central and Eastern Africa

INTRODUCTION

THE INTERNATIONAL CONTEXT OF MIGRATION AND DEVELOPMENT

Modern migrations in Western Africa have been extensively surveyed in an International African Institute book of that title which may be regarded in part as the sister volume to this (Amin 1974). As its title indicates, however, the present volume is not exclusively concerned with modern migratory patterns. Rather, it looks more broadly at a range of factors which mediate the development of social processes in both town and country: as well as migration, there is the ebb and flow of beliefs, ideologies, and educational and occupational opportunities. These may become located in a particular town or rural area but, insofar as they involve specific groups of people, remain responsive to developments affecting distant urban or rural members of the same social groups.

The volume, then, starts from the now generally accepted view that the rural and urban areas of East and Central Africa have to be regarded as part of a single field of relations made up of a vast criss-crossing of peoples, ideas, and resources. Indeed, it depends on the particular problem being investigated as to where the boundaries of this field are drawn. Though the spread of innovative ideas and ideologies may be extensive, the movement of people, cash, and material resources is generally more controlled by political and administrative factors, and this, if anything, justifies the isolation of East and Central Africa as a socio-geographical field of enquiry within which links have been established through labour migration. For the countries in which the studies making up this volume were carried out are Uganda, Kenya, and Tanzania ('East Africa'), and Zambia, Malawi, and Rhodesia or Zimbabwe ('Central Africa'), which, as part of their common colonial past under the British, were subject to a variety of attempts at economic integration. There was

4 *Introduction*

the colonial attempt in 1953 to translate the common fiscal and transportation system of Central Africa into a Federation, which broke up in 1963, shortly before Zambia's independence. There was also an abortive attempt in the early 1960s by the independent governments of East Africa to become a Federation on the same colonial foundation. The East African Economic Community set up in 1967 has, as yet, achieved very little. The East African Common Services Organization continues to deal with the shared network of railways, harbours, and posts and telecommunications, but the prospect of a Federation is remote. Political developments in the twelve years or so since independence in East and Central Africa have already redefined the colonial pattern of connections including those of labour migration, as we shall see. But important traces remain including the extensive use of English in various domains, and similar judicial and administrative systems, with Tanzania most removed from the colonial pattern. This said, it is unfortunate that budgetary limitations on space precluded contributions to this volume based on studies in, say, non-Anglophone Zaïre or Ethiopia, against which comparisons might have been made.

In view of the extensive West African bibliographical coverage and recent publication date of the volume edited by Amin, I have tried to confine references and comparisons in this introduction to work in East and Central Africa. This said, the volume on West African migrations raises important issues, one of which can here be used as a comparative starting-point. Thus, in his introduction Samir Amin stresses the integrated nature of migratory flows within and between nations in West Africa. He says, 'Despite the balkanization of West Africa, migrations have not been hindered too much by national frontiers and retain a largely international character' (1974: 70). How far is this also true of East and Central Africa?

Just as the European Economic Community originally envisaged an unrestricted mobility of labour between member countries to enable jobless areas to service those needing labour and to distribute skills where they were required, so did the proponents of both the East and Central African Federations. But the flow of labour between the countries of what would have been the two Federations has been considerably reduced since independence as each state has stressed the distinctiveness of its own national philosophy and politico-economic objectives. Chilivumbo (*infra:* 309) refers to the return of many Malawian labour migrants from Zambia, Rhodesia, and South Africa as both a consequence of political positions taken by each of these countries and, in turn, a major determinant of

Town and Country in Central and Eastern Africa 5

urbanization within Malawi. Ohadike also points to tighter immigration control into Zambia as partly responsible for the decline in numbers of foreign workers and for the refusal of those already in the country to be identified as such (*infra:* 140). Similarly, the exodus of many Kenyan migrants from Uganda predicted on the basis of data in the early sixties (Parkin 1969a: 11) seems gradually to have been generally confirmed.

More generally, Uchendu (*infra:* 176) explains that such barriers have arisen because '. . . increasing industrialization and rising unemployment in African countries have led to competition between international migrants and local labour'. This is, as Uchendu says, a consequence of the trend in much of Africa toward 'economic nationalism'. But over and above this trend particular political alignments and disengagements between nations may also influence the direction and, alternatively, the cessation of migratory flows between them, as is well demonstrated by the situation in East and Central Africa. The disengagements have been mentioned. Thus, Uganda's unorthodox though undeniably independent line under President Amin is reflected in the rejection of Kenyans and Tanzanians and, to a lesser extent, Rwandan refugees, just as Malawi's ambivalent political position in relation to white-controlled Southern Africa and independent Zambia partly explains the return home from these areas of many Malawians. Conversely, the relatively recent political links between Tanzania and Zambia, expressed most obviously in the joint construction of the Tanzam railway following the Rhodesian unilateral declaration of independence, may well grow in other directions also and so accelerate the limited but already significant movement of men and resources between the two countries. The imminent independence of Lusophone (Portuguese-speaking) Africa may, of course, alter such emerging political configurations and the extent to which neighbouring governments erect or lift formal and informal barriers to the movements of their respective peoples. So far, however, Tanzania and Zambia are really the only exceptions to an apparent tendency to separatism in East and Central Africa.

While any tendency to economic nationalism may be seen as an understandable response by national political leaders to give employment priorities to its own citizens and thence to reduce international labour migration, we should not ignore the influence of the less visible industrial connections across Africa made up of major, mainly foreign-owned, enterprises based in various capitals of the industrialized world.

The role and power of the multi-national corporations is recog-

6   *Introduction*

nized and much debated with reference to North America, Europe and other parts of the world. But a similar process involving foreign companies generally is also evident in Africa, in which labour is seen as the most abundant resource and therefore relatively cheap. It has to be recognized that much of the unemployment perceived as such by individual African governments and as necessitating economic nationalism, is often really the shortfall in people's expectations of how many jobs will be generated by industry set up with foreign money. Such new industry tends to be capital- rather than labour-intensive, even though cheap labour is supposed to be the main attraction for foreign investors (ILO Report 1972: 184–7).

Capital-intensive industry thus moulds the official definition of unemployment. It may be highly productive but requires a labour force of white-collar, skilled and to a lesser extent unskilled workers which is small compared with that required in indigenous non-industrial modes of production, or in those based on intermediate technology (defined in Schumacher 1974: 128, 143–59; examples in Uchendu *infra:* 171). The emphasis by such industry on select white-collar and trained skills happens to fit in with a colonially inherited educational system strongly geared to producing clerks. Thus, each East and Central African country has a growing abundance of young, increasingly more educated people who aspire to the limited white-collar and skilled jobs for which, they have been taught to believe, their education has qualified them. As long as so many job-seekers share such aspirations and view other forms of employment, often of an independent nature, as no more than temporary and indeed as a form of 'unemployment', then major employers, including government, will continue to use formal educational criteria as defining suitability for employment. The association in people's minds that education and superior job opportunities go together is reinforced by the growing tendency for proportionally more, as well as the best, secondary school places to be made available in urban rather than rural areas, as Gould demonstrates for Uganda (*infra:* 250–62), so further increasing the rural-urban flow of young people.

There is a second characteristic of capital-intensive industry which derives from the fact that it is either largely foreign-owned or set up by foreign aid and development funds. This is the preference sometimes exercised by the national government as well as the external development agency that the enterprises that they finance should be oriented to produce goods for export. Amin posits a case from Senegal (1974: 86–87) in which the theoretical choice is

Town and Country in Central and Eastern Africa　7

between funds for a dam which would improve Senegalese self-sufficiency by providing hydro-electricity and irrigation but would not directly boost export production, and a ground-nut scheme which would do so and is preferred for that reason. There is obvious sense in creating export possibilities. But it can surely be reasonably argued that a balance must be maintained. For, unless money is also given genuinely to improve the possibilities of economic self-sufficiency within an underdeveloped nation, the result will be to increase its dependency on external market conditions and on foreign financial institutions. This is all the more the case when, as E. Brett has suggested capital-intensive industry, including highly mechanized agriculture, also creates a *continuing* demand for imported technological equipment and replacement parts, e.g. in the maintenance of tractors, long after the enterprise itself has been set up and paid for. One possible consequence of such continuing dependency is an increasing power of foreign investors and aid donors to dictate the actual physical location of new urban and agricultural industry, not always where it is most needed from the viewpoint of balanced regional development.

Though no conspiracy theory is suggested, it can clearly be seen how, within and sometimes between nations, such factors influence the direction of migratory flows, the scale and social composition of migrants, and even where government and many migrants themselves draw a definitional line between wage employment, unemployment, and underemployment.

In this respect, it is interesting to note that migratory patterns on the one hand, and the political and administrative directives and limitations arising from colonial rule on the other, were *both* grouped together by Mitchell (1960: 171, 1966: 49) and Southall (1961: 5) as external determinants of urban social relationships. It can reasonably be suggested that during the colonial era also it was political decisions of government in pursuit or defence of economic interests which greatly determined the volume and direction of migratory flows and that these, in turn, provided the 'extrinsic' context in which urban and rural social relations developed. There are, in other words, different levels of external determinancy. Then, as now, this will continue to apply to those independent African countries where national economies are increasingly tied to markets, technology, and suppliers located in the industrialized world, and whose indigenous modes of production and distribution providing at least partial self-sufficiency are being permanently set aside.

The discussion so far has considered modern migratory processes

8 *Introduction*

in East and Central Africa as responsive to wider political and economic forces at both the national and international level. It is not forgotten that extensive population movement in East and Central Africa was also a pre-colonial feature of indigenous colonization and settlement, and of trade and marketing, as it was, though probably more so, in West Africa (Meillassoux 1971: 67–76 and 197–281). But such movement was not based on the supply of labour for capital-intensive enterprises nor for those concerned with producing exportable commodities, unlike much modern migration. It is true that most contemporary migrants in wage-employment may not themselves be working for capital-intensive organizations directly concerned with producing exports. But the large capital-intensive enterprises often set up by or with the help of non-African foreign funds, whether private or in the form of external aid, do seem to act as foci around which arise other economic activities generating employment, including jobs not even recognized nor officially enumerated by government departments of labour. So, in this sense, even parts of this so-called informal sector of employment (e.g. urban migrant women independently providing cheap food and other services to low-paid men employed in offices and other workplaces, as described by Obbo, *infra:* 290), may to some extent be controlled by the development of such enterprises.

The foregoing are, of course, generalizations on which further research needs to be done. Few of the contributors to the seminar on which this volume is based pay direct attention to the influence of such international factors linking African nations to those outside. But many explicitly recognize the influence which is then taken for granted rather than analysed. Following the tradition of the International African Institute seminars, intensive studies of particular situations were provided which, if analysed independently in the context of the possible development of external relative economic dependency in East and Central Africa, show to what extent local groupings are affected by national, international, and global factors beyond their control. This is surely an important corrective to the generalizations of the kind given above and to the models of some development economists which, once stated, may swiftly become truisms if they cannot accommodate the many variations of social process within relatively small populations. This is not to argue against the formulation of such generalizations. Indeed, Southall (*infra:* 267) rightly chastizes urban anthropology for having neglected them. It is only to insist that intensive analyses of small-scale situations continue to be produced and that the generalizations be tested against them.

Town and Country in Central and Eastern Africa

Models of migratory process should, no less than developmental models set up by economists, be manipulable over a range of different social situations. The first section of this volume includes four papers which in two cases explicitly propose new models (Mitchell, and Garbett), and in two cases consider old ones (Ohadike, and Parkin).

MODELS OF MIGRATORY PROCESSES

In discussing some of the factors precipitating labour migration, the Seminar inevitably asked how much analytical emphasis should be placed on the individual migrant as being free to decide between alternative courses of action, and how much on the wider political, economic, and ecological factors directing and constraining migratory flows of particular groups. Amin discusses this problem and argues firmly that '. . . the decision of the migrant to leave his region of origin, is then completely predetermined by the overall strategy determining the "allocation of factors" ', i.e. the overall strategy of development for a country or region. Stated or inferred motivations for choices made by migrants, though highly variable, are seen as rationalizations of a situation basically determined by factors beyond the migrants' control (Amin 1974: 88–9 and 93).

Even more forcible is his assertion that 'the survey of motivations, by which some sociologists believe they can separate economic from extra-economic motivations, is in reality useless because the economic reason is there in every case and *its ideological guise is equally general*' (92, my italics). My own paper (Parkin *infra*: 146) notes that earlier studies of migration in colonial Africa did not need to consider wage unemployment. They looked closely at the choices taken by migrants as to whether or not, or where, they should move. It is possible that a short, transitional period existed between the early colonial demand for labour and a later saturation point, when migrants had a slightly wider range of alternatives open to them. But they never had the bargaining power on which are based true 'choices' regarding the disposition of one's labour. Certainly, nowadays, we are obliged to consider unemployment and the consequences of there being little or no such choice.

My analysis views the urban end of migratory flows in the context of a competition between ethnic or regionally-based groups for scarce urban jobs and housing. It suggests that the circulatory migration first identified by Mitchell (1959: 259–79) of men more or less voluntarily moving in and out of employment, and in and out of urban and rural home areas, can now be viewed as comprising

10 *Introduction*

increasingly larger numbers of relatively well-educated, young job-seekers who move for long periods between town and country, and between different towns (see especially Gutkind 1967 and 1968). Circulatory migration persists but its social composition and intensity have changed.

This is clearly sympathetic to Amin's approach but not to the extent of dismissing ideological or socio-cultural factors as seemingly impotent 'guises'. It is accepted, as Mitchell and others demonstrated long ago, that economic factors are prime determinants of migration. But it cannot be accepted that 'extra-economic motivations', insofar as they are culturally consistent, ideological justifications for behaviour and not simply idiosyncratic ones, are insignificant and 'equally general'. For this would mean disregarding the influence of, for example, a pronounced localized, segmentary patrilineal ideology on the effects of rural emigration which, as Watson (1958: 112–36) showed for the Mambwe of Zambia, may facilitate less breakdown of rural households than a matrilineal ideology such as that of the Bemba, or its variable influence on urban migrant organization as in the case of Luo, Luyia, Ibo, and Tiv with their distinctive pyramidal structure of urban ethnic associations (Southall *infra*, 1975, and Parkin 1966, 1969a). Ethnic relations clearly provide the framework within which much competition for jobs and housing occurs and so have an immediate effect on migratory patterns. And, since an ethnic group is distinguished overall by the summation of its socio-cultural and ideological attributes, these latter do require special analysis. Ethnicity in Africa may well be a form of false consciousness or mystification which deflects migrants' attention from the fundamental cleavage arising from their displacement from a peasant to an industrial mode of production. If this is so, then there is all the more reason to analyse it and its constituent 'ideological guises'.

The distinction between economic and ideological (or cultural) variables in migration partly parallels that made by Mitchell (1959) between the *rate* of migration based primarily on economic needs and the *incidence* of migration as based on 'social' needs and predispositions. These latter refer to the range of customary roles and beliefs which have normative and symbolic value for a migrant by virtue of his membership of an ethnic or cultural group. In this sense they are ideological.

These customs, symbols and values have their overall effect on a society through their cumulative use by participant members of it. Thus, one person uses a spate of believed witchcraft activity in a village as his justification for emigrating; another claims that fre-

Town and Country in Central and Eastern Africa

quent quarrelling between competing half-brothers is his reason for leaving; another gives as his reason the need to acquire cash for bridewealth; others variously pick on acknowledged events, obligations, and beliefs in their culture, as justifying their departure. The repertoire of possible 'reasons' for leaving are wide, being limited only by what is recognized and therefore acceptable in that particular culture. The point here is that a stated so-called 'economic' reason for migrating, e.g. for bridewealth, is as much a cultural phenomenon as wishing to leave for fear of being bewitched: both are no more than justifications made intelligible to fellow-members by virtue of shared cultural experiences. It is true that in some societies bridewealth is much more valuable, as among the Korekore (Garbett *infra:* 122), than in others and can only be earned through labour migration. But the economic significance of such high bridewealth as a 'cause' of emigration can only be understood in the context of the totality of economic demands and opportunities. This totality of economic factors, buttressed largely by external political and administrative directives and restrictions of the kind I have mentioned, determine the *rate* of migration. By contrast, the *incidence* of migration is expressed in individual appeals to a common cultural system of values and beliefs.

Mitchell's paper on rural male absenteeism in Rhodesia (*infra:* 93) is concerned with the *rate* rather than *incidence* of this phenomenon. That is to say, he is not here concerned with the cultural or ideological variable. This is because the study is entirely based on quantitative data which are analysed statistically. As he points out, the study is intended to provide a 'contextual' basis for more intensive studies. His model aims to show how rural male absenteeism may vary in the context of eight other variables which are: a region's population density; its proportion of male job-seekers; their educational level; regional wage differences; distance from employment opportunities; proportions of non-foreign persons employed locally, and of persons employed by trading stores; and the type of agro-ecological region to and from which migrations take place. The prime variable is the extent to which a region has agro-ecological advantages and, as is likely to be the case in Rhodesia, a European farming community located in it. The densely populated Chiduku area in Makoni district has European farms and towns in it which retain a high proportion of the local labour whose earnings approximate those of the national average. By contrast the thinly populated Chipise area in the Beit Bridge district is very dry and suitable only for extensive cattle ranching and is distant from European towns and farms. It offers wages which are below

12 *Introduction*

those of the national average and so drives out its local labour but does bring in the labour of even more disadvantaged areas, including a high proportion of foreign workers from outside Rhodesia.

But there are also those areas which do not come directly within an environment of such capitalist economic development and in which intervening variables are critical, such as educational level and the proportion of trading stores able to offer employment. Many of the local people of thinly populated Urungwe have no education and do not seek wage employment either within or outside their area, and the number of foreign employees who have moved in is proportionately high. The people of more densely populated Gwande and Brunapeg, on the other hand, are highly educated jobseekers for whom local wages and opportunities are higher than average. Other workers from other areas within Rhodesia join them but few foreigners are represented. Finally, Binga is an example of an area which is both isolated and severely underdeveloped economically, having very few trading stores, lacking wage and cash-cropping opportunities, and providing a high rate of male absenteeism.

It is important to note that Mitchell does not see the absentee rate of males as necessarily *directly* related to the demographic and economic conditions and educational levels of the rural areas from which men emigrate. Rather, it is the quality of the wider agro-ecological region encompassing such local areas which governs the degree of relevance of such factors. In a plural society, of which colonial southern Africa is a type, favourable agro-ecological regions tend to be controlled by the dominant group which demands and is able to hold labour from within the region. But in less developed regions the local distribution of economic opportunities and the educational level determine how many men move out to the developed regions, how many remain either employed locally or unemployed, and how many move in from within and outside Rhodesia. The metaphorical image conveyed is that of an international weather chart which depicts broad currents which are determined by major troughs of high and low pressure but within which there are variations immediately dependent on local conditions.

Mitchell's analysis is concerned with macro-level phenomena and not with the decisions of actors in particular localities to migrate or not to migrate. For Mitchell, these two levels of analysis are not incompatible but are simply different approaches to the same problem and pose different questions. The first is the macro-context which can be taken as a 'given' in the micro-scopic study of the social interactions of migrants and non-migrants. This is sensible.

Town and Country in Central and Eastern Africa   13

However, one might still argue that, since a macro-context *does* change over time (e.g. governments and political systems are altered, economic expansion alternates with recession, etc.), then the relationship between its changing nature and alterations in the choices open to individuals requires analysis at both levels. How can this be accomplished?

With regard to the micro-context I have suggested that we can view individual decisions as cultural or ideological justifications. This gives such decisions the significance of a general variable, for their intelligibility and acceptability differ according to whatever cultural group a migrant belongs to. The macro-context of labour absenteeism and migration is, as Mitchel states, 'primarily a reaction to the national (and I would add, international) economic and political situation. . . .' (*infra:* 111). In other words, this variable is directly dependent on the positions of dominance and subordination between competing interest groups. Change in the one variable, i.e. in the repertoire of culturally accepted reasons given for migrating or not migrating, may be linked to changes in the relative positions of interest groups. To understand such linked changes, we analyse the two variables as being interdependent. I believe that this view comes close to that expressed by Cohen (1974), who demonstrates the interplay of the two variables of symbolic behaviour and group power relations.

Garbett (*infra:* 114–17) considers in detail the significance of the wider politico-economic forces of colonial society over which the individual has little control. Then, taking such facts as given, he constructs a decision model to explain circulatory migration in Rhodesia. He wants to go beyond the kinds of decisions taken by migrants obeying culturally defined rules and to consider also the strategies which they adopt out of sheer self-interest. In other words, the potential migrant is confronted with a possible multiplicity of choices, some culturally sanctioned, others not so. The decision model is centrally concerned with the effects that decisions taken by other people have on a migrant, and with the effects that past choices made by himself have on his present choices. The cumulative and patterned nature of such past choices acts as a field of constraints on any future ones. The model therefore presents migrants as having only partial and not total freedom in what they decide. This characteristic enables Garbett to reject the simple 'rational choice/maximization models' of some economists, which necessarily neglect the 'non-rational' and subjective pressures and obligations to which any person must also respond. He also rejects the so-called 'push-pull' model as placing too much emphasis on general economic determinants of migration to the

14 *Introduction*

exclusion of social, or what I would call cultural and ideological, factors.

I think the value of Garbett's model is in showing how core cultural incentives and constraints do in fact persist and that migrants are constantly having to find ways not of flouting them, but of *adapting* their aims and actions to them. Let me elaborate on an example given by Garbett (*infra:* 122) which illustrates this.

The institution of bridewealth in many, though by no means all, African societies represents one of the largest financial commitments which young men enter into, not unlike mortgages taken on by young, first-time house-buyers in Western countries. Bridewealth is by no means an atrophying institution. It has frequently taken the form of money rather than, say, livestock, and become inflated along with other costs. Some societies insist on complete payment of bridewealth within a short time. Others, perhaps increasingly in view of its often inflated value, accept drawn-out payments. The Korekore are of this kind, and a man may be indebted to his father-in-law for many years. But should a man wish to work in a distant town and to take his wife with him, his father-in-law may demand that a large part of the bridewealth be paid immediately. Few men can afford to do this, and the usual compromise is to take a job in a nearby European farm and to leave the wife with her father. Husband and wife can then visit each other fairly regularly. The compromise also suits the man's father-in-law who may benefit from the cash, gifts, and agricultural assistance which his son-in-law's visits to his wife may bring. The overall consequence is three-fold: migrants working on European farms mostly come from nearby common home areas; they experience relatively little dis-continuity in social relations between rural home village and work-place; and they can obviate potentially conflicting conjugal interests and affinal obligations. From being a comprise solution of a con-flict of customary obligations, this set of choices has now become normative, that is to say, a cultural preference among Korekore. The economic gains from working in either a distant town or nearby European farm may be roughly comparable. So much for the under-lying economic factor. But from this example we see the significance also of a cultural factor, in this case that centring on the important institution of bridewealth, in deciding which of the two European-dominated workplaces should be preferred.

The colonial domination of the politico-economic bases of migra-tion is fundamental. But by studying the interplay of cultural and politico-economic factors, we understand variations within migra-tory flows. We might, for instance, expect a different response to

Town and Country in Central and Eastern Africa   15

that of the Korekore from members of a society operating under the same politico-economic constraints but among whom bridewealth is of low value. Garbett's analysis of migratory behaviour, i.e. the 'incidence' of migration, thus complements that by Mitchell of migratory 'rates' in this volume. The next step is to integrate the two models, for, as Garbett remarks, ultimately it is necessary to explain the interrelationship between micro- and macro-processes (*infra:* 117). A beginning in this direction might be made by investigating whether and how Korekore compete with other African groups for jobs both within and outside their home area. How much, in other words, is the Korekore decision to work near their rural homes rather than in distant towns also affected by ethnic competition in a labour market basically controlled by European enterprises?

Ohadike's model compares with Mitchell's in being exclusively concerned with the use of quantitative data to depict migratory rates. Ohadike distinguishes 'first-time' and 'plural movers' and measures how many moves migrants in Lusaka have made and within what time-period. In this way he is able to modify the distinction in static models between the migrant and the 'settled' rural or urban non-migrant and to see instead the gradations of differences between persons variously involved in migration at some time or other in their lives. Whereas Mitchell looked at migration from the rural viewpoint, Ohadike takes Lusaka, the capital of Zambia, as his standpoint. He relates differences in the rate and volume of migratory flows in and out of the city to differences of 'class', ethnic or cultural group, and their residential location in Lusaka. A number of findings emerge from Ohadike's study of Lusaka which can be fitted into general discussions regarding the consequences of urban migration on educational opportunities and the development of a socio-economic hierarchy of residential areas. One general finding requires special mention in the present discussion.

Ohadike estimates that Lusaka has expanded at successive annual growth rates of 5·3 per cent, 10·9 per cent, and 11·8 per cent during the five-year periods of 1953–8, 1958–63, and 1963–8. During this last period, ten per cent of the annual increase has been through immigration. But, Ohadike emphasizes, there has been a radical change in the migratory process into Lusaka. At the beginning of this fifteen-year period, most migrants moved to Lusaka straight from their rural homes and most were first-time movers. At the end of the period most had come via other towns and the distances travelled from their rural homes by first-timers was significantly higher. This must surely be an increasingly more common develop-

16   *Introduction*

ment in East and Central African countries. For the majority of
their towns approximate to that designated by Southall as Type B
(1961: 6–13), which are relatively modern centres of capital-intensive industry, and of commerce and administration (like Lusaka),
set up through the use of labour rapidly moving from a relatively
high degree of agricultural self-sufficiency to partial dependence on
wage employment. This implies a development also of greater discontinuity in urban and rural political, economic, and cultural
relations, and perhaps of increasingly distinct urban and rural
groups and categories: an urban proletariat on the one hand, and
a possibly impoverished rural sector on the other. How far has this
occurred? We can begin to answer this by looking at the relationship
of migration to rural development and underdevelopment.

MIGRATION AND RURAL DEVELOPMENT

Ohadike's paper distinguishes urban-to-urban from rural-to-urban
migration. To the extent that at least some circulatory migration
persists and that, even after many years in towns, most workers
still retire to their rural homes, then it is possible to talk of urban-
to-rural migration also. The fourth possibility, inter-rural migration, is the subject of Uchendu's paper (*infra:* 165) and is also
dealt with in Mushanga's (*infra:* 159). According to Mushanga,
Uganda has had an unusually long-established pattern of labour
migration between rural areas, particularly to and from Buganda
(Richards 1955), but also to other cotton-growing areas in southern
and eastern parts of the country. He notes a pronounced shift
from this to a rural-urban movement of labour and argues that rural
development policies aimed at stemming this flow must be accompanied also by an institutional decentralization of the major towns
of employment, Kampala and Jinja. Thoden Van Velzen (*infra:*
178) also takes as the starting-point for his analysis of Tanzanian
village development Frank's model (1969: 6) that in poor countries
a few metropoles dominate and exploit a vast number of much
smaller satellite communities.

   The deliberate resiting of national capitals is indeed often advocated
both as a partial means of urban decentralization and of reducing
regional imbalances in the nation's rural development. This can be
a costly measure. Malawi is transferring its capital from Zomba
to newly-built Lilongwe, though Blantyre is by far the largest
city; and it is reported that in 1974 Tanzania designated the
small inland town of Dodoma as its new capital instead of Dar-
es-Salaam and had its National Assembly meet there for the first

Town and Country in Central and Eastern Africa   17

time on October 22nd of that year (*The Times* 23rd October 1974). Small towns can act as intermediary rural foci of urban and regional decentralization without having to become capitals, and their importance as a special type facilitating the combined activities of agriculture, trade and local administration (see Middleton 1966: 31 Gutkind 1969) has recently attracted intensive research in this part of Africa (Vincent 1971, Jacobson 1973, Lang 1974, Pain 1975, and see also Abrahams 1961 and Thoden Van Velzen (*infra:* 178).

Uchendu emphasizes, however, that inter-rural labour migration already accounts for a large proportion of economic activities but that this is not generally recognized either by scholars or by governments. He asks, how is it that with only 10 per cent of its population actually living in towns at any one time the African continent can be described as over-urbanized? On the contrary, he argues, the high rate of urban unemployment shows how the urban economy has failed to generate enough jobs and that it is still the rural sector of the economy which, at least, sustains most people. The problem of urban unemployment is seen as a problem of how further to develop agricultural jobs. Together with deliberate policies of rural investment, inter-rural migration is seen as a rational allocation of land and labour if it enables people to move from land-deficient areas to those with surplus land. Uchendu adds the *caveat* that labour migration between rural areas should only be encouraged under the direction of a national land tenure policy (*infra:* 175). A crucial question is whether to impose ceilings on private land ownership in land-surplus areas to prevent gross regional inequalities occurring as a result of migrants from land-hungry areas becoming wholly dependent on 'landlords' in more favoured ones.

Here it should be noted that regions or parts of regions are often also differentiated by ethnic as well as administrative boundaries, a feature going back to colonial rule (Southall 1970). A national policy which imposed ceilings on land ownership would have to overcome the resistance that members of agro-ecologically favoured regions, sharing a common culture, might exert against less advantaged immigrants, for whom the prospective benefits of permanent settlement would probably outweigh those of simply supplying their labour. The allocation to immigrants of genuinely *unused* land through settlement schemes does seem to offer a partial solution, provided the possibly high expense (Moris undated: 79–80) and organizational problems (Apthorpe undated: 5–13, Chambers 1969: 257–62 and Shorter 1974: 118–32) can be avoided or dealt with. It can lessen the development of a division between peasant employers and landless employees. It can also clearly define the zones

18 *Introduction*

beyond which further settlement may not occur, so alleviating fears by the indigenous group that immigrants will eventually encroach on their own, cultivated land. Such schemes presuppose intensive agriculture using intermediate technology rather than shifting cultivation. They need to be specially fitted to the situations of nomadic pastoralists whose territorial requirements are necessarily large, at least if they are to be encouraged more in their pre-colonial and pre-capitalist role of maintaining ecological balance rather than being forced to overgraze in restricted areas (Spencer 1974, see also Rigby undated: 42–52).

Uchendu notes that, to a greater extent than in West Africa, much inter-rural migration in East and Central Africa has been between the large agricultural estates resulting from white settlement. This combines with the movement of labour to, say, the coffee, and banana and cotton zones worked by small-holders in Buganda (see Richards *et al.* 1973), Kilimanjaro and Bukoba (Tanzania), to produce an overall pattern which, as discussed in the first section of this introduction, was markedly international but has recently become much less so. It will be of interest to see whether national land tenure policies and the effect that these have on the general pattern of inter-rural migration will differ according to the extent to which independent nations have large agricultural estates as part of their colonial legacy.

Three ecologically distinct areas located in Uganda, Tanzania and Kenya and now highly productive, are presented by Uchendu as demonstrating the different effects of migration on rural development in the context of differing national policies. In all three areas new farm lands have been settled by immigrants. In one case, that of Teso district in Uganda, it is the Teso people themselves who have farmed the new land, doing so originally in response to planned development under the fiscal control of colonial government as early as 1910. Through their early acceptance of the ox-plough, Teso were able to grow cotton independently of outside migrant labour. The ox-plough itself is a form of intermediate technology which, while reducing dependence on outside labour, does not eliminate the labour-intensive element in agricultural work. The generally successful results of its use contrast strikingly with more recent findings from research on Teso in 1972–4 by E. Brett which show how the adoption by co-operatives of modern tractors has greatly helped the large, entrepreneurial farmers but not the many small holders who, as fellow contributing members of the co-operatives, effectively subsidize the former and yet supply them with labour (personal communication).

Town and Country in Central and Eastern Africa 19

The other two cases of high rural development, in Kisii district of Kenya and in Geita district of Tanzania, were achieved without any radical changes in agricultural technology. As tsetse fly was eradicated in the uninhabited areas of Geita during the late thirties, people from land-hungry areas of Sukumaland moved in to settle there. All farmed, some of them later worked in the short-lived gold mines, and still later some traded. The money so earned was invested in the cultivation of cotton as a cash crop. But, unlike the Teso, the Sukuma settlers in Geita have depended on the seasonal migrant labour of workers from Ruanda and Urundi. The people of Kisii first worked as labour migrants on nearby mines and tea plantations between 1930 and 1950 and then migrated to the Kisii highlands, which had previously been used for cattle-grazing. There they invested their accumulated earnings and became expert at growing maize which they supplied to workers on the nearby plantations, later diversifying into such high-value crops as pyrethrum, tea, exotic cattle and specialist kinds of maize. Like the Teso they do not use external labour as do the people of Geita. Instead, prosperous farmers hire the labour of fellow-Kisii cultivators who are themselves short of land. This internal class development in Kisii has recently been studied quite independently by A. Manners (unpublished papers) and seems, then, to have developed early by comparison with the other two areas. Geita has been able to draw on non-Sukuma seasonal migrant labour from outside, and in Teso the early use of the ox-plough probably delayed the need for extra labour. As mentioned, the recent adoption of tractors there has accelerated the differentiation of wealth and land ownership, and of employers and labourers.

Uchendu does not say how far Tanzania's land tenure policy has affected the distribution of farmland in Geita, which in Kisii and Teso has become increasingly uneven. All three districts fit into one of three types of rural area identified by Amin in West Africa (1974: 94). This type includes those areas 'organized for large-scale export production which have already entered the capitalist phase, which implies private appropriation of the land and the availability of wage labour.' His other two types, one supplying the wage labour for but not itself much involved in agricultural export production, and the other neither supplying wage labour nor producing cash crops, certainly exist also in East and Central Africa. Uchendu's paper refers to migration from the densely-populated West Nile district of Uganda to Buganda and from Ruanda and Urundi to both Buganda and Geita, and these may be taken as examples of the former type. Increasingly rare examples of the latter type of

20 *Introduction*

area, which neither supply wage labour nor engage in cash-cropping for export, may include such East African peoples with a predominantly pastoralist orientation as the Karamojong, Turkana, Masai, Samburu and Gogo, who are not yet or are only peripherally organized into intensive cattle-ranching, and such hunters and gatherers as the Hadza of Tanzania and, in some instances, the Dorobo and Aliangulu or Sanye of Kenya.

The question of the current relationship of relatively prosperous Geita district to the Tanzanian policy of balanced regional development raises a possible parallel with the even more prosperous coffee-producing area of the Chagga people around Mount Kilimanjaro. The high productivity of particular Chagga farmers achieved through peasant capitalism has occasionally brought them into conflict with the socialist ideology as expressed in the Arusha declaration of 1967 by the government party, the Tanzania African National Union (TANU) (Stahl 1969: 221–2, Moore, forthcoming). Conflict at the ideological level is inevitable, but what are the unintended effects of Tanzania's distinctive policy designed to ensure that peasants remain in control of their own production of crops, cash or otherwise?

Thoden van Velzen's intensive study (*infra:* 178) of an administrative centre of about 1,000 people in Rungwe district focuses on the political and economic relationship between the salaried civil servants and wealthy peasants on the one hand and the more numerous poorer peasants on the other. The civil servants have genuinely been responsible for the development of community projects but, because they are set apart from the peasants as an élite dependent on relatively high government salaries rather than farming, they develop a correspondingly distinct life-style which further reinforces the separateness of their material interests. There is a continuing tendency, dating back to the colonial administration but apparently still followed by the people, for the wealthiest, i.e. most 'progressive', farmers to be elected onto local government councils. Thus thrown together, the local civil servants and wealthy farmers inevitably account between them for an improportionate amount of funds channelled into community development by the central government. This is a consequence not so much of the machinations of ideologically unfaithful individuals but more of a structural situation in which an informal alliance of government officers and wealthy farmers has come to constitute a 'class' which perpetuates and widens inequalities in land distribution which originated before Tanzania's independence.

At first, the particular form of this division seems to be charac-

Town and Country in Central and Eastern Africa   21

teristic of many parts of Africa and the third world in which peasant capitalism is emerging, examples of which in Kenya have been analyzed by Lamb (1974), Leys (1971), and Parkin (1972). Lamb shows how a rural élite of coffee-growers in the Murang'a district of Central Province is able to appropriate a large share of limited central government funds and subsidies through their complementary exercise of power at the level of the local community. I describe how rural development loans in Kilifi district, Coast Province, are awarded on a meritocratic basis to those deemed to be the most successful farmers. Leys, while arguing that a clear polarization of large capitalist farmers and rural and urban proletariats will take a long time, even in Kenya's economically advanced Central Province, accepts that the process has begun even to the extent of a developing peasant political consciousness being selectively directed at members of the national élite.

Thoden Van Velzen emphasizes that the wealth which the Tanzanian central government puts into the peasantry actually exceeds that which is extracted for investment in urban areas, so that in this respect the country does follow a distinctive policy. But since such external funds are allocated by the civil servants in consultation with the wealthy farmers, the privileged position of this rural élite enables it to take a 'toll' as the money passes through them to the community as a whole. Are the general consequences for economic development, then, no different in spite of sharply contrasting policies between the two nations (see Hyden 1969: 37–60)?

The consequences, if unchecked by formal limitations on private land ownership in Tanzania, may indeed become more than superficially similar and converge to a common pattern. Prognoses can be made now but the real test is long-term and is surely whether genuinely large estate owners emerge in Tanzania who are able to perpetuate their holdings through the formation of future family dynasties whose local political dominance is transferred to the national and urban context. Minor differences of rural inequality which do not survive beyond a generation or two as a result of major fluctuations in world market demand for cash crops reflect peasants' external dependency. But, paradoxically, such oscillating inequality need not be the basis of enduring classes among them. The constantly changing horizon of entrepreneurial status noted by some anthropologists as characteristic of pre-capitalist, primarily redistributive 'traditional' economies, may indeed be a continuing feature of some contemporary peasant regions of Africa isolated from the main-stream of national political decisions on economic policy and yet dependent on the production of crops for export.

22 *Introduction*

Again, national and international factors beyond the control of local populations can be critical in deciding the extent of their internal socio-economic differentiation. It follows that a full understanding of particular peasant communities heavily engaged in cash-cropping for export can only be had by tracing the links between them, the metropoles or urban centres through which their produce passes, and the markets to which it is directed, and by analysing the roles of those who control these links, i.e. the gatekeepers, as they have been called, who operate at different levels of the distributive network. It also follows that the extent to which relations of external dependency develop among peasants is very much a function of national government policy in the early stages of development. In this regard, Tanzania since independence has surely shown a comparatively high degree of consistency in the exercise of its ideology of national self-reliance and balanced regional development, even at the 'cost', as some would put it, of a lower GNP rate than might otherwise have been achieved by greater concentration on export production in such favoured agro-ecological regions as that of the Chagga around Mount Kilimanjaro.

Some inequalities between rural regions can be explained primarily in terms of the planned development of favoured agro-ecological areas, other inequalities can arise more directly from the location of heavy plant and industry, not necessarily within existing towns, and still others from a combination of this and agro-ecological advantages. Examples of the latter two emerge from Colson and Scudder's study (*infra:* 190).

The Kariba dam was built to serve all three countries of the abortive Central African Federation, Malawi, Zambia and Rhodesia, and in fact straddles the border between the latter two, now contributing significantly to the self-sufficiency in electricity of each of them. Similarly the railway in Zambia was built in the colonial era to carry minerals from that country and Rhodesia through southern Africa to world markets and has now assumed extraordinary significance in the pattern of development occurring within Zambia itself. Colson and Scudder have for a number of years studied the effects of those two massive projects on the people of southern Zambia.

The Kariba dam project uprooted some 56,000 Tonga of the Gwembe valley in Zambia and Rhodesia, who were then resettled as whole villages in different areas of the same district in 1958. One such village is Mazulu, which is now fifty miles from the new town of Kafue and ninety from the Zambian capital of Lusaka. It now occupies a favourable agro-ecological site but also falls within a

Town and Country in Central and Eastern Africa   23

wider area of industrial development which includes all of Zambia's Southern Province and the line of rail as far north as Lusaka. It is thus a highly productive rural village yet is set within and with excellent access to urban markets and alternative employment opportunities. As in the example provided by Uchendu from Teso (*infra:* 171) immediate acceptance of plough cultivation in Mazulu has enabled this village to exploit its agricultural advantages rapidly. Though distant, the large towns are significant outlets for the village's cash crops and, in turn, provide regular links enabling younger men to work in them. A high level of rural productivity and re-investment and readily seized opportunities to earn 'surplus' cash through urban employment have reinforced the ties between village and town in spite of the distance separating them. Indeed, Colson and Scudder point out, the mobile villagers do not themselves perceive an urban-rural dichotomy, and, in view of the mutually reinforcing nature of economic ties and investment, neither can the analyst. Mazulu therefore benefits from a combination of agro-ecological and industrial advantages and has actually prospered from re-settlement. Nevertheless, the authors warn, already younger villagers are beginning to prefer urban to rural involvement.

The second village studied, called Musulumba, was sited within the tsetse fly belt. Its people cannot therefore rear cattle nor use them to pull ploughs for the cultivation of cash crops on any significant scale. They continue to practise hoe agriculture for subsistence purposes. Consequently they have depended much more on wage labour, usually at the nearby construction works. They have lost the agricultural self-sufficiency they possessed prior to re-settlement. The two types of villages, the one prospering through a combination of rural cash cropping and urban wage labour, and the other languishing through lower-paid rural wage labour and subsistence agriculture, do show the range of rural diversification likely to be found in Africa and other parts of the developing world (cf. T. S. Epstein's contrast of two Indian villages, 1962). But they are also representative of emerging inequalities. The critical factor is the extent to which wage employment, whether urban or rural, erodes peasant agricultural self-sufficiency as has happened in Musulumba. It should be noted that though this has not occurred in the other village, the growing preference there by younger people for urban wage employment over rural farming suggests that even this story of peasant 'success' may be of short duration.

The greater availability of urban wage employment in Zambia compared with other East and Ceneral African countries may make this an exceptional case. Nevertheless, it could also signalize future

B

24 *Introduction*

trends in these other countries in which land scarcity and a slow but definite expansion, in absolute terms, of urban employment opportunities may eventually have the same effect.

The extensive development in Africa of a true urban proletariat, wholly dependent on wage employment by virtue of being landless or unable to subsist through peasant production alone, may not be imminent (Elkan 1972). Its emergence is likely to be gradual, for one reason because the provision of urban jobs is still increasingly outweighed by the number of young immigrants seeking them. Nevertheless, an urban population growth rate roughly thrice that of the rural surely provides ideological pre-conditions for the development of urban proletariat *consciousness*, some of which is increasingly expressed in trade unionism (see Grillo 1974: 125–43, including bibliography). Whether mythical or factual, the popular assumption that urban opportunities exceed rural ones perpetuates itself through this continuing imbalance of town and country populations. The 'bright lights' theory of migration has been discredited or at least rejected as being of secondary importance to one stressing economic factors as fundamental causes. In the form in which it was originally presented, its rejection is justified. We must not, however, forget that the rationalization of economic advantage almost invariably takes ideological form. As is clear from a number of the papers in this volume, many men and especially many women living in overcrowded urban conditions and working, if at all, in underpaid jobs, still do not seriously question the assumption held by many of them that 'town' in some way offers a better life than 'country'. Income and expenditure levels apart, the criteria by which such attitudes can be measured are subjective. We move here to consider the formation of ideas, beliefs, and values and their transmission, not just from townsmen to rural folk at home, but to town by the greater number of rural emigrants travelling in this direction.

THE RURAL-URBAN FLOW OF LANGUAGE, BELIEF, AND EDUCATIONAL OPPORTUNITY

While it is true that ideas can be spread by other media than mobile populations, the latter are particularly significant in Africa through the various kinds of circulatory migration between and within rural and urban areas by workers, job-seekers, and their family dependants. The diffusion of language is a phenomenon of the same order as the spread and intermingling of 'traditional' or customary values and religious beliefs and practices. All result from the regular or sustained interaction of distinctive cultural groupings among

Town and Country in Central and Eastern Africa   25

whom new concepts need to be articulated or old ones simply communicated. The towns of East and Central Africa are not the only areas of concentrated multi-cultural populations, which can also be found in rural settlement schemes, plantations or estates, and market and administrative centres. The papers by Rigby and Lule, Kashoki, and Gould, focus on the Zambian and Ugandan capitals of Lusaka and Kampala, which may be taken as strong examples of how people from diverse rural cultural and linguistic backgrounds may preserve their distinctiveness and yet evolve common assumptions, expectations, languages and codes in town.

Rigby and Lule (*infra:* 213) analyse the operation in Kampala of 'traditional' Ganda religion, in which they include magic, witchcraft, divination, healing, and beliefs and practices associated with ancestors. Much useful material on witchcraft beliefs and accusations in urban and industrial situations in East and Central Africa has been documented. Recourse to diviners, ritual cure and protective medicines is also undoubtedly widespread in towns, as presumably, it is in western and southern Africa. The persistence of such beliefs and practices is no less a response to uncertainties of human endeavours and conditions than in rural areas. If there is change or difference of belief and ritual action in the urban situation, then it is because the kinds of misfortunes that occur there have no conceptual nor explanatory parallel in the rural.

Mitchell's analysis of the way in which misfortunes are explained in Salisbury, Rhodesia, was the first systematic attempt to explore the urban dimension of such phenomena (1965: 192–203). He identifies two structural situations characteristic of heterogenous and shifting urban populations which determine whether and to what extent a misfortune may be blamed on another person's witchcraft. First, the urban family stresses cohesion rather than fragmentation and so its members in town are unlikely to accuse each other. Second, in the context of competitive urban occupational relationships a victim is less likely to blame his misfortune on a workmate and more likely to accept the diviner's verdict that it is due to the anger of ancestor spirits located in the rural area. This is because, in Salisbury, the illegality of outright witchcraft accusations can be enforced relatively easily in the tightly structured administrative situation there. Initial accusations of witchcraft may, for this reason, later be reinterpreted as due to rural ancestral wrath. In this way the misfortune is at least satisfactorily explained even though the victim is unable to take direct retributive action against a suspect.

This is a persuasive hypothesis which may be modified according to how closely the urban administration enforces the illegality of

26   *Introduction*

witchcraft accusations. In Salisbury the enforcement appears to have been strong. Data from other towns in East and Central Africa are varied. I have analysed a long-standing quarrel in Kampala between two male cross-cousins which never included witchcraft accusations, even though one of them suffered a number of misfortunes at the time. The quarrel was finally reconciled when one of the cousins had a dream in which his dead maternal grandmother (i.e. the paternal grandmother of his rival) urged him to end the dispute for the sake of the 'family' name (1969a: 125–6). It is only now that I see that this may fit the first part of Mitchell's two-fold hypothesis, that the need for urban family cohesion inhibits witchcraft accusations among close relatives. Regarding the second part, we may note from this case that a rural ancestor was used to reconcile the quarrel, though not quite to explain the misfortune. However, urban misfortunes *are* sometimes explained as having rural causes.

In another case, one of two Luo friends who were living next door to each other in Kampala was sacked from his job. There followed a quarrel between the two men, supported by their wives, which was marked by accusations and counter-accusations of sorcery (i.e. the use of mystically harmful objects). But there was no need in this case to suppress the idiom of sorcery, since no family cohesion was under threat. Disengagement was affected by the simple expedient of one couple voluntarily leaving the neighbourhood (*ibid.*: 66–7). As an inverse instance, this is consistent with Mitchell's argument.

In neither this nor the preceding case was the illegality of making witchcraft accusations a deterrent. Nor, in recent reports by Grillo in Kampala (1973 : 142–6), Kapferer in Broken Hill (1969: 202–8), and La Fontaine on Kinshasa (1970: 182–7), do explanations of misfortune in terms of rural ancestral displeasure appear to predominate over those of urban witchcraft. But, as is well known, the analytical distinction between witchcraft, sorcery, and affliction by ancestral or other spirits is often shaky if only because the people themselves do not always draw a hard and fast line between them, either terminologically or conceptually. Perhaps we can look at the material from a different viewpoint.

The above data, including some which I have on Luo in Nairobi, suggest a more general distinction between those explanations of urban misfortune for which the mystical causative agent is seen as located in the town, and those for which the mystical cause is rural-based (see also Grillo 1973: 54; 144, La Fontaine 1970: 185–6). How do we account for the tendency of some townsmen to interpret and sometimes reinterpret the causes of urban misfortunes in these

Town and Country in Central and Eastern Africa   27

alternative ways? In Salisbury this tendency results from the deterrent effects of a tightly controlled urban administration. Such control is an aspect of a town's political structure which, in Salisbury, is dominated by Europeans. Africans in Salisbury are in no political position to regard the city as a permanent base complementing their rural homes. Insofar as they have any control over their destinies, it is in their rural homes, and it is by referring there that they tend also to explain and control personal misfortunes. Similarly, Luo in Kampala in the mid-sixties and in Nairobi at present time regard themselves as having less permanent status in those cities than the acknowledged, politically dominant host groups, the Ganda and the Kikuyu respectively. They make clear distinctions between urban and rural causes and, in Nairobi at least, seem to place most emphasis on the latter when diagnosing witchcraft and malevolent spirits.

From these slender data an hypothesis can be suggested which is too broad as it stands but may be worth testing. The more alienated a migrant group is from the political and economic control of the city in which it works, like the Cewa and Yao of Salisbury as the extreme example, the more likely it is, when using mystical explanations of misfortunes, to ascribe them to rural rather than urban causative agents. This must assume that the group retains some rural interests and that at least some of its members circulate between town and country. The corollary would be that the politically dominant host group 'discovers' a larger proportion of urban causes or simply makes little distinction between them and rural ones. Before relating this hypothesis to further ideas about the development of ideology and political consciousness among such groups, we need to know which kind and what proportion of misfortunes are explained in mystical terms rather than as being due to, say, outright 'exploitation' by the dominant group or 'subversion' by the subordinate.

All this rests on the assumption that townsmen conceptualize behaviour and values as being different between town and country. Most do, it seems, often in the face of factual evidence (Grillo 1973: 184). But where urban and rural economic interests reinforce each other strongly, as among the Gwembe Tonga of Mazulu village, people may ignore such putative differences of value and behaviour and consequently have more 'conceptual space', so to speak, in which to explain misfortune as arising in both rural and urban areas indiscriminately (Colson and Scudder *infra:* 201–2).

How does the material presented by Rigby and Lule on Ganda religion in Kampala fit into this? The position of Ganda in Uganda

28   *Introduction*

as a whole has changed radically in the twelve years since independence. Though this has inevitably diminished the degree of control which they have been able to exert in Kampala relative to other African groups, they are still by far the most numerous and are well represented at all levels of the occupational hierarchy. Their political influence can hardly be said to have disappeared but is, perhaps, held in abeyance. In this respect it parallels their traditional religion, which never 'died' even in the face of extensive conversion to Christianity and Islam. Rather, it has been 'kept in store', so to speak, to be released on crisis situations as a rallying call for all Ganda, as when the Kabaka was exiled by the British from 1953 to 1955 and again, after independence, from 1966, and later, after his death, at the expectation of his son's return in 1971.

Not only has there been a resilient continuity of core elements of Ganda religion over many generations but its urban and rural dimensions are also largely continuous, with the special exception of rural *misambwa* spirits which are associated with natural features like hills and rivers and so are less easily transplanted in the city. Otherwise there is a striking formal continuity of rituals, medicines, shrines, and beliefs between rural and urban contexts. Their meanings and functional significance are, however, adapted to Kampala. Thus: the *mayembe* (divinatory spirits for both good and evil) are even more widely used in Kampala for healing, and also to catch *mizimu* (spirits of the recently dead); the Ganda in Kampala draw constant parallels in urban ritual between the sometimes humble urban *ssabo* (shrines) and the tombs of kings and notables, buried a little way from the city; some dozen *lubaale* (possessionary spirits of Ganda gods and mythical heroes) are known by Ganda in Kampala and figure prominently there. But while these represent the incorporation of rural beliefs in an urban setting, there are more complex rituals concerning difficult cases of urban infertility, which can only be carried out in the rural village.

The status of Ganda as host people in Kampala and the relative lack of discontinuity for them of urban and rural social and economic relations parallels the comparatively unbroken flow of their religious ideas between town and country. We may note that unlike the Cewa and Yao in Salisbury discussed by Mitchell, or the Luo in Kampala and Nairobi, or the African population of colonial, white-controlled Leopoldville described by La Fontaine, ancestral spirits (*mizimu*) among the Ganda actually move, so to speak, to Kampala and afflict their descendants there rather than at a distance from the rural area. The Ganda in Kampala can draw from within the city on almost their total range of mystical agents

Town and Country in Central and Eastern Africa   29

to explain misfortunes experienced there and do not normally interpret them as originating from the rural area.

This seems to be consistent with the above hypothesis. Nevertheless, apart from having to justify the tautological implications of arguing that people who live adjacent to a city can preserve greater continuity of ritual beliefs and action, much more data are needed to see whether changes in the political relationship of Ganda to Kampala before and after independence correlate with any differences in the extent to which Ganda in Kampala see their personal misfortunes as explained by rural as against urban causes.

The process by which rural beliefs and practices are rejected, or selected and translated in urban contexts, is similar to that whereby different ethnic vernaculars undergo change in interaction with each other and with urban lingua francas. We may ask here how far it is a characteristic of an urban host community that its language as well as its ritual concepts will come to be borrowed by others. Ganda diviners in Kampala have a large clientele which includes many non-Ganda. The Ganda language (Luganda), too, is widely used as a limited lingua franca in the city. Much depends on the size and influence of a host community as to how much of its language and culture will be adopted by fellow-townsmen and migrants. But its size alone is insufficient. Thus, the Zaramo, whose home area surrounds that of Dar es Salaam, accounted for nearly two-fifths of the city's population in 1957. They played an important role as host community in the early development of the city (Leslie 1963: 33). But the spread of Islam and of the lingua franca, Swahili, blurred cultural and linguistic distinctions between them and other groups, and their political and economic influence now appears to be negligible compared with that of Ganda in Kampala and Kikuyu in Nairobi.

By contrast, Nyanja has easily outstripped Bemba and Tonga-Ila as the most widely spoken lingua franca in Lusaka. Ohadike shows that this occurred as the number of Nyanja-speaking migrants from Zambia's Eastern Province a) exceeded that of Tonga-Ila speakers from Central Province, who were the host people in Lusaka before 1950, and b) remained above that of Bemba-speakers from Northern, Luapula, and Copperbelt Provinces (*infra:* 138). Here the acquisition and loss of host status in Lusaka correlates directly with the proportional expansion, restriction and contraction of the three rival African lingua francas.

In the Copperbelt towns of Zambia, a special urban form of Bemba is the most extensive lingua franca, with Nyanja second (Richardson 1961). English is regarded by many people as a language

30   *Introduction*

of prestige competition (Epstein 1959), as in many other urban centres in East and Central Africa, with the particular exception of Tanzania where fluent and elegant Swahili can attract deference (Whiteley 1969). It is characteristic of the heavy industrial basis of the Copperbelt towns that a specifically 'workers' language is also used there, known as Kabanga or Chilapalapa and imported from South African towns where it is known as Fanagala or Kitchen Kaffir, and arose primarily from the interaction of Zulu and English. While recognizing the extraordinary diversity of these Copperbelt lingua francas, Kashoki (*infra:* 228) concentrates on Bemba. By tracing the origins of key loan words and their approximate periods of incorporation he is able to assess the influence of migration on the development of Copperbelt Bemba. His thesis is that this development was not simply the result of European contact with Bemba speakers in town. Rather, as Bemba-speakers engaged in rural–urban circulatory migration, they adopted non-Bemba vocabulary from a variety of non-European and European rural sources.

Interestingly, some of these sources were themselves earlier migratory routes of Arab traders, using Swahili. The Catholic White Fathers' rural missions also used Swahili extensively, as well as English, and provided further sources of loan words. Circulatory migrants, in turn, carried these loan words to Copperbelt towns, where they were further diffused. There, Bemba- and Nyanja-speakers borrow from each other. Lexical complexity thereby increases and provides constant specialization of reference and meaning within and between the widening scale of town and country.

People continue, then, to move between urban and rural areas and, in doing so, modify these lingua francas lexically, phonologically, and syntactically. Nevertheless distinctive urban languages and codes are emerging. Copperbelt Bemba and Kabanga, Nyanja in Lusaka, Swahili in Nairobi, and Swahili and Luganda in Kampala (Parkin 1971, 1974; Scotten 1972), and Lingala in Kinshasa (La Fontaine 1970: 45) are each sufficiently specialized to differ significantly from their rural counterparts, where these exist. In all these and other towns, their use jostles, cheek by jowl, with the languages of former colonial administrations.

The dense polyethnic, multi-racial, and socio-economically divisive contexts of urban wage employment draw out the ambivalent connotations of these lingua francas. In some contexts Swahili in Nairobi or Kampala undoubtedly connotes brotherhood and equality and the ability to transcend ethnicity. But its use by, say, an educated English-speaker addressing an uneducated non-speaker of English, can emphasize the socio-economic differences between them and

Town and Country in Central and Eastern Africa 31

unwittingly cause resentment. Or the connation may be intended. Epstein gives an illustration from the Copperbelt before Zambia's independence in which a European abusively addresses an African Education Officer in Fangalo but angrily snubs him when the African replies in English (1959: 237f5).

This symbolic relationship between the use of a 'colonial' language and an indigenous lingua franca is widespread. Describing a comparable relationship between French and Swahili in Lubumbashi in Zaïre, Polomé says that the linguistic situation '. . . is a clear reflection of the historical growth of the town under the colonial régime' (1971: 371). And even in Tanzania the Second Vice-President expressed dismay that ten years after independence some people were still so inhibited by a 'colonial hangover' that they despised Swahili and preferred using English and French (Whiteley 1974: 4).

Lingua francas thus have comparable significance to beliefs and practices dealing with misfortunes. They are carried to and fro between town and country by people for whom they are indispensable. They facilitate the transmission of ideas between the two areas while their forms, whether lexical or symbolic, are specially adapted to the concepts of particular urban or rural situations.

In the same way that increasing education is said to reduce beliefs in indigenous ritual practices, so English or French are sometimes seen as a threat to African languages. But, as the papers in this volume show, the confrontation is not that clear-cut and there is much mutual borrowing. Results of the Kenya Language Survey of 1968–9 suggest that there may in fact be something of a paradox. For instance, Swahili in Kenya increasingly thrives in towns and yet the incentives to acquire education and, through it, English are greater and can be more easily attained in towns (Whiteley 1974: 6). Similarly, the growth and social complexity of urban populations increases rather than reduces the need for as wide a range as possible of indigenous methods of dealing with misfortune. Yet it is in town that the best modern health services are avail ble, employing highly educated and trained people.

Both education and modern medicine were originally brought in by Christian missionaries, who set up the first schools and hospitals, with the divisive and also contradictory result that a 'public' and even official stereotype has developed that the uses of Western and 'traditional' medicines are respectively the marks of education and illiteracy, even though in practice people of all educational levels may resort to both forms of therapy (see Beidelman 1974: 244–5). The ambivalent and situationally varying positions taken by ordinary

32 *Introduction*

people regarding the merits and demerits of traditional and Western medicine parallel the uncertain attitudes of most governments towards the use of a traditional lingua franca like Swahili, and a former colonial one like English.

Official attitudes to the educational system itself may also be ambivalent. Much of its colonially inherited content is recognized as inappropriate as well as socially divisive. But the existing system is still viewed by people as the biggest key to opportunities and so it is not surprising that the post-independence years have seen considerable stress placed by governments on the value of widespread and, eventually, universal education for development and, more ideologically, as an indisputable right in itself. Gould (*infra:* 250) shows how genuine efforts were made in Uganda immediately after independence to reduce regional inequalities by providing new secondary schools. But then policy changed and budgetary criteria determined that expansion should now be through enlarging existing schools. It has been cheaper to enlarge urban day-schools, for which neither food nor accommodation for pupils needed to be found, than boarding schools, which tend to be outside towns. The policy has provided many more secondary school places at least cost and so in this respect has been successful. But it has had the two unintended consequences of adding to the rural-urban flow of boys and girls and of requiring them to find urban board and lodging with relatives who may themselves have housing and employment difficulties. Insofar as employment opportunities for holders of good 'O' level school certificates are almost all in urban areas (*infra:* 262), we can see how the effect of this policy has been to reinforce people's perceptions that high education is a pre-requisite for 'acceptable' employment, and that this must be urban rather than rural.

This final example of the mutual reinforcement of policies, perceptions, and ideological thinking takes us on to consider the very fact of urban settlement and the part played by continuing rural links and relationships in shaping the structure and social composition of the expanding towns of East and Central Africa.

THE RURAL LINKS IN URBAN SETTLEMENT

(*a*) *The role of ethnicity*

Leslie describes how the migratory routes to early Dar es Salaam of different ethnic groups terminated as distinct residential quarters of the city. Ethnic groups whose routes crossed or coincided developed informal mutual help and alliance relationships, called *utani* (1963:

Town and Country in Central and Eastern Africa 33

33). Little of this remains nowadays but it is a good illustration of how a town's ethnic residential structure may be influenced by continuing rural links. In this volume Hirst (*infra:* 319) shows that Kampala's structure continues to be influenced by ethnic migratory differences, but he also stresses the importance of socio-economic status as an intervening variable. For Mombasa, Stren (1972: 97–115) gives a detailed analysis not only of how host and migrant peoples gravitate towards different residential areas, but also of how host dwellings tend to be privately owned and let by Africans themselves, while those of up-country migrants are more likely to be rented on a public housing estate.

Colonial restrictions and, latterly, dire housing scarcities in the towns of East and Central Africa may have limited the options open to distinct immigrant groupings as to whether they locate themselves separately from each other. But ethnic enclaves are variously reported and, with rapidly growing urban populations having to rely more and more on self-built housing in 'unauthorized' areas, seem likely to increase. By contrast, the new public housing estates do not officially cater for particular ethnic groups.

Again, Southall's distinction between two types of town can be used to demonstrate this new development. It will be remembered that Type A towns like Kampala, Dar es Salaam, Mombasa, and Blantyre had the characteristics of many West African cities in facilitating the residential separateness and localized corporateness of extended families, home-based groupings and ethnic enclaves. The tight administrative residential structure of such 'newer' Type B towns as Nairobi, Salisbury, Lusaka, Ndola and other Copperbelt and 'line-of-rail' towns was characterized by clearly zoned non-African (including European) and African areas, housing in the latter being controlled by municipalities or public employers such as police, railways, telecommunications, and sometimes by large private employers. Type A towns have had these kinds of controlled housing estates added, so to speak, to their basically pre-colonial residential structure as a result of colonial administration (see Southall and Gutkind 1957: 46–9 for Kampala, Stren for Mombasa (*op. cit.*), Chilivumba *infra:* 310–11 for Blantyre, and, in West Africa, Marris 1961 for Lagos).

Type B towns have, in a sense, undergone change in the opposite direction. To their controlled housing estates have recently been added increasingly larger areas of so-called uncontrolled or unauthorized housing in which distinct mono-ethnic as well as poly-ethnic 'villages' have developed. Sometimes the common regional origins of most of the residents of such a settlement are reinforced

34 *Introduction*

by their shared religious and/or political party affiliations as in the remarkable case of Kapipi in Lusaka, in which a branch of the now banned opposition political party, the African National Congress, effectively authorized the organization of trade and housing in the absence of police and local government officials (Boswell, forthcoming and 1974). The famous Mathare valley 'squatter' development in Nairobi is really an extending belt of self-help villages in which people have solved the problem of scarce housing through their own initiative (Ross 1973: 91), an achievement that has now been given some limited official recognition by the Nairobi city council (Nelson, forthcoming papers).

The point about self-help villages established in unauthorized urban areas is that, as in the essentially pre-colonial Type A towns, they do enable immigrants some greater choice in organizing domestic and ethnic settlement patterns than is possible in officially organized housing estates. We do not want to over-idealize to the extent of denying the serious over-crowding, poor amenities and sometimes high rents demanded by landlords for structurally deficient dwellings. But, to harp on an old theme, improving their services and existing lay-out where possible seems a preferable alternative to that of razing them to the ground and re-building new housing estates.

It has yet to be proved that the preservation of ethnic enclaves which may result from such official recognition is necessarily a bad thing. There is no evidence that residential urban ethnic enclaves play a fundamental role in fostering ethnic divisiveness, for which the underlying contemporary cause is surely more likely to be found in ethno-regional inequalities in the nation as a whole, as discussed in a previous section. Indeed, the trite point is worth emphasizing that urban residential ethnic enclaves provide security in a situation of economic uncertainty and, as part of this, provide both migrants and longer-established townsmen with continuous links with rural home areas. Insofar as such rural continuity may offer an admittedly slender alternative to total dependence on urban employment, through a return to peasant self-sufficiency, then such ethnic enclaves may actually be seen as an expression of resistance, so to speak, against capital-intensive urban development on the Western model, and of the preservation of rural ties.

Poly-ethnic urban settlements in unauthorized areas may be built around a core of long-established residents including landlords who have no more than nominal rural ties if that, as in the predominantly Muslim Pumwani (Bujra 1974: 197), and Kibera (Clark 1973) of Nairobi. Those of relatively recent origin, in which residents still

Town and Country in Central and Eastern Africa 35

value the maintenance of rural relationships, are at a kind of cross-roads. Their polyethnic composition does not restrict landlords to accepting only tenants of their own ethnic group. There is an absence of the informal 'moral' constraints which might otherwise be exerted on landlords in a recently established ethnic enclave, where the market for tenants is to some degree regulated by a continuing system of rural obligations. And yet, simply because they are recently established, residents in new poly-ethnic urban villages are still involved in their respective webs of rural relationships. For them, one road points to the development of a 'melting-pot' residential 'community' in which, over generations, ethnic differences are subordinated to a common cultural expression of shared urban interests. Another road points to persisting poly-ethnic differences within a settlement which separately articulate distinctive urban occupational specializations, and a third to the perpetuation of residential poly-ethnicity through distinctive interests which are more or less equally rural and urban.

The fourth possible direction is the extent to which residents are able to exercise any preference for moving to, or setting up, an ethnic enclave. This may depend on the degree of control they themselves have over the urban housing market. In this they are potentially in conflict not only with urban authorities but with other ethnic groups living in the city. Urban settlements which start out as ethnic enclaves are more likely to conflict with each other over territorial expansion, which is at least theoretically amenable to settlement by arbitration involving recognized community leaders whose legitimation may be reinforced by a continuing system of rural relationships.

Given the existence of an expanding, if unofficial, private housing market, a growing economic and political differentiation between landlords and tenants is inevitable in both poly-ethnic and mono-ethnic urban settlements. Such differentiation seems to be the case also in urban neighbourhoods which are developed as 'site and service schemes'. Here residence is based on home ownership by private individuals. Investment in a concrete block house built to a standard acceptable to the authorities indicates a permanent stake in urban residence. The stake may be heightened by the high incidence of inter-ethnic marriage. Lusaka's Kaunda Square is such an example. (Isla Schuster, personal communication). This apart, settlements which voluntarily organize themselves on a mono-ethnic basis seem most likely to retain for their residents over a relatively long period of time, the two options of self-sufficient peasant production and urban wage employment. Ultimately, of course, the extent to which these are viable options depends, as mentioned, on national planning

36   *Introduction*

policy regarding the nature of rural as against urban investment and on the avoidance of gross regional inequalities.

A strong continuity of urban and rural relationships is possible even when members of an urban ethnic group do not live near each other. They may come together at special ethnic 'events', being recruited through extensive interpersonal networks, as Weisner (1972) has shown for a Luyia sub-group in Nairobi among whom lineage affiliations remain important. Additionally, they may be organized into formal ethnic associations, about which so much has been written in Africa as a whole. It is now accepted that a host urban community is less likely to form such associations, which are more commonly found among peoples whose rural homes are at some distance from the town. Kampala is already a familiar example of this and so it is worth noting that Leslie (1963: 39) also briefly draws special attention to the 'flourishing associations' in Dar es Salaam of such 'up country' peoples as the ubiquitious Luo, and the Chagga and Pare. Apart from distance from town being a possible pre-condition, the different forms of rural social organization of urban migrant communities may influence the structure of any urban associations which do emerge (see Southall *infra:* 267 and accompanying references).

Southall is right to argue that one must analytically disentangle rural social organization from membership or otherwise of the urban host community, as distinct influences on the forms of urban organization adopted by different ethnic groups. In Type A towns, the two often went together so that a pre-colonial city would also be the capital of a kingdom with a system of rural stratification which inevitably acted as a template for further urban development of the city in colonial times. Kampala is the best example of this in East and Central Africa (see Gutkind 1963), with its dual division into two focal growth points: one of the host Ganda, and the other of the British and, under them, predominantly non-Ganda peoples. From Hirst's study (*infra:* 330–31) we see how, even nowadays, the distinction between host and migrant peoples in Kampala to some extent perpetuates and is in turn perpetuated by their 'choice' of residential location through ethnic chain migration.

The relatively recent urban host ethnic groups of Kikuyu in Nairobi, 'Nyanja-speakers' in Lusaka, or 'Bemba-speakers' in the Copperbelt towns, have no such historical template of urban organization and are more immediate products of colonialism and post-colonial industrialization. They may or may not have originally stemmed from a pre-colonial centralized political system. The Kikuyu did not, while the Bemba to some extent did, and though

Town and Country in Central and Eastern Africa 37

such differences in rural social organization are not irrelevant in urbanism even nowadays, they less directly influence the structure and social composition of the Type B towns in which their people work than is the case of the Ganda in Kampala. As mentioned above, little work has been done on the smaller townships and trading centres, identified by Middleton as Type C, though presumably their future development too, will be much moulded by the extent to which either the local or a distant ethnic group dominates the opportunities provided by expansion.

I have laboured the three distinctions between Type A and B towns, between host and migrant ethnic groups, and between precolonial centralized and non-centralized political systems, because I believe that they may continue to influence contemporary forms of urban organization, and that it is relevant to our analyses to understand how far this is the case. For instance, we may ask whether, in view of their increasing involvement in international forces governing industrial location and labour supply, Type A and B towns are converging to a common pattern. The distinction between host and migrant groups is surely relevant where ethnicity or regional identification is the primary, publicly recognized idiom of urban political and economic confrontation. Not all host groups are dominant. As mentioned above, the host people of Lusaka, identified as Tonga-Ila speakers from Zambia's Central Province and comprising mostly Sala, Sali and Lenje, have been losing their dominant influence from about 1950 onwards to Nyanja-speakers from the more distant Eastern Province. In Mombasa, Kenya, the local Mijikenda frequently complain of being 'dominated' by up-country peoples like Kikuyu, Luo and Luyia. By contrast in Nairobi it is only since Kenya's independence in 1963 that the Kikuyu have been regarded unambiguously, even by Luo, as the controlling host community in place of Europeans, whose earlier control of the city was recognized if not accepted by Kikuyu themselves (see Werlin 1974: 79–80, 126).

The distinction between pre-colonial centralized and uncentralized political systems and their possible modern relevance is the most contentious. It is obviously true that all such political systems have long been subordinated to first the colonial and later the independent state. But we must note also the persisting influence of formal and informal colonial policies of indirect rule, which made use of existing territorial units and communication channels, frequently falsifying their significance and in the end creating far sharper ethnic cultural differences than originally existed (Southall *infra:* 265).

38 *Introduction*

Let me give an example of this and its effects on rural–urban relations. In Kampala, the Ganda and Luo have highly contrasting ideologies of kinship. Ganda who achieve higher social status are not strongly obliged to continue to help large numbers of relatives, whereas Luo are. What accounts for this difference? The persisting strength of the Ganda kingdom and its constituent strata, upheld by the British, reduced the importance of extensive lineage and kin ties in town as well as in the country. By contrast, among the uncentralized Luo the British artificially froze the pre-colonial territorial divisions of lineages of varying levels, and used them for administrative purposes. Thus entrenched, such territorial divisions and the lineage principle generally have remained important and in some respects have been strengthened during the increasing involvement of Luo in wider scale political and economic developments. In town, agnatic ties among them have practical as well as ideological relevance in job-finding, in providing accommodation, in arranging marriages, as well as in upward social mobility. Also, rural home divisions of lineage and 'sub-tribe' are crucially important in the conduct of national political elections in both urban and rural areas (Okumu 1969). These two examples of the Ganda and Luo suggest that, while pre-colonial political systems, *qua* political systems, are by definition non-existent, it is wrong to argue that the organizational and ideological patterns set up by such differences have ceased to have relevance in contemporary industrial contexts (*pace* Grillo 1973: 180).

Any attempt at high-level generalizations of the kind represented by these three distinctions necessarily glosses over particular variations. Halpenny (*infra:* 281–6) is right to emphasize how, among the host Ganda in Kampala, there is in fact much more variation in their *internal* pattern of migration than among other ethnic groups. For the independent status of Ganda women, who are called *nakyeyombekedde*, results in distinctive female modes of migration which not only differ from those of women of other ethnic groups but also from those of their own Ganda menfolk. On the other hand, when considering the totality of inter-ethnic relations in Kampala, Ganda female emancipation stands in some marked contrast to the status of other women, a contrast which can be explained by the broad cultural differences of kinship organization outlined above and by the proximity of rural land-owning opportunities for Ganda women in Kampala.

The migration of another category of 'independent' or 'emancipated' females depends less on ethnic affiliation than on education and vocational training. When access to these is not related to mem-

Town and Country in Central and Eastern Africa   39

bership of a particular ethnic group, a new urban-based, sub-élite status group which is poly-ethnic and self-aware may emerge, partly as a result of the nationalization of the skilled labour force. Schuster (forthcoming) describes such a process in Zambia.

(*b*) *Independent women in low income urban areas.*

Halpenny and Obbo (*infra:* 288–93) provide rich material on the ways in which the presence or absence of rural and urban opportunities for women provides the conditions for the emergence of distinctively female urban 'sub-cultures' which frequently cut across ethnic differences held to be important by men. Data from Nelson on Kikuyu and Bujra (1973) on Muslim women in Nairobi support those of Halpenny and Obbo in confirming the trend in East and Central African towns for women increasingly to engage in beer-brewing, distilling, food-preparation and sale, house-letting, as well as prostitution, and so to provide services for male urban employees. Whereas men can work in both the so-called formal and informal sectors of urban employment, most opportunities for unskilled women are confined to the informal sector.

There may be the germ of an hypothesis here. Given that urban employment opportunities are so sharply divided between men and women, and that women must first achieve relatively independent status in order to take advantage of those available to them, we may hypothesize that the common interests of women of all ethnic groups will increasingly be expressed in distinctive female life-styles and marital preferences; and that the development towards a common urban female sub-culture may stand in contrast to the persistence of ethnic cultural differences among urban males. The persistence of ethnic differentiation among males depends on their control of female out-marriage rates and/or on consistent paternity claims as a means of perpetuating group distinctiveness over succeeding generations. Therefore, any developing cross-sexual cultural transformations, in which women come to control marital arrangements and have custody of children born to them, have important implications for the future nature of urban inter-ethnic relations as well as simply relations between men and women. The growing informal sector of the urban economy is one increasingly influenced by women and so, in this respect, the prospective patterns of political and economic relationships in urban Africa do seem to turn much more on the innovatory roles of women than of men.

At present, the marked ethnic difference between the statuses of, say, Ganda and Luo women might seem too great to warrant the above hypothesis, which is deliberately stated in broad terms. But

40 *Introduction*

Obbo's study of a low-income area in Kampala, in which women from different ethnic groups together form the backbone of the informal economy, demonstrates the convergence to a more common female pattern of expectations, aspirations and techniques for survival, which is already assuming its own distinctive ethos.

There is even the possibility of a partial reversal of male and female statuses from those customarily associated with 'pre–urban' conditions. Men, as explained, are increasingly encouraged by the educational system to seek white-collar work in towns built up or expanding on the basis of capital-intensive enterprises. Women, by contrast, generally have little opportunity to enter such employment and must use their own initiative in getting to town and finding and creating work there, usually within the informal sector. As a generalization, it is possible to argue that men's aspirations are more likely to lead them to dependency on employment beyond their immediate control than is the case with women, who, though hardly unexploited, have more direct control over their own forms of productive enterprise.

It has to be acknowledged that, though the migration of women to towns in East and Central Africa seems proportionally on the increase, as Ohadike shows for Lusaka (*infra:* 132), most are still economically dependent wives who are unlikely in the near future to assume the independent status of the women described by Obbo and Halpenny. These latter are more directly the products of allegedly low income[1] urban areas in which so-called informal types of employment flourish. But the proportionate urban expansion of such areas surely points to a relative growth in their numbers and, in view of the importance of the services which they provide, of their economic and, indeed, political influence.

Given the continuing expansion of low-income urban areas, the transition by women from economic dependency on males to some degree of economic emancipation rests on five general attributes which are implicitly considered in Obbo's paper.

(1) Women form the backbone of the informal economy in low-income urban areas, just as they have often supported rural agricultural economies.

(2) Employment in such areas depends on personal initiative rather than on special training or education, so that women are not in this respect disadvantaged.

(3) While among both men and women economic factors are fundamental in generating urban immigration, the precipitating

[1] In fact data from Nelson on the Mathare valley women beer brewers suggest incomes as high as the formal sector average.

Town and Country in Central and Eastern Africa   41

factors among women probably encompass a wider range and relate to such rural stigma as pregnancy outside of marriage, and divorce or separation, and to such restrictions on self-advancement as inability to inherit or acquire land, or limited educational opportunities compared with brothers.

(4) Though limited, the urban informal economy offers women a wider range of careers than is normally possible in rural areas, and yet, in later life, may enable them to re-invest income in rural assets.

(5) The constant process of marital and family re-definition, which in different forms is world-wide and neither wholly urban nor rural, finds its greatest expression in urban areas providing opportunities for informal employment.

This is not the place to make comparisons with the economic status of women in West Africa, except to acknowledge that there it has generally advanced far beyond reliance on occupational opportunities offered in low-income areas of the Namuwongo-Wabigalo and Kisenyi type described in this volume (Little 1973: 45–6).

(c) The control of urban residence
Like Halpenny, Van Velsen (*infra:* 296) stresses the contribution to the urban and, indeed, national economy by both the men and women of these areas, who are usually officially labelled as 'unemployed'. He asks why it is, then, that the city authorities in Lusaka still tend to view the areas in a negative light as fit only for demolition. The plethora of adjectives used to describe these settlements, including 'squatter', 'slum', and 'shanty', reinforce this negative image. The most telling is that of 'unauthorized'. For Van Velsen argues that in Lusaka, and presumably in other African towns, this term derives from planning regulations dating back to a colonial system of local urban government which was geared to controlling, among other things, the town's racial distribution of residents. Arising out of such policies, the broad racial division into European, Asian and African residential areas is nowadays increasingly giving way to one based on status groups and classes, as described in this volume by Chilivumbo for Blantyre and by Ohadike for Lusaka, and an invariable feature of all major towns in East and Central Africa.

By a systematic contextual analysis of a Zambian newspaper editorial condoning the demolition of an 'unauthorized' 'squatter' settlement in Lusaka, Van Velsen suggests that the city planners are trapped by essentially colonial regulations and legalistic definitions which have no bearing on the real needs of an independent urban

42   *Introduction*

African population, however much they may previously have suited Europeans.

Thus, the official view is, or until recently was,[2] that squatters in Lusaka constitute a 'problem' because they have taken over what was called Crown Land in colonial times. Yet, looked at from the viewpoint of Zambians themselves, it is in fact public land and so presents none of the difficulties inherent in the status of squatter settlements built on privately owned land, as is commonly the case in Latin America. Van Velsen's argument is that, if urban authorities could recognize the economic contribution made by people living in such areas, then, unhampered by costly and time-consuming negotiations with private land owners for compensation, they could easily convert the settlements into self-help schemes enjoying better facilities. This point is well taken. For, Grohs suggests (1972: 165), the decision to destroy and rebuild from scratch is often favoured simply because it is also administratively the least complicated of alternatives, as well as conforming to established practice.

A number of the official justifications for removing unauthorized settlements in Lusaka are shown by Van Velsen to be mythical: the areas are not largely inhabited by bachelors but include a significant proportion of families; the distribution of occupations broadly corresponds with that of municipal housing areas; they are not overrun by rural emigrants seeking jobs; and, given the high percentage of men in wage employment in Zambia, these areas accommodate not 'squatters' but an important proportion of the country's labour force.

With its considerable mineral wealth, Zambia does not have anywhere near the same degree of 'under- and unemployment' as do other countries of East and Central Africa, and so it is not surprising to find relatively little difference in demographic and socioeconomic patterns between authorized and unauthorized urban residential areas.

Though in this respect exceptional, the case nevertheless illustrates

[2] Schuster comments: 'The official view is no longer that squatters in Lusaka constitute a "problem". The notion that squatters were a "solution" was current in Lusaka in the years 1971–3 and the subject of a campaign by a group called "Social Action in Lusaka". Squatters: Problem or Solution was the SAIL slogan. SAIL is a voluntary association run by Zambians and expatriates who ran a series of articles in the newspaper, appeared on radio and generally publicized this view while working on the local level on development projects. Partly as a result of SAIL's activities, squatter policy seems to have changed in 1973, and urban authorities are increasingly receptive to the economic contribution of squatters, or at least increasingly realistic about accepting the existence of these compounds, which, however, are still viewed as "eyesores" to be hidden away from visitors to the country'.

Town and Country in Central and Eastern Africa 43

a more general contradiction, pushed very much further, between an ex-colonial urban planning philosophy and the needs of a town's population. Examples from non-Zambian towns of the destruction of unauthorized and their replacement with authorized dwellings are perhaps early manifestations of this contradiction. This happened in parts of Pumwani, Nairobi (Bujra forthcoming) but was, creditably, partially reversed in the case of settlements in the city's Mathare valley (see also ILO Report 1972: 227).

It is now becoming recognized that the conversion of unauthorized settlements into self-help schemes requires a lowering of the often unrealistically high building standards required by officialdom (see Gugler: 7; Safier: 31; Rado and Wells: 222; all in Hutton (ed.) 1972). It takes little imagination to envisage the possible beginnings of yet another contradiction between the common-sense policy of self-help house building through intermediate technology and the interests of city planning authorities, should these latter become heavily involved in the fortunes of private construction firms using capital-intensive technology and materials. The economic advantage of a labour-intensive house-building policy from a national view-point, is in making use of under- and unemployed urban immigrants and so conceivably enabling money which would otherwise be spent on satisfying high building standards to be diverted to rural improvement schemes.

Consideration of such policy raises the question of how the balance is weighted between rural and urban opportunities and incomes. The seminar considered this issue at length. The main methodogical problem was how to reconcile the mutually irreducible criteria of social or humanitarian as against economic benefits as measures of whether townspeople are or are not better off than rural residents. If 'purely' economic criteria can be isolated, it should be possible to determine who subsidizes whom. In Zambia there is evidence to argue that the real incomes of small family farmers have declined, even though their agricultural output has increased, while those of urban workers have risen (Fry 1975). On the other hand, it could be argued, as does Van Velsen, that the so-called 'squatters' of Lusaka contribute considerably to the urban economy yet receive few services in return. Or, one could argue more generally that continuing and increased dependency on urban wage employment reduces a worker's and his family's chances of exercising the option of returning to rural peasant production for self-sufficiency. However, the explanation of personal advantages and disadvantages in terms of differing rural and urban terms of trade must not ignore the continuing involvement in their rural areas of most townsmen,

44 *Introduction*

as has been stressed by many papers in this volume. Nor must it blind us to the fact that the terms of trade in both rural *and* urban areas, with their growing proportions of educated job-seekers, are still becoming increasingly unfavourable in the third world as a whole compared with industrialized nations, even allowing for the very geographically limited exception of major oil-producing countries. We come back, then, to the viewpoint originally expressed in the first section of this introduction, that the migratory, ideological, cultural, and organizational links between town and country may in the first instance be patterned by the distribution of resources and opportunities within the nation, but that ultimately they are to be understood as responses to international factors which are becoming increasingly beyond the control of local populations. That East and Central Africa are not alone in this, does not lessen the immediacy of their predicament.

Introduction
French Version

LE CONTEXTE INTERNATIONAL DE LA MIGRATION ET DU DEVELOPPEMENT EN AFRIQUE

Les migrations contemporaines en Afrique de l'Ouest ont fait l'objet de multiples études, certaines regroupées dans un ouvrage de l'Institut International Africain (Amin 1974) que l'on peut, à certains égards, considérer comme le pendant du présent volume. Cependant, et comme son titre l'indique, celui-ci ne traite pas uniquemeut des migrations contemporaines. Il s'attache plutôt à étudier une série de facteurs intervenant dans le développement de processus sociaux, en milieu urbain comme en milieu rural: au même titre que les migrations, le flux et le reflux des croyances et des idéologies, les possibilités ouvertes en matière de formation et d'emploi. Ces phénomènes peuvent être circonscrits à une ville ou à une zone rurale bien définie; cependant, dans la mesure où ils concernent des groupes sociaux, ils sont influencés par les changements qui affectent les membres éloignés, citadins ou ruraux, de ces mêmes groupes.

Cet ouvrage postule, au départ, que les zones rurales et urbaines d'Afrique Centrale et d'Afrique de l'Est font partie d'un même champ de relations, constitué par d'intenses brassages de peuples, d'idées, de ressources. C'est, en fait, le problème étudié qui définit les limites dans lesquelles ce champ s'inscrit. Alors que la diffusion des idées et des idéologies novatrices s'opère à grande échelle, les mouvements de populations, de fonds et de biens matériels sont, en général, plus étroitement contrôlés par les instances administratives et politiques, ce qui justifie, s'il en était besoin, la délimitation de l'Afrique Centrale et de l'Afrique de l'Est en tant que champ d'enquête socio-géographique, au sein duquel les migrations de travail ont tissé leurs liens.

Les études qui composent ce volume ont été menées dans les pays suivants: l'Ouganda, le Kenya, la Tanzanie, pour l'Afrique de de l'Est; la Zambie, le Malawi, la Rhodésie—ou Zimbabwe—pour l'Afrique Centrale; tous pays qui, au cours de leur passé colonial sous domination britannique, furent soumis à diverses tentatives d'intégration économique. En 1953, une entreprise coloniale, visant

46 *Introduction*

à transformer les services communs pour la fiscalité et les transports en une fédération, échoua en 1963, peu avant l'indépendance de la Zambie. Au début des années 60, une autre tentative, avortée celle-là, des gouvernements indépendants de l'Afrique de l'Est pour constituer une fédération sur des bases identiques. La Communauté est-africaine, n'a, jusqu'à présent, que très peu de réalisations à son actif. L'Organisation des Services Communs d'Afrique de l'Est (EACSO) continue à administrer le réseau ferroviaire commun, les ports, les postes, les télécommunications, mais le projet de fédération reste lointain. Les événements politiques survenus ces quelques douze dernières années, depuis les indépendances, ont déjà redéfini le modèle colonial des contacts, y compris, comme nous allons le voir, celui des migrations de travail. Cependant, des survivances persistent, au nombre desquelles une large utilisation de l'anglais, dans des domaines variés, des appareils administratifs et judiciaires similaires, la Tanzanie étant la plus affranchie du modèle colonial. Ceci dit, il est regrettable que le manque de crédits n'ait pas permis d'inclure dans cette publication certaines contributions, par exemple des études consacrées au Zaïre ou à l'Ethiopie non anglophones, qui auraient pu servir de points de comparaison.

Compte tenu de la richesse de la littérature concernant l'Afrique de l'Ouest et la parution récente de l'ouvrage de S. Amin, j'ai essayé de me cantonner, dans cette introduction, et pour ce qui est des références et des comparaisons, à l'Afrique Centrale et l'Afrique de l'Est. Le volume traitant des migrations en Afrique de l'Ouest soulève des problèmes importants; l'un d'entre eux nous servira de point de départ, à titre comparatif.

Dans son introduction, S. Amin souligne le caractère intégrateur des flux migratoires en Afrique de l'Ouest. Il écrit: 'Malgré la balkanisation de la région, il s'agit encore de migrations qui ne sont pas gênées outre mesure par les frontières d'Etat et qui gardent de ce fait un caractère largement international' (1974: 8). Dans quelle mesure cette assertion s'applique-t-elle à l'Afrique de l'Est et à l'Afrique Centrale?

Les artisans des Fédérations d'Afrique de l'Est et d'Afrique Centrale se rendirent aux prévisions que la Communauté Economique Européenne avait avancées à l'origine, à savoir la libre circulation de la main-d'œuvre entre les Etats membres, qui autorise un transfert de la main-d'œuvre des régions sans débouchés vers celles qui en proposent, aussi bien qu'une répartition des qualifications au gré des besoins. Mais, le flux de main-d'œuvre circulant entre les pays qui auraient pu constituer deux fédérations, s'est considérablement ralenti depuis les indépendances car, à compter de ce moment,

La ville et la campagne en Afrique   47

chaque Etat s'est attaché à singulariser l'originalité de son idéologie nationale et de ses objectifs politico-économiques. Chilivumbo (*infra:* 309) présente le retour au Malawi, de Zambie, de Rhodésie et d'Afrique du Sud, d'une nombreuse main-d'œuvre migrante, à la fois comme une conséquence des options politiques de chacun de ces pays, mais aussi comme un facteur important d'urbanisation du Malawi. Ohadike signale lui aussi que le strict contrôle de l'immigration en Zambie est en partie à l'origine de la diminution du nombre de travailleurs étrangers et du refus de ceux qui s'étaient déjà installés d'être identifiés en tant que tels (*infra:* 140). De la même façon, le départ d'Ouganda de nombre de migrants kényans, prévisible dès le début des années 60 (Parkin 1969a : 11), semble se confirmer graduellement.

Sur un plan plus général, Uchendu (*infra:* 176) explique que de telles barrières se sont érigées parce que : '. . . l'industrialisation croissante et le chômage naissant dans les pays africains ont conduit à une rivalité entre main-d'œuvre internationale et main-d'œuvre locale'. Ce qui est, comme le note Uchendu, une conséquence de la propension au 'nationalisme économique' propre aux États africains. Mais, par-delà cette propension, les alignements ou ruptures politiques entre nations peuvent également infléchir l'orientation et, inversement, entraîner l'arrêt des flux migratoires, comme en témoigne si bien la situation en Afrique Centrale et en Afrique de l'Est. Nous avons parlé de ruptures. Ainsi, la ligne politique de l'Ouganda, qui—pour ne pas être orthodoxe—est incontestablement indépendante, sous le président Amin, trouve un écho dans le refoulement des Kényans et des Tanzaniens, et, à un moindre degré, des réfugiés rwandais; tout comme l'ambivalence de la position politique du Malawi vis-à-vis de l'Afrique du Sud, dominée par les Blancs, et de la Zambie, indépendante, explique le retour chez eux de nombreux Malawiens qui avaient émigré dans ces pays.

Inversement, les liens politiques relativement récents entre la Tanzanie et la Zambie, que traduit à l'évidence la décision de construire en commun le chemin de fer Tanzam, après la déclaration unilatérale d'indépendance de la Rhodésie, peut se prolonger dans d'autres directions et, ce faisant, accélérer les échanges (limités, mais d'ores et déjà significatifs) d'hommes et de biens entre les deux pays. L'indépendance imminente de l'Afrique d'expression portugaise peut évidemment modifier les configurations politiques naissantes; au même titre que les décisions des gouvernements voisins d'ériger, ou de renforcer, les barrières officielles ou tacites qui font obstacle aux mouvements de leurs populations respectives. Jusqu'à présent, la Tanzanie et la Zambie sont les deux seules

48   *Introduction*

exceptions échappant à une évidente tendance au séparatisme en Afrique de l'Est et en Afrique Centrale.

Alors qu'on peut interpréter tout attachement au nationalisme économique comme une réaction des dirigeants politiques pour protéger l'emploi en faveur des ressortissants de leur pays, et qui vise, partant, à réduire la migration de main-d'œuvre internationale, il ne faut pas, pour autant, négliger de prendre en compte l'incidence, moins tangible, du réseau industriel implanté à travers l'Afrique par les grandes entreprises étrangères (dont les directions se trouvent dans les capitales du monde industriel).

Le rôle et la puissance des sociétés multinationales sont reconnus et largement débattus, référence faite à l'Amérique du Nord, à l'Europe et à d'autres parties du monde. Mais un processus analogue —impliquant des compagnies étrangères—se dessinne en Afrique, où la main-d'œuvre est considérée comme une ressource, au demeurant la plus abondante de toutes et, partant, la moins onéreuse. Il faut savoir que, dans une large mesure, le chômage tenu comme tel par les différents gouvernements africains, et à l'origine de l'orientation vers le nationalisme économique, n'est souvent la déception de l'attente de ceux qui escomptaient de nouveaux emplois grâce à l'implantation d'une industrie financée par des capitaux étrangers. La finalité de telles industries est de faire fructifier un capital, beaucoup plus que d'employer massivement la main-d'œuvre locale, même si son bon marché constitue l'attrait déterminant pour les investisseurs étrangers (ILO Report 1972: 184–7).

Cette industrie à intensité capitalistique modèle, par conséquent, la définition officielle du chômage. Ce type d'industrie peut être hautement productif mais faire appel à une main-d'œuvre d'employés administratifs, de travailleurs qualifiés et, dans une moindre part, à une main-d'œuvre non qualifiée, mais, en fait, peu de monde par rapport à la main-d'œuvre requise par les formes de production non industrielles, ou même par rapport à celle que requiert une technologie intermédiaire (définie par Schumacher 1974: 128, 143–59; exemples dans Uchendu, *infra:* 171). Les besoins d'une industrie de ce type en employés et ouvriers qualifiés répondent parfaitement à la finalité du système d'enseignement, hérité de l'époque coloniale, orienté vers la formation d'agents de production. Ainsi, chaque pays d'Afrique Centrale et d'Afrique de l'Est dispose d'une jeunesse toujours plus nombreuse, de citoyens toujours plus instruits qui aspirent aux emplois administratifs ou qualifiés auxquels, les a-t-on incité à croire, leur formation leur permet de prétendre. Aussi longtemps qu'autant de personnes à la recherche d'un emploi partageront de telles aspirations et considéreront toute autre forme de travail,

La ville et la campagne en Afrique 49

souvent de nature indépendante, comme un pis-aller temporaire, voire même une forme de 'chômage', les plus gros employeurs, gouvernments compris, continueront à évaluer l'aptitude à exercer un emploi sur des critères officiels de niveau d'instruction. La conviction générale que diplômes et emplois supérieurs vont de pair est renforcée par la tendance croissante à installer les écoles secondaires, en plus grand nombre et de meilleure qualité, en milieu urbain plutôt qu'en milieu rural, comme le montre Gould pour l'Ouganda *infra:* 250–62), tendance qui encourage ainsi le mouvement des jeunes qui affluent de la campagne vers la ville.

Une deuxième caractéristique de cette industrie à intensité capitalistique procède du fait qu'elle est, la plupart du temps, propriété étrangère ou qu'elle s'établit grâce à un apport étranger et aux fonds de développement. Le gouvernement et l'organisme de développement étranger font parfois valoir leur préférence, pour que les entreprises qu'ils financent orientent leur activité vers la production de biens destinés à l'exportation. Amin cite un cas au Sénégal (1974 : 26–7) où une option théorique entre deux possibilités devait être arrêtée : d'une part, l'affectation de fonds à la construction d'un barrage, propre à conforter l'indépendance sénégalaise en produisant de l'électricité et en offrant une solution d'irrigation, mais qui n'aurait aucune incidence sur la production destinée à l'exportation; d'autre part, un projet arachidier qui renforcerait cette production et qui est choisi pour cette raison. Il est, de toute évidence, intéressant de créer des possibilités d'exportation. Mais on est tout aussi raisonnablement fondé à rappeler qu'un certain équilibre doit être préservé. A moins que l'argent ne soit réellement donné pour améliorer les possibilités d'indépendance économique d'un pays sous-développé, un don déguisé de cet argent ne contribuera qu'à accentuer sa dépendance vis-à-vis des conditions du marché extérieur et des instances financières étrangères. Et cela d'autant plus quand cette industrie à intensité capitalistique, y compris l'agriculture hautement mécanisée, instaure un besoin *durable* d'équipement technologique importé, de pièces de rechange, à savoir tout ce qui se rattache à l'entretien des tracteurs, besoins qui persistent bien après que l'entreprise elle-même soit achevée et amortie. Une conséquence probable à cette dépendance persistante est une ingérence accrue des investisseurs étrangers ou bailleurs de fonds pour imposer leurs choix quant à l'implantation d'une nouvelle industrie, en milieu agricole ou urbain, sans considération particulière prêtée à l'équilbre du développement régional.

Bien qu'on ne veuille pas, ici, engager une polémique, il est évident qu'au sein d'une nation, et parfois entre nations, de tels facteurs

50 *Introduction*

pèsent sur l'orientation des flux migratoires, sur leur ampleur et sur la condition sociale des migrants, et même sur l'intangible différence qu'Etat et migrants instituent entre salariat, chômage et sous-emploi.

Il est intéressant de noter à ce propos que Mitchell (1960: 171; 1966: 49) et Southall (1961: 5) établissent tous deux un rapport entre les structures migratoires d'une part, les instructions et les restrictions, tant administratives que politiques, léguées par le régime colonial, d'autre part, les tenant pour des agents extérieurs des relations sociales en milieu urbain. On est fondé à penser qu'en toute vraisemblance, au cours de la période coloniale, ce sont les décisions politiques du gouvernement, pour promouvoir ou protéger les intérêts économiques, qui ont déterminé dans une large mesure le volume et l'orientation des flux migratoires; et, qu'inversement, ces derniers créèrent le contexte 'extrinsèque' au sein duquel les relations sociales rurales et urbaines se développèrent. En d'autres termes, les agents externes renvoient à différents niveaux où s'opèrent les déterminations. Ce qui continuera à s'appliquer à ceux des pays africains indépendants dont les économies nationales sont trop étroitment tributaires des marchés, de la technologie, des fournisseurs du monde industrialisé et dont les méthodes traditionnelles de production et de distribution, qui leur permettent au moins une indépendance partielle, sont toujours négligées.

Cet exposé nous a permis jusqu'à présent d'étudier les mécanismes des migrations contemporaines en Afrique Centrale et en Afrique de l'Est sous l'angle de leur vulnérabilité aux forces politiques et économiques, tant au niveau national qu'international. Nous n'oublions pas que les grands déplacements de population ont été généralement unt trait des processus de peuplement précoloniaux en Afrique de l'Est et en Afrique Centrale, ainsi que du commerce et de l'organisation des marchés dans ces régions, tels qu'ils le furent, peut-être plus encore, en Afrique de l'Ouest (Meillassoux 1971: 25–35 et 197–281). Mais, contrairement aux migrations contemporaines, le moteur de ces déplacements n'était pas l'apport de main-d'œuvre aux industries à intensité capitalistique ou produisant des biens pour l'exportation. Il est vrai que la plupart des migrants salariés d'aujourd'hui peuvent ne pas travailler tous dans ce secteur. Mais les grandes entreprises de rentabilisation capitalistique installées par (ou avec) l'aide de fonds non-africains—sous forme d'aide privée ou d'aide étrangère—semblent jouer le rôle de foyers autour desquels se cristallisent d'autres activités économiques créatrices d'emplois, y compris les petits travaux qui ne sont ni reconnus ni officiellement recensés par les ministères du travail de ces pays.

La ville et la campagne en Afrique 51

Ainsi, dans ce sens, même certains aspects de ce secteur appelé informel (femmes migrantes en milieu urbain fournissant indépendamment une nourriture bon marché et d'autres services à des hommes peu rémunérés dans des bureaux ou des ateliers, comme le décrit Obbo, (*infra:* 290) peuvent, jusqu'à un certain point, dépendre de l'implantation de telles entreprises.

Toutes ces idées ne sont bien entendu que généralités qu'il convient d'approfondir par des recherches ultérieures. Peu de participants à ce séminaire ont prêté suffisamment attention à l'incidence de ces facteurs internationaux qui lient les nations africaines au monde extérieur. Cependant, nombre d'entre eux en ont clairement reconnu l'influence, en l'admettant toutefois plus qu'en l'analysant. Se conformant à la tradition des séminaires de l'Institut International Africain, on entreprit des études poussées de situations très partielles qui, si on les analyse indépendamment du contexte d'une éventuelle extension de la dépendance économique vis-à-vis de l'extérieur de l'Afrique de l'Est et de l'Afrique Centrale, montrent dans quelle mesure des groupements locaux se trouvent affectés par des facteurs nationaux, internationaux et globaux qui les dépassent totalement. Ce qui apporte un correctif important aux généralités énoncées ci-dessus, ainsi qu'aux modèles de développement de quelques économistes qui, sitôt énoncés, ne sont que truismes s'ils ne peuvent rendre compte de tous les aspects du processus social qui se réfractent au sein de populations relativement restreintes. Ceci dit sans volonté d'entamer une polémique à l'encontre de la formulation de telles généralisations. Et c'est à juste titre que Southall stigmatise l'anthropologie urbaine pour les avoir négligés, et pour insister sur le fait qu'on persiste à produire des analyses approfondies de situations à très petite échelle et qu'il convient de les confronter aux généralisations pour tester l'exactitude des conclusions avancées.

Les modèles des mouvements migratoires devraient, au même titre que les modèles de développement élaborés par les économistes, être applicables à tout une gamme de situations sociales. La première partie de ce livre comprend quatre articles qui, pour deux d'entre eux, proposent clairement de nouveaux modèles (Mitchell et Garbett) et, pour les deux autres, examinent des modèles déjà anciens (Ohadike et Parkin).

MODÈLES DE PROCESSUS MIGRATOIRES

Le débat sur les conditions qui précipitent les migrations de travail a inévitablement conduit à s'interroger sur la part que l'analyse doit faire au libre arbitre du migrant—qui choisit une solution parmi

52 *Introduction*

d'autres—et celle qu'elle doit ménager aux facteurs politiques, économiques, écologiques qui induisent et déterminent les flux migratoires de groupes spécifiques. Amin aborde ce problème et écrit sans ambiguïté: '. . . le choix du migrant de quitter sa région d'origine est [donc] tout entier *prédéterminé* par la stratégie d'ensemble qui détermine les "dotations en facteurs" ', c'est-à-dire la stratégie globale de développement d'un pays ou d'une région. Les motivations explicites ou implicites ayant présidé aux choix effectués par les migrants sont appréhendées comme autant de rationalisations d'une situation essentiellement mue par des facteurs qui échappent au contrôle du migrant (Amin 1974: 28, 32). Plus vigoureusement encore: 'L'enquête des motivations, par laquelle le sociologue croit qu'il pourra trancher entre la motivation économique et la motivation extra-économique, est en réalité sans intérêt, car la cause économique est réelle dans tous les cas, et son *habillement idéologique* également général'. Mon propre article (Parkin *infra:* 146) remarque que les études antérieures du phénomène migratoire en Afrique coloniale n'avaient pas à tenir compte du chômage. Elles cernaient de près les choix auxquels les migrants s'arrêtaient, quand ils avaient à décider de l'opportunité et de la direction d'un déplacement. Il se peut qu'ait existé une courte période transitoire, entre la demande coloniale initiale de main-d'œuvre et un seuil ultérieur de saturation, lorsqu'une gamme quelque peu plus étendue de solutions s'offrait à eux. Mais ils ne disposèrent jamais du réel pouvoir d'opter indifféremment—condition même du choix, au sens vrai du terme. Nous sommes, de nos jours, tenus de prêter attention au phénomène du chômage et aux conséquences qu'entraîne l'absence, ou la rareté, de tels choix.

Mon analyse tient compte de la finalité urbaine des flux migratoires, celle d'une rivalité entre groupes ethniques, ou régionaux, pour les quelques rares emplois et non moins rares logements. Elle suggère que ces déplacements rotatifs, que Mitchell a identifiés le premier, déplacements d'hommes passant plus ou moins volontairement d'un emploi au chômage, d'une zone urbaine à une zone rurale, et vice-versa, regroupent, en fait, un nombre toujours croissant de jeunes hommes, relativement bien instruits, à la recherche d'un emploi, qui se déplacent entre la ville et la campagne, ou vont de ville en ville (cf. spécialement Gutkind 1967 et 1968). Les migrations rotatives persistent, mais leur composition et leur intensité ont changé.

Tous arguments qui abondent dans le sens de l'approche de S. Amin, pas suffisamment toutefois pour écarter les aspects idéologiques ou socio-culturels comme autant d''habillements' inopérants.

La ville et la campagne en Afrique 53

Il est reconnu, voilà longtemps que Mitchell et bien d'autres l'ont démontré, que les facteurs économiques sont des agents essentiels de migration. Mais on ne peut se rendre à l'argument que les 'motivations extra-économiques', dans la mesure où ce sont des justifications culturellement cohérentes et pas seulement des idiosyncrasies, ne sont que peu importantes ou 'également générales'. Ce qui signifierait qu'on néglige, par exemple, l'influence d'une idéologie patrilinéaire, localement bien affirmée, sur les effets de l'émigration rurale qui, Watson l'a montré pour les Mambwe de Zambie (1958: 112–36), est mieux à même de prévenir l'éclatement de concessions rurales qu'une idéologie matrilinéaire—telle que celle des Bemba— ou sa rémanence dans l'organisation urbaine des migrants—telle dans le cas des Luo, Luyia, Ibo et Tiv, une structure pyramidale spécifique d'associations ethniques urbaines (Southall *infra*: 1975; et Parkin 1966, 1969a). Les relations ethniques constituent le cadre au sein duquel s'exerce une rivalité pour obtenir emplois et logements, et infléchissent donc directement les structures migratoires. Or, dans la mesure où un groupe ethnique se distingue par la somme de ses traits socio-culturels et idéologiques, il convient d'analyser ces traits pour eux-mêmes. L'ethnicité, en Afrique, pourrait bien être une sorte de fausse conscience ou une mystification détournant l'attention des migrants de la rupture fondamentale consécutive au passage d'un mode de production paysan à un mode de production industriel. S'il en est ainsi, on en est d'autant plus fondé à analyser le phénomène et ses 'habillements idéologiques'.

La distinction entre variables économiques et variables idéologiques (ou culturelles) du phénomène migratoire recoupe en partie celle que fait Mitchell (1959) entre *taux* d'émigration, fondé principalement sur les besoins économiques, et *incidence* de la migration, fondée sur les besoins et préférences 'sociales'. Celles-ci renvoient aux rôles et croyances traditionnels ayant, pour un migrant et en vertu de son appartenance à un groupe ethnique ou culturel, valeur normative ou symbolique. Dans ce sens, ils sont idéologiques.

Ces coutumes, symboles et valeurs ont un effet global sur une société, puisque les citoyens s'y réfèrent constamment. Ainsi, un individu prend pour prétexte les pratiques de sorcellerie exercées à son encontre pour justifier sa décision d'émigrer; un autre prétend que ce sont les fréquentes querelles de demi-frères qui le font partir; un autre allègue qu'il doit amasser de l'argent pour payer une 'compensation matrimoniale'; d'autres recourent au prétexte d'événements, d'obligations ou de croyances connues de tous pour justifier leur départ. Le répertoire des 'motifs' possibles de départ est étendu, ses limites sont celles de l'admis et du plausible

54 *Introduction*

dans la société de référence. C'est donc qu'un prétexte de départ soi-disant 'économique', par exemple pour constituer une 'compensation matrimoniale', relève autant du phénomène culturel que du désir de partir par peur d'être ensorcelé : les deux niveaux d'explication ne sont que justifications mais que les partenaires comprennent parce que leurs références culturelles sont communes.

Il est vrai que dans certaines sociétés, la compensation matrimoniale est lourde, chez les Korekore par exemple (Garbett *infra:* 122), et ne peut être constituée que grâce aux salaires perçus en migration. Mais, la signification économique d'une compensation matrimoniale d'un montant si élevé—entraînant émigration—ne peut s'appréhender que si on la replace dans le contexte général de l'offre et de la demande. Cet ensemble de facteurs économiques, façonné par des directives et des restrictions politiques et administratives émanant de l'extérieur, dont j'ai évoqué la nature, détermine le *taux* d'émigration. Par contre, l'*incidence* de la migration s'exprime, pour chaque individu, en termes de préférences dans un système de valeurs et de croyances.

L'article de Mitchell sur l'absentéisme rural masculin (*infra:* 93) traite plus du *taux* que de l'*incidence* de ce phénomène. Ce qui revient à dire qu'il n'évalue pas des variables idéologiques ou culturelles, parce que son étude repose sur des données quantitatives, relevant de l'analyse statistique. Comme il le fait remarquer, son étude se propose de fournir une base 'contextuelle' à d'autres études plus complètes. Son modèle veut démontrer comment l'absentéisme rural masculin peut varier en fonction de huit autres variables : la densité de peuplement de la région; la proportion d'hommes à la recherche d'un emploi; leur niveau d'instruction; l'éventail des salaires pratiqués dans la région; la distance les séparant de possibilités d'emploi; la proportion d'habitants employés sur place et de personnes employées dans des boutiques; enfin, le type agro-écologique de la région de départ et celui de la région d'arrivée.

La variable première, ce sont les avantages agro-écologiques qu'offre une région et l'existence d'une communauté européenne de cultivateurs, comme c'est le cas en Rhodésie. La région de Chiduku, dans le district de Makoni, densément peuplée, compte des fermes et des villages européens qui offrent en quantité des emplois locaux, dont les rémunérations sont équivalentes à la moyenne nationale. Par contre, dans la région de Chipise, dans le district de Beit Bridge, faiblement peuplée, très sèche et ne convenant qu'à l'élevage extensif de bovins, éloignée des villages et des fermes européens, les salaires proposés sont inférieurs à la moyenne nationale, ce qui provoque une fuite de la main-d'œuvre locale, mais

La ville et la campagne en Afrique   55

également draîne celle de régions encore plus déshéritées, ainsi qu'une forte proportion de travailleurs étrangers. Mais existent également des régions qui ne s'inscrivent pas dans un tel environnement de développement économique capitaliste, pour lesquelles les variables sont difficiles à quantifier : niveau d'instruction, nombre d'établissements offrant des emplois.

La plupart des habitants de la région peu peuplée d'Urungwe n'ont reçu aucune instruction et ne cherchent pas d'emploi salarié, que ce soit dans leur région ou ailleurs; le nombre de travailleurs étrangers qui s'y sont installés est proportionnellement élevé. Par contre les habitants des régions plus densément peuplées de Gwande et Brunapeg, dont le niveau d'instruction est élevé et qui recherchent un emploi, bénéficient de possibilités locales dont le niveau de rémunération est supérieur à la moyenne nationale. Des travailleurs en provenance d'autres régions de Rhodésie, parmi lesquels on compte peu d'étrangers, se joignent à eux. Enfin, Binga offre l'exemple d'une région à la fois isolée et sous-développée, d'un point de vue économique : elle compte fort peu d'établissements de commerce, peu de possibilités d'emploi, peu de marchés pour négocier les récoltes; le taux d'absentéisme masculin y est élevé.

Il est important de remarquer que Mitchell n'établit aucune relation de cause à effet entre le taux d'absentéisme masculin d'une part, les conditions démographiques et économiques et le niveau d'instruction d'autre part, pour les zones rurales désertées par les hommes. C'est plutôt le caractère de la région agro-écologique plus vaste, englobant plusieurs de ces zones, qui confère à ces facteurs leur degré de pertinence. Dans une société plurale, du type de celle de l'Afrique méridionale coloniale, les régions agro-écologiques les plus fertiles sont sous la coupe du groupe le plus puissant qui appelle, ou peut retenir à l'extérieur, la main-d'œuvre étrangère.

Mais, dans les régions moins développées, la répartition locale des ressources économiques ainsi que le niveau d'instruction déterminent l'importance des départs masculins vers les régions développées, la proportion de ceux qui restent sur place, pour y travailler ou pas, le nombre enfin de ceux qui quittent la Rhodésie ou bien y arrivent. Une métaphore peut rendre compte de cette situation, celle d'une carte météorologique retraçant de larges courants déterminés par les principales zones de basse et de haute pression, à l'intérieur desquelles des variations de moindre amplitude dépendent directement des conditions locales.

L'analyse de Mitchell traite du macrophénomène, et non pas des décisions individuelles, prises en un lieu précis, d'émigrer ou pas.

c

56 *Introduction*

Pour Mitchell, ces deux niveaux d'analyse ne sont pas compatibles et constituent des approches différentes du même problème; elles connotent des interrogations de niveau différent. La première concerne le contexte global que l'on peut considérér comme 'donné' dans l'étude microscopique des interactions sociales entre migrants et non migrants. Ce raisonnement est fondé. On peut, cependant, argumenter que, dans la mesure où un contexte global évolue au fil du temps (les gouvernements et les systèmes politiques changent; à l'expansion fait suite la récession), le rapport entre cette nature changeante et les modifications qui s'ensuivent au niveau des choix offerts aux individus requiert une analyse à deux niveaux. Comment peut-on y parvenir?

Nous avons suggéré que les décisions individuelles peuvent être appréhendées sous l'angle de justifications idéologiques et culturelles. Ce qui leur confère la valeur d'une variable, leur intelligibilité et leur acceptabilité variant suivant le groupe culturel auquel le migrant appartient. Le contexte absentéiste global, dont s'assortit le phénomène migratoire, est une stratégie qui, comme le dit Mitchell, répond à une situation politique et économique nationale (j'ajouterais internationale) (*infra:* 111). En d'autres termes, cette variable dépend directement des rapports de domination et de subordination de groupes d'intérêts rivaux. Le changement dans une variable, à savoir dans le répertoire des raisons culturellement recevables—qui expliquent qu'on choisit ou pas d'émigrer—peut être lié aux modifications intervenues dans les positions relatives des groupes d'intérêt. Pour comprendre ces changements, nous considérons dans notre analyse les deux variables comme interdépendantes.

Je crois cette optique proche de celle de Cohen (1974) qui démontre l'interpénétration de ces deux variables : conduite symbolique et rapports de force entre groupes.

Garbett (*infra:* 114–17) étudie de près les forces politico-économiques de la société coloniale dont la maîtrise échappe à l'individu. Puis, cette certitude établie, il élabore un modèle de décisions propre à expliquer les migrations rotatives en Rhodésie. Il entend aller au-delà des types de décisions prises par les migrants qui se conforment à des règles socialement définies, et étudier les stratégies auxquelles ils recourent dans leur seul intérêt. En d'autres termes, le migrant potentiel se trouve confronté à une multiplicité de choix possibles, au nombre desquels certains sont sanctionnés par sa société, d'autres pas. Le modèle de décision concerne essentiellement l'incidence qu'ont, sur un migrant, les décisions prises par des tiers, ainsi que l'influence de ses choix personnels passés sur ses choix présents. La nature cumulative et

La ville et la campagne en Afrique 57

structurante des choix antérieurs agit comme un faisceau de contraintes sur les choix à venir. Le modèle définit donc le migrant comme partiellement, et non totalement, responsable de ses décisions. Ce qui permet à Garbett de rejeter les modèles simplistes du type 'choix rationnel/maximisation' proposés par certains économistes, qui ignorant les pressions non rationnelles et subjectives, les obligations auxquelles tout individu doit satisfaire. Il récuse également le modèle dit 'push-pull', qui accorde trop d'importance aux facteurs économiques, à l'exclusion des facteurs sociaux ou des facteurs que j'appellerais culturels et idéologiques.

Le mérite du modèle de Garbett est de dégager la persistance de contraintes et de motivations sociales et l'effort constant des migrants pour ne pas les enfreindre, mais concilier leurs préférences et ces nécessités contraignantes. L'explication et l'exemple que propose Garbett (*infra:* 122) illustrent ce propos. L'institution de la 'dot' représente, dans certaines sociétés africaines, un des engagements financiers les plus importants que les jeunes hommes contractent, assez semblable aux prêts contractés par les jeunes occidentaux qui acquièrent un premier logement. Cette institution n'a rien d'atrophiant. Elle est fréquemment constituée par de l'argent, de préférence à du bétail, et s'assortit d'autres dépenses. Certaines sociétés tiennent au paiement intégral en un court laps de temps. D'autres, escomptant peut-être tirer avantage de l'inflation, acceptent des règlements échelonnés. C'est cette dernière solution qui est en vigueur chez les Korekore: un homme peut s'endetter envers son beau-père pour plusieurs années. Mais que cet homme souhaite partir travailler dans une ville éloignée et emmener sa femme, le beau-père peut exiger sur le champ le règlement de la majeure partie de la compensation matrimoniale. Rares sont les hommes qui en ont les moyens financiers. Aussi, le compromis auquel ils recourent le plus fréquemment est de trouver du travail dans une ferme européenne voisine et de laisser leur épouse chez son père. Mari et femme peuvent ainsi se voir assez souvent. Ce compromis agrée également au beau-père qui peut tirer profit de l'argent, des dons, de l'aide agricole reçus à l'occasion des visites de son beau-fils à sa fille. Les conséquences sont de trois ordres: les migrants qui travaillent dans des fermes européennes viennent, dans la majorité des cas, des mêmes régions avoisinantes; la discontinuité dans leurs relations sociales, entre le village d'origine et le lieu de travail, est relativement réduite; ils parviennent à concilier des intérêts conjugaux potentiellement conflictuels et des obligations imposées par les relations d'alliance. De solution de compromis face à un conflit d'obligations traditionnelles, cet ensemble de choix est devenu

58 *Introduction*

normatif, c'est-à-dire qu'il constitue une préférence culturelle chez les Korekore. Que le migrant travaille dans une ville éloignée ou une ferme européenne proche, les avantages économiques respectifs sont comparables. Mais cet exemple permet de mettre en évidence l'importance complémentaire d'un facteur culturel, dans le cas présent cette polarisation sur l'importante institution de la compensation matrimoniale, pour décider celle des deux possibilités de travail, toutes deux dépendantes des Européens, qu'il convient de retenir.

L'emprise coloniale sur les bases politico-économiques de migration est fondamentale. En étudiant l'interaction des facteurs culturels et politico-économiques, nous comprenons les variations qui interviennent dans les courants migratoires. Nous pouvons, par exemple, escompter un type de réponse différent de celle apportée par les Korekore de la part d'une société qui, tout en subissant des contraintes politico-économiques identiques, n'accorde pas à la compensation matrimoniale une valeur aussi importante. L'analyse de Garbett du comportement migratoire, de l'*'incidence'* de la migration, est complémentaire de celle de Mitchell qui parle, dans ce volume, de 'taux' de migration. L'étape ultérieure consiste à intégrer ces deux modèles car, ainsi que le remarque Garbett, il est finalement souhaitable d'expliciter la relation qui intervient entre micro-processus et macro-processus. On progresse vers cette étape en cherchant si les Korekore rivalisent, et de quelle manière, avec d'autres groupes africains pour les mêmes emplois, tant à l'intérieur qu'à l'extérieur de leur région d'origine. En d'autres termes, dans quelle mesure la décision des Korekore de travailler à proximité de leurs foyers ruraux plutôt que dans des villes éloignées résulte-t-elle d'une rivalité ethnique sur un marché du travail essentiellement dominé par des entreprises européennes?

Confronté à celui de Mitchell, le modèle de Ohadike d'évaluation des taux migratoires repose exclusivement sur des données quantitatives. Ohadike distingue la 'première' migration des déplacements 'ultérieurs' et décompte les déplacements des migrants à Lusaka en les inscrivant dans le temps. Il peut, de cette façon, modifier la distinction faite, dans les modèles statiques, entre le migrant et le non migrant, 'fixé', paysan ou citadin, pour s'attacher à considérer des degrés de disparité entre individus impliqués dans des processus migratoires à un moment ou à un autre de leur vie. Tandis que Mitchell appréhende le phénomène migratoire du point de vue rural, Ohadike prend Lusaka, capitale de la Zambie, comme point de référence. Selon lui, les différences de taux et de volume des flux migratoires qui entrent et sortent de la ville s'expliquent par

La ville et la campagne en Afrique 59

des différences de 'classe', de groupe ethnique ou culturel, et par leur implantation résidentielle dans Lusaka. Un certain nombre de faits saillants se dégagent de l'étude que Ohadike consacre à Lusaka, qui trouveraient leur place dans des discussions générales ayant trait aux conséquences de la migration urbaine sur les possibilités d'instruction, ainsi que sur l'émergence d'une hiérarchie socio-économique des quartiers résidentiels. Un de ces faits mérite qu'on le développe.

Ohadike estime que Lusaka s'est développé aux taux annuels successifs de 5,3 pour cent, 10,9 pour cent et 11,8 pour cent au cours des périodes quinquennales suivantes: 1953–8, 1958–63, 1963–8. Pour cette dernière période, l'immigration contribue pour dix pour cent dans l'accroissement annuel. Mais, souligne-t-il, un changement radical du processus migratoire vers Lusaka est intervenu. Au début de cette période de quinze ans, la plupart des migrants à Lusaka arrivaient droit de leur région rurale d'origine et migraient, dans la grande majorité des cas, pour la première fois. Mais à la fin de cette même période, la plupart avaient transité par d'autres villes avant d'arriver à Lusaka; les distances couvertes par ceux qui se déplaçaient pour la première fois étaient considérablement supérieures. Tendance qui doit être encore plus prononcée dans les pays d'Afrique orientale et centrale. Car la majorité des villes approchent de la ville de type B définie par Southall (1961: 6–13), centres relativement modernes où se regroupent l'industrie, le commerce et l'administration (comme à Lusaka), l'appel de main-d'œuvre assurant la transition rapide d'une autosuffisance agricole relativement prononcée à une dépendance partielle par rapport au travail salarié. Ce qui implique un facteur de discontinuité dans les relations urbaines et rurales, au plan tant politique que socio-économique, et peut-être même un clivage de plus en plus net entre groupes et catégories urbains et ruraux: un prolétariat urbain d'une part, un secteur rural peut-être appauvri d'autre part. Ces faits se produisent-ils? Nous pouvons apporter un élément de réponse en examinant le rapport entre migration et développement ou sous-développement rural.

MIGRATION ET DÉVELOPPEMENT RURAL

Dans son article, Ohadike opère la distinction entre migration urbaine-urbaine et migration rurale-urbaine. Dans la mesure où persiste au moins une migration rotative et où, même après plusieurs années passées en ville, la plupart des salariés retournent à leur village d'origine, il est également possible de parler de migration

60 *Introduction*

urbaine-rurale. La quatrième possibilité, la migration rurale-rurale constitue le sujet de l'article de Uchendu (*infra:* 165); il est également abordé par Mushanga (*infra:* 159). Selon ce dernier, l'Ouganda a connu pendant une période particulièrement longue des migrations de travail entre régions rurales, tout particulièrement en provenance et en direction du Buganda (Richards 1955) mais aussi vers d'autres régions de culture du coton au sud et à l'est du pays. Il remarque un changement prononcé à la faveur d'un mouvement rural-urbain des travailleurs et soutient que les politiques de développement rural, dont l'objectif était d'endiguer ce flux, doivent se conjuguer avec une décentralisation officielle des grands centres urbains où l'on trouve du travail, Kampala et Jinja. Thoden Van Velzen (*infra:* 178) prend également comme point de départ de son analyse du développement d'un village tanzanien le modèle de Frank (1969) selon lequel en pays pauvre quelques métropoles dominent et exploitent un grand nombre de communautés périphériques.

Le transfert délibéré des capitales nationales est souvent préconisé, à la fois comme un moyen partiel de décentralisation urbaine et de réduction des déséquilibres régionaux du développement rural de la nation. Mesure qui peut se révéler onéreuse. Le Malawi transfère sa capitale de Zomba à Lilongwe, bâtie récemment, bien que Blantyre soit, et de loin, la plus grande ville; il est rapporté qu'en 1974 la Tanzanie a désigné comme nouvelle capitale, au lieu de Dar es Salaam, la petite ville intérieure de Dodoma; l'assemblée nationale s'y réunit le 22 octobre 1974 pour la première fois (*The Times*, 23 octobre 1974). Les petites villes peuvent servir de relais de la décentralisation régionale et urbaine, sans devenir pour autant des capitales; leur singularité, facilitant la pratique d'activités conjuguées: agriculture, commerce et administration locale (cf. Middleton 1966: 31; Gutkind 1969), exerce sur la recherche une attraction qui a suscité de études détaillées sur cette région de l'Afrique (Vincent 1971; Jacobson 1973; cf. également Abrahams 1961 et Thoden Van Velzen *infra*).

Uchendu souligne, cependant, que les migrations de travail inter-rurales sont d'ores et déjà source d'une large part des activités économiques, fait qui n'est généralement reconnu en tant que tel ni par les chercheurs ni par les gouvernements. Et il interroge: comment se peut-il qu'on dise le continent africain sur-urbanisé alors que 10 pour cent seulement de sa population vit effectivement dans des villes? En revanche, affirme-t-il, le taux élevé du chômage urbain témoigne de l'échec de l'économie urbaine à créer suffisamment d'emplois et c'est encore le secteur rural qui fait vivre la majorité de la population. Le problème du chômage urbain est

La ville et la campagne en Afrique 61

abordé en termes d'accroissement des débouchés agricoles. Conjuguée à une politique délibérée d'investissements dans le secteur rural, la migration inter-rurale apparaît comme une redistribution rationnelle de terres et de travail dans la mesure où elle permet aux paysans de se déplacer d'une région où le manque de terres se fait sentir vers une autre où elles sont en excédent. Uchendu ajoute une mise en garde : les migrations de travail d'une région rurale à une autre ne devraient être encouragées que dans le cadre d'une politique nationale en matière de propriété foncière (*infra:* 175). Une question cruciale est de savoir s'il convient d'imposer des plafonds à la propriété privée dans les régions excédentaires pour éviter les inégalités régionales trop prononcées, dont résulterait une entière dépendance des migrants venus des régions pauvres envers les gros propriétaires des régions prospères.

Il convient ici de remarquer que les régions, ou parties de région, sont délimitées par des frontières tant ethniques qu'administratives, particularité qui renvoie au passé colonial (Southall 1970). Une politique nationale imposant des plafonds à la propriété foncière devrait vaincre la résistance que les habitants des régions jouissant de conditions agricoles et écologiques favorables, et appartenant à un même ensemble culturel, pourraient opposer aux immigrants issus de régions moins favorisées, pour qui l'avantage d'une installation définitive prévaut probablement sur celui de simplement fournir leur travail. L'attribution à des migrants de terres réellement neuves dans le cadre de projets de colonisation agricole semble offrir une solution partielle, dans la mesure où les frais élevés (Morris, s.d. : 79–80) et les problèmes d'organisation (Apthorpe, s.d. : 5–13; Chambers 1969 : 257–62, Shorter 1974 : 118–32) sont évités ou réglés. Elle peut colmater la brèche qui se creuse entre employeurs paysans et salariés agricoles dépourvus de terres. Elle peut également définir sans ambiguïté les zones au-delà desquelles d'autres implantations ne sont pas possibles, apaisant ainsi les craintes du groupe indigène à l'encontre des immigrants qui pourraient éventuellement empiéter sur leurs parcelles. De tels projets présupposent une pratique de l'agriculture intensive et le recours à des techniques semi-mécanisées plutôt qu'une agriculture itinérante sur brûlis. Ils doivent être tout particulièrement adaptés aux situations des pasteurs nomades qui ont impérativement besoin de territoires étendus, du moins si l'on souhaite les encourager dans leur rôle précolonial et précapitaliste de préservation de l'équilibre écologique et non les forcer à faire paître leur bestiaux sur des espaces restreints (Spencer 1974; cf. également Rigby, s.d. : 42–52).

Uchendu remarque que, à une échelle plus vaste qu'en Afrique

62 *Introduction*

occidentale, la plupart des migrations inter-rurales en Afrique de l'Est et en Afrique centrale sont intervenues entre les grands domaines agricoles à la suite de l'implantation européenne. Elles se sont articulées avec les déplacements de la main-d'œuvre vers les régions de culture du coton, de la banane, du café, cultivées par de petits exploitants au Buganda (cf. Richards *et al.* 1973) au Kilimandjaro et au Bukoba (Tanzanie) et se sont traduites en un schema général qui, nous avons déjà eu l'occasion de le dire dans la première partie de cette introduction, pour avoir été nettement international, l'est beaucoup moins depuis peu. Il sera intéressant de savoir dans quelle mesure les politiques nationales en matière de tenure foncière ainsi que leurs effets sur l'orientation générale des migrations rurales-rurales, se différencieront suivant l'importance des domaines agricoles que l'héritage colonial aura dévolu à ces nations indépendantes.

Uchendu illustre sa démonstration des différents effets des migrations sur le développement rural, dans la perspective de politiques nationales différentes, en présentant trois zones écologiquement distinctes et actuellement hautement productives, situées en Ouganda, en Tanzanie, au Kenya. Dans ces trois régions, les immigrants ont implanté leurs fermes sur de nouvelles terres.

Dans le district de Teso, en Ouganda, ce sont les habitants de la région qui ont eux-mêmes colonisé les terres neuves, l'initiative revenant, à l'origine, à une décision du gouvernment colonial, en 1910, en faveur d'un développement planifié sous contrôle fiscal. L'emploi de la charrue à bœufs, auquel les Teso ont eu très tôt recours, leur a permis de cultiver le coton sans le recours à une main-d'œuvre extérieure. L'emploi de cette technique aratoire correspond à un stade de technologie intermédiaire, laquelle, tout en atténuant la dépendance vis-à-vis de la main-d'œuvre étrangère, n'élimine pas pour autant l'aspect 'intensif' du travail agricole. Les résultats, généralement excellents, qu'elle permet d'obtenir contrastent étonnament avec les récentes conclusions d'une recherche faite en pays Teso par E. Brett, qui montre comment l'introduction, par les coopératives, de tracteurs modernes a considérablement avantagé les fermiers des grandes exploitations, au détriment des petits qui, en tant que membres des coopératives, non seulement les subventionnent, mais en outre mettent leur force de travail à leur disposition (communication personnelle).

Les deux autres cas de développement rural intensif, dans le district de Kisii au Kenya et dans le district de Geita en Tanzanie, ont été atteints sans que la technologie agricole ait à subir des changements radicaux. Dans les années trente, la région de Geita, qui

La ville et la campagne en Afrique   63

était inhabitée, fut débarassée de la mouche tsé-tsé, aussi les habitants de Sukumaland, une région touchée par la pénurie de terre, commencèrent à s'y installer. Tous cultivèrent la terre; certains d'entre eux travaillèrent plus tard dans les mines d'or pendant le peu de temps où celles-ci furent exploitées; ultérieurement, certains devinrent commerçants. L'argent qu'ils gagnèrent ainsi, ils l'investirent dans la culture du coton considérée comme culture de rapport. Mais, contrairement aux Teso, les colons sukuma dépendaient des migrations saisonnières de travailleurs venant du Rwanda-Urundi. Les Kisii furent tout d'abord employés comme main-d'œuvre migrante dans les mines proches et les plantations de thé entre 1930 et 1950, puis ils émigrèrent vers les hautes terres kisii, qui servaient jusqu'alors de pâtures. Là, ils investirent la totalité de leurs gains et se spécialisèrent dans la culture du maïs, qu'ils fournirent aux travailleures des plantations voisines, ils diversifièrent par la suite leur activité en s'orientant vers la culture de variétés hautement rentables, telles que le pyrèthre, le thé et diverses sortes de maïs. Contrairement aux habitants de Geita, mais comme ceux de Teso, ils ne font pas appel à la main-d'œuvre extérieure. Les fermiers prospères rétribuent plutôt les services de cultivateurs kisii à court de terres. Cette stratification interne chez les Kisii a récemment fait l'objet d'une étude particulière de A. Manners (articles non publiés) et semble s'être manifestée plus précocement que dans les deux autres régions. Geita a pu draîner de la main-d'œuvre saisonnière extérieure; en pays Teso l'emploi de la charrue a probablement retardé le moment où la main-d'œuvre extérieure devient nécessaire. Comme nous l'avons dit, l'introduction des tracteurs a aiguisé les différences, fondées sur la fortune et la propriéte foncière, entre salariés agricoles et fermiers.

Uchendu ne précise pas dans quelle mesure la politique foncière de la Tanzanie a affecté la répartition des terres cultivables au Geita, mais au Kisii et au Teso l'inégalité s'est accentuée. Ces trois districts correspondent à l'un des trois types de campagnes distingués par S. Amin en Afrique de l'Ouest (1974: 33–4). Ce type comprend les régions 'organisées pour la production d'exportation à grande échelle, qui sont déjà entrées dans l'ère capitaliste et sont avancées en direction d'un processus de différenciation de type capitaliste, qui implique l'appropriation privée du sol et la disponibilité d'une main-d'œuvre salariée'. Les deux autres types (l'un, les régions dévolues au rôle de réserves de main-d'œuvre salariée; l'autre, les campagnes qui ne fournissent pas de main-d'œuvre et qui ne sont pas vouées aux cultures de rapport) existent certainement en Afrique orientale et en Afrique centrale. En illustration du premier type, l'article

64 *Introduction*

d'Uchendu traite des migrations qui s'effectuent du district, densément peuplé, de West-Nile (en Ouganda) en direction du Buganda, et du Rwanda et du Burundi vers le Buganda et le Geita.

Les exemples du troisième type sont de plus en plus rares, qui ne fournissent ni main-d'œuvre salariée, ni cultures d'exportation. On peut, à ce titre, compter les populations d'Afrique orientale à forte tendance pastoraliste, telles les Karamojong, les Turkana, les Masaï, les Samburu et les Gogo, n'ayant que peu ou pas pratiqué l'élevage intensif; on y compte également des chasseurs et des cueilleurs comme les Hadza de Tanzanie et, dans quelques cas, les Dorobo et les Aliangulu ou Sanye du Kenya.

La question des rapports actuels entre le district de Geita, relativement prospère, et la politique tanzanienne de développement régional équilibré, incite à une éventuelle mise en parallèle avec le pays Chagga, une zone plus prospère de culture de café, près du mont Kilimandjaro. La forte productivité obtenue par certains planteurs Chagga, dans le cadre d'une agriculture capitaliste, les a parfois inscrits en contradiction par rapport à l'idéologie socialiste, exposée par le parti unique, la TANU, dans la déclaration d'Arusha de 1967 (Stahl 1969: 221–2. Moore à paraître). Un conflict sur le plan idéologique est inévitable, mais quelles sont les incidences non recherchées de la politique bien particulière de la Tanzanie visant à garantir que les paysans gèrent leur propre production?

L'étude de Thoden van Velzen (*infra:* 178) d'un centre administratif de mille personnes environ du district de Rungwe est centrée sur les rapports économiques et politiques existant entre fonctionnaires salariés et riches agriculteurs d'une part, la majorité de la petite paysannerie d'autre part. Les fonctionnaires sont les véritables artisans de la mise en œuvre des projets de la communauté. Mais, dans la mesure où ils se démarquent des paysans en tant qu'élite jouissant de traitements relativement élevés—et non pas de revenus agricoles—leur mode de vie se différencie à proportion, ce qui renforce la disparité entre leurs intérêts matériels. Une constante persiste, qui date de l'administration coloniale, mais qu'apparemment les gens respectent encore: les agriculteurs les plus riches, c'est-à-dire les plus 'progressistes', sont élus aux conseils locaux. Ainsi mêlés, fonctionnaires locaux et riches agriculteurs ont inévitablement à justifier, entre eux, de l'utilisation des crédits et des fonds accordés par l'Etat pour le développement communautaire. Cette situation n'est pas tant la conséquence des machinations tramées par des individus dont l'intégrité idéologique aurait failli, que celle d'une faiblesse structurale qui a toléré l'instauration d'une collusion entre fonctionnaires et riches agriculteurs. Ces derniers

La ville et la campagne en Afrique 65

forment une 'classe' qui perpétue et aggrave les inégalities, apparues avant l'indépendance en matière de répartition des terres.

En premier lieu, le principe de cette répartition semble typique de plusieurs régions d'Afrique et du tiers-monde, qui voient émerger un capitalisme paysan, et dont Lamb (1974), Leys (1971) et Parkin (1972) ont analysé des exemples au Kenya. Lamb montre comment une élite rurale de planteurs de café, dans de district de Murang'a de la Province centrale, peut s'emparer d'une large part des fonds et subsides de l'Etat central, par le jeu de l'exercice du pouvoir au niveau de la communauté locale. J'indique comment, dans le district de Kilifi, province de la Côte, des prêts destinés au développement rural sont attribués, sur des critères de méritocratie, aux agriculteurs dont on estime qu'ils obtiennent les meilleurs résultats. Bien que Leys estime qu' une nette polarisation autour des grands exploitants agricoles d'une part, du prolétariat rural et urbain d'autre part, ne sera pas immédiate, même dans la province centrale dont le niveau économique est élevé, il reconnaît que ce processus est engagé— avec début de prise de conscience politique paysanne.

Thoden van Velzen fait ressortir que les subventions que le gouvernement tanzanien accorde à la paysannerie excèdent les revenus tirés des investissements en milieu urbain; dans cette mesure, la campagne suit une politique distincte. Mais ces fonds extérieurs étant accordés par les fonctionnaires, en accord avec les riches agriculteurs, la position privilégiée de cette élite rurale lui permet de détourner à son profit une 'part' au passage. Les conséquences générales sur le développement économique sont-elles insignifiantes, en dépit du contraste frappant entre la politique des deux pays (voir Hyden 1969: 37–60)?

Les conséquences, même si elles échappent à la règlementation concernant la propriété privée du sol en Tanzanie, peuvent révéler une similitude moins superficielle et converger vers un modèle unique. On peut essayer de prévoir, mais le véritable critère est à long terme; les grands propriétaires terriens existeront-ils en Tanzanie, ceux capables de perpétuer leurs domaines parce qu'ils auront jeté les bases de dynasties familiales dont la domination politique, au niveau local, se répercute à l'échelon urbain et national. La non-persistence, au-delà d'une génération ou deux des faibles variations de l'inégalité en milieu rural (résultant des fluctuations importantes de la demande sur le marché mondial des cultures commerciales) témoigne de la dépendance des agriculteurs vis-à-vis de l'étranger. Mais, paradoxalement, cette inégalité changeante n'amorce pas nécessairement la formation de classes. L'instabilité intrinsèque du statut d'entrepreneur, que certains anthropologues tiennent pour

66 *Introduction*

caractéristique des économies 'traditionnelles', pré-capitalistes, essentiellement redistributives, pourrait bien être un trait toujours vivace de certaines régions agricoles de l'Afrique contemporaine, qui restent à l'écart des décisions politiques nationales sur l'orientation économique (du pays) mais qui, pourtant, dépendent des cultures d'exportation.

Encore une fois, des facteurs intervenant à l'échelon national et international, par conséquent tout à fait hors du contrôle des populations locales, peuvent définir de façon décisive la portée de la différenciation socio-économique interne de ces populations. Il s'ensuit que la connaissance des communautés agricoles pratiquant, sur un mode intensif, les cultures commerciales passe par une reconstitution des liens qui les unissent aux métropoles ou centres urbains par lesquels leurs produits transitent, aux marchés auxquels ils sont destinés; elle passe aussi par l'analyse du rôle que jouent ceux qui manipulent ces liens, les gardes-barrières comme on les a surnommés, et qui interviennent à différents niveaux du réseau de distribution. Il en découle également que le degré de développement des relations de dépendance des agriculteurs est fonction de la politique appliquée par le gouvernement lors des premières phases du développement. . . . A cet égard, la Tanzanie témoigne, depuis son indépendance, d'une assez grande stabilité par rapport à son idéologie d'indépendance nationale et d'équilibre du développement régional, même si c'est au prix—diraient d'aucuns—d'un taux de PNB plus faible, qui aurait pu être meilleur si le gouvernement avait opté pour une plus forte concentration de la production destinée à l'exportation dans les régions dont les conditions agro-écologiques sont particulièrement favorables, telle la région de Chagga, près du Kilimandjaro.

Certaines inégalités entre régions rurales s'expliquent essentiellement en termes de planification du developpement des zones aux conditions agro-écologiques favorables; d'autres inégalitiés proviennent plus directement de l'implantation des industries, qui ne se fait pas forcément dans des villes déjà constituées; d'autres inégalités, enfin, par une conjonction de ces deux facteurs. Les études de Colson et de Scudder (*infra:* 190) dégagent des exemples à ce propos. Le barrage de Kariba fut construit pour alimenter les trois pays de l'ancienne Fédération d'Afrique Centrale (Malawi, Zambie et Rhodésie); il chevauche en fait la frontière entre la Zambie et la Rhodésie, et contribue efficacement, en les alimentant, à l'indépendance énergétique de chacun de ces deux pays. De la même façon, le chemin de fer de Zambie fut construit à l'époque coloniale pour le transport des minéraux, de ce pays et de Rhodésie, à travers

La ville et la campagne en Afrique   67

l'Afrique du Sud à destination des marchés mondiaux; il assume maintenant une fonction particulièrement efficace pour le developpement qui intervient en Zambie. Colson et Scudder ont étudié, pendant plusieurs années, l'impact de ces deux grands projets sur la population de la Zambie du Sud.

Le projet de barrage de Kariba déracina quelque cinquante six mille Tonga de la vallée du Gwembe en Zambie et en Rhodésie; ils furent réinstallées en 1958 par villages entiers dans différentes secteurs du même district. Un de ces villages, Mazulu, se situe maintenant à une cinquantaine de miles (quatre-vingts kilomètres environ) de la nouvelle ville de Kafue, et à cent cinquante kilomètres environ de Lusaka, capitale de la Zambie. Il occupe dorénavant un site agro-écologique privilégié et se situe dans une zone de développement industriel qui englobe toute la province méridionale de la Zambie et la ligne ferroviaire, au nord, jusqu'à Lusaka. C'est donc un village agricole en plein essor dont l'implantation ménage d'excellents accès aux marchés urbains et des possibilités d'emploi. Comme dans l'exemple cité par Uchendu (*infra:* 171), l'adoption immédiate de la charrue à Mazulu a permis à ce village de tirer rapidement parti de ses atouts agricoles. Bien qu'elles soient distantes, les grandes villes constituent une possibilité d'écouler les récoltes et, à leur tour, ces liens réguliers permettent aux jeunes gens d'y trouver des emplois.

Le niveau élevé de productivité agricole et des réinvestissements, des occasions qu'on a saisies pour gagner 'plus' d'argent en travaillant à la ville, renforcent les liens entre le village et la ville, en dépit de la distance qui les sépare. En vérité, Colson et Scudder le soulignent, ces villageois mobiles ne perçoivent aucune dichotomie ville-campagne, pas plus que ne le peut l'analyste, vu le renforcement mutuel des liens économiques et des investissements. Mazulu bénéficie donc de la conjonction d'avantages agro-écologiques et industriels; sa réimplantation l'a rendue plus prospère. Cependant, avertissent les auteurs, certains villages nouveaux commencent à préférer l'insertion en milieu urbaine à l'implantation rurale.

Le deuxième village étudié, Musulumba, se trouve dans le rayon d'action de la mouche tsé-tsé. Les villageois ne peuvent donc pas élever de bétail, ni faire tirer leurs charrues par des bœufs pour pratiquer des cultures commerciales à grande échelle. Ils assurent leur subsistance en labourant la terre à la houe. Ils dépendent, par conséquent, beaucoup plus du travail salarié, généralement sur des chantiers de construction proches. Ils ont perdu l'indépendance agricole qui était la leur, précédemment à la réimplantation. Les deux types de villages, l'un prospère grâce à vivotant l'agriculture

68 *Introduction*

de marché et au salariat urbain, l'autre végétant du travail agricole sous-payé et d'agriculture de subsistance, témoignent de la diversification rurale existant en Afrique, ainsi que dans d'autres régions du monde également en voie de développement (cf. la mise en contraste, par T. S. Epstein, de deux villages indiens, 1962). Mais ils témoignent aussi d'inégalitiés naissantes. Le critère est le degré auquel le salariat—urbain ou rural—entame l'autarcie rurale, comme c'est arrivé à Musulumba. Il faut remarquer que, même si cela ne s'est pas produit dans l'autre village, la prédilection marquée des jeunes gens pour le salariat urbain, au détriment de l'agriculture, conduit à penser que cette histoire du 'succès' paysan risque d'être sans lendemains.

Les grandes possibilités de travail urbain salarié en Zambie, par rapport à d'autres pays d'Afrique orientale et centrale, peuvent en faire un cas exceptionnel. Il peut également auguer des tendances futures qui verront le jour dans ces pays, où la pénurie en valeur de terres, et une expansion lente mais assurée—dans l'absolu—des perspectives d'emploi urbain peuvent, an définitive, avoir le même effet.

En Afrique, la formation d'un vrai prolétariat urbain, totalement dépendant du travail salarié, n'est peut-être pas imminente (Elkan, 1972). Son émergence sera probablement graduelle et cela pour une raison: les offres d'emplois urbains sont encore largement supérieures au nombre de demandes émanant des jeunes migrants. Cependant, un taux de croissance de la population urbaine triple de celui de la population rurale fournit les conditions idéologiques préalables pour le développement, en milieu urbain, d'une *conscience* de classe prolétarienne qui s'exprime en partie dans le syndicalisme (cf. Grillo 1974: 125–43, avec bibliogr.). Utopique ou fondée, la croyance populaire qu'à la ville les possibilités sont plus grandes qu'à la campagne se perpétue à la faveur des déséquilibres entre population urbaine et population rurale. La théorie mettant l'accent sur l'attraction exercée par les 'lumières de la ville' s'est trouvée discréditée, ou—à tout le moins—rejetée, pour être secondaire par rapport aux théories qui accordent la primeur aux facteurs économiques. Vu la présentation initiale, le rejet est justifié. Il ne faut pas oublier, cependant, qu'une rationalisation des avantages économiques revêt presqu'invariablement une forme idéologique. Ce qui se dégage clairement des articles composant ce volume, c'est que nombre d'hommes, et surtout de femmes, qui vivent dans des conditions de surpeuplement urbain, et qui sont employés—quand ils travaillent—à des taches sous-payées, ne remettent pas sérieusement en question la certitude que beaucoup partagent, que la 'ville'

La ville et la campagne en Afrique 69

offre une vie meilleure que la 'campagne'. Niveaux de revenus et de dépenses mis à part, les critères qui permettent d'évaluer une telle attitude sont subjectifs. Cela nous incite à nous tourner vers la formation des idées, des croyances et des valeurs, ainsi que vers leur mode de transmission, non seulement dans le sens citadins—famille villageoise d'origine, mais aussi de la campagne vers la ville.

LE FLUX DE LA CAMPAGNE VERS LA VILLE, DU LANGAGE, DES CROYANCES ET DES POSSIBILITÉS D'INSTRUCTION

S'il est vrai que la mobilité des populations n'est pas elle seule facteur de propagation des idées, son efficacité, en Afrique, est particulièrement décisive du fait des différents types de migrations rotatives, en direction des zones rurales ou des zones urbaines, qu'effectuent tout à la fois les travailleurs, ceux qui cherchent un emploi et leurs parents à charge. La diffusion des langues relève d'un phénomène du même ordre, tout comme la propagation et l'interpénétration des valeurs 'traditionnelles' ou coutumières, des croyances et pratiques religieuses. Ce sont les contacts, réguliers ou fréquents, entre groupements culturels distincts qui en constituent le point de départ: de nouveaux concepts doivent être trouvés, les anciens sont transmis. Les villes d'Afrique de l'Est et d'Afrique centrale ne sont pas les seuls foyers où se concentrent des populations culturellement hétérogènes; on les retrouve également dans les nouvelles zones de peuplement rurales, dans les plantations ou sur les domaines, dans les centres commerciaux et administratifs. Les articles de Rigby et de Lule, de Kashoki et de Gould, sont centrés sur les capitales de la Zambie et de l'Ouganda—Lusaka et Kampala —qui constituent des exemples probants illustrant la manière selon laquelle des ruraux issus de milieux culturellement et linguistiquement disparates peuvent préserver leur singularité tout en partageant des certitudes, des espérances, des langages et des codes urbains identiques.

Rigby et Lule (*infra:* 213) analysent le fonctionnement, à Kampala, de la religion 'traditionnelle' ganda, qui inclut la magie, la sorcellerie, la divination, les guérisons, les croyances et pratiques associées au culte des ancêtres. Quantité de précieux matériaux ayant trait aux croyances et accusations de sorcellerie en milieu urbain existent pour l'Afrique de l'Est et l'Afrique centrale. Le recours aux devins, aux soins rituels et aux objets magiques est également fort répandu en milieu urbain, aussi fréquent qu'il l'est en Afrique australe et en Afrique occidentale. La persistance de ces

70 *Introduction*

croyances et pratiques n'en constitue pas moins qu'en milieu rural une réponse aux incertititudes que doivent affronter les entreprises et les destinées humaines. Si les croyances et pratiques rituelles changent ou évoluent en milieu urbain, c'est que les difficultés graves qu'on doit y affronter n'ont pas d'équivalents, au plan conceptuel ou explicatif, en milieu rural.

L'analyse, par Mitchell, de la façon dont les difficultés rencontrées à Salisbury sont expliquées, représente la première tentative d'exploration systématique de la dimension urbaine du phénomène (1965 : 192–203). Il identifie deux situations structurelles caractéristiques de populations urbaines hétérogènes et changeantes qui déterminent si c'est l'adversité qu'il faut incriminer, ou les pratiques malveillantes d'une autre personne, et dans quelle mesure respectivement. Tout d'abord, la famille urbaine privilégie la cohésion plus qu'elle ne favorise la division et il est peu vraisemblable qu'en ville des parents citadins en viennent à s'accuser mutuellement. En outre, dans le contexte urbain, l'émulation qui marque les relations professionnelles, une victime est moins portée à accuser un compagnon d'être la cause de ses malheurs qu'à s'en remettre à la sentence du devin, à savoir que ces malheurs sont le fait de la colère des esprits de ses ancêtres ruraux. Ceci parce que, à Salisbury, l'illégalité des accusations de sorcellerie peut être facilement sanctionnée, eu égard au rigoureux contrôle administratif qui y règne. C'est pourquoi les accusations initiales de sorcellerie doivent être transposées et interprétées en fonction de la colère des ancêtres. Ainsi peut-on au moins expliquer la cause d'un malheur de façon satisfaisante, même si aucune action efficace ne peut être entreprise à l'encontre d'un suspect. Cette hypothèse, convaincante dans ce cas précis, demande à être adaptée en fonction de la rigueur avec laquelle les autorités administratives urbaines répriment l'illégalité des accusations de sorcellerie. A Salisbury, l'application de la loi semble être sans faille. Les informations sur d'autres villes d'Afrique de l'Est et d'Afrique centrale sont diverses, J'ai analysé une vieille querelle de famille mettant aux prises, à Kampala, deux cousins croisés : les accusations de sorcellerie ne furent jamais portées à aucun moment, alors même que l'un des deux protagonistes avait, à l'époque, été l'objet de malveillances. La querelle s'apaisa quand l'un des cousins fit un rêve dans lequel l'âme de sa grand-mère maternelle (c'est-à-dire la grandmère paternelle de son rival) lui enjoint de mettre un terme à cette dispute 'au nom de la famille' (1969a : 125–6). Je me rends compte, maintenant, que ce dénouement corrobore la première partie de la double hypothèse de Mitchell, à savoir que le besoin de cohésion familiale en milieu urbain inhibe les accusations de

La ville et la campagne en Afrique 71

sorcellerie entre parents proches. Quant à la deuxième partie de son hypothèse, nous remarquons que c'est l'intervention d'un ancêtre paysan qui met fin à la querelle, même si elle ne l'explique pas entièrement. Mais les difficultés de la vie en milieu urbain *sont* parfois expliquer d'avoir une origine rurale.

Autre cas, celui de deux amis luo, voisins immédiats à Kampala; l'un se trouve renvoyé de son travail: une dispute s'ensuit entre les deux hommes, stimulés par leurs épouses, avec accusations et contre-accusations de sorcellerie (c'est-à-dire utilisation d'objets investis d'une puissance surnaturelle maléfique). Dans ce cas, rien n'obligeait à passer la sorcellerie sous silence, puisque la cohésion familiale n'était pas en cause. L'un des couples quitta volontairement le quartier, et c'est ce qui mit fin à la querelle (*ibid.*: 66–7). Ce qui accrédite l'hypothèse de Mitchell, bien que la démarche soit inverse.

Jamais, ni dans l'un ou l'autre cas, l'illégalité du recours à la sorcellerie ne fut dissuasive. Pas plus que dans les récents travaux de Grillo sur Kampala (1973: 142–6), de Kapferer sur Broken Hill (1969: 202–8) ou de La Fontaine sur Kinshasa (1970: 182–7) où les explications du malheur comme signe du mécontentement des ancêtres paysans, prévalent sur celles formulées en termes de sorcellerie. Mais, c'est bien connu, la distinction entre *witchcraft*, *sorcery* et tourments infligés par les ancêtres ou autres esprits, est très ténue. Les gens eux-mêmes ne les distinguent pas clairement, ni sur le plan de la terminologie, ni au niveau conceptuel. Peut-être pouvons-nous aborder ce sujet sous un autre angle.

Les informations ci-dessus, ainsi que celles dont je dispose sur les Luo de Nairobi, donnent à penser, cependant, que ces explications se répartissent selon deux pôles: d'une part, celles qui attribuent le malheur survenu en milieu urbain à un agent surnaturel ayant pour demeure la même ville; d'autre part, celles qui postulent une cause surnaturelle d'origine rurale (cf. également Grillo 1973: 54, 144; La Fontaine 1970: 185–6). Comment peut-on expliquer cette propension de certains citadins à interpréter, et parfois ré-interpréter, l'origine des malheurs qui les assaillent en ville selon ces deux pôles? A Salisbury, cette propension s'explique par l'effet dissuasif d'un contrôle administratif très sévère. Une telle contrainte témoigne de l'organisation politique d'une ville, en l'occurance régie par des Européens. La situation des Africains à Salisbury n'est pas telle qu'ils considèrent la ville comme un point d'attache permanent. C'est en milieu rural qu'ils maîtrisent, si tant est qu'ils le peuvent, leur destinée. Ce milieu tend par conséquent à constituer leur pôle de référence pour expliquer et surmonter leur mauvaise fortune. De la même façon, les Luo de Kampala au milieu des années 60, ceux

72 *Introduction*

de Nairobi actuellement, estiment que leur situation dans ces villes est bien moins affermie que celle des communautés d'accueil, respectivement les Ganda et les Kikuyu, qui les dominent politiquement. Causalité urbaine et causalité rurale sont clairement distinguées, et, tout au moins à Nairobi, cette dernière semble prévaloir dans la diagnose de la sorcellerie et des diables malévoles.

A partir de ces quelques données, nous pouvons avancer une hypothèse qui—trop vague telle quelle—mérite d'être soumise à examen. Plus l'intégration d'un groupe migrant au milieu économique et politique de la ville où le travail est faible, plus ses membres imputeront leurs malheurs à des agents ruraux, et non pas urbains. Ce qui laisse présumer que le groupe conserve des attaches rurales et que certains de ses membres assurent la jonction entre la ville et le village. Le corollaire veut que le groupe d'accueil —celui qui domine politiquement—'allègue' des causes d'origine urbaine pour la plupart, ou, simplement, fasse peu de différence entre motifs 'ruraux' et motifs 'urbains'. Avant de rattacher cette hypothèse à d'autres éléments sur l'éveil de la conscience politique et idéologique chez ces groupes, il nous faut savoir dans quelle proportion, et pour quels types d'entre elles, ils appréhendent leurs malheurs sous l'angle du surnaturel, plutôt que de dénoncer leur 'exploitation' pure et simple par le groupe dominant, ou la 'révolte' de ceux qui y sont soumis.

Tout ceci repose sur le postulat que, pour les citadins, les valeurs et conduites qu'ils conceptualisent ne sont pas identiques en milieu urbain et en milieu rural. La plupart le réalisent à la faveur de circonstances qui les font se rendre à l'évidence (Grillo 1973: 184). Alors que là où les intérêts économiques ruraux et urbains se complètent—tel est le cas chez les Gwembe Tonga du village de Mazulu—ces différences présumées de valeurs et de conduites n'existent pas; en conséquence, le 'champ conceptuel' dans lequel trouver des explications aux malheurs subis est plus vaste; les infortunes surviennent sans discrimination, tant en milieu urbain qu'en milieu rural (Colson et Scudder, *infra*: 210–12).

Les matériaux présentés par Rigby et Lule sur la religion ganda à Kampala épousent-ils ce postulat? La situation des Ganda en Ouganda a radicalement changé au cours des douze années qui ont suivi l'indépendance. Bien que ce changement ait inévitablement amoindri la domination qu'ils ont exercée à Kampala sur les autres groupes africains, ils restent, et de loin, les plus nombreux et sont fort bien représentés à tous les niveaux de la hiérarchie professionnelle. On ne peut dire que leur influence politique ait disparu; mais peut-être qu'elle est temporairement reléguée. Elle renvoie, à

La ville et la campagne en Afrique 73

cet égard, à celle de leur religion traditionnelle, qui n'a jamais complètement disparu, même lors des conversions massives au christianisme et à l'islam. Elle s'est plutôt mise en 'réserve', pour apparaître, en situation de crise, comme le point de rassemblement de tous les Ganda (quand, par exemple, les Britanniques exilèrent le Kabaka de 1953 à 1955, puis, à nouveau, en 1966 après l'indépendance; puis quand il mourut, dans l'attente du retour de son fils en 1971).

Il y a eu non seulement préservation d'aspects fondamentaux de la religion ganda, pendant plusieurs générations, mais, en outre, ses dimensions urbaine et rurale sont restées stables, à la seule exception des esprits ruraux *misambwa* qui sont associés à des aspects topographiques—tels les collines ou les rivières—et donc moins facilement transposables en milieu urbain. A ceci près, la perpétuation en milieu urbain des rituels, des objets magiques, des autels et des croyances est frappante. Cependant, leur signification et leurs fonctions se sont adaptées à Kampala. Ainsi a-t-on plus fréquemment recours, à Kampala, aux *mayembe* (esprits à la fois bienveillants et malveillants) pour soigner, et aussi pour attraper les *mizimu* (esprits des trépassés); à Kampala, les Ganda font un parallèle constant, dans les rituels urbains, entre les tombeaux de la ville (*ssabo*), parfois modestes, et les tombeaux des rois et notables enterrés non loin de la ville; les Ganda de Kampala connaissent une douzaine de *lubaale* (esprits de possession des divinités ganda et des héros-fondateurs) qui y sont éminents. Ceci représente la greffe de croyances rurales en milieu urbain; mais d'autres rituels plus complexes, concernant des cas difficiles d'infécondité en ville, doivent être accomplis dans le village.

Le statut de communauté d'accueil des Ganda à Kampala, et la relative continuité des relations économiques et sociales ville-campagne, auxquelles ils participent, est à mettre en parallèle avec la permanance de leurs croyances religieuses, identiques dans les deux milieux. Remarquons que, contrairement à ce qui se passe pour les Cewa et les Yao de Salisbury, étudiés par Mitchell, ou les Luo de Kampala et de Nairobi, ou encore les populations africaines de Léopoldville, décrites par La Fontaine, chez les Ganda les esprits ancestraux se déplacent—si l'on peut dire—jusqu'à Kampala pour y tourmenter leurs descendants sur place plutôt qu'à distance. Les Ganda de Kampala trouvent dans la ville la quasi-totalité des agents surnaturels qui leur servent à expliquer les malheurs qu'ils y subissent et ne font normalement pas intervenir l'univers rural.

Ce qui semble cohérent par rapport à l'hypothèse ci-dessus énoncée. Néanmoins, et si ce n'est qu'il reste à justifier les impli-

74 *Introduction*

cations tautologiques d'une argumentation selon laquelle les groupes vivant près d'une ville préservent mieux leurs croyances et pratiques rituelles, il faut beaucoup plus d'informations pour établir si les changements qu'ont connu les Ganda à Kampala, eu égard à leur position politique, avant et après l'indépendance, correspondent à des variations dans les explications qu'ils donnent de leurs propres malheurs, dont ils tiendraient les causes pour 'rurales', par opposition à des causes 'urbaines'.

Croyances et pratiques rurales sont rejetées, ou sélectionnées et adaptées dans des contextes urbains. De même, les différentes langues vernaculaires se transforment par interaction et au contact des langues véhiculaires urbaines. Jusqu'à quel point la diffusion de sa langue—comme de ses concepts rituels—caractérise-t-elle une communauté d'accueil urbaine? Les devins ganda de Kampala ont une clientèle étendue, qui comprend de nombreux non-Ganda. La langue des Ganda, le luganda, est aussi largement employée comme langue véhiculaire dans la ville. Selon son importance et son influence, une communauté d'accueil diffusera plus ou moins sa langue et sa culture parmi les migrants et les citadins. Mais l'importance ne suffit pas. Ainsi les Zaramo, dont le territoire d'origine entoure Dar es Salaam, représentaient en 1957 près des deux cinquièmes de la population de la ville. Ils jouèrent un rôle important en tant que communauté d'accueil lors des premiers développements de la ville (Leslie, 1963: 33). Cependant l'expansion de l'islam et du swahili comme langue véhiculaire estompèrent les distinctions politiques et culturelles entre eux et d'autres groupes. Maintenant leur influence politique et économique semble négligeable si on la compare à celle des Ganda à Kampala ou des Kikuyu à Nairobi.

A l'opposé, à Lusaka le nyanja l'a aisément emporté comme langue de relation sur le bemba et le tonga. Ohadike montre que pendant cette expansion le nombre de locuteurs Nyanja venant de la province orientale de Zambie dépassait celui des locuteurs Tonga-Ila originaires de la province centrale, qui jouèrent le role de communauté d'accueil à Lusaka avant 1950. Les Nyanja étaient également plus nombreux que les locuteurs Bemba originaires des provinces du Nord, de Luapula et du Copperbelt (*infra:* 138). Dans ce cas l'acquisition ou la perte du statut de communauté d'accueil est en liaison directe avec l'expansion, la limitation, le repli des trois langues véhiculaires africaines rivales.

Dans les villes du Copperbelt de Zambie, c'est une variété particulière du bemba qui est la langue de relation la plus répandue, le nyanja venant en second. L'anglais y est considéré par beaucoup

La ville et la campagne en Afrique 75

comme une langue de prestige (Epstein: 1959), comme dans bien d'autres centres urbains d'Afrique orientale et centrale. La Tanzanie fait exception, le maniement avec aisance d'un bon swahili pouvant y entraîner la considération (Whiteley: 1969).

Caractéristique de la forte assise industrielle des villes du Copperbelt est l'emploi d'un parler propre aux travailleurs dénommé kabanga ou chilapalapa. Ce parler a été importé des villes sud-africaines, où il est fanagala ou cafre populaire. Il s'y est développé à partir du zulu et de l'anglais. Tout en reconnaissant l'extraordinaire diversité de ces langues véhiculaires du Copperbelt, Kashoki (*infra:* 228) s'est intéressé au bemba. En étudiant les origines des principaux termes d'emprunt et en reconstituant les dates de leur adoption, il a pu évaluer l'influence des migrations sur l'évolution du bemba parlé dans le Copperbelt. Il conclut que ce développement n'a pas été simplement le résultat du contact urbain entre Européens et locuteurs Bemba. C'est plutôt à la faveur des migrations rurales-urbaines que les 'Bembaphones' ont adopté des termes étrangers d'origine rurale, européennes et non-européennes.

On notera que certaines de ces foyers correspondent à d'anciens points de passage de commerçants arabes parlant le swahili. Les missions rurales des Pères Blancs employaient également le swahili, tout comme l'anglais: elles furent une autre source de termes d'emprunt. A leur tour, les migrants temporaires entraînèrent ces termes d'emprunt jusqu' aux villes du Copperbelt d'où ils furent diffusés encore plus loin. Dans ces villes, locuteurs Bemba et Nyanja se font des emprunts réciproques; de ce fait, la complexité du vocabulaire s'accroît, entraînant une spécialisation constante de référence et de signification à l'échelle de la ville et du pays.

Ainsi les mouvements de population entre zones rurales et zones urbaines modifient les langues véhiculaires sur les plans du vocabulaire, de la phonologie et de la syntaxe. Cependant, on assiste à l'émergence de langages et de codes spécifiquement urbains. Le bemba et le kabanga du Copperbelt, le nyanja de Lusaka, le swahili de Nairobi, le swahili et le luganda de Kampala (Parkin 1971; 1974; Scotton 1972) et le lingala de Kinshasa (La Fontaine 1970: 45), tous ces parlers sont assez spécialisés pour se différencier significativement de leurs homologues ruraux, là où ceux-ci existent. Dans ces villes comme dans d'autres, ces parlers rivalisent avec les langues des anciennes administrations coloniales. Les conditions de l'emploi salarié urbain—exercé dans un contexte pluri-ethnique, multi-racial et de division socio-économique—mettent en lumière les connotations ambivalentes de ces langues de relation. Dans certains con-

76 *Introduction*

textes, l'emploi du swahili à Nairobi ou à Kampala connote la fraternité, l'égalité, le dépassement de l'ethnicité. Mais son emploi par un anglophone instruit s'adressant à un illetré qui ignore l'anglais peut souligner leurs différences sur le plan socio-économique et entraîner involontairement un ressentiment. Cette connotation peut être intentionnelle. Epstein en donne un exemple : dans le Copperbelt, avant l'indépendance de la Zambie, un Européen s'adresse en fangalo abusivement à un délégué africain à l'éducation, mais manifeste son mécontentement quand l'Africain lui réplique en anglais (1959 : 237 p5).

Ce rapport symbolique entre l'emploi d'une langue 'coloniale' et une langue véhiculaire autochtone est très répandu. Décrivant un rapport analogue entre le français et le swahili à Lubumbashi (Zaïre), Polomé dit que la situation linguistique 'y reflète nettement la croissance de la ville sous le régime colonial' (1971 : 371). Même en Tanzanie le second vice-président a déploré que, dix ans après l'indépendance, certains soient encore si inhibés par 'le relent colonial' qu'ils méprisent le swahili et préfèrent employer l'anglais ou le français (Whiteley 1974 : 4).

Ainsi les langues véhiculaires se rapprochent des croyances et pratiques liées à l'adversité. Elles circulent entre villes et campagnes, véhiculées par des gens auxquels elles sont indispensables. Elles facilitent la transmission des idées entre les deux zones tandis que leurs formes, lexicales ou symboliques, s'adaptent aux concepts des situations spécifiques, rurales ou urbaines.

L'on affirme parfois que le développement de l'éducation affaiblit les croyances aux rites traditionnels. De même l'anglais ou le français sont parfois considérés comme dangereux pour les langues africaines. Cependant, comme le montrent les articles présentés dans ce volume, la confrontation n'est pas si nette et il y a de nombreux emprunts réciproques. Les résultats de l'enquête linguistique effectuée au Kenya en 1968–9 indiquent une situation quelque peu paradoxale. Ainsi au Kenya, le swahili se développe dans les villes, mais c'est dans les villes que les besoins d'éducation—celle-ci conduisant à l'acquisition de l'anglais—sont les plus importants et les plus aisés à combler (Whiteley 1974 : 6).

De même, l'importance et l'hétérogénéité des populations urbaines accroissent le besoin d'un vaste éventail de méthodes indigènes de 'traitement' de l'adversité. Pourtant c'est en ville que l'on trouve les meilleurs services de santé modernes, employant un personnel hautement qualifié.

L'éducation et la médecine moderne furent initialement apportées par les missionnaires chrétiens qui fondèrent les premiers hôpitaux

La ville et la campagne en Afrique 77

et écoles. Le résultat fut le développement d'un stéréotype quasi officiel, voyant dans l'utilisation des médecines occidentale ou traditionnelle les attributs respectifs de l'instruction ou de l'analphabétisme bien qu'en pratique tous les niveaux d'éducation fassent appel aux deux formes de thérapie (voir Beidelman 1974: 244–5). La position, ambivalente et variant selon la situation, de tout un chacun quant aux avantages et inconvénients de la médecine occidentale et de la médecine traditionnalle fait écho aux attitudes incertaines de la plupart des Etats quant à l'emploi d'une langue véhiculaire traditionnelle comme le swahili et d'une ancienne langue coloniale comme l'anglais.

Les attitudes officielles envers le système éducatif lui-même peuvent également être ambivalentes. Une grande partie de son contenu, hérité du colonialisme, est reconnu comme inadéquat et comme facteur de divisions sociales. Mais le système existant est encore considéré comme la meilleure voie vers le succès. Aussi, pendant les années suivant l'indépendance, les gouvernements ont souligné la valeur d'une éducation largement répandue et si possible généralisée, comme facteur de développement mais aussi—de façon plus idéologique—comme un droit en soi. Gould (*infra:* 250) montre comment de réels efforts furent faits en Ouganda peu après l'indépendance pour réduire les inégalités entre régions en ouvrant de nouvelles écoles secondaires. Mais par la suite la politique changea et les critères financiers poussèrent à une extension fondée sur l'agrandissement des écoles déjà existantes. Il était moins onéreux de développer les externats urbains, où l'on n'avait pas à fournir aux élèves nourriture et logement, que les internats généralement situés loin des villes. Cette politique a permis d'offrir davantage de places dans le secondaire à un moindre coût; de ce point de vue elle a réussi. Mais elle a eu deux conséquences inattendues: augmenter les migrations des jeunes vers les villes, les contraindre à trouver en ville logement et pension auprès de parents qui peuvent eux-même avoir des problèmes d'emploi ou de logement. Dans la mesure où les possibilités d'emploi pour les détenteurs de certificats du niveau 'O' sont presqu'exclusivement dans des zones urbaines (*infra:* 262) il apparaît que cette politique a renforcé la conviction générale qu'une éducation de haut niveau est un préalable indispensable à un emploi 'acceptable' et que cette éducation doit être urbaine plutôt que rurale.

Ce dernier exemple du renforcement mutuel des politiques, des convictions et des considérations idéologiques nous amène à considérer le fait même de l'implantation urbaine et la part jouée par les attaches et rapports continus avec le monde rural dans la forma-

78 *Introduction*

tion de la structure et de la composition sociale des villes en expansion d'Afrique orientale et centrale.

ATTACHES RURALES ET IMPLANTATION URBAINE

(*a*) *Le rôle de l'appartenance ethnique*

Leslie a décrit comment les routes de migrations des divers groupes ethniques vers l'ancienne Dar-es-Salaam aboutirent à des quartiers différents dans la ville. Des groupes dont les routes se croisèrent ou se rejoignirent établirent des rapports d'aide et d'assistance mutuelle denommés *utani* (1963: 33). Il ne subsiste plus grand'chose de tout cela aujourd'hui mais on voit par là comment la structure ethnique d'une ville peut être influencée par des attaches rurales se perpétuant. Dans cet ouvrage Hirst (*infra:* 319) montre que la structure de Kampala continue à être influencée par les différentes migrations ethniques, mais il souligne l'importance du statut socio-économique comme variable intermédiaire. Pour Mombasa, Stren (1972: 7–115) analyse en détail la façon dont habitants et immigrants se répartissent dans des zones résidentielles distinctes; il souligne aussi que les demeures des hôtes sont généralement propriété privée, louées par les Africains eux-mêmes alors que celles des migrants sont plus fréquemment louées dans des lotissements publics.

Les restrictions coloniales et, dernièrement, un sérieux problème de logement dans les villes d'Afrique centrale et orientale ont pu limiter la liberté de choix des divers groupes d'immigrants quant à l'installation séparée de chaque groupe. Cependant des enclaves ethniques sont signalées et augmenteront vraisemblablement, les populations urbaines en expansion rapide étant amenées à recourir à des implantations spontanées dans des zones 'non-autorisées'. A l'opposé, les nouvelles unités d'habitation du secteur public ne sont pas destinées à des groupes ethniques particuliers.

Ici aussi, la distinction de Southall entre deux types de villes peut servir à souligner cette évolution. On se rappelle que les villes de type A, comme Kampala, Dar-es-Salaam, Mombasa, Blantyre, présentaient les caractéristiques de nombreuses villes d'Afrique occidentale, favorisant la ségrégation résidentielle et l'organisation à l'échelon local des familles étendues, les regroupements basés sur le pays d'origine et les enclaves ethniques. Plus étroitement déterminée par l'administration, la structure résidentielle des villes plus récentes de type B, telles Nairobi, Salisbury, Lusaka, Ndola et autres villes du Copperbelt et liées au chemin de fer, était caractérisée par un zonage séparant nettement quartiers non africains (y compris les

La ville et la campagne en Afrique   79

quartiers européens) et quartiers africains. Dans ces derniers, le logement était contrôlé par les municipalités, les employeurs publics —Police, Chemins de Fer, Télécommunications,—parfois par de grands employeurs privés. Dans les villes de type A, ces lotissements officiels se sont ajoutés, pour ainsi dire, à la structure urbaine précoloniale, comme produit de l'administration coloniale (voir Southall & Gutkind 1957: 46–9, pour Kampala; Stren pour Mombasa, *op. cit.: Chilivumbo infra:* 310–11, pour Blantyre; Marris 1961, pour Lagos).

Les villes de type B ont évolué dans un sens opposé. Aux lotissements officiels se sont ajoutées récemment des implantations spontanées ou illégales où se sont développés des 'villages' mono et pluri-ethniques. Les résidents d'un tel ensemble ont parfois en commun non seulement une région d'origine, mais encore des croyances religieuses et/ou des affiliations politiques. Tel est le cas de Kapipi à Lusaka où un parti d'opposition, maintenant interdit, le Congrès National Africain, contrôlait effectivement l'organisation du logement et du commerce, devant la carence de la police et des autorités locales (Boswell, à paraître & 1974). La célèbre zone de squatting de la vallée du Mathare à Nairobi est de fait une couronne de villages spontanés dont les habitants ont résolu de leur propre initiative les problèmes de la crise du logement (Ross 1973: 91). Cette réalisation est maintenant à peu près reconnue par le conseil municipal de Nairobi (Nelson, articles à paraître).

Il faut souligner, à propos de ces villages spontanés établis sur des zones urbaines non autorisées, qu'ils permettent aux habitants— comme dans les villes précoloniales de type A—davantage de liberté dans l'implantation domestique et ethnique que les lotissements officiels. Il ne s'agit pas d'idéaliser et de nier l'entassement, le manque de confort, les loyers parfois élevés exigés par les propriétaires pour des demeures dépourvues de confort. Mais—pour reprendre un thème ancien—il semble préférable d'améliorer l'organisation et le tracé des implantations existantes que de les raser complètement pour rebâtir à zéro.

La préservation des enclaves ethniques—qui résulterait de cette reconnaissance officielle—n'est pas forcément mauvaise. Il n'a nullement été prouvé que des enclaves ethniques en milieu urbain attisent les divisions entre groupes. Actuellement, la cause sous-jacente de ces divisions est plutôt l'existence d'inégalités ethniques et régionales dans l'ensemble de la nation, comme on l'a précisé plus haut. Il est bon de rappeler le fait bien connu: les enclaves ethniques assurent sécurité dans une situation économique incertaine et, entre autres, permettent aux migrants récents comme aux citadins plus

80 *Introduction*

anciennement installés de maintenir les liens avec leur foyer rural. Dans la mesure où le maintien d'attaches rurales offre une alternative, certes précaire, à une dépendance totale envers l'emploi urbain par un retour à l'autarcie paysanne, ces enclaves ethniques peuvent être considérées comme l'expression d'une résistance, pour ainsi dire, au développement urbain par accumulation de capital selon le modèle occidental et comme un mode de préservation des relations avec le milieu rural.

Des implantations urbaines non-autorisées de type pluri-ethniques peuvent se constituer autour d'un noyau d'habitants de longue date, dont les attaches rurales ne sont plus que nominales comme chez les Pumwani (Bujra 1974: 197) et Kibera (Clark 1973). Les implantations d'origine plus récentes, où les habitants valorisent encore le maintien de leurs attaches rurales, sont à un carrefour. Leur composition pluri-ethnique n'oblige pas les propriétaires à n'accepter que des locataires de la même ethnie. Il n'y a pas de contraintes 'morales' implicites qui pourraient jouer pour les propriétaires dans une enclave ethnique récente où le marché du logement est régi par un système permanent d'obligations rurales. Et cependant, simplement parce qu'ils sont installés depuis peu, les habitants de ces nouveaux villages multi-ethniques sont encore impliqués dans les mailles de leurs attaches rurales respectives. Trois voies leur sont ouvertes: l'une conduisant au développement d'une communauté résidentielle 'brassée' où les différences ethniques s'estomperont, à travers les générations, face aux intérêts urbains communs; l'autre menant à la persistance de différences ethniques qui s'articulent sur des situations professionnelles hétérogènes; la troisième assurant la perpétuation de la pluri-ethnicité résidentielle à travers des intérêts distincts, tant ruraux qu'urbains.

Les possibilités offertes aux habitants de manifester leurs préférences en rejoignant ou en établissant une enclave ethnique dépendent du contrôle qu'ils peuvent exercer sur le marché du logement urbain. Il y a là conflit potentiel non seulement avec les autorités municipales, mais encore avec d'autres groupes ethniques demeurant dans la ville. C'est sur des problèmes d'expansion spatiale qu'éclateront vraisemblablement les conflits entre les implantations urbaines ayant démarré comme enclaves ethniques. Ces conflits sont—en tout cas en théorie—susceptibles de règlement par arbitrage faisant appel à des chefs de communauté reconnus, dont la légitimité peut être renforcée par leurs attaches rurales.

Etant donné l'existence d'un secteur privé du logement—en expansion bien que non reconnu officiellement—une differenciation économique et sociale accrue entre propriétaires et locataires est

La ville et la campagne en Afrique   81

inévitable dans les implantations urbaines, mono-ethnique et pluri-ethniques. Ceci mis à part, les implantations qui s'organisent volontairement sur une base mono-ethnique offriront probablement plus longtemps à leurs habitants les deux options de l'autarcie paysanne et de l'emploi salarié urbain. En dernier ressort, évidemment, il s'agit d'options viables ou non en fonction de la politique de planification nationale quant aux investissements ruraux ou urbains et quant à la réduction des inégalités criantes entre régions.

La perpétuation des rapports urbains-ruraux est possible même quand les membres d'un groupe ethnique n'habitent pas ensemble en ville. Ils peuvent se réunir à l'occasion d' 'evenements ethniques', se recrutant à travers des réseaux interpersonnels étendus. C'est ce qu'a montré Weisner (1972) pour un sous-groupe luyia de Nairobi où les affiliations lignagères restent importantes. De plus, ils peuvent être organisés en associations ethniques structurées qu'on a beaucoup étudié dans l'ensemble de l'Afrique. Il est maintenant reconnu qu'une communauté d'accueil formera plus rarement de telles associations qui sont plus fréquentes parmi les groupes d'origines rurales lointaines. Kampala est un exemple déjà familier de cette situation et nous noterons que Leslie (1963: 39) souligne également brièvement la 'floraison d'associations' à Dar-es-Salaam parmi les 'gens de l'intérieur' tels que les Luo (installés partout), les Chagga et les Pare. Les diverses formes d'organisation sociale rurale des groupes émigrant vers les villes peuvent influencer la structure des associations urbaines susceptibles de se constituer (voir Southall, *infra:* 267 et ses références), la distance à la ville étant sans doute une condition préalable.

Southall considère justement que l'analyse doit distinguer l'organisation sociale rurale et les liens avec la communauté urbaine d'accueil qui influencent séparément les formes d'organistion urbaine adoptées par les différents groupes ethniques. Dans les villes de type A, les deux allaient souvent de pair et une ville précoloniale était également la capitale d'un royaume doté d'un système de stratification rurale qui servait inévitablement de modèle pour la croissance ultérieure de la ville à l'époque coloniale. Kampala en est le meilleur exemple en Afrique centrale et orientale (voir Gutkind 1963): la ville s'organise autour de deux pôles de croissance, l'un regroupant les occupants ganda, l'autre les Anglais et, dans leur mouvance, les populations non-ganda. L'étude de Hirst (*infra:* 330–31) montre comment, même de nos jours, la distinction hôtes— migrants se maintient à Kampala et est à son tour perpétuée par leur 'choix' de résidence à travers la chaîne des migrations ethniques.

Les communautés d'accueil plus récentes, tels les Kikuyu à

82 *Introduction*

Nairobi, les Nyanja à Lusaka ou les Bemba dans les villes du Copperbelt n'ont pas un tel modèle historique d'organisation urbaine et sont plus directement liées au colonialisme et à l'industrialisation post-coloniale. Elles peuvent avoir surgi d'un système politique précolonial centralisé ou non : ce n'était pas le cas des Kikuyu, c'était jusqu'à un certain point celui des Bemba. Bien que l'importance de telles différences dans l'oraginsation sociale rurale soit sensible aujourd'hui encore, elles influencent moins directement les structures et la composition des villes de type B. Comme on l'a mentionné plus haut, on n'a guère écrit sur les petites villes et centres d'échange dénommés par Middleton villes de type C; l'on peut présumer que leur croissance future sera déterminée selon que ce seront les ethnies locales ou les ethnies lointaines qui auront maîtrisé les possibilités offertes par l'expansion.

J'ai souligné les trois distinctions—entre villes de type A et de type B, entre groupes ethniques d'accueil et immigrants, entre systèmes politiques précoloniaux centralisés ou non centralisés— parce qu'il me semble qu'elles peuvent continuer à influencer les formes actuelles de l'organisation urbaine et qu'il est pertinent pour nos analyses d'apprécier l'étendue de cette influence.

Ainsi nous pouvons nous demander si—en tenant compte de leur implication accrue dans les tendances internationales qui gouvernent les localisations industrielles et les offres de travail—les villes de type A et de type B ne convergent pas vers un schème commun. La distinction entre groupes d'accueil et immigrants est certainement pertinente là où l'ethnicité ou l'appartenance régionale est le mode d'expression majeur, officiellement reconnu, des confrontations politiques et économiques en milieu urbain. Tous les groupes ethniques d'accueil n'occupent pas une position prééminente. On l'a vu plus haut, la communauté d'accueil des Tonga-Ila (originaires de la province centrale de Zambie) a perdu à Lusaka sa situation dominante à partir de 1950 au profit des locuteurs Nyanja originaires de la plus lointaine province orientale. A Mombasa (Kenya), les gens du pays, les Mijikenda, se plaignent fréquemment d'être 'dominés par des populations de l'intérieur, Kikuyu, Luo, Luyia. A l'opposé, ce n'est que depuis l'indépendance du Kenya, en 1963, que les Kikuyu ont été considérés—sans hésitation, même par les Luo—comme la communauté d'accueil prééminente en lieu et place des Européens dont l'emprise antérieure sur la ville était reconnue, sinon acceptée, par les Kikuyu eux-mêmes (voir Werlin 1974 : 79–80, 126).

La distinction entre systèmes politiques précoloniaux centralisés et non centralisés est sûrement la plus controversée. Certes, tous ces

La ville et la campagne en Afrique 83

systèmes politiques sont depuis longtemps dominés par l'Etat, d'abord colonial puis indépendant. Cependant il faut noter l'influence persistante des politiques coloniales, déclarées ou non, d'administration indirecte qui ont utilisé les unités territoriales et les réseaux de communication existant, gauchissant fréquemment leur signification et créant en fin de compte des différences culturelles inter-ethniques beaucoup plus accentuées que dans la situation originelle (Southall *infra:* 265).

Voici un exemple de ce phénomène, et de son effet sur les relations villes—zones rurales. A Kampala, les Ganda et les Luo ont des attitudes très différentes vis-à-vis de la parenté. Les Ganda qui atteignent un statut social élevé ne sont pas obligés de continuer à aider un large cercle de parents, alors que les Luo le sont. Comment expliquer cette différence? La persistance du royaume ganda (et des couches sociales le composant), soutenu par les Anglais, réduisit l'importance des liens lignagers, en ville comme dans les zones rurales. A l'opposé, chez les Luo au système politique non centralisé les Anglais empêchèrent toute evolution de l'organisation spatiale précoloniale et utilisèrent les territoires associés aux lignages d'extension différents à des fins d'administration. Ainsi renforcées, ces divisions territoriales et le principe lignager ont gardé de l'importance et ont, dans une certaine mesure été renforcées lors de l'implication accrue des Luo dans le développement économique et social à grande échelle. En ville, les liens agnatiques ont pour eux une importance pratique, autant qu'idéologique, pour trouver un emploi ou un logement, arranger un mariage, s'élever dans l'échelle sociale. Les divisions rurales originelles (lignages, 'sous-tribus') ont une importance articulaire dans les élections nationales, tant dans les zones urbaines et que dans les régions rurales (Okumu 1969). Ces deux exemples suggèrent que, bien que les systèmes politiques précolohiaux soient inexistants en tant que régimes politiques, les modes d'organisation et de pensée différents établis par eux ont encore de l'importance (*pace* Grillo 1973: 180).

Toute tentative de généralisation, telle ces trois distinctions, passe forcément sous silence les variations spécifiques. Halpenny (*infra:* 281-6) a raison de souligner que, chez les Ganda de Kampala il y a en fait beaucoup plus de variations dans la structure interne des migrations que parmi les autres ethnies. En effet le statut indépendant des femmes ganda, appelées *nakyeyombekedde*, conduit à des modes de migrations spécifiquement féminins, qui se différencient de ceux des femmes des autres ethnies, mais également de ceux des hommes ganda. D'un autre côté, quand on considère l'ensemble des relations inter-ethniques à Kampala, la situation émancipée des

84   *Introduction*

femmes ganda se différencie nettement de celle des autres femmes; ce contraste peut être expliqué par les différences d'organisation familiale évoquées plus haut et par la possibilité d'acquisition de terres dans le voisinage pour les femmes ganda de Kampala.

(b) Femmes indépendantes dans les quartiers urbains pauvres.

Halpenny & Obbo (*infra:* 288–93) montrent comment l'existence de chances d'enrichissement dans les zones rurales ou urbaines détermine l'apparition de 'sous-cultures' féminines qui transcendent souvent les différences ethniques que les hommes valorisent. Les données de Nelson, sur les femmes kikuyu, et de Bujra (1973) sur les musulmanes de Nairobi confirment celles de Halpenny & Obbo quant à la tendance des femmes des villes d'Afrique centrale et orientale à entreprendre brassage de bière, distillation d'alcool, préparation et vente de nourriture, location de garnis, prostitution; elles offrent ainsi un ensemble de services aux travailleurs urbains. Alors que les hommes peuvent s'employer dans les secteurs formel et informe de l'emploi urbain, il n'y a guère de possibilités pour les femmes sans qualifications en dehors du secteur informel.

On voit ici poindre une hypothèse. Etant donné la différenciation des possibilités d'emploi en ville offertes aux hommes et aux femmes, et puisque les femmes doivent tout d'abord acquérir un statut relativement indépendant afin de profiter des possibilités qui leur sont offertes, on peut prévoir: que les intérêts communs des femmes de tous les groupes ethniques s'exprimeront de plus en plus par l'adoption de styles de vie typiquement féminins et de préférences matrimoniales; le développement d'une sous-culture féminine urbaine contrastant avec la persistance des différences ethniques chez les hommes. Cette persistance dépend elle-même du contrôle exercé par les hommes sur la proportion de mariages féminins contractés hors groupe, et/ou sur la revendication des droits paternels comme moyen de perpétuer les différences entre groupes par delà les générations successives. Par conséquent toute transformation des rôles sexuels par laquelle les femmes viennent à contrôler les unions matrimoniales et ont la garde des enfants qui leur sont nés aura des conséquences importantes sur l'avenir des relations inter-ethniques en zones urbaines aussi bien que sur celui des rapports entre hommes et femmes. Le secteur informel en expansion de l'économie urbaine est de plus en plus influencé par les femmes et, sous ce rapport, l'avenir des relations politiques et économiques en Afrique urbaine semble faire davantage appel au rôle novateur des femmes qu'à celui des hommes.

A l'heure actuelle, les différences entre les statuts, par exemple, des femmes luo et ganda peuvent sembler trop importantes pour confirmer cette hypothèse qui est volontairement présentée de façon très large. Cependant l'étude présentée par Obbo d'un quartier pauvre de Kampala où les femmes divers des groupes ethniques forment l'ossature de l'économie informelle, montre la convergence vers un modèle féminin d'aspirations et de techniques de survie qui assume déjà sa morale particulière.

Les statuts masculins et féminins contrasteront sans doute avec ceux que l'on associe généralement aux conditions 'préurbaines'. Les hommes, comme on l'a vu, sont poussés par le système éducatif à rechercher du travail en col blanc, dans des ville bâties ou se développant grâce à des entreprises financièrement puissantes. A l'opposé, les femmes ont généralement peu de chances de trouver de tels emplois et doivent faire preuve d'initiative, venir en ville, y trouver et y créer du travail, généralement dans le secteur informel. On peut affirmer que les aspirations des hommes les conduiront probablement à dépendre d'un emploi qu'ils ne contrôlent pas alors que les femmes, bien qu'elles soient exploitées, ont davantage de contrôle sur leurs enterprises de production.

Il faut reconnaître que, bien que les migrations des femmes vers les villes d'Afrique orientale et centrale semblent croître plus vite que celles des hommes (Ohadike l'a montré pour Lusaka, *infra*: 132) la plupart sont encore des épouses économiquement dépendantes qui n'assumeront probablement pas dans un proche avenir le statut indépendant décrit par Obbo et Halpenny. Ces femmes indépendantes sont plus directement le produit des quartiers pauvres où les emplois dits informels sont légion. Mais la croissance de ce genre de quartier permet de prévoir une augmentation du nombre de ces femmes indépendantes et, étant donné l'importance des services qu'elles assurent, de leur influence économique et même politique.

Etant donné l'expansion continue des quartiers populaires, la transition de la dépendance économique à l'émancipation économique repose, pour les femmes, sur cinq attributs généraux implicitement énumérés dans l'article d'Obbo :
1) Les femmes forment l'ossature de l'économie informelle dans les zones urbaines à bas revenus, tout comme elles ont fréquemment assuré le fonctionnement d'économies agricoles rurales.
2) Dans ces zones, l'emploi dépend de l'initiative personnelle, non d'une formation ou d'un apprentissage, aussi les femmes ne sont-elles pas désavantagées.
3) Chez les hommes comme chez les femmes, les facteurs économiques jouent un rôle majeur dans le développement de l'immigration

86 *Introduction*

urbaine; cependant les facteurs déterminants sont plus variés chez les femmes et se rapportent à des opprobres tels qu'une grossesse extra-maritale, un divorce, une séparation, ou à des obstacles à l'avancement personnel, telle l'impossibilité d'hériter ou d'acquérir de la terre ou l'étroitesse de la voie d'accès à l'éducation.

4) Bien que limitée, l'economie urbaine informelle offre aux femmes un éventail de carrières plus large que normalement dans les zones rurales tout en leur permettant, plus tard dans la vie, de réinvestir dans des biens ruraux.

5) Le processus continu de la redéfinition conjugale et familiale, qui sous diverses formes est mondial, et qui n'est pas complètement rural ou urbain, s'exprime surtout dans les zones urbaines offrant des possibilités d'emplois informels.

Ce n'est pas ici le lieu d'esquisser des comparaisons avec le statut économique des femmes en Afrique occidentale, sauf pour reconnaître que là-bas, ce statut a généralement largement dépassé les chances d'emploi offertes dans les quartiers pauvres tels que le Namuwongo-Wabigalo et Kisenyi décrits dans ce volume (Little 1973: 45–6).

(c) Le contrôle du peuplement urbain.

Tout comme Halpenny, Van Velsen (*infra:* 296) souligne la contribution apportée à l'économie urbaine et même nationale par les habitants de ces quartiers, souvent qualifiés officiellement de 'chômeurs'. Pourquoi, demande-t-il, les autorités municipales continuent-elles à vouer ces quartiers à la démolition. Les termes employés pour les décrire: taudis, bidonville, 'zone de squatting', renforcent cette vision négative. Le terme le plus significatif est celui de zone 'illégale'. Van Velsen firme qu'à Lusaka—et probablement dans d'autres villes africaines—le terme dérive de règles de zonage remontant à un système colonial d'administration municipale qui visait à contrôler la répartition raciale des habitants. Née de ce système, la division en quartiers européens, africains et asiatiques est à présent progressivement remplacé par le découpage découlant de l'appartenance à des groupes ou des classes sociales; c'est ce que décrivent ici Chilivumbo pour Blantyre et Ohadike pour Lusaka, et c'est ce que l'on peut observer dans toutes les grandes villes d'Afrique centrale et orientale.

Par une analyse contextuelle systématique d'un éditorial paru dans un journal de Zambie approuvant la démolition d'une implantation 'illégale' à Lusaka, Van Velsen suggère que les autorités municipales sont prises au piège de réglementations coloniales et de définitions légalistes qui n'ont aucun rapport avec les besoins réels

La ville et la campagne en Afrique 87

d'une population urbaine africaine indépendante, quelle qu'ait pu étre leur utilité antérieure pour des Européens.

Ainsi, l'opinion officielle récemment était que les squatters de Lusaka representent un 'problème' parce qu'ils se sont appropriés des terres dénommées 'terres de la couronne' à l'époque coloniale. Pourtant, du point de vue des Zambiens eux-mêmes, il s'agit simplement de terres d'appartenance publique; les difficultés présentées par les cas d'implantation spontanée sur des terres d'appartenance privée —ce qui est frequemment le cas en Amérique latine—ne jouent donc pas ici. Van Velsen affirme que, si les autorités urbaines reconnaissaient les apports économiques de ces populations elles pourraient (n'étant pas handicappées par des négociations longues et coûteuses avec des propriétaires au sujet de leur indemnisation) facilement convertir ces implantations en cités de Castors jouissant de meilleures facilités. La remarque est pertinente. En effet, comme le suggère Grohs (1972: 165), la décision de tout raser et de rebâtir à zéro est souvent prise parce qu'elle est la plus simple du point de vue de l'administration, et aussi parce qu'elle est conforme aux pratiques antérieures.

Van Velsen montre que de nombreuses justifications officielles de ces démolitions sont mythiquës: ces zones ne sont pas peuplées surtout de célibataires, mais comprennent de nombreuses familles; la distribution des emplois y correspond à peu près à celle des lotissements officiels; elles ne sont pas envahies de migrants d'origine rurale en quête d'emplois et enfin, étant donné le pourcentage élevé de salariés en Zambie, elles n'abritent pas des 'squatters', mais une proportion importante de la force de travail du pays.

Etant donné ses richesses minières considérables, la Zambie connaît moins le sous-emploi et le chômage que les autres pays d'Afrique centrale et orientale; aussi n'est-il pas surprenant d'y trouver peu de différences sous l'angle démographique et socio-économique entre zones d'habitation légales et franges illégales.

Bien qu'exceptionnel de ce point de vue, le cas zambien illustre cependant une contradiction plus générale, et qui va beaucoup plus loin, entre une conception de la planification urbaine héritée du système colonial et les besoins de la population d'une ville. Des cas de destruction d'implantations illégales et de leur remplacement par des lotissements officiels, dans des villes non-zambiennes, sont peut-être des manifestations précoces de cette contradiction. C'est ce qui est arrivé dans certaines zones de Pumwani, Nairobi (Bujra à paraître), mais cette politique a heureusement été abandonnée dans le cas de implantations de la vallée de Mathare à Nairobi (voir aussi le ILO Report 1972: 227).

D

88 *Introduction*

On reconnaît maintenant que la transformation d'implantations ceux-ci se lient au sort d'entreprises de bâtiment privées utilisant des des normes de construction officielles, souvent trop élevées pour être réalistes (voir Gugler: 7, Safier: 31, Rado & Wells: 222, tous trois dans Hutton, ed., 1972). Il faut peu d'imagination pour envisager l'apparition d'une autre contradiction entre la politique de bon sens de construction avec les moyens du bord, en recourant à des techniques simples, et les intérêts des planificateurs urbains si ceux-ci se lient au sort d'entreprises de bâtiment privées utilisant des technologies et des matériaux qui impliquent accumulation capitaliste. D'un point de vue national, l'avantage économique d'une politique de construction faisant appel à la force de travail, plutôt qu'à l'accumulation capitaliste, est d'utiliser des immigrants au chômage ou sous employés et de permettre ainsi d'utiliser l'argent qui aurait été dépensé pour satisfaire à des normes élevés de construction, à des programmes de développement rurale.

Envisager une telle politique pose le problème de l'équilibre entre possibilités de développement et de revenus dans les zones rurales et les zones urbaines: le colloque a longuement étudié ce sujet. Le principal problème méthodologique était la conciliation des critères irréductibles des bénéfices sociaux (ou humanitaires) et des bénéfices économiques comme mesures du bien-être respectif des citadins et des ruraux. Si l'on peut isoler des critères 'purement' économiques, on devrait pouvoir déterminer qui subventionne qui. Les données concernant la Zambie montrent que les revenus réels de la petite ferme familiale ont décru en dépit d'un accroissement des productions agricoles alors que ceux des travailleurs urbains ont cru (Fry 1975). D'un autre côté on peut dire de façon plus générale que les soi-disant squatters de Lusaka contribuent largement à l'économie urbaine mais en reçoivent peu en échange. On pourrait également affirmer qu'une dépendance continue et accrue envers l'emploi salarié urbain réduit les chances qu'a un travailleur, et sa famille, d'exercer son choix éventuel de retour à un mode de vie paysan centré sur des activités de subsistance. Cependant l'explication des avantages et inconvénients individuels, selon les termes de l'échange des zones urbaines et zones rurales, ne doit pas ignorer les liens continus entretenus avec leurs régions rurales d'origine par bien des citadins comme l'ont souligné de nombreux exposés dans ce volume. Nous ne devons pas oublier que les termes de l'échange dans les zones rurales *et* urbaines, avec leurs proportions croissantes de demandeurs d'emploi diplômés, se dégradent encore dans l'ensemble du tiers-monde par rapport aux nations industrialisées, même avec l'exception limitée des principaux producteurs de pétrole.

La ville et la campagne en Afrique 89

On revient, par conséquent, à l'opinion exprimée au début de cette introduction. Les liens migratoires, culturels, idéologiques, institutionnels entre la ville et la campagne peuvent être en premier lieu déterminées par la distribution des ressources et des possibilités dans la nation; cependant en dernier ressort il faut les considérer comme des réponses à des facteurs internationaux qui échappent toujours davantage au contrôle des populations locales. Que l'Afrique de l'Est et l'Afrique centrale ne soient pas seules à connaître ceci ne diminue pas l'urgence de leurs problèmes.

PART II
SPECIAL STUDIES
MODELS OF MIGRATION

Factors in rural male absenteeism in Rhodesia[1]

J. C. MITCHELL

SPECIFIC AND GENERAL CONTEXTS IN THE STUDY OF LABOUR MIGRATION

Labour migration, or rather, labour absenteeism—the temporary absence in wage labour of some sections of a given population from their usual place of residence—seems particularly to be characteristic of, though not peculiar to, what have been called 'plural societies'. These societies, like the colonial societies of Southern Africa, of which Rhodesia is an example, are composed of population segments who restrict their voluntary social relationships largely to their own kind, who are located in different parts of the country, command different shares of the national product and who have unequal involvement in making important political decisions. Yet labour migration in Rhodesia has not yet been subjected to much systematic analysis, partly because of the paucity of information on a nationwide basis which could provide the foundation of study of this scope. Such studies as exist have dealt either with the particularistic set of circumstances of specified local areas (Garbett 1960, 1967; Sister Mary Aquina 1964), with inter-territorial migration (Scott, 1954), or with a circumscribed aspect of migration (Johnson 1964; Barber 1960, 1961).

The purpose of this analysis is to bring together some information in official statistics of various kinds, that relate to the country as a whole, so as to provide a general context within which more detailed studies may be located.

CONTEXTUAL AND ECOLOGICAL VARIABLE

It is important, however, at the outset to distinguish between phenomena at different levels of analysis. Practitioners of different analytical disciplines such as geographers, economists, social psychologists, social anthropologists or sociologists necessarily subsume

[1] I am grateful to the International African Institute Seminar on Town and Country in East and Central Africa and also to my wife, Hilary Flegg Mitchell for useful comments on an earlier draft of this paper.

94 *Special Studies*

the same apparent 'real' phenomenon such as labour migration into different analytical frameworks. The phenomena are only apparently similar because what is germane in labour migration, say, to a social psychologist may not necessarily be so to, say, an economist; the common-sense label of 'labour migration' may have quite different connotations to specialists in different subject disciplines. In effect the topics of theoretical significance to practitioners in these different fields lead them to ask different questions about the common-sense phenomenon in question.

Within subject disciplines a similar disparity is apparent between those approaches which concentrate on the macroscopic or molar as against the microscopic or molecular aspects of societal organization. The sort of question a social anthropologist adopting a structural frame of reference asks about labour migration is different from the sort of question one adopting an interactionist frame of reference asks. This does not mean that one approach necessarily invalidates the other; it only means that the different approaches assume different aspects of the common-sense phenomenon to be relevant.

It is useful on this basis to draw the distinction between the context in which social actions take place and the social actions themselves. The context, itself a proper topic of study, may be taken as given in the study of social action. Insofar as the study of labour migration is concerned the broad features of geographical locations, and economic, political and administrative structure may be taken for granted if the analyst's purpose is primarily to examine the decisions of actors, in some restricted locality, to migrate or not to migrate. These contextual features, are, after all, common for all the actors in that locality. Equally, the particular set of personal circumstances in which the individual migrant is involved may be treated as epiphenomena if the analyst's main interest is in the broader structural framework within which the migrant is operating. In reality of course the framework and the individual action are indivisible: it is only for the analytical convenience that we treat them as phenomena at different levels of abstraction.

The hazards in the analytical separation of contextual from individual perspectives have been well appreciated in what has come to be known as the 'ecological fallacy' (Robinson 1950, see also Cartwright 1969; Alkers 1969; Valkonen 1969). This arises when data are available in aggregate form, as for example, for geographical areas and when analysts attempt to deduce from their existence at the aggregate level the relationships of variables to one another at

Factors in rural male absenteeism in Rhodesia 95

the individual level. It is fairly easy to show that although variables at the aggregate level may correlate quite highly, there may in fact be no relationship between the variables at the individual level. The fallacy arises essentially from the conflation of different levels of analysis: regularities in phenomena at the aggregate level apply essentially to units of analysis at that level while regularities in what appear to be the same phenomena at the individual level apply essentially to *individual* behaviour. The argument may be caricatured by stating that a common-sense phenomenon may in fact be distinct phenomena at different levels of analysis.

CONTEXTUAL ELEMENTS IN MALE ABSENTEEISM IN RHODESIA

Studies in labour migration at both the contextual and individual levels, have isolated some fairly general variables with which the rates of migration seem to be associated. Some of these variables are, for example, the opportunities for earning cash locally, the ease of access to wage earning opportunities, the supply of labour, and the extent to which migrants must separate themselves from local social involvements if they are to become engaged in wage earning. Typically however these variables are related in the context of some limited local area and the generality of the relationships among these variables must be based upon 'analytic induction' which Znaniecki characterizes as 'inducing laws from a deep analysis of experimentally isolated instances' as against what he calls 'enumerative induction'. (1934: 237). Here I wish to explore the relationships among some variables whose connections may be established by analytic induction but which may be tested on data relating to the whole of Rhodesia in 1962.

The units of analysis were sixty-eight geographical areas identified in Table III of the official census of the African population in 1962 (Central Statistical Office 1964) as 'Tribal Trust Lands' (Land Apportionment Act 1931). These areas varied considerably in terms of natural resources and their proximity to the towns, mines and European farming areas which constitute the main centres for wage employment for Africans in Rhodesia. They are located on Map 1. The proportion of males absent from these areas—also varied from one area to another and this covariance of labour absenteeism with ecological variables and indicators of general social conditions provides a means of identifying some of the determinants of the context of male absenteeism.

SELECTING, DEFINING AND OPERATIONALIZING THE VARIABLE

1. *Male absenteeism*

The phenomenon which we wish to explain, of course, is the extent to which the population normally resident in an area is absent from it at a particular moment of time. We are able, on the basis of our general knowledge of circumstances in Rhodesia, to make the reasonable assumption that males absent from Tribal Trust Lands will almost certainly be away working on mines or farms or in towns either in Rhodesia or outside it. Unfortunately no attempt has been made in the census to estimate the proportion of males so absent from the Tribal Trust Lands. Accordingly I have sought to estimate this figure from the *de facto* age and sex distributions of the population in the

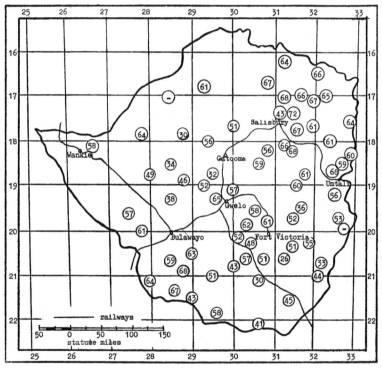

Estimated rates of male absenteeism from areas of labour supply: Rhodesia, 1962

Note: The circles contain the estimated rates of male absenteeism from the labour supply areas located approximately at the centre of the circle.

Factors in rural male absenteeism in Rhodesia

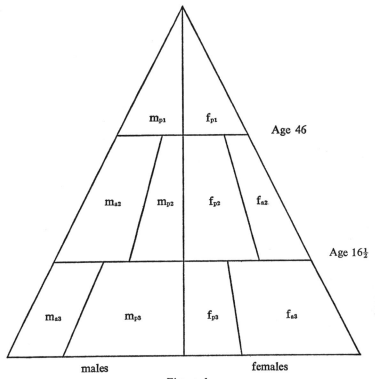

Figure 1
Population categories used in the estimation of male absenteeism

Tribal Trust Lands. The census enumerated males and females in the age categories 0–16½, 16½–46 and 46 and over. A marked disparity of males or females aged 16½–46 in relation to the numbers in the other age and sex categories would indicate a high degree of absenteeism. The position might be visualized in terms of Figure 1. The areas of the population diagram marked m_{p1}, f_{p1}, m_{p2}, f_{p2}, m_{p3} refer to the numbers of males and females in different age categories present in the locality at the time of the census. The areas m_{a2}, f_{a2}, m_{a3} and f_{a3} refer to the numbers of males and females in different age categories who were absent. The problem is to estimate the numbers of males absent aged 16½–46. The basic procedure is to estimate the total numbers of males aged 16½–46 to be expected in the population from the numbers of males and females in the other age and sex categories on the basis of the proportions in the age and sex categories of a standard population. For this purpose the struc-

98 Special Studies

ture of a stable population with an expectancy of life at birth of 50 and a natural rate of increase of $3\frac{1}{2}$ per cent per annum was used,[2] since these rates were characteristic of the African population of Rhodesia as a whole. In this procedure the number of absent males and females aged $0-16\frac{1}{2}$ was estimated by applying a fixed ratio to the number of females aged $16\frac{1}{2}-46$ estimated to be absent from the population.

It is not easy to test the validity of procedure. The absentee rate for males $16\frac{1}{2}-46$ from rural areas for the whole of Southern Rhodesia computed from this expression was 54·0 per cent. The actual absentee rate computed from the known distribution in town and European farms was 52·46 per cent when no allowance was made for absenteeism outside Rhodesia or 54.9 per cent when an allowance of 30,000 was made for absentees outside Rhodesia, which suggests that overall the estimate is reasonable. Data for comparison in local areas however are not easily available. The following rates have been derived from various anthropological and sociological surveys and provide a rough test of the validity.

Table 1

Comparison of estimates of male absenteeism rates derived from social surveys with rates derived from estimation of age and sex structure of the population

Social survey	Date		Census area (1962)	This estimate
Mangwende	1958	52·4[1]	Mangwende	60·7
Dibilishaba	1964	48·4[2]	Dibilishaba	43·1
Wenlock	1964	54·0[2]	Wenlock	68·2
Chilimanzi	1964	56·8[3]	Chilimanzi	57·6
Victoria	1964	33·3[4]	Ntilikwe	25·8
Mudande	1961	72·0[5]	Sipililo	67·1

[1] Garbett (1960) Table 8.   [2] Mitchell, H. F. (1967) Table 3.   [3] Sister Mary Aquina (1965) Tables 3 and 4.   [4] Estimated from Sister Mary Aquina Ph.D. Thesis.   [5] Garbett (1967) p. 310.

[2] Table West Mortality 14 from Coale, Ansley J. and Demeny, Paul (1966). The expected number of males aged $16\frac{1}{2}-46$ turned out to be:

$$(E)\ m_{p2} = \frac{{}^{w}1z^{m}p1}{2} + \frac{{}^{w}2z^{f}p1}{2} + \frac{{}^{w}3z^{m}p3}{2} + \frac{{}^{w}4z^{f}p3}{2} - {}^{w}5z^{f}p2$$

where w_i are the weights to take account of the reliability of the estimates (in this case the communalities of a factor analysis of the ratios in the age structures of the areas concerned) and z_i the ratios of the different age and sex categories to the number of males aged $16\frac{1}{2}-46$ in a standard population. The actual expression in this analysis was:

$$(E)m_{p2} = 2 \cdot 130\ m_{p1} + 1 \cdot 570\ f_{p1} + \cdot 455\ m_{p3} + \cdot 430\ f_{p3} - 1 \cdot 018\ f_{p2}$$

Factors in rural male absenteeism in Rhodesia 99

Variations in dates of survey and of the local coverage of some of the sociological studies reduces the value of these comparisons to some extent but the overall agreement appears reasonable in that the estimating procedure used here predicts fairly well the level of absentee rates derived from sociological surveys.

The estimates for male absentees gave negative results for two areas: Kariba and Mutema area in Chipinga. In both of these areas the proportion of persons aged $16\frac{1}{2}$–46 was much higher than in other areas suggesting that there may have been migration of families into these areas thus rendering the estimation procedure invalid. These two areas marked on Map 1 on p 96 by a dash within circles, have therefore been excluded from the rest of the analysis.

A number of indicators were available from the censuses and official records which could be construed as variables which could affect the level of male absenteeism from any given area. These were:

2. Density of population

The density of population in the area of supply of labour is an obvious factor if we are trying to relate absenteeism to the extent that local resources are being pressed upon. The 1962 Census Report Table III, pp. 47–58 (Central Statistical Office 1964) provided total *de facto* population figures for individual Tribal Trust Areas, Purchase Areas, towns, European farms, forest reserves and other types of settlement. The physical juxtaposition of Tribal Trust Lands enabled several of these to be combined to provide population units varying from 100,130 to 4,610 in size. The areas of these localities were not available from records. I therefore measured them with a planimeter from a 1:1,000,000 Land Apportionment map on which they could be easily identified. Each area was measured with the planimeter three times. A linear regression of planimeter readings of units for which the actual areas were known from other sources on to those areas provided a means of taking account of measurement errors. The areas of the units in square miles were derived from the planimeter readings in the linear regression expression and from these areas the population densities.

3. Proportion of men seeking work

The Census Report Table XII, p. 71 (Central Statistical Office 1964) provided details of the number of men who said that they were 'seeking paid work'. A return of this kind could not be an accurate measure of the extent to which local wage-earning opportunities outstripped the supply of labour. It could represent the extent to

100 *Special Studies*

which local men merely defined themselves as being potential wage-earners. Expressed as a proportion of men aged 16½–46 the figures varied from zero in Binga to 21·5 in Bulalima-Mangwe. I have interpreted it here as an indicator of the disparity between local expectations and local opportunities.

4. *Proportion of men with no education*

Table XI, p. 70 of the Census Report (Central Statistical Office 1964) displays the proportion of adult males with different levels of formal education. I have used the proportion of adult males with no formal education as the variable here. This measure may be construed in several different ways. One way would be to view the proportion of men with no education in the area as reflecting the degree to which they possess or do not possess one of the requisites for earning a reasonable wage. But it could also be taken to reflect the extent to which the area in question lacks schools and is therefore an indicator of general backwardness or of a lack of development resources.

5. *Difference between local and average wage*

One of the factors which may effect absenteeism is the extent to which local wages fall below the mean wage level obtainable elsewhere. Table XI of the Census of Employees (Central Statistical Office 1965) records wage levels with and without rations and housing allowances in the various districts of Rhodesia. For purposes of this analysis the mean cash wage without rations or housing allowances was subtracted from the mean cash wage in the district in which the unit was located. The difference therefore, reflects the extent to which cash wages obtainable locally compared with those that were available further afield. Since most of the units in the analysis were Tribal Trust Lands the wages available locally mainly on European farms were considerably lower than the national average but these differed appreciably from one area to another.

6. *Mean opportunity distance*

The likelihood that men would migrate from any locality in search of wages would also be affected by the distance they would have to travel to find work. In this analysis an attempt was made to estimate this by computing the direct distance from the approximate geographical centre of a locality to the geographic centres of main wage earning employment. The distances were calculated directly from the latitudes and longitudes of the locality in question and the

Factors in rural male absenteeism in Rhodesia 101

particular wage earning centre. These distances were then weighted by the number of men employed at each distance derived from the Census of Employees Table VI (Central Statistical Office 1965) and the mean weighted distance from the locality computed from these weighted totals.[3]

7. *Proportion of non-foreign persons employed locally*

Absenteeism could well be affected by the extent to which local employment was available to men of foreign origin in the sense that places remote from developed areas would not be likely to attract foreign workers. The Census of Employees Table VI (Central Statistical Office 1965) sets out figures of the proportion of men employed in districts of foreign or of Rhodesian origin. Unfortunately the figures do not break down the Rhodesian totals into those which come from localities close at hand as against those from further afield in Rhodesia. It could best be used as an indicator of the extent to which the area is subject to labour competition from distant as well as local sources.

8. *Number of persons per trading store*

One of the deficiencies in this analysis is the lack of a measure which could be used to gauge the extent to which local opportunities exist for cash earning through the sale of crops and stock or through trade. An indirect measure of this might be the number of trading stores which exist in any locality in relation to the total population in that locality. The argument would be that the number of trading stores that can operate in an area depends on the amount of cash circulating in that area. Hence in an area where there is little economic development there would be few trading stores to serve a population of given size while in a locality where there was more development there would be more trading stores for the same population. The Native Commissioner's Report for 1962, Table I, p. 33 (Southern Rhodesian Government 1962) sets out the number of trading stores in districts of Southern Rhodesia. These were related to the population in those districts in 1961 to provide an indicator for use in this analysis.

---

[3] The distance in statute miles from A to B would be:

$$\frac{6080}{5280} \cdot 60. \text{ arc cosine (sin Lat A. sin Lat B.} + \cos \text{ Lat A. cos Lat B. cos (Long A} - \text{Long B))}.$$

The mean opportunity distance would be $\Sigma d_i w_i / \Sigma w_i$ where d_i are the distances to the wage centres 'i', w_i the numbers of men employed at those centres and Σw_i the total number of all men employed.

102 *Special Studies*

9. *Agro-ecological region*

Wage absenteeism is also likely to be related to the basic natural resources of a locality. These are difficult to measure in their full complexity but the agro-ecological region in which the area is situated might be taken as a crude indicator of them. Agro-ecological regions may be thought of as categories of natural habitats classified by their soil types, rainfall, relative humidity, temperature and topography in relation to their potential agricultural utility. The Agro-ecological Survey of Southern Rhodesia (Phillips 1962) determined five major agro-ecological types. These in brief outline were:

(1) Areas suitable for intensive livestock production and general diversified production.
(2) Areas suitable for intensive agricultural production by mixed farming systems.
(3) Areas suitable for semi-intensive beef production.
(4) Areas suitable for semi-extensive livestock production.
(5) Areas only suitable for extensive beef production.

The agro-ecological survey produced a map showing the distribution of these regions. The sixty-eight areas used in this analysis could be located on this map and the agro-ecological regions into which they fell could thus be determined. Several of the areas in fact straddled several regions. The five types of region used in the agro-ecological region were therefore elaborated into ten ordinal types which could take into account the mixture of regions in any one area, ranging from those suitable for most intensive mixed farming at one extreme to those suitable only for extensive beef production at the other.

For computational purposes the coded number between 1 and 10 was treated as a point on an interval scale with 1 representing the most advantageous agro-ecological circumstances and 10 the least advantageous.

THE ANALYSIS OF THE DATA

Statistics derived from official sources, of course, involve a number of difficulties when they are used for sociological analysis. The first difficulty is that the official statistics are produced for administrative purposes and are created in terms of definitions which presumably are meaningful primarily for those purposes. Sociological analysis on the other hand must be conducted in terms of concepts to which the official statistics may refer only obliquely. The statistics may

Factors in rural male absenteeism in Rhodesia 103

have to be redefined for sociological purposes and possibly manipulated if they are to represent the phenomena in which the sociologist is interested. This implies that the characteristic of real sociological interest is often only indirectly reflected in the statistics and that any attempt by the sociologist to manipulate the statistics to make them reflect the characteristic in which he is interested, may be fraught with danger. Official statistics have been used as indicators requiring varying degrees of reinterpretation in each of the nine variables discussed so far. Clearly the indicators used could be given other interpretations leading to different conclusions from the findings. But the process of any analysis inevitably involves constructing variables from available data. The test of utility of the constructions lies in the extent to which the indicators behave in accordance with the analyst's expectations.

The second difficulty is that the official statistics, like all other data, are subject to error. Obviously the amount of error will differ according to the topic to which the data refer. The number of Africans in employment recorded in the census is probably fairly reliable, but if the total enumerated as 'seeking paid work' is to be taken as an accurate reflection of the amount of unemployment then it is possible that there could be serious error. The data on employment, that is the wages, numbers in employment and origin of labour were collected from employers and are presumably reasonably accurate. The number of trading stores comes from the Native Commissioner's records. The population statistics, including those on age and sex distributions, the number of men without educational qualifications, the number said to be seeking paid work were derived from census enumerators and are no doubt subject to the range of error familiar in African census taking. In terms of census taking as a whole the Rhodesian census is probably as good as any but not too much store should be put on the face value of the various statistics used in this analysis.

The statistical analysis of the material, in fact, is in terms of general measures of association—measures which estimate the over-all relationship between the variables. Individual variations in the accuracy of the statistics would not affect the measures too seriously if the errors in them were unbiased. For purposes of analysis I have in fact assumed that the errors in the statistics are unbiased.

The over-all association among the variables was in fact estimated by the correlation coefficients. Table 2 sets out the product-moment correlations among these variables.

One of the points that emerges from this table is that areas in which there appears to be a high proportion of men absent tend

Table 2

Correlations among variables associated with male absenteeism

	1	2	3	4	5	6	7	8	9
1. Agro-ecological region	—	·715	·596	·540	·302	·300	·274	·082	·177
2. Mean opportunity distance	·715	—	·587	·434	·238	·166	·364	·195	·106
3. Population density (reflected)	·596	·587	—	·249	·220	·143	·155	·367	·090
4. Per cent non-foreign labour	·540	·434	·249	—	·143	·433	·457	—·151	·178
5. Wage differential	·302	·238	·220	·143	—	·127	·168	—·187	·035
6. Male absenteeism (reflected)	·300	·166	·143	·434	·127	—	·139	·058	—·019
7. Per cent seeking paid work	·274	·364	·115	·457	·168	·139	—	—·297	·176
8. Per cent males no education	·082	·195	·367	—·151	—·187	·058	—·297	—	·280
9. No. persons per store	·177	·106	·090	·178	·035	—·019	—·176	·280	—

Note: The directions of the variables of population density and of male absenteeism have been reversed in order to make the table more easily interpretable. The correlations should be read therefore as showing a correlation, when positive, of a *low* density or a *low* male absenteeism rate with *high* value in the other variable.

Factors in rural male absenteeism in Rhodesia 105

also to be those in which there is a high proportion of foreign labour employed. This mildly puzzling relationship is almost certainly due to the fact that in those regions where economic opportunities are good, local men are able to find jobs with good wages close at hand. In areas where economic conditions are poor, however, local men tend to migrate further afield to labour centres where wages are higher while the relatively poorly paid local jobs are taken by migrants predominantly from Mozambique and Malawi.[4] At the same time the generally advantageous economic circumstances in the region imply that more of the local population can meet their cash needs from economic activities inside the local areas as for example by growing crops for cash sale. This latter interpretation is supported by the relatively high concentration of the areas with few men absent in the advantageous agro-ecological regions.

THE PATTERN AMONG THE VARIABLES

The interconnection among the variables associated with areas from which there are high or low proportions of men absent makes it difficult to estimate the effects of any one variable on male absenteeism since indirect effects of other variables may be compounded in the zero order correlations reported in Table 2. The fact that some variables appear to be closely connected with others suggests that multiple regression procedures may not be very trustworthy.[5] I have attempted, therefore, to disentangle the effects of the variables by principal components analysis. Principal components analysis attempts to reduce variables to a smaller set which by definition may be uncorrelated with one another. The smaller set of variables can be thought of as components or dimensions of the original set of relationships which reflect some common underlying characteristic of the original variables. The relations of the eight independent variables to the underlying dimensions to which they may in part be reduced is set out in Table 3.[6]

This analysis separates three analytically distinct features of the areas. The main dimension which accounts for just over one-third

---

[4] I made a similar observation in respect to the Mount Darwin and Sipililo Districts in an earlier paper on wage labour in Southern Rhodesia. See Mitchell 1961 : 230.

[5] Because of multi-collinearity effects.

[6] Unities were used in the leading diagonal of the correlation matrix. All vectors with eigenvalues of less than 0·95 have been ignored. The three dimensions displayed here accounted for 70·0 per cent of the total variance of the variables. The values in Table 3 are those derived from a Varimax rotation.

106 *Special Studies*

Table 3

Associations of attributes with underlying dimensions

Population density (ref)	·804	−·048	·048
Mean opportunity distance	·743	−·374	·082
Agro-ecological region	·688	−·468	·206
Wage differential	·189	−·283	−·027
Per cent males not educated	·455	·544	·299
Per cent seeking work	·135	−·617	−·189
Per cent non-foreign labour	·244	−·667	·263
No. persons per store	·085	·049	·708
Per cent of variance explained	36·8	21·0	12·2

of the total variance, differentiates between areas on the basis of the extent to which they are close to, or distant from, major locations of wage employment and activities based on the cash economy. These are either the more favourable agro-ecological regions in which towns or European farms are located or, conversely, the poorer agro-ecological regions which are distant from towns or European farms where the labour opportunities are concentrated. Associated with these regions, depending upon the end of the continuum at which they fall, are either high densities of population, a high proportion of non-foreign labour and a small differential between local and national wage levels or conversely, a low population density, a high proportion of foreign labour and a large differential between local and national wage levels. The areas at one extreme of the dimension are thus situated either in the richest and most favourable farming regions many parts of which in terms of the Land Apportionment Act were allocated to European farmers or near the line-of-rail. European farmers were also, of course, large employers of African labour, and the towns were also main centres of employment in this dimension. When African areas are located in the superior agro-ecological regions the carrying capacity of the land is *high* and the population densities are accordingly *high*. In addition there is a tendency for there to be a higher proportion of the population with some education in these areas than in areas at the other end of the continuum. These three attributes then, the agro-ecological region, the mean opportunity distance for wage

Factors in rural male absenteeism in Rhodesia 107

employment and the density of population are the main character-istics of this first dimension.

A Tribal Trust area which illustrates this extreme is the Chiduku area in Makoni District. This area has a high density of population (173 per square mile) in a relatively good farming area and it is relatively close to employment centres. At the other extreme is the Chipise area in the Beit Bridge District which is a very dry region categorized by agricultural officers as suitable only for extensive cattle ranching. It carries a density of only $6\frac{1}{2}$ persons per square mile, and is relatively distant from areas of labour demand. This dimension therefore relates to the basic natural resources of the area which in turn is reflected in the density of the African population living in areas along the continuum and also in the relative distance from places where employment may be found.

The second dimension, which accounts for 23·4 per cent of the total variance, distinguishes areas by the extent to which the men in them have responded to labour demands regardless of the area's location in respect of local resources and employment. The features which characterize this dimension are a low proportion of males classified as 'seeking work', a high proportion of males with no formal education, a low proportion of non-foreign labour and a relatively small difference between the local average and the national average wage levels. At the one extreme we have isolated areas like Urungwe in which there is a high proportion of people with no education but where relatively few define themselves as 'seeking work'. What local employment opportunities exist are for work which is relatively poorly paid and is taken up mainly by men from outside Rhodesia. Areas at this extreme of the dimension are those in which the population does not respond easily to demands for labour. At the other extreme are areas like Gwanda and Brunapeg where a relatively high proportion of the males defined themselves as 'seeking work', a relatively small proportion of males have no education, a high proportion of the population employed in the area comes from within Rhodesia and where local mean wage levels are somewhat higher than the national average. These are areas in which the population is oriented towards wage earning employment and exploits the available local opportunities.

The third dimension, which accounts for 12·2 per cent of the total variance is one which is particularly characterized by the small number of shops in relation to the population. A relatively high proportion of uneducated men is also moderately associated with this dimension. Areas at one extreme would be characterized by a general lack of opportunities of earning money either by labour or

108 *Special Studies*

by cash-cropping. These are areas marked by a general backwardness of social development. Binga is an example of such an area with over three thousand persons per store as against the national average of 666 and with 94·5 per cent of the men in the area with no education as against the national average of 50 per cent. At the other extreme is Umzingwane which has 262 persons per store and only 36·7 per cent of the men with no education indicating its relatively high level of local development.

These three dimensions with which the variables are correlated as set out in Table 2, are constrained by the method of analysis to be uncorrelated with one another while at the same time passing as nearly as possible through the points representing the areas characterized by the eight variables. These points, of course, are deemed to be located in a three-dimensional space. We can, however, relax this constraint and allow the dimensions to reflect the correlations amongst them.[7] In this case the correlations among the dimensions are as set out in Table 3. The dimension representing the agro-ecological region correlates with that representing general employment response to the extent of ·2086 and with that representing local development to the extent of −·2732. These two latter dimensions however are virtually independent of one another ($r = ·0641$).

A SUGGESTED CAUSAL STRUCTURE OF FACTORS INFLUENCING THE LEVEL OF MALE ABSENTEEISM FROM LOCAL AREAS

The components analysis used thus far merely makes the implicit regularities among the variables explicit: it does not of itself suggest what factors may lead to high or low male absenteeism from local areas. The components analysis has suggested, however, that the underlying factors may be looked upon as falling into two rather different categories. The first is related to the extent to which the areas were contiguous with localities in which there has been substantial capitalized economic development involving as it does a considerable demand for labour. The first dimension designated as 'agro-ecological region' falls into this category. The second category is related to the general social and economic isolation of the local areas themselves: the second and third dimensions designated as 'labour opportunities', and 'local development' fall into this category.

[7] In effect this is done by a rotation of axes to an oblique solution. In this case an Oblimin rotation was used.

Factors in rural male absenteeism in Rhodesia   109

These considerations suggest that the variables available for use in this analysis may be fitted into a causal model in which the level of male absenteeism is the final dependent variable. This suggested model is set out in Figure 2. The model makes the assumption that the agro-ecological region in which the area falls is logically prior to all others. The existence of favourable natural resources and capitalized economic developments which has arisen because of them, will determine both the extent to which labour opportunities exist and the circulation of cash and general level of development in the neighbouring African areas. These two sets of circumstances we may assume are logically dependent on the agro-ecological region in which the areas are located but in turn logically prior to the level of male absenteeism. In this model, therefore, the response to the labour demand and the level of development in the local area are construed as variables which intervene between the basic variable, the agro-ecological region and male absenteeism which is the phenomenon we wish to explain.

It is possible to determine from weights derived from the principal components analysis (as set out in Table 2) and the value each area has on each of the eight variables the position of each area on each dimension.[8] We may use the values thus derived on each of the dimensions to examine the influence of each of these underlying factors on male absenteeism. The correlations of male absenteeism with the agro-ecological regions factor is in fact ·1740 with local labour opportunities as ·2844 and with local development 0·0431.

Perhaps the first observation that needs to be made is that the hypothetical variables we have constructed from the original eight empirical variables account for only 9·0 per cent of the variance of the level of male absenteeism.[9] The presumption must be that the sort of variables we have been able to construct from official statistics have in fact omitted others which are considerably more important. From our knowledge of labour circulation in general we might suspect that one crucial variable which is missing is that which relates the standard of living to which Africans aspire in Tribal Trust Lands to the opportunities they have of earning the wealth locally to achieve it.

Given then that we are operating with a restricted set of variables we are still able to examine the extent to which they do in fact support the model we have postulated. To do this however we need

[8] These are in fact the factor scores based on the oblique factor structure.
[9] The multiple correlation coefficient of the level of male abstenteeism with the scores on the three dimension was in fact ·3091.

to go beyond zero order correlation coefficients since they may compound in them the effects of the operation of all the background variables since they are themselves to some extent all intercorrelated. Accordingly causal path coefficients have been computed and entered on Figure 2. The full set of path coefficients and residual paths are set out in Table 4.

The path coefficients estimate the direct effect of any given factor upon variables dependent on it, by removing the effect of other variables which operate upon that variable indirectly through the factor. For example the correlation between agro-ecological region activity and male absenteeism is ·1740. This means that areas in good agro-ecological zones are likely to a slight degree to have higher male absentee rates. But about half of this relationship arises because local development and the response to labour opportunities are also related to both agro-ecological zone and to the rate of male absenteeism. The *direct* effect of the agro-ecological zone on the rate of labour absenteeism excluding the indirect effects of the level of local development and the response to labour opportunities is much less.

This model suggests that areas in which both the level of social and economic development is better than average and the response

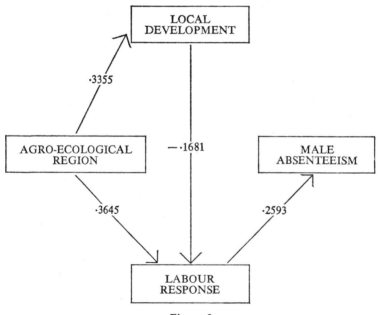

Figure 2

Factors in rural male absenteeism in Rhodesia   111

Table 4

Correlations, path coefficients and residual paths between hypothesised factors and male absenteeism

	Agro-ecological region	Local develop-ment	Path coefficients Response to labour demand	Male absenteeism
Agro-ecological region	1·0	·3355	·3645	·0852
Local development	·3355	·9420	—·1681	·0264
Response to labour demand	·3081	—·0458	·9381	·2593
Male absenteeism	·1740	·0431	·2844	·9541

Note: The values in the diagonal are the residual paths representing the extent to which the preceding variables have failed to explain the variance in the variable in question.

to labour opportunities higher than average are associated with more favourable agro-ecological regions. But the relationship is not straightforward. Among the areas in which local development is lower than average, whether in rich or poor agro-ecological regions, there are about the same proportion of areas in which the response to labour opportunities is high. But among areas in poor agro-ecological regions where local development is better than average there is a far higher proportion of areas in which the labour response is low. In richer agro-ecological regions where the local development is better than average, however, there is a much larger proportion of areas in which the labour response is high. In other words the level of local development is a variable intervening crucially between the type of region and the local response to labour opportunities but its effect in good agro-ecological areas is opposite to what it is in poorer regions. It is this reversal of relationships which leads to the negative path coefficient between local development and response to labour opportunities in the model.

The model also suggests that areas with higher absentee rates will be associated with those in which the response to local opportunities is high and not with the level of local development. A more detailed examination of the data, not reported here, shows, however, that the areas showing the highest absentee rates and those showing the lowest *both* fall in the better agro-ecological regions. What distinguishes the areas in the better agro-ecological zones which have high absentee rates from those that have low rates is that they are areas in which the local response to labour oppor-

112 *Special Studies*

tunities has been high while good agro-ecological zones where the absentee rates are low are areas in which the response to labour opportunities is low. One possibility is that areas in good agro-ecological regions with low response to labour opportunities and low absentee rates are far from labour centres so that people in them meet their cash needs from agricultural activities while those with high response to labour opportunities are close to labour centres and are able to find cash earning wage employment close at hand. In terms of the way in which 'local economic activity' has been defined here a plausible hypothesis might be that labour absenteeism at the molar level is primarily a reaction to the *national economic and political situation* and that activities at the local level are not connected directly with these. The test of this suggestion, however, can only be made with molecular data collected on a comparative basis in several areas in which the level of absenteeism differs appreciably but the other characteristics of the areas are as balanced as possible.

Circulatory migration in Rhodesia: Towards a decision model

G. K. GARBETT

Circulatory labour migration, in which men seek paid employment away from their homes, possibly for some years, return for a period then set out again, often repeating this process many times during their working lives, is a phenomenon which has been reported from various parts of the world in addition to East, Central and Southern Africa (Alvarez 1967; Appleyard 1962; Böhning 1970; Jackson 1969; OEDC 1967; Richmond 1967; Rose 1969; Thistlethwaite 1969). It is commonly, though not exclusively, associated with capitalist modes of production occurring within political structures in which labour migrants perceive a disparity between the rights and privileges which they may claim in their place of employment as against those accorded them in their home areas (cf. Mitchell 1969: 177). Typically, circulatory migration has been a prominent feature of colonial societies in Africa and elsewhere, though by no means confined to them. It has been most persistent in those societies such as Rhodesia, where it is in the political and economic interest of a dominant section of the population to maintain a high degree of residential and social segragation, to control the allocation of political rights, and hence, to influence wage rates and the flow of migration.

In this paper, after outlining some of the major variables at the macro-level which have influenced labour migration rates in Rhodesia, I consider certain problems which arise in analysis when, as sociologists, we turn to consider data at the micro-level. I suggest that a significant improvement in analysis at this level can be obtained by applying a 'decision-model'. The notion of an individual exercising choice under conditions of risk and uncertainty is familiar. Allied to the concept of strategy, it has been widely applied in economics, in political sociology, in the study of interpersonal relations and of social exchange (cf. von Neumann, J. and Morgenstern, O. 1947; Bernard, J. 1954; Boulding, K. 1963; Schelling, T. C. 1963; Blau, P. 1964; Bailey, F. G. 1969; Goffman,

114 *Special Studies*

I. 1970; Kapferer, B. 1972). Here I link the concept of an individual exercising strategic choices in the pursuit of multiple alternatives to the concepts of social network, field, and the emergent properties of systems. I suggest that with these basic elements, a model can be constructed which may aid analysis at the micro-level by enabling one to rise above the description of the actions of particular individuals in particular contexts and thereby achieve broader generalizations. In addition, it may enable the oft-neglected inter-relationship between micro- and macro-level processes to be examined. I present the model in an as yet unrefined state and as a logical, not a predictive one, I simply illustrate some of its elements with data drawn from Rhodesia and Central and Southern Africa.

The major variables operating at the macro-level to influence the flow of labour migrants in Rhodesia derive from the ecological, economic and political processes set in motion by the establishment of the colonial régime. Initially, Africans were unwilling to enter wage employment. A hut tax was imposed in the 1890s and raised several times to stimulate a supply of labour for the mines and to cover the administrative costs of the British South Africa Company (BSAC Report 1899: 20). However, once labour migration had begun, it increased rapidly as new wants arose.

In addition, as the African population began to expand, the effects of the alienation of large tracts of land to the white population began to be felt. The pressure of population on the available resources led to a rapid decrease in soil fertility and to declining crop yields. In some areas this situation had already been reached by the early thirties; by the end of the Second World War, it was general (Yudelman 1964). Administrative measures had only limited success in controlling a deteriorating situation (cf. Floyd 1961; Garbett 1963; Yudelman 1964). For many families it became essential for one or more of its members to seek work to earn cash to purchase additional foodstuffs (cf. Johnson 1965: 2; Jordon 1965: 67).

Furthermore, the post-war demand for education among Africans, increased the need for cash to pay school fees (Johnson 1965: 2; Aquina 1968: 21; Hollman 1969: 125). Few Africans were able to market sufficient produce to fulfil their cash needs and the fact that marketing arrangements on the whole were organized in such a way as to prevent African producers gaining access to the prices prevailing in the markets to which White producers had access, tended to discourage any spontaneous innovation and development in African agriculture (Yudelman 1964: 179ff; Arrighi 1967: 33).

Circulatory migration in Rhodesia 115

After the Second World War, increased international investment in S. Rhodesia, together with a large influx of white settlers, led to a rapid expansion in industry and commerce as well as in agriculture (Yudelman 1964: 44; Arrighi 1967: 41). This greatly increased the demand for labour. In addition, the stricter enforcement of the Land Apportionment Act led to the displacement of large numbers of African families from what was designated as European land creating still further pressure on the Tribal Trust Lands (Reserves). Johnson (1963) has estimated that by 1961, of African men aged 15–50, some 53 per cent were in wage employment. In 1962, of Rhodesian-born African men, 48 per cent were resident in the Tribal Trust Lands, 22 per cent on White farms and 30 per cent in the towns (Final (1962) Census Report 1964: 13). It is clear that by this time a high proportion of the able-bodied men in the African population had already been drawn into wage employment (cf. Jordon 1965: 74). This led to the encouragement of migrant labour from other territories. By 1961, some 46 per cent of Africans working in S. Rhodesia were foreign born (Census of Employees 1961; 1965: table 6). The availability of a large external pool of labour relieved the labour shortage and, since unionization of African labour was illegal, wages remained low (cf. Census of Employees 1961; 1965). There is some indication that, since the unilateral declaration of independence in 1965, the internal rate of labour migration may have fallen to around 27 per cent and that the influx of foreign-born Africans has also declined. However, the proportion of Rhodesian-born Africans migrating to other countries may have increased giving an overall labour migration rate of around 35 per cent (estimated from Interim (1969) Census Report 1971: 21).

Low wages contributed to the inability of most Africans to support their families entirely from wage labour and the high cost of living in Rhodesian towns meant that wives and children generally had to be left in the Tribal Trust Lands (cf. Bettison in Plewman Report 1958: 180ff.). As Mitchell (1969: 176) has argued, those who remitted part of their earnings to their kin and families in the Tribal Trust Lands therefore tended to be young unmarried men and men unaccompanied by their families. My own observations and those of Sister Mary Aquina (1964: 34) and Johnson (1964: 107) confirm this and show that in general labour migration is a means of income supplementation rather than an alternative source of income.

In many areas the average income per head expressed in cash terms of rural production is falling. The result is that, at worst, men

116 *Special Studies*

must migrate in order that their families shall survive and that, at best, they may gain a little extra to meet the cost of education, clothing and various consumer goods. One element in the circulation of labour in Rhodesia, therefore, is the need for men to divide their time between assisting in maintaining production in the rural areas and working in the towns or on the European farms. The extent to which labour migrants have to contribute to maintaining rural production depends upon the degree to which productive roles in the Tribal Trust Lands can be taken over by women, children and the elderly. This will depend upon the type of farming practised, the fertility of the soil and, for a particular family, the stage that it has reached in the domestic life-cycle. Seasonal migration in which most men returned to their rural homes at time of planting or harvesting characterized labour migration during the inter-war period. Since the end of the Second World War, however, while men may set out for work after planting or harvesting, they may then be away from home for some years. Similarly, the decision to return home after several years in employment may coincide with the time for the preparation of the fields. Thus, there is always an influx of men at times of planting and harvesting and an egress after these periods, but different men are involved from year to year and there is no longer a regular inflow and outflow involving most able-bodied men (Bell 1963: 26; Johnson 1965: 85; Mitchell 1969: 173).

In the light of this, Barber's (1961) argument concerning the annual seasonal movement of labour migrants between their places of work and their home areas must be modified. He is correct in assuming that some male labour is required to maintain rural production but these inputs of labour need not be annual (cf. Mitchell 1969: 72). Furthermore, his argument that the need to maintain rural production is the sole reason for the circulation of labour, since, thereby, migrants are maximizing their returns from both the subsistence and cash sectors of the economy, does not account for the fact that there is a proportion of men who have good jobs, who earn relatively high wages, and who have their wives and children with them but who still maintain contact with their areas of origin, which they visit from time to time, and to which they eventually return (cf. Mitchell 1969: 72).

Part of the behaviour of all these men can be explained in relation to the general insecurity of life for Africans outside the Tribal Trust Lands. In S. Rhodesia the majority of African workers have no sickness or social security benefits. In sickness or in old age, a man's only ultimate security is to be able to return to subsist on

Circulatory migration in Rhodesia 117

the land. He must therefore maintain access to land, usually through his connection with his rural kin. Furthermore, legislation has been promulgated since the arrival of the white settlers in the 1890s to control the entry and residence of Africans in towns and European areas. Whilst much of the most irksome and repressive measures were amended or abolished in the late fifties and early sixties, during a brief period when relatively liberal political policies were pursued, some of these measures were reinstituted after 1965. The municipalities as landlords have always had the power to evict tenants for the non-payment of rent. The various home-ownership schemes begun in the late fifties also suffered from a fairly high rate of defaulting tenants. The intense political rivalry which developed between the two major African political parties and which led to faction fights, resulted in massive police and military intervention throughout the early sixties. This also contributed to the general insecurity of life in town.

Thus far, I have outlined the principal ecological, economic and political variables affecting the character and rate of circulatory migration in Rhodesia. The variations in the rate, either temporally or spatially, can be accounted for in large measure by the co-variation of these variables. An analysis at this level, therefore, provides an explanation of modal behaviour. If, however, we shift our level of analysis to explain the behaviour of particular sets of migrants and to comprehend the range of variation in migratory behaviour, we need an explanatory model which both takes into account the effects of processes occurring at the macro-level and variables involved in processes occurring at lower levels of abstraction (cf. Mitchell 1969: 177). Initially we can take as constant the relationship among the variables operating at the macro-level, at least for limited spans of time, though ultimately we must aim at explaining the inter-relationship between processes operating at all levels of analysis.

Recently, Kapferer and I (1970) pointed to the inadequacy of a number of models currently used to explain circulatory migration. In particular, we criticized the so-called 'push-pull' model, which has frequently been applied by social anthropologists, and the simple 'rational choice/maximization models' applied by economists. Whilst the explanation of circulatory migration in terms of poor socio-economic conditions 'pushing' migrants from their rural homes whence they are 'pulled' to town by the attraction of better opportunities may account for the initial migration, it does not help in understanding the persistence of the circulation or the range of variation in migratory careers. Additional explanations to accom-

118 *Special Studies*

modate labour circulation within the 'push-pull' model such as the concept of the target worker (cf. Elkan 1969), or the reverse 'push' caused by the general economic uncertainty of town life (cf. Gluckman 1960; van Velsen 1963), or the necessity for regular inputs of labour to sustain rural production (cf. Barber 1961) all prove inadequate on close examination. Similarly, the behavioural models of the economists, in which the stress is on the rational maximization of money income to the exclusion of other social considerations, do not adequately account for the circulation or for the range of variability in migrant behaviour. As Mitchell (1959, 1969) has indicated, for East, Central and Southern Africa, economic conditions provide necessary, but not sufficient conditions for migration because the decision of a migrant to move from his rural home at one particular time rather than at another may be due to a quarrel with a kinsman, failure to succeed to political office or even trouble with the police.

In searching for a more adequate model for understanding circulatory migration it might be useful to review briefly two orientations which have been applied to the understanding of social processes in general: these may be designated briefly as the 'institutional' and the 'statistical'. In the 'institutional' orientation the behaviour of individuals is seen as normatively constrained. The difficulty here has been to relate models constructed from normative rules to actually observed patterns of behaviour (cf. van Velsen 1967; Keesing 1967; Garbett 1970). The 'statistical' orientation proceeds from the observed incidence of patterns of behaviour in a population. Leach (1960, 1961) has strongly urged the case for this approach, arguing that the concept of social structure can sometimes be regarded 'as the statistical outcome of multiple individual choices' (1960: 124); a 'by-product of the sum of many individual human actions of which the participants are neither wholly conscious nor wholly aware' (1962: 300). The difficulty here is that while one may analyse the correlation of one or more distributions of patterns of behaviour with other individual attributes to determine their co-variation, the process by which these patterns are themselves generated is difficult to determine (cf. Barth 1966). This is partly because two different aspects of social behaviour become confused in the 'statistical' orientation. Firstly, in some situations individuals do take cognizance of culturally defined rules, but, secondly, they also pursue strategies in terms of their self-interest as they perceive this. In the first case, while individuals may take cognizance of rules, they may circumvent them in various ways— some regular, others irregular (cf. Bailey 1968; Nicholas 1968) and,

Circulatory migration in Rhodesia 119

in the second case, while they may pursue strategies, they may be unaware, or only partially aware, of the consequences which flow from their actions, some of which may display persistent regularities. In both cases, therefore, regularities arise—which we observe as statistical distributions of patterns of behaviour—but from different sources. It would seem useful, therefore, to develop a third orientation which will accommodate, without confusion, both the fact that in some situations cultural constraints—rules—produce determinate outcomes, while in other situations outcomes can only be understood by considering the range of alternatives confronting an individual and his evaluation of these in the light of the multiple strategies which he is pursuing. We can thus take account of 'custom' —cultural constraints—and evaluations in cultural terms, as well as the fact that individuals in pursuit of their interests may deliberately manipulate, and in some cases fabricate rules. Keesing (1967) has recently stressed the advantage of this type of orientation, which he has termed the 'decision model', for the understanding of social processes in general, and Blau *et al.* (1965) have developed a similar orientation for the understanding of occupational choice and the analysis of career and mobility patterns, whilst Graves (1966) has advocated the application of this type of model for the analysis of aspects of rural-urban migration among the Navaho Indians.

In the 'push-pull' model discussed earlier, there is an implicit assumption that individuals are evaluating alternatives and, of course, in the models of economists this is explicit and fundamental. Sister Mary Aquina (1965: 28) for example, while her analysis of labour migration from Chilimanzi is essentially of the 'push-pull' type, gives an interesting case of a family which consciously pursued a number of strategies in order that one of them could qualify as a teacher (cf. also Gluckman 1940 (1958): 22ff.). Van Velsen (1960, 1963) has also stressed the way in which the Tonga of Malawi consciously maintain and exploit rural-urban relationships.

In an earlier paper (1967), in which I had begun to formulate a relatively elementary choice or decision model, I reviewed statistical evidence which showed in essence that in any Korekore village the more remote a man's kinship connection with the village headman and his primary patrilineal kin, the higher the probability that he would be a migrant. At that time, I argued rather statically, from this and other evidence, that Korekore men who continue in wage labour for as long as possible 'appear to be those who, even if they wished, could not advance their position within the "traditional" system'. Mitchell (1969: 174) drew attention to one of the case

E

120   *Special Studies*

histories I presented of a Korekore man, a mine-foreman, who had been in continuous employment in town for fourteen years, who had married and raised children there, but who, upon the death of his brother—an event which put him next in line to succeed to a village headmanship—forsook his town life, inherited his brother's widow and returned to settle in the Zambezi valley. Rightly, correcting my static mode of interpreting the evidence, Mitchell argued that men who are disadvantageously placed for achieving status in the rural systems do not completely withdraw from it. They simply pursue their interests 'for the time being where it is most advantageous for them to do so. But their positions in both the rural system and at the labour centres are not static. Events in either of the two localities may alter the balance of advantages for a migrant at any time'. In other words, in considering the alternatives confronting a migrant we have to be aware of the dynamics of the social field, spanning both rural and urban contexts, in which the migrant is involved (cf. Gluckman 1947: 223; Mitchell 1959: 297; Middleton 1969; Cohen, 1969).

Kapferer and I (1971), in developing a decision model in relation to circulatory migration, located the migrant in a social field, part of which consisted of a network of social relationships. We criticized the view, frequently only implicit, in the work of economists and sociologists which regards the individual as an independent decision maker and we stressed the need to regard the individual as one who has his decisions constrained by his position in a particular set of social relationships. Here, we took stimulus from Mayer's (1961) work on Xhosa Red and School migrants. It is apparent from Mayer's work that the networks of Red migrants are dense ('close-knit' in Bott's terms (1957)) and span both town and country, whilst those of School Xhosa are less dense and can be partitioned into two virtually disjoint sets so that there is relatively little 'feed-back' between the town and the rural sets of relationships. Essentially, this means that the behaviour of a Red migrant is constrained not only by members of his network in town but also by his rural kin and friends. Any action he may take in relation to one member of his network may have wide repercussions among other members both in town and country. By contrast, the less dense network of the School migrant, and the fact that it is partitioned into disjoint sets, means that he is free to pursue a variety of courses of action, some of which may endanger a particular relationship within his network, without necessarily endangering any other in either town or country.

A similar situation is found among Korekore of the Zambezi

Circulatory migration in Rhodesia 121

valley, although the discrete cultural categories similar to the Red-School division among Xhosa do not exist. In 1961, from a census which I conducted in the chiefdom of Muzarabanhi in the Darwin district, I estimated that over 70 per cent of men aged 15–50 were then labour migrants. From an analysis of labour migration histories of older men and the few men who were 'resting' between jobs, it is clear that particularly since the end of the Second World War the majority of Korekore men have found jobs on the European farms which were developed after the war along and near the escarpment of the Zambezi valley. For Valley Korekore of the Darwin and Sipolilo districts these farms are at the most a day and a half's journey away. The remaining relatively few migrants who go further afield to find work in the towns and on the mines are by contrast widely dispersed. Those who migrate to the farms often return to the same farm, trip after trip, or to neighbouring farms. Men from the same neighbourhood often take work at the same farm or an adjoining one. They are therefore in frequent contact with one another, meeting at a farm shop, or drinking beer together at weekends and on rest days. As they return home, or are joined by fellows from their villages or neighbourhoods, they carry news and gossip with them, so that between farms and villages there is a constant interchange of information which, among other things, serves to regulate the behaviour of both migrants and villagers. Migrants are expected to transmit cash regularly to their rural kin and, although on the low wages which most Korekore earn, these are often only small amounts, they are vital to the continuation of the rural economy (v. Garbett, 1967). By contrast, I visited several Korekore living in African townships who were working in Salisbury and was always struck by their lack of detailed knowledge of either what was happening at home or of the activities and whereabouts of other migrants from their home areas whom I knew to be living in the same town. They were less inclined to give cash assistance to their visiting rural kin and, when they suffered a misfortune, resorted to urban rather than rural diviners and herbalists. My data show that these men tend to be among the long-term migrants who are sometimes away from their areas of origin for ten years or more. Here, it would appear that network structures are related to the volume of migration, to the clustering of migrants on the farms, and to the distances involved. This appears to produce effects similar to those described by Mayer for the Xhosa migrants although I lack the detailed evidence from urban areas fully to support my argument.

Locating the individual in a network of relationships which is

122 *Special Studies*

part of a social field enables us to determine to what extent he is affected by choices which others make in regard to him. In addition, it enables us to assess the migrant's differential involvement in the social field and to determine the extent to which he has a rural or an urban orientation (cf. Mayer 1961). Finally, cultural constraints, norms, rules and values, can be accommodated within the wider system of which the field itself is part (cf. Swartz 1969: 12) and their differential effects on the decision-making process assessed.

Many Korekore migrants, for example, as I have indicated elsewhere (1967), tend to be younger men, many of whom are still in debt to their fathers-in-law since bridewealth is relatively high. No man can easily evade this debt and, consequently, a man may be subservient to his father-in-law for many years. Should a man wish to take his wife with him to work in some distant town, his father-in-law may insist that a substantial portion of the bridewealth be paid. A father-in-law also favours having his son-in-law in employment nearby since this means that the young man will visit his wife fairly regularly, bringing gifts and cash. He will also be available, if need be, to help in the preparation of new fields. Most men, therefore, find it more convenient to leave their wives behind and take work on the nearby European farms whence they can visit their wives from time to time, or be visited by them for short periods. This in turn leads to the reinforcement of the dense network structures found among migrants on the farms and gives the social field which embraces farm and village its particular character.

This example also illustrates another important assumption of the decision model which Kapferer and I have put forward: that individuals attempt to maximize in terms of multiple alternatives and that the inter-play of these acts as a constraint. Here we see that a son-in-law achieves a compromise which enables him to seek wage labour, to see his wife from time to time, to know that she is well cared for while he is away, and to fulfil his obligations to his affines, all at relatively low cost. Most men have selected this choice and this has produced a regular pattern of behaviour which has now become a generally *expected* pattern. Thus, what was *normal* has become *normative*.

Finally, in considering decision models, one has to be aware of the dynamic effects of the decision-making process. I have already touched on the inter-play of the pursuit of multiple alternatives, which itself has a dynamic effect, but one must also consider the consequences of current choices since they may have a constraining effect on future choices. Specific alternatives become relevant at certain stages in an individual's career but not at others. Factors

Circulatory migration in Rhodesia 123

such as increasing age, marriage and children, may limit the range of choices open to an individual and result in some which were not previously attractive becoming more so. The case of the mine-foreman to which I have already referred, is a good example of this latter point. Blau *et al.* (1965: 543) have argued, in relation to occupational choice, that by applying a decision model at crucial turning-points in the lives of individuals, it is possible to analyse the effects of a succession of earlier decisions on the final choice of occupation. It is also possible by analysing the labour histories of migrants and abstracting patterns of mobility and of careers to gain some understanding, albeit retrospectively, of the effects of past choices. Among Valley Korekore there appears to be a high probability that men who first migrate to seek work on the nearby European farms remain in this type of employment for the rest of their working lives while those who seek work further afield in the towns and mines of Rhodesia experience more varied labour careers. There are a number of reasons for this. A migrant who seeks work on the farm is locked into a whole structure of social relationships with their concomitant obligations. He also acquires particular skills which tend to limit the range of occupations for which he is equipped. Men who migrate long distances often have their wives with them (or marry in town, thus avoiding the commitment to rural affines). They acquire skills which they can exploit in the industrial field where the rewards are higher than in agriculture. They tend to be much more mobile and to move from job to job in search of higher wages, better working conditions, or to avoid unemployment. Data collected among the Zezuru of the Musami district of Rhodesia (cf. Garbett, 1960) suggest that men with little formal education who eventually escaped from the poorly paid occupations succeeded because, at some point in their labour careers, the occupations they chose to enter gave them access to new skills or informational advantages. The few men, for example, who began work as domestic servants but who eventually became policemen did so either after having served for a period in the army or after having worked as servants for European policemen. Similarly, men who later became carpenters, bricklayers and house painters learnt their trades whilst working as labourers for European artisans.

CONCLUSION

I have shown how at the macro-level in Rhodesia, circulatory labour migration can be understood as an aspect of a plural social system. At this level such matters as the opportunities for wage labour,

124 *Special Studies*

minimum wage rates, the siting of industries, the extent and distribution of land holding, and so forth, are controlled by the dominant white minority. At this level, too, economic fluctuations caused by changes in international markets or climatic disturbances and population pressure on limited rural African resources, producing a decline in soil fertility, also have their effect. The labour migrant has no control over these matters. They provide a set of constraints, some constant, others variable over periods of time, within which the migrant exercises choice. It is the fact that the migrant exercises choice and responds to the changing attractions of various alternatives caused by processes of which he may be unaware, occurring at the macro-level, that explains some of the gross patterns of migrant behaviour. For at this level, the constraints can be conceptualized as operating as biases on choice, so producing the constancies which we understand in the statistical sense as rates. But the migrant is confronted by alternatives at other levels, some at the level of interpersonal relationships, some at the level of different sub-systems. It is the processes occurring at these other levels which add the complexity to a migrant's behaviour. I suggest that one of the means by which this complexity of behaviour may be analyzed and the effects of the constraints operating at these various levels understood is by applying a decision model.

To reiterate, in abstract, the decision model is constructed around the notion of an individual set in a network of social relationships. The constraints of these relationships act variably to affect the strategies pursued by the individual according to the particular context and according to the individual's degree of investment in and commitment to particular relationships. The individual is conceptualized as pursuing multiple objectives in different contexts. The choices the individual makes in relation to the various alternatives are seen, in varying degrees, as constraining one another. The individual is envisaged as moving through time along a career path which is full of fateful choices. Having committed himself to one line of action, other alternatives become impossible or more difficult to pursue.

The set of relationships in which the individual is enmeshed is conceptualized as being part of a field. The field is a socio-cultural space in which forces of variable intensity are operating (cf. Lewin 1951; Turner 1968). On the one hand, the forces arise from the wants, aspirations and perceptions of the individual and those with whom he is in relationship, and on the other, from the cultural, ecological, economic and political processes operating in the system of which the field is part. This concept of field, I feel, enables one

Circulatory migration in Rhodesia 125

to take cognizance of both normative constraints—which may produce determinate outcomes, and the constraints generated by strategic actions—which may produce probabilistic outcomes. Finally, the system of which the field is part is conceptualized as composed of a number of analytical levels, each emergent from the others. Each level has a degree of autonomy but affects, and is affected by processes occurring at adjacent higher and lower levels. At which level one begins analysis is to some extent a matter of personal inclination and the availability of data, but by conceptualizing the total system in this way, ultimately one may be able to relate processes occurring at micro- and macro-levels by moving from one emergent level to another without any necessary logical discontinuity. In addition, the often marked dichotomy between 'actor-oriented' and 'institutional' types of analysis (cf. Emmet and MacIntyre, 1970) may be avoided. I have indicated here how such a model may be applied to the study of circulatory labour migration but it could also be applied to the analysis of other types of migration and to other social processes.

The evolving phenomena of migration and urbanization in Central Africa: A Zambian case

PATRICK O. OHADIKE[1]

DEFINITION AND MEASUREMENT OF AFRICAN MIGRATION

The African migrant, like many others elsewhere, has been defined in different ways depending on the type and organization of available data. The commonest definition is the one based on the records of the birthplaces of persons, the implicit assumption being that migrants are persons born in places other than the localities where they are enumerated.

In spite of their common application, birthplace data mask the identification of persons who have made several other moves to places other than where they happen to be counted. Besides, they fail to show the duration over which migrants have been away from their places of origin. These defects are true of studies of migration in Zambia (see Mitchell 1954: 30–6; Harries-Jones 1965: 124–246; Ohadike 1971) which used information on the place of origin of labour employed in commerce and industry.

Migrants have also been designated according to the last place where individuals resided permanently. Where this information exists along with that on the place of birth, as in the 1969 National Census of Zambia, some knowledge of plural movements can be acquired without, of course, the finer details of the actual number of moves made. In the final analysis, there appears to be no adequate substitute for an *ad hoc* study of the number of movements made and the duration of residence in the various places where the migrants settle. For purposes of assessing the degree and extent of social integration, assimilation and change, the time dimension showing the length of exposure to novel influences is very important. By doing this, we carry our analysis beyond the dichotomous migrant/

[1] The writer is at present employed by the United Nations Economic Commission for Africa, Addis Ababa, and wishes to state that the views expressed in this paper are his, and not those of the United Nations.

The evolving phenomena of migration and urbanization   127

non-migrant differentiation to one in which gradations of differences among migrants coming at different periods can be studied.

Tribal or linguistic groupings have also been sparingly used to measure the rate of emigration from respective home districts or places of birth. This has been done through subtracting the size of the enumerated tribal or language group in a home district from the total number of the same tribe or linguistic groups recorded in the census. This method yields what one of the users (Southall 1961: 157–92) terms 'emigration rate' from the home area. More important, it shows the variations in the flow of migrants to job centres. Its main weakness, in a period of unbridled migration, lies, with reference to internal migration, in overestimating the rate of movements out of the home districts because it records 'second-generation migrants' or the children born to migrants while in towns or employment centres as members of the tribal or linguistic groups not resident in the home areas and therefore as having moved physically. Furthermore, there is the problem arising from linguistic assimilation in towns and from marriage between partners of different ethnic or language groups. In the first instance, depending on how the language question is phrased and put to respondents, there is the possibility that a significant number of persons particularly children, who have acquired languages other than their mother tongue, will be missed in the estimate for one home area while being included in the estimate for the home area, the language of which they have acquired. In the second place, depending on the pattern of social organization (patrilineal or matrilineal) and, more important, the tilt of the husband-wife dominance in the home, children of mixed tribal or linguistic marriages may be differently and erroneously classified by language or tribal groups. In fact, because children mostly spend their time with their mothers, the likelihood is greater that they would pick up the language of their mothers whereas, in effect, they may have been expected to speak their fathers' language.

Sex ratios for regions have also been used (Harries-Jones, *idem*) to infer the relative rate of in- or out-migration from designated localities. The rationale for doing so derives from the fact that migration to towns in Africa selects more males than females, and from the rather narrow expectation that, but for population movements, the numbers of the sexes should almost balance. Thus, within a country, regions have high or low levels of out-migration if they have high or low levels of male/female sex ratio. But the equilibrium of the sex ratio is also disturbed by factors other than differential population movements. Differences in mortality arising

128 *Special Studies*

from male/female variations in the exposure to health hazards and death, obviously disturb the balance of the sex ratio, and any measure of the rate of out-migration based on the relative levels of the sex ratio ought to take these factors into account, especially where there is evidence of regional variations in mortality and health conditions.

One other method employed has been the direct method or the actual enumeration of migrants on the move at various check points. This has been used by Prothero (1957: 251–61) in his study of seasonal labour migration in Northern Nigeria. It will, of course, be agreed that with so many unguarded borders in Africa, this method cannot give an accurate picture of the volume of migration because many illegal movers will be left out. But by enabling the migrants to be interviewed while on the move, the method fosters, granting the adequacy of the questions and probing, a reasonable understanding of migration attitudes and motivations. In fact, the dividend will be more rewarding if, after the initial interview of the migrants on their outward journey, a follow-up study is subsequently made either at their destination or preferably on their homeward journey. This will be useful in improving the reliability and accuracy of measures of migration attitudes.

Two important definitions not effectively and commonly used in the study of African migration are the indirect statistically derived balancing equation method and the survival ratio method of estimating net migration. Their lack of frequent use is tied up with the general lack of adequate and reliable census and vital registration data on a continuing basis, as such data are the requisite ingredients for the computation of the migrant population between any two dates (United Nations 1970: 5–39; Zachariah 1962: 175–83).

THE 1968–9 SURVEY DATA

A survey of households for information on the place of birth, place of last permanent residence and personal characteristics of their members provides the bulk of the information for the present study. The data represent part of a wider socio-demographic sample survey collected by the writer between December 1968 and March 1969 in Lusaka. Respondents were selected by a stratified random sampling method, using the following sampling fractions in each universe-stratum: ·33 in the highly developed low density areas, ·071 in the settled municipal suburbs and shanty towns, and ·142 in the only peri-urban area of Chelston included in the study. In this presentation, account is taken of this variation

The evolving phenomena of migration and urbanization   129

in the size of the sampling fractions by weighting the results of each stratum with the reciprocal of the sampling fraction used and then summing the results for the three strata to produce composite figures for the whole city. Such figures will be referred to in the analysis as weighted data.

The survey definition of a household conforms to the international standard of a group of individuals who share living quarters and their principal meals (UN Demographic Dictionary 1965: 4). However, individuals living by themselves were included as single-member households, while institutional households consisting of people living in hostels, hospitals, prisons and other such institutions were omitted. As will become obvious later in the analysis, Lusaka households were predominantly migrant and therefore provided an ideal setting for the present study.

RECENT RATES OF MIGRATION AND URBANIZATION IN LUSAKA

After all the rather impressionistic guesses, one is now in a fairly good position to make reasonable estimates of the rate of urbanization in Lusaka from quantitative information. All such evidence clearly underlines the very high rate of increase which has taken place in the town, particularly in recent years. The Doxiadis Associates (1969: 90–1) show that whereas the average annual growth rate of the Greater Lusaka Area was 5·3 per cent during 1953–8, it soared to 10·9 per cent during 1958–63 and 11·8 per cent during 1963–8. The major part of the increase is accounted for more by net immigration than by natural increase. Thus, of the total population increase of 94,000 in the Greater Lusaka Area during 1963–8, 83 per cent or 78,000 were migrants in private households. By adding migrants in 'collective households', the authors estimate that the average annual rates of growth through net migration and natural increase were respectively 10·0 per cent and 1·8 per cent.

These estimates are in line with those made for the Central Province and its major town of Lusaka from the 1963 Census data and from the preliminary figures of the 1969 National Census of Zambia. Although the whole area attracted migrants, it turned out that the majority of migrants to the Province, 78·3 per cent, settled in Lusaka. Consequently, the contribution of net migration to total increase between 1963 and 1969 was 82·9 per cent for Lusaka and only 60 per cent for the Central Province. From these figures, the average annual contribution of net migration to total increase during 1963–9 was 10 per cent for the Ceneral Province and 13·8 per

130   *Special Studies*

cent for Lusaka. Also emphasizing to a significantly greater degree the tremendous growth of Lusaka through urbanization is the estimated ratio of the volume of net migration to the population in 1963. Whereas the Central Province showed only a ratio of 24·0 per cent, Lusaka more than trebled this with 77·0 per cent.

Information drawn from the 1968–9 survey of Lusaka also provides additional evidence of the rapid urbanization of the city. A record of persons who came to Lusaka in the last 12 months preceding the survey and of the total number of live births which occurred in the period was made. Admittedly, since the survey was retrospective, the relevant data on births and migrants in the last 12 months refer only to surviving migrants and births.

Table 1

Rate of Urbanization and Natural Increase in Lusaka,
Survey 1968–9

Enumerated persons arriving in the year	$=$	17,820
Enumerated births in the year	$=$	5,309
Enumerated population increase in the year	$=$	$17,820 + 5,309$
	$=$	23,129
Enumerated total population	$=$	126,807
Enumerated population at beginning of year	$=$	$126,807 - 23,129$
	$=$	103,678
Enumerated total mid-year population	$=$	$103,678 + \frac{1}{2}(23,129)$
	$=$	115,243
Total increase over mid-year population	$=$	20·1 per cent
Increase (births only) over mid-year population	$=$	4·6 per cent
Increase (migrants only) over mid-year population	$=$	15·5 per cent
Births as per cent of total increase	$=$	22·9 per cent
Migrants as per cent of total increase	$=$	77·1 per cent

The estimated rates of urbanization and natural increase for the year are indicated in Table 1, and these, as already stated above, further underscore the overriding contribution of population mobility to urban growth. Presumably, the population of Lusaka increased by slightly over 20 per cent in the year and of this growth, well over three-quarters was due to net migration, and under one quarter to natural increase. This estimate of the rate of net migration (15·5 per cent in the year) appears reasonably higher than those made from the 1963 and 1969 censuses and also from the survey by the Doxiadis group, mainly because the information is more recent and is less affected by mortality and return-migration in the sense of whittling down the number of surviving migrants. Also because the rate of in-migration, as shown by the Doxiadis estimates and as will be subsequently illustrated in this paper, has grown with the

The evolving phenomena of migration and urbanization 131

years, it is to be expected that this more recent survey data on in-movement will show higher levels. In fact, the survey record, adjusted for over-enumeration due to the timing of the date of arrival over the survey period, indicates that out of a total of 85,111 migrants found in the households, 17,820 or 20·9 per cent came to Lusaka in the last 12 months. The proportion would have been higher if we had based the calculation on the actual number of persons (20,929) who claimed they came in the last 12 months.

MIGRANTS / NON-MIGRANTS: CHARACTERISTICS AND LOCATION IN LUSAKA

The relatively more developed, salubrious and middle-class low density suburbs had the highest proportion of the new migrants. Although this might be related to recent transfers of administrative and executive staff from other regions of the country, the flow to the low density suburbs is associated more with the migration of young school leavers employed there as domestic servants. Army and police quarters came next to low density areas, and one might attribute this to the rather frequent physical mobility of members of the armed forces.

Table 2

Percentage distribution of non-migrants, migrants in the last 12 months and those before by civic location (all ages), Lusaka Survey 1968–9

| | | MIGRANTS COMING | | | |
Civic location	Non-migrants	Last 12 months	Before	Total	N
Low Density Areas (Woodlands, Olympia Park, Rhodes Park, Sunningdale, Roma, etc.)	19·3	27·1	53·6	100·0	4,126
Authorized Municipal High Density Areas including New Kanyama	34·6	15·2	50·2	100·0	75,215
Army and Police Barracks (Wardroper and Arrakan)	19·4	26·7	53·9	100·0	4,984
Unauthorized Squatter Settlements	24·1	22·3	53·6	100·0	31,666
Total	30·5	18·1	51·4	100·0	115,991

Of the two lower class civilian areas, unauthorized squatter compounds proportionately had more of the new migrants than the authorized municipal suburbs, which contain some of the oldest, settled locations in the city, and are inhabited by a more per-

Special Studies

manently settled group than is found in squatter compounds with a higher proportion of floating population. That, to a significant degree, the proportion of non-migrants is highest in the authorized suburbs is another indication that life in these areas is more sedentary and less transient. It is, as such, very difficult for the often impoverished newcomers to acquire accommodation there unless their employers have pre-arranged this. For such persons, if they do not want to live as 'hangers-on', the only alternative is to find accommodation in the squatter compounds. There, people can build or rent houses, no matter how bad, more cheaply and quickly. To many squatters, the choice was seen as a temporary measure, but many have had to stay longer than expected because of the difficulty of securing homes in the authorized locations. Already, in every major Zambian town, the demand for homes in the authorized areas is formidably high, and it seems that as long as uncontrolled migration continues in the face of limited time and money for new homes, the inevitability of the squatter 'problem' in towns has to be accepted by Governments and critics alike, first, as a palliative not as a panacea for the acute shortage of housing for urban workers and their families, and, second, as a means for individuals to exercise a free choice of the location and design of their own homes.

As would be expected, most of the migrants who came to Lusaka in the last 12 months preceding the survey differed significantly both from non-migrants and also from migrants who arrived years before them. In terms of average age, they were much older than non-migrants but were significantly younger than their counterparts who came to Lusaka earlier on. The proportion of children under 15 years of age was 44·2 per cent among migrants who came in the last 12 months and only 29·2 per cent among those who came earlier. In fact, the rather low proportion of children among the long-standing migrants is related to the very high proportion (88·5 per cent) among non-migrants or persons born in Lusaka. The high proportion in the latter case reflects the fertility contribution of the non-migrants as well as of migrants whose children fell into the non-migrant category because they were born to them while in the town.

The male/female sex ratios for the migrant/non-migrant categories also show meaningful differences. At 102, non-migrants had only a few more males than females, while at 120, the long-standing migrants had an abnormally high masculinity ratio. What is perhaps intriguing and indicative of the increasing flow of females to the city, to be demonstrated later, is the fact that in the last 12 months more female migrants had come to Lusaka as shown by the male/

The evolving phenomena of migration and urbanization   133

female ratio of 95. Migrants in the last 12 months also differed from those who came earlier in terms of their origins. One would have expected that more of those who came in the last 12 months would have come from places where they were born. A higher proportion, 70·6 per cent, of the migrants who came before the last 12 months came from their birthplaces as against only 64·5 per cent of those who came in the last 12 months. As the difference appears considerable, an indication of the new direction of flow will be made later in the analysis.

Table 3

Selected characteristics of non-migrants, migrants in the last 12 months, and migrants arriving before the last 12 months, Survey 1968–9

Selected characteristics	Non-migrants	Migrants last 12 months	Other migrants
		ALL PERSONS	
N (total persons)	35,427	20,929	59,590
% children under 15 years	88·5	44·2	29·2
% adults above 15 years	11·5	55·8	70·8
Mean age at migration	. . .	16·8	17·2
Internal migrants (% distribution)	—	27·3	72·7
External migrants (% distribution)	—	18·1	81·9
Sex ratio (M/F)	102	95	120
% from places same as birthplace	—	64·5	70·6
% from places not their birthplace		35·5	29·4
		Adults only	
% adults without education	42·7	26·4	25·3
% adults with up to 6 years schooling	22·7	34·1	35·6
% adults with 7 or more years schooling	34·6	39·5	39·1
% in white-collar jobs	7·7	10·3	14·7
% in skilled manual jobs	4·1	9·6	15·4
% other jobs	10·5	15·9	20·5
N (Adults only)	6,538	10,110	39,536

Whether migrants had arrived in the last 12 months or earlier, they were generally better placed educationally and occupationally than the non-migrants. It is also obvious from table 3 that, while the difference between migrants who came to the town in the last 12 months and those before was not very pronounced, there was a general tendency for the latter with longer migration history to be more educated and in better jobs. Presumably, having stayed longer in the city, they have taken advantage of the more generously supplied urban educational facilities and of gaining promotions in their jobs. Finally, an indication of a change in the age-pattern of migra-

134   *Special Studies*

tion can be inferred from the mean age at which migrants in the last 12 months and those before came to Lusaka. The tendency is towards lower ages, because those arriving in the last 12 months had come at a lower average age of 16·8 years as against 17·2 for those who came earlier.

ORIGIN AND CHARACTERISTICS OF LUSAKA MIGRANTS

It is not uncommon to assume that all migrants in the town are persons coming from the rural areas and/or that they are 'first movers'. On the contrary and depending on the general level of population mobility in the country, a significant proportion of migrants, wherever located, would have also migrated before. The greater the number of moves made, the greater the degree of exposure to novel influences and to the impact of social change. Technically, it is possible to ask direct questions about the number, destination and duration of earlier moves and relate these to variables for the study of change.

In the present survey, no attempt was made to use the above procedure, but information on the place of birth and the place of last residence of respondents was compared in the coding stage of the analysis to give the category of migrants who came to Lusaka from their birthplace and of those who came from other places. The categories are not exclusive, for it can be argued that some persons coming to Lusaka from their birthplace may have been to other places before returning home and then proceeding to Lusaka. For those who came to Lusaka from places other than their birthplace, there is a failure to take account of the duration of residence in the places they have been to as well as the degree of urbanization in such places. But despite these limitations, observed differences between the two major groups of migrants are interesting. Of the entire number of migrants in the survey, 69·4 per cent moved into Lusaka from places which were their birthplace as well as their last place of residence. The last place of residence of the balance, 30·6 per cent, was not their birthplace. The latter group proved to be older than both the former and the non-migrants, who were the youngest of the three groups. The respective proportions aged 15 years or more were 11·6, 65·7 and 68·9 per cent for non-migrants, migrants from their birthplaces and those not from their birthplaces.

No sex ratio differences existed between the two migrant categories, but both clearly exhibited higher masculinity ratios than the non-migrants. Having migrated elsewhere before coming to Lusaka,

The evolving phenomena of migration and urbanization 135

the adult 'plural movers', aged 15 years or more, were not only more educated than those who moved from their birthplaces but also surpassed those born in the town. Non-migrants who were never at school constituted 41·4 per cent as against 28·4 and 20·0 per cent respectively for migrants whose last residences were the same as their birthplaces and for those who came from places other than their birthplaces. The respective proportions in the three groups with seven or more years of schooling were 35·2, 35·1 and 47·5 per cent. Thus migration to Lusaka selected more persons with education, and persons with longer migration history tended to have more education.

As the levels of industrialization and urbanization increased in Zambia, the tendency for migrants to move direct from their place of birth to Lusaka diminished. With minor fluctuations, shown in Table 4, the proportion of persons involved in this type of migration declined from slightly over three-quarters of all migrants in the period before 1960 to slightly over seven-tenths during 1960–4, after which, it further fell to nearly thirteen-twentieths in the last five years, 1965–9.

Table 4

Distribution of migrants coming to Lusaka from their birthplace and those from elsewhere by date residence began in Lusaka

	Birthplace and residence			
Date residence began	Same	Not same	Total	N (weighted)
Before 1950	75·7	24·3	100·0	2,791
1950–54	77·3	22·7	100·0	5,074
1955–59	78·9	21·1	100·0	7,222
1960–64	70·8	29·2	100·0	18,524
1965–69	64·9	35·1	100·0	45,556
Total	69·4	30·6	100·0	79,167

Apart from migrant origins of the types discussed above, there are also the more specific ones in terms of administrative districts or provinces. Previous studies of labour migration in Zambia have shown that the various urban areas attract more workers from certain districts than others. In particular, the Copperbelt towns tended to rely more on labour from adjacent districts in the Northern, Luapula and North-Western provinces than from the remote districts in the Southern, Eastern and Western Provinces. Over the years, most migrants to Lusaka, whether defined in terms of birthplace or place of last residence, came predominantly from the Eastern Province and secondarily from the Central and Northern

136 *Special Studies*

Table 5

Descending order of the proportion of Lusaka migrants from various Provinces by birthplace and place of last residence

(A)

Province of birth	% all migrants	Province of last residence	% all migrants
Eastern	31·0	Eastern	29·5
Central	15·9	Central	14·3
Northern	13·3	Copperbelt	12·6
Southern	8·8	Northern	11·8
Copperbelt	8·0	Southern	9·3
Western	4·6	Western	4·5
Luapula	2·4	Luapula	2·1
North-Western	2·2	North-Western	1·7
Outside Zambia	13·8	Outside Zambia	14·2
Total	100·0	Total	100·0
	N = 85,111		N = 84,243

(B)

Province of birth	% migrants last 12 months	Province of last residence	% migrants last 12 months
Eastern	28·0	Eastern	26·4
Northern	15·6	Copperbelt	17·2
Central	15·5	Central	14·3
Copperbelt	11·3	Northern	13·4
Southern	11·2	Southern	12·1
Western	3·6	Western	2·6
Luapula	2·6	North-Western	2·5
North-Western	2·1	Luapula	2·3
Outside Zambia	9·8	Outside Zambia	7·9
No entry	0·3	No entry	1·3
Total	100·0	Total	100·0
	N = 20,929		N = 20,929

provinces. Birthplace data clearly support this observation, and the fact that the Northern Province was relegated to a fourth position below that of the Copperbelt Province in the distribution by place of last residence does not really nullify the point being made. The displacement merely underlines the industrial potential of the Copperbelt to which some migrants in Lusaka would have been previously. The Northern Province, by reasons of proximity and history, sends the largest number of migrants to the Copperbelt and, no doubt, a significant proportion of Lusaka migrants (by place of last residence) from the Copperbelt include persons born in the

The evolving phenomena of migration and urbanization 137

Northern as well as other provinces. In fact, judging from the survey results, an estimated 5,000 persons born in other provinces were migrants from the Copperbelt by place of last residence.

Examples of the differences implied above show up clearly in Table 5. Heading the list among provinces with more migrants by place of last residence than by place of birth is the relatively most industrialized Copperbelt Province. The others in this category (Southern and North-Western) show differences which are not large enough for serious inferences. In the case of the Copperbelt, the difference (4·6 per cent more migrants by last residence) derived from the data for all migrants irrespective of the time of arrival and that derived from the data on migrants who came in the last 12 months (4·9 per cent) are impressive, but the latter is also suggestive of recent and possible future increase in the number coming to Lusaka from the Copperbelt. Lusaka's political, economic and administrative stature has grown since independence and many firms and organizations including the mining companies have shifted their administrative headquarters to Lusaka. This has therefore been accompanied by transfer of some members of staff and has also, by creating more job opportunities, attracted other migrants to the town. Clearly the Lusaka migrants from the Copperbelt have made many more moves than those from most of the other provinces as shown not only by their having higher proportions of migrants by place of last residence than by birthplace but also by their remarkably high proportion (see Table 6) of the migrants who came to Lusaka from places not their birthplace.

In addition to the provinces discussed above, the Southern Pro-

Table 6

Provincial distribution of migrants coming to Lusaka from their birthplace and of those from elsewhere

	% migrants by last residence			
	Birthplace and residence			
Province	Same	Not same	Total	N
				(weighted)
Central	70·4	29·6	100·0	12,061
Southern	60·7	39·3	100·0	7,855
Copperbelt	33·1	66·9	100·0	10,593
Eastern	82·5	17·5	100·0	24,850
North-Western	60·2	39·8	100·0	1,406
Luapula	73·7	26·3	100·0	1,752
Northern	78·7	21·3	100·0	9,929
Western	85·1	14·9	100·0	3,752
Outside Zambia	66·7	33·3	100·0	12,045
Total	69·4	30·6	100·0	84,243

138 *Special Studies*

vince has also sent many migrants to Lusaka. The significance of the respective contributions made by the main sending provinces has acquired some cultural dimension in the sense that the major languages spoken in those provinces are the predominant ones in Lusaka. Of particular significance is Nyanja, spoken largely and originally in the Eastern Province and now virtually the *lingua-franca* in Lusaka and the surrounding districts. In the survey, the proportion of persons, migrant and non-migrant, who spoke Nyanja as their mother tongue was 41·0 per cent; Bemba including Mambwe and Inamwanga, originally spoken in parts of the Northern and Luapula provinces and, by acculturation, in the Copperbelt Province, was next to Nyanja and was spoken by 23·0 per cent of the survey respondents. Also, because of the sizeable number of migrants from the Central and Southern provinces, Tongo-Ila speakers, represented 14·1 per cent of the survey respondents.

THE CHANGING LEVELS, DIRECTION AND PATTERN OF FLOW

The pattern of the flow of migrants from various points of origin to Lusaka has undergone some changes over the years. Table 7 presents the distribution of migrants by province of birth and by date residence began in Lusaka. It should, of course, be noted that the validity of the inferences to be made from this table rests on the assumption that differences in the rates of mortality and of return migration are slight or non-existent. It then appears that before 1950, most migrants to Lusaka were from the Central Province in which the town lies. Of the enumerated migrants from the province, 6·6 per cent came before 1950. Next in importance before 1950 were people from the Eastern Province (3·4 per cent) and North-Western Province (3·3 per cent), closely followed by those from the Northern and Southern provinces with 2·9 per cent of their groups coming before 1950. Part of the reasons for the differences, especially in the case of persons from the Central and Eastern provinces include proximity and accessibility in terms of transportation and communication links with Lusaka. During the next quinquennium, 1950–4, persons from the Eastern Province appeared to have caught up with those from the Central Province in terms of the increase in their respective proportion in Lusaka. Respectively, 7·1 per cent cent and 6·9 per cent of their members enumerated in the survey came there during 1950–4. It can be seen from Table 7 that with the total sample proportion coming during the period at 6·4 per cent, both provinces appeared to have increased or maintained their flow

The evolving phenomena of migration and urbanization 139

Table 7

Distribution of migrants by Province of birth and by date residence began in Lusaka, Survey 1968–69

Province	Before 1950	1950–54	1955–59	1960–64	1965–69	Total	N
Central	6·6	6·9	11·4	21·5	53·6	100·0	12,224
Southern	2·9	4·7	5·4	20·3	66·7	100·0	6,871
Copperbelt	1·8	1·8	4·2	20·3	71·9	100·0	6,233
Eastern	3·4	7·1	10·2	23·2	56·1	100·0	24,223
North-Western	3·3	6·1	5·3	29·7	55·6	100·0	1,581
Luapula	1·8	3·8	3·9	28·8	61·7	100·0	1,992
Northern	2·9	6·1	6·5	18·9	65·6	100·0	10,746
Western	1·8	3·8	6·7	29·6	58·1	100·0	3,645
Outside Zambia	3·3	9·6	13·8	30·1	43·2	100·0	11,281
Total	3·6	6·4	9·1	23·4	57·5	100·0	79,167

significantly more than some of the other provinces (Copperbelt, Southern, Luapula and Western) with proportions well below the average. Although the proportion (6·1 per cent) of those from the Northern and North-Western provinces remained below the total average, the increases in their flow, representing part of the overall swing of the trend and direction of migration to Lusaka, has been in the period quite as remarkable as those for persons from Eastern and Central Province, which over the next five years, 1955–9, continued to dominate the flow. Significantly also, persons from the Copperbelt Province and Western (Barotse) Province increased their flow, the former from 1·8 per cent to 4·2 per cent and the latter from 3·8 per cent to 6·7 per cent.

After 1960, a new pattern of flow of migrants to Lusaka emerged. Although more and more people came from all the provinces, more people came to the town from the less traditional and dominant sending areas of the Central and Eastern provinces. In particular, and as can be seen by comparing the period 1955–9 with 1960–4, the flow from Luapula, North-Western and Western (Barotse) provinces have, in that order of importance, been very pronounced. The increases shown for those from the Southern, Copperbelt and Northern provinces during the period was low but, in any case, significantly higher than those for persons from the traditional sending provinces.

While 1960–4 could be regarded as the 'take-off' stage of rapid migration from all provinces to Lusaka, the period after independence in 1964 would more or less represent the era of sustained rapid growth. Clearly, most migrants to the city, well over half the total in this survey, came during 1965–9. They came from all provinces but the proportion from the Copperbelt, Northern,

140 *Special Studies*

Southern, Luapula and Western (Barotse) provinces exceeded the average in that order of importance. The proportional changes between 1960–4 and 1965–9 virtually tell the same story, and clearly show that the flow of migrants to Lusaka increased in this order of importance: Copperbelt (51·62), Northern (46·7 per cent), Southern 46·4 per cent), Luapula (32·9 per cent), Eastern (32·9 per cent), Central (32·1 per cent), Western (28·5 per cent) and North-Western (25·9 per cent). By using 1960–4 as a watershed, it can be shown that migrants from five provinces (Copperbelt, Southern, Northern, Luapula and Western) increased their respective numbers much more rapidly than others including those from the Eastern and Central provinces. The figures also indicate the uncontested dominance of flow of migrants from Central and Eastern Provinces during most part of the period before 1960.

The part played by external migrants has also been important. They came in quite substantial numbers after 1950; over half (53·5 per cent) came between 1950 and 1964. Their rate of increase has, however, since declined, presumably as a result of tighter immigration control, which has made entry difficult and may also have forced some external migrants already in the country to refuse to be identified as such. There is also the less important point that alternative economic opportunities in some of the sending countries, such as Malawi and Tanzania may have discouraged migration to Zambia.

Table 8

Date of arrival of migrants with reference to selected socio-economic characteristics, Lusaka Survey, 1968–69

| | *Selected characteristics* | | |
	Sex ratio (M/F)	*Mean age at migration*	*N (total weighted)*
Non-migrants	101	. . .	35,647
Migrants arriving			
Before 1950	196	17·8	2,410
1950–1959	131	17·5	11,127
1960–1969	114	16·9	60,227
Total Migrants	112	17·0	73,764

	Per cent adults (15+) never been to school	*N (adults) weighted*
Non-migrants	42·7	6,412
Migrants arriving		
Before 1950	43·6	2,324
1950–1959	26·1	10,136
1960–1969	24·4	37,147
Total Migrants	25·6	49,607

The evolving phenomena of migration and urbanization 141

The external migrants, including those who did not state their date of arrival, were Rhodesians (5,294), Malawians (4,054), South Africans (813), Zairians (688), Tanzanians (500), Tswanas and South West Africans (223), persons from Mozambique (206) and other countries not listed (568).

The change in the pattern of the regional flow of migrants to Lusaka was also accompanied by changes in the characteristics of the migrants. These reflect the general pattern of modernization occurring in the country as a whole. One significant development in this respect is the higher educational attainment of the more recent migrants, but more so is the normalization of the sex ratio towards parity. From a very high one of 196 males to 100 females in the period before 1950, the ratio fell to 131 during 1950–9 and 114 during 1960–9. As already mentioned this process indicates not only the increasing tendency of single females to migrate alone but also the move towards more family movements.

Another significant area of change has been the rejuvenescence of the city's population as indicated by the ever growing proportion of young able bodied persons, mostly children and those in the working age group. Apart from the rising rate of natural increase, possibly due more to falling death rates than rising fertility, part of the explanation for this is related to the fall in the age at which people come to the city. Thus, it has been shown earlier on that migrants who came in the last 12 months tended to be younger than those who came before, just as they also showed lower age at migration than the migrants who came earlier. Migrants dated as coming to the city in recent years also migrated at younger ages than those dated as coming earlier. Before 1950, the average age at migration was 17·8 years. This fell very slightly to 17·5 years during 1950–9 and more rapidly to 16·9 years during 1960–9. With higher educational attainment and better employment skills (Ohadike 1969: 60), external migrants arrived at older ages (18·2 years) than most internal ones (17·0 years). Partly because wives tended to be very much younger than their husbands, and partly because men stayed longer at school and spent more time in acquiring skills, the average age at which females came to Lusaka, 16·1 years, was lower than the average for males at 17·9 years. The overall average age at migration to Lusaka does not, however, reflect the average for persons generally moving for the first time from their villages to towns anywhere. The average for such 'first-movers' will, no doubt, fall below the survey total average age of migration to Lusaka. Thus, if we assume that most persons who came to Lusaka from their birthplaces were 'first movers', their average age at migration (16·2 years)

142 *Special Studies*

to Lusaka was not only lower than the overall average of 17·0 years but far below that of persons who came to Lusaka from places which were not their places of birth at an average age of 19·1 years. In the survey, migrants whose birthplaces or places of last residence were distant came at older ages than those from places near Lusaka. Consequently, the relationship between distance and mean age at migration was positive. For persons nearer to Lusaka or any other town for that matter, distance and transportation do not constitute as much of a motivational problem as for those living farther away, and the nearer ones migrated at younger ages.

Table 9

Sex ratio (M/F) of internal migrants by distance of birthplace and place of last residence to Lusaka

Distance covered (miles)	Birthplace			Last residence		
	% male	% female	Sex ratio	% male	% female	Sex ratio
Under 200	22·8	24·8	103	25·8	27·5	105
200–299	24·1	26·5	104	27·8	29·5	106
300–399	22·0	21·2	118	21·3	19·8	121
400–499	16·1	14·1	131	12·4	11·5	123
500 or more	15·0	13·4	133	12·7	11·7	122
Total	100·0	100·0	114	100·0	100·0	113
	N = 38,553	33,845	...	38,266	33,996	...

Distance and transportation do not seem to affect the sexes equally, and female response to them presumably differs from that of males. Females are in the special position of often migrating as dependent adults of their husbands, and are, as spinsters, not as free to migrate as the men. Tradition imposed this restriction while, in the case of Zambia and most Central African countries, colonial administration reinforced this attitude by discouraging the employment of females in towns and by not providing adequate housing for men to bring their wives to the city. Even under different and changed circumstances, tradition still frowns on the idea of single girls going a long distance to live alone without some relatives to take charge of them. In this survey, considering the ratio of males to females travelling through given distances, males definitely covered longer distances than females. From Table 9, it can be seen that the relationship between the distances covered and the sex ratios is positive. In fact, the shorter the distance, the lower the sex ratio, and therefore, the greater the number of females involved in the short-distance movements. Conversely, the longer the distance involved, the higher the sex ratio and consequently the more males than females involved

The evolving phenomena of migration and urbanization 143

in the long-distance movements. This observation is further supported by the figures for the overall mean distance of the place of last residence from Lusaka: 300·4 miles for males and 291·7 miles for the females. This difference between the sexes will, no doubt, gradually even out as development and industrialization foster more and more opportunities for females.

Table 10

Mean distance covered by migrants between place of birth and Lusaka by the date residence began, Survey 1968–69

Date residence began	Mean distance	N (weighted)
Before 1945	265·7	986
1945–54	305·6	5,116
1955–64	308·9	19,692
1965–69	322·4	38,815
Total	313·3	64,609

Already, the impact of modernization can be seen in the relationship between the average distance covered by migrants and the dates they took up residence in Lusaka. The flow of migrants to Lusaka initially tended to be dominated by districts adjacent to Lusaka. Later on, the migrant composition became more heterogeneous and more people came from districts more remote from Lusaka in response not only to growing political and administrative needs, but also to increased diversification and spread of industrialization. The increase in the average number of miles travelled by migrants to Lusaka over the years, as will probably be true of migration to most other towns in Zambia, falls in line with the development just outlined. Table 10 presents data on the mean distance covered in miles by migrants between their place of birth and Lusaka for various years. The average number of miles covered rose over the years from 265·7 miles in the period before 1945 to 322·4 miles during 1965–9.

SUMMARY AND CONCLUSION

Although urbanization does not necessarily develop as a result of industrialization, it seems accurate to say that most Zambian towns have grown mainly in response to increasing industrialization and the concomitant growth of administration.

From its beginnings as a village and, later in 1905, a small railway siding, Lusaka became the political and administrative headquarters of the country known as Rhodesia in 1931 and began to expand in

144 *Special Studies*

population. Its growth gathered momentum in the period after the Second World War, and especially in more recent years following Independence, by which time the population had reached the 110,000 mark. As the premier political and administrative centre in independent Zambia, further economic and industrial developments have been established, and these developments have served as magnets for migrants from within and outside the country.

To the extent that available data permit, the salient features of the development of Lusaka have been analysed in this paper. A reasonable estimate of the rate of urbanization of Lusaka in recent years has been between 10 and 15 per cent, with the probable average figure, based on estimates from all sources over the last ten years, around 13·1 per cent. Internal migration, much more than natural increase, has been the most important single factor and accounts for more or less than three-quarters of its remarkable growth.

New migrants gravitate mostly to areas where employment and other opportunities can be found, as is illustrated by the fact that many were found in low density areas with jobs for domestic servants, and at locations where accommodation could more easily be found, i.e. the squatter locations. The squatter problem in relation to migration undoubtedly presents a vicious circle for the Government. It is not easy to control migration and it is not easy to provide urgently-needed accommodation.

The overall industrial, political and administrative development in Zambia has generated changes in the pattern of migration flow as well as in the characteristics of migrants to Lusaka. No longer do persons from the Eastern and Central provinces tend to dominate the migration stream to the city; those from the more distant provinces such as the Northern, Luapula and the North-Western have significantly increased their rate of migration. The Copperbelt Province, by reason of its economic potentials and the link between its industries and their representatives in Lusaka, has also increased the flow of its migrants. More of the recent arrivals had migrated to other towns before coming to Lusaka than had those who came earlier. Apart from the change in the pattern of flow, the characteristics of migrants have also changed. The earlier marked sex imbalance is now being adjusted. The educational and occupational placement of migrants has improved tremendously with the years and, as would be expected, migrants are coming at younger ages and consequently the population has been growing younger and more enlightened.

Migration, settlement, and the politics of unemployment: A Nairobi case study

DAVID PARKIN

INTRODUCTION

In an important early paper on the causes of labour migration, important enough to be re-published in 1970 (Middleton), Mitchell (1959) distinguished between 'centripetal' and 'centrifugal' forces which operate in three different combinations to direct the flow of rural-urban migration in particular areas and to determine whether or not it is circulatory. Like other scholars at the time (Gulliver 1955, Powesland and Southall both in Richards 1954), he saw economic factors as necessary preconditions for migration but saw also that they need not, by themselves, be sufficient: a particular nexus of *social* (as opposed to economic) obligations or 'needs' might impede or encourage migration by tipping the economic balance, so to speak.

The distinction between economic and social needs is based on stated reasons or motivations for migrating (or not migrating), backed up by the fieldworker's own observations. Economic needs are those of acquiring cash for taxes, bridewealth, financial support for families, and, we might suppose, children's school fees, and consumer articles. Social needs are satisfied by the 'psychological security' (Mitchell, p. 34 in Middleton, 1970) of membership in a network of personal and family relations, whether, for the new urban migrant, those of his rural home or, for the established urban migrant, those of his adopted town (e.g. neighbours, workplace associates, friends, etc., whose interaction is frequently symbolized through a common prestige system). In Mitchell's analysis social needs are given equal weighting with economic needs: their 'pull' may be sufficiently strong to counteract that of economic needs. For example, men may be economically dependent on urban wage employment but, unless their social needs are also satisfied there, they will eventually be drawn back to the rural nexus of social needs and obligations. Mitchell has also made a similar useful distinction

146 *Special Studies*

between urban commitment, the satisfaction of economic but not social needs, and involvement, the satisfaction of both.

Though it is unlikely that Mitchell would now make the distinction he made then between economic and social needs, or to dwell at all on the concept of need (see 1969 (a): 177–8) it is interesting to reproduce the three combinations of forces posited as determining the migratory pattern:

(1) When profitable rural cash cropping inhibits or eliminates the need for migration for (urban) wage labour, 'economic needs' can be satisfied in the rural area and rural social involvement prevails.

(2) When the absence of rural economic opportunities prompts urban labour migration but does not result in the satisfaction of 'social needs' in the town of employment: economic needs pull the migrants to town, but social needs pull them back to the rural areas, resulting in 'circulatory' or 'recurrent' labour migration.

(3) When both economic *and* social needs can be satisfied in town, i.e. migrants become both economically committed and socially involved in town and lessen their rural social obligations, migration ceases and the previous migrants become settled townsmen.

This is of course a simplification of a sophisticated analysis. As an exploratory model, how has it stood the test of time?

THE PROBLEM OF UNEMPLOYMENT

We can begin to answer this by bringing up to date an assumption on which the model is based. At the time of their studies neither Mitchell nor other scholars concerned with labour migration needed to consider the possibility of large-scale wage unemployment as a factor in migration. The analyses assumed the steady availability of jobs and concentrated on why migrants *chose* either to work at home, work in town, or shift their labour between them. By contrast, nowadays we are obliged to consider also the *consequences* of there frequently being no such choice (cf. Elkan 1969, Frank 1968, Gutkind 1967, 1968, Grillo 1969, Hutton 1966, 1973, Parkin 1969a, Todaro and Harris 1968).

It is true to say that 'unemployment' in the African context is to some extent a matter of definition. The 'problem' of unemployment has of course become a political issue in newly independent African countries so that the definition of what constitutes unem-

Migration, settlement and the politics of unemployment 147

ployment may now seem on the surface more clear-cut than it really is. But in East Africa and other parts of Africa certain recent trends (see Jolly 1969, and Sheffield 1967), which largely coincide with the emergence to independence of the new African nations, provide some crude parameters:

(1) an increasingly inverse ratio in the number of job-seekers and available wage jobs;
(2) an increasing imbalance in the education-manpower ratio— i.e. educational levels are rising but job opportunities are nevertheless decreasing proportionally;
(3) a rate of urban population increase (6 per cent) which is roughly twice that of the national increase and thrice that of the rural.

Even the usual elementary conclusions based on these trends suggest radical demographic changes in the towns so affected: the ratio of urban unemployed to employed is increasing; an increasing proportion of the unemployed are younger and more educated than those already established in employment. It may be old hat to see in this development the creation of a politically alienated majority but the possibility cannot be discarded. From the observational view, at least, the politics of unemployment does seem to underlie many contemporary urban social processes in Africa, frequently along ethnic or national lines of conflict.

THE CASE OF NAIROBI

(a) A settled urban ethnic group
I consider the significance of these factors among a particular section of an ethnic community whom I have studied in Nairobi, capital of Kenya. These are the Luo, who, with the Kikuyu, Kamba and Luhya, are one of four main ethnic groups in Nairobi together making up about 90 per cent of the city's African population of 407,736 (1969 Kenya Census) with Kikuyu over 45 per cent, and Luo, Luhya and Kamba around 14 per cent and 15 per cent each. In 1968 and 1969 I worked in the city council housing estate of Kaloleni which had a population of nearly 5,000 in late 1968 according to my own survey. Luo were the most numerous (about 40 per cent) in the estate, even outnumbering the Kikuyu (14 per cent) who are otherwise by far the largest of the four groups in Nairobi. The household heads of these particular Luo are long-settled townsmen in secure and relatively prestigious jobs. They have a median length of residence in Nairobi of 17·6 years and include only 10 per cent who are

148 *Special Studies*

unskilled workers. Have their long residence in Nairobi, their relatively high incomes (median Shs 539/-) and secure jobs, and their participation in local political activities in fact resulted in an investment of urban economic and social interests which has reduced their need for and dependence on rural ones?

We find that two-thirds of them are members of urban ethnic associations of various kinds and that a half are trade union members. Most are married (309 out of 333 or 93 per cent) and most will have their wives with them in Nairobi for at least part of the year. It is clear that this particular section of Nairobi Luo have indeed developed important economic interests in the city: as well as receiving above average incomes in jobs demanding above average skill and training, over 13 per cent of them are self-employed, a proportion almost equalling that of Kikuyu on the estate in self-employment (15·6 per cent) who elsewhere in Nairobi dominate this category. As well as having more members of their families with them in Nairobi than other ethnic groups in the estate, Luo send significantly more children to schools in Nairobi.

But there is no evidence that this intense social and economic involvement of Luo in Nairobi is resulting in a lessening of rural relationships and commitments. In fact, as Ross (1968) noted for a different area of Nairobi, the higher status and more securely placed townsmen among all groups are most likely also to have made a number of corresponding rural investments. They may have bought more farming land, built a house, sometimes of mud and wattle but increasingly of plaster with corrugated iron roofs, and even to have branched out into a rural 'business' such as a shop or transport service. It is clear, as we might expect, that those who most succeed in town are most likely to exploit new economic opportunities available in their home rural areas. This is a familiar enough phenomenon in modern Africa which hardly needs to be elaborated. It certainly applies to the better-off Luo whom I studied in Kaloleni.

Are these high-status Luo, then, no more than a new kind of absentee rural entrepreneur, operating by proxy, so to speak, from their urban base? It is certainly true that they are unlikely to relinquish urban employment. It is too scarce a commodity for them to run the risk of being unable to return to a job. Their annual leave amounts to no more than a few weeks. Physically, therefore, their absence in the rural area may be somewhat conspicuous. In the Nairobi housing estate I studied, I have come across cases of men in their fifties and sixties who have worked away from home for up to forty years with short periods spent at home during this time

Migration, settlement and the politics of unemployment 149

amounting in some cases to little more than a year or two. There is no evidence that their economic and social involvement in rural relations has lessened, though it may be said to have taken a different form. Indeed, they are greater sources of patronage for rural kin than they might otherwise be had they remained at home.

It might be assumed that the financial expense which must result from maintaining two sets of social relations in this way would deter men from retaining many rural ties. Undoubtedly, demands are avoided or shirked if possible. But most men have little choice but to accept that rural economic interests or even simply a rural base, have to be paid for. Sending remittances home or helping out relatives or fellow Luo in town may be seen by some as an unwarranted drain on resources. But the overall consequence is that obligations of this kind can act as an investment system. More than 'security' may be protected. For the most successful townsmen, land and property interests may also be protected.

It is true that, so far, less than 15 per cent have actually *bought* land (in addition to what they have or will inherit) either from other Luo or, to a lesser extent, on a settlement scheme, and even fewer have significant rural 'businesses'. As we move progressively down the social ladder, however, we still find the same high rate of rural 'involvement': relatives from home are rarely refused urban board and lodging, remittances continue to be sent home, and there is the same constant switching of children and wives between town and country residences.

The point I want to make is that Luo household heads of all socio-economic levels in the housing estate show a low job turnover, show signs of persisting in urban employment (and in their present jobs) until retirement, are likely to join urban ethnic associations and, to a lesser extent, trade unions, yet are also likely to continue to invest economically in their rural home areas: though at present less than 15 per cent have bought land, more (at present over 25 per cent) have built 'permanent' homes (i.e. with corrugated iron roofs and sometimes plaster walls), while nearly all have this intention.

There are two ideologically important practices which have the consequence of enabling urban Luo to maintain rural interests. One is the circulatory movement of wives and children between town and country, and the second is the custom of providing board and lodging in town to a wide range of job-seekers who are usually relatives but also rural neighbours and friends, and of 'contacts' of these. These two features are, again, typical of most urban African groups. But they are pronounced among Luo. Regardless

150 *Special Studies*

of socio-economic status, Luo households tend to be larger at any one time than those of other ethnic groups. More importantly, because the Luo polygyny rate is very much higher than that of other ethnic groups, household heads have on average a larger number of children as well as wives (figures in Parkin 1974). Much of Luo rural society continues to be organized into localized patrilineal descent units segmentarily arranged. This means that the Luo 'blue-print' or cognitive map for classifying people in town has a consistency based on a modified but basically corresponding segmentary principle. That is to say, there is a likelihood that the home local origins of a fellow Luo encountered in town can be made more 'meaningful' by being articulated within an extensive genealogy. It is therefore relatively easy for Luo to 'place' each other and to appeal for help including accommodation on the basis of common membership in a descent unit or an affinal 'alliance' or matrilateral tie.

There are certainly a number of expedient reasons which townsmen may give for switching wives and children between town and country: urban houses are small; co-wives are customarily prohibited from sharing a single room and, anyway, quarrel under such congested conditions; not all a man's children can be found places in Nairobi schools, so that some, especially the younger, must go to rural ones; it is cheaper to keep half rather than all one's family in town; and so on. It would be fruitless to do more than reproduce these stated reasons. We must focus, again, on the consequences of this rural-urban circulatory movement of family members, relatives and others. Since it is particularly marked among Luo, then the consequences must be greater. The consequences themselves may be summarized as keeping the urban household head in constant contact with rural developments in his area. He may thereby be informed of the availability of land which he wishes to develop, or of a shop or other business which he wishes to acquire or become a partner in, or simply of local-level political developments: it is important to know who the present councillors are or who the intending Member of Parliament is. Information on such matters is crucially important for men who, at all status levels, already or intend to invest economically in the ways I have mentioned.

(b) Urban settlement in its political context

It could be argued, of course, that Nairobi is one of those ex-British colonial capitals in which the opportunity for urban settlement and home ownership was always virtually non-existent. It would follow that townsmen had no alternative, even in the days

Migration, settlement and the politics of unemployment   151

when jobs were more easily available, but to look to their rural areas for their future security and livelihood (Van Velsen, pp. 240–1, in Southall 1961). This is indisputable and, as a persisting tendency, may partly explain why Luo and other groups nourish a rural as well as an urban system of relations. But the fact remains that very high-status Luo, men in the professions as well as politicians, continue to invest in both systems simultaneously. Some of these top Luo have followed a larger number of Kikuyu counterparts in buying up some of the substantial houses in areas of Nairobi like Eastleigh, which have been vacated by Asians who have left Kenya; the same Luo buy and expand rural businesses from the profits acquired by letting out these urban houses. Again, perhaps this is to be expected of an ethnic elite.

The real test of whether there is an emerging category of Luo who are, to parody Mitchell, beginning to sink all their economic and social investments in Nairobi to the exclusion of corresponding rural interests, is to focus on a middle range who are not rich enough to belong to the new capitalist elite but have secure and well-paid jobs, and to ask whether they have been tempted to buy any of the houses recently, since Kenya's independence in 1963, made available for tenant-purchase by the Nairobi city council. And this is where we begin to understand why Luo have no alternative but to continue to maintain rural as well as urban interests.

The biggest planned home owernship housing estate built by the post-independence Nairobi city council is called Uhuru, appropriately after the independence Swahili slogan 'freedom'. The houses on Uhuru were first sold through city council mortgages at the end of 1967. They are very desirable economic assets to the middle-range category of townsmen. The repayments are over fifteen to twenty-five years and are from about Shs. 120/- to 150/- monthly and so are not very much greater than rents for inferior city council houses and are often less than rents for single rooms in privately-owned houses in areas like Eastleigh.

I have records on only the first 604 houses allocated in Uhuru and already well over 90 per cent of the new owners were Kikuyu. Many more houses, for which I had no records, had been sold by late 1969 when I left the field, but the predominance of Kikuyu ownership appeared to have continued. Whenever these houses become available an announcement by the city council appears in the press, but the application lists are closed almost immediately. Such is the demand that the number of applicants vastly exceeds the supply of houses. Since the ending of the Kenya Emergency in 1959, the proportion of Kikuyu in Nairobi has not only swung

152   *Special Studies*

back to its pre-Emergency level but seems actually to have exceeded it. Even without the special factor of alleged inside help from particular city council offices, this simple fact of numerical predominance makes it inevitable that other home ownership schemes will follow Uhuru in being overwhelmingly Kikuyu.

A large proportion of Luo in Kaloleni not only expressed a wish for one of these homes but had actually queued outside the city council offices to get one. Though, objectively, we can say that little conscious and deliberate discrimination had actually been responsible for these frustrated attempts by certain individual Luo (and other non-Kikuyu) to claim a stake in Nairobi's development, it is not surprising that this is invariably the cause cited. It parallels similar allegations regarding: (*a*) the increasingly predominant Kikuyu population in Nairobi and, it is assumed, in employment, and (*b*) market stalls and shops which are undeniably increasingly dominated by Kikuyu as well.

It would be facile, futile and grossly exaggerated to lay the blame for such imbalance at the door of Kikuyu mutual favouritism. It should not be forgotten that there are many poor and homeless Kikuyu in Nairobi. The main point is that once an imbalance of this kind is under way, it generates its own force: non-Kikuyu accept the fact as a *fait accompli* and see themselves as almost alien members of their capital city. It was possible for Southall to write, quite justifiably on the basis of its colonial history, that Nairobi was not looked upon by most Africans as their city (1966). In fact, there can be little doubt now that, though the proportion of Kikuyu who have actually bought homes in Nairobi may still be few, they and other ethnic groups already regard it as an essentially Kikuyu city. Kikuyu are swiftly assuming 'host' status, more by reference to their increasing control over its governmental and commercial institutions, relative to other Africans, than by their rural home proximity.

Yet, this has only recently become so. The Kenya Emergency of 1952–9 resulted in the imprisonment and detention of large numbers of Kikuyu and significantly reduced their numbers in Nairobi. It was during this period that Luo may be said to have emerged as the key ethnic group. Admittedly under the conditions of the Emergency this provided limited benefits. But they were able to establish a strong footing in Nairobi in certain markets, residential areas and in the employment structure generally as well as in trade unions. The subsequent reversal of Kikuyu and Luo fortunes in Nairobi undoubtedly strongly influenced the dissolution of the independence Luo-Kikuyu political party alliance of KANU and the emergence

Migration, settlement and the politics of unemployment 153

of KPU (now banned), which is strongly though not exclusively associated with Luo.

If I may confine myself to consideration of Luo in Nairobi, it seems that we must distinguish between their economic and their political incorporation in the city's institutions.

There seems little doubt that they are economically incorporated: Luo actually in jobs suffer no loss of privileges and they, for their part, remain dependent on employment. But their urban economic interests do not displace rural ones. On the contrary they subsidize and supplement them. For the Luo elite the reason that this may be expected to continue is simply that it is profitable: the two sources of income become mutually reinforcing investment spheres, whose benefits exceed obligatory payments to family, kin and 'supporters'. For the ordinary mass of Luo, the reason is that Nairobi is no longer regarded as a 'neutral' place of employment: proportionally fewer *new* jobs and houses are coming their way. The two sets of onerous rural and urban social ties may constitute a drain on resources but at least they keep open both options.

Changes in the city's ethnic power structure correspond with these economic changes and are thus seen by Luo to diminish their chances of full political representation and incorporation in Nairobi. For example, the disqualification of all KPU candidates at the Nairobi city council election of 1968, though defended by the city council returning officers on legalistic grounds, inevitably strengthened this impression among Luo. In this situation, the constant movement of wives, children, relatives and others between country and town, between a man's rural homestead and his urban household is both an unconscious 'ritual' statement of their common political predicament as an ethnic group and a means also of making the most of two apparently diminishing systems of economic opportunity.

CONCLUSION

However subjective it may sometimes be, it is pointless to deny that there is openly stated and almost universally believed competition and conflict between Luo and Kikuyu in Nairobi. The main source of the cleavage is a diminishing pool of employment in Nairobi relative to the numbers seeking it, and an associated scarcity of housing. As mentioned in my introduction, unemployment was not a factor of significance in the model of migratory causes proposed by Mitchell. Though more figures would be needed to substantiate this fully, it can be argued generally that unemploy-

154 *Special Studies*

ment has nowadays had the effect of 'freezing' most circulatory migration for wage labour: of the 'employable' population only the unemployed job-seekers circulate between town and country or between town and town;[1] those in secure employment prefer to remain secure and so show a low labour turnover and rarely leave employment. Their contact with rural areas is maintained through the various personnel mentioned who move between them and the country.

If this is generally so, then we can suggest a modification of some 'causes' giving rise to the second and third situations making up Mitchell's model. I have not the space to consider the first situation, the 'all-rural' one, though it too could be shown to be responsive to the political and economic problems of wage unemployment.

The second situation, that of circulatory migration, characterizes the growing pool of job-seekers who may move between towns, thus expanding the overall urban population, as well as between country and town. The circulatory or recurrent nature of their migration would seem to have little to do with conflicting social and economic 'needs', since, as illustrated with reference to the Luo at least, no such conflict exists: both urban and rural social relations are highly maintained and are in fact used for job-seeking or, for those already in employment, for economic and political security and investment.

In the absence of such conflict it follows that the third situation, that in which migration actually ceases, cannot arise from a resolution of this conflict. It is true that individual Luo in town who are fortunate to have jobs frequently complain of the irksome demands made on them by relatives and other fellow Luo. But it is doubtful that they continue to heed these requests simply out of respect for custom. I do not think that it is crudely utilitarian to suggest that

---

[1] Weisner (1969) shows that some circulatory migration among a Kisa sub-group in low status employment does persist, though since it appears to be restricted to relatives and others standing in close relation to each other, it would seem that the same cluster of urban jobs are held in perpetuity by what is in effect an exclusive grouping. This kind of personnel replacement probably typifies unskilled rather than skilled occupational monopolies. In view of the risks involved of permanent loss of employment, such cases may concern a minority of Nairobi's 'conventional' or 'official' labour force, but may characterize much more widely the 'informal' or 'unofficial' employment sector, whose importance in the urban context in providing a range of inexpensive services grows considerably in accordance with the rapid general increase in the urban population. This hypothesis is worth testing.

Migration, settlement and the politics of unemployment 155

economic benefits and political refuge[2] constitute the pay-offs. The ideological demands of kinship, descent, affinity and general ethnic solidarity between people moving between country and town are not the 'cause' of a continuing system of rural-urban relations. They are the most ideologically potent way in which the system and its pay-offs must be expressed, recognized, and legitimated within the terms of a single culture.

Further to this, we must clarify a distinction between two types of conflict. One is that discussed by Mitchell, Gulliver, Southall and others, namely the *personal* conflicts an individual may experience between his social obligations to others and his own economic self-interest or 'needs'. The second is that of conflicts between principles of social organization. In Nairobi there is a conflict between continuing economic dependence by Luo on jobs in Nairobi and their apparently growing exclusion from political control of the city. In the context of unemployment affecting much of Africa, it is this conflict, indeed contradiction of organizational principles, with its implications of uneven regional development, which I regard as most likely to explain sociologically the cessation, persistence, and nature of migration of distinctive social groups and categories. For some groups and catetgories have more choice in resolving personal conflicts than others.

Group-focussed and actor-focussed perspectives are indeed different levels of abstraction (Mitchell 1969(b): 10, and see also Garbett *infra:* 113) and the study of inter-group and inter-personal relations must be accommodated within the same analysis. The scale of the problem, how macro- or micro- it is and whether it refers to a short or a long time-span, prescribes which perspective is most emphasized. So, whatever the analytical weight placed on the range of choices open to individuals, significant changes in the ranges themselves must surely be demonstrated ultimately by changes in the differential access to and control of resources held by socio-cultural groups and categories.

[2] See J. Okumu's analysis (1969) of a parliamentary by-election in a Luo rural area for an illustration of the crucial interconnection of urban and rural political forces. I can add, also, that the importance of rural 'clanship' in contemporary politics as emphasized by Okumu was parallelled by the way in which in Nairobi Luo ethnic associations (clan, location and the central Union) mobilized Luo opinion, interests, and involvement in the by-election.

MIGRATION AND RURAL
DEVELOPMENT

Notes on migration in Uganda

TIBAMANYA mwene MUSHANGA

Human migration is an inherent element of the processes of industrialization, urbanization and development in general. In Uganda, as in most developing areas, two main causes are responsible for large-scale human movements: (1) the introduction of a monetary economy and, (2) population increase. Within the overall context of these two factors educational, political and other changing social factors are responsible for local variations of migratory processes. Since the introduction of a money economy in Uganda some eighty years ago, large groups of people have been moving from rural areas to urban centres and industrial areas in search of employment opportunities. A large proportion of these migrant workers move from rural areas to places of work for only short periods of time, sometimes for a few years but usually for some months. The other migrants, made up of professionally trained employees such as teachers, clerks, policemen, nurses and other government employees, move for much longer periods, usually within their home districts, but sometimes to other areas distant from home. It is common today to see large numbers of school leavers, both boys and girls, in large cities and trading centres looking for employment. With some education, however elementary, the young school-leaver expects and is expected by his family, to get paid employment which is usually in urban or peri-urban areas.

Improved medical care and hygiene have reduced the death rate and increased the live birth rate with the result that, in a district such as Kigezi in south-west Uganda, the population density in some parts reaches 800 persons per square mile. With a population of 642,300 occupying a little less than 2,000 square miles, Kigezi as a whole has an average density of 320 persons and is one of Uganda's most thickly populated districts. The resultant scarcity of land has undoubtedly been the main factor behind the large-scale migration to work outside this district. But it is not only urban areas which have attracted such migration: an historically long-established pattern of inter-rural migration has persisted even as certain rural economies became monetized.

160 *Special Studies*

In the late 1920s and early 1930s, coffee began to be grown on a large scale in Uganda and cotton was established as a second cash crop especially in Buganda and the Eastern Region. To those who saw the cultivation of these cash crops as an assured means of earning an income, new land was necessary, and this brought about inter-rural migration of the intending growers which was followed by inter-rural migrant labourers as they came to work on the new fields. Great numbers of migrant labourers from rural Ruanda, Kigezi and Ankole went to Buganda (now Central province of Uganda) to work for Ganda coffee and cotton growers (Dak 1968: 6). The Ruanda, the Alur and the Lugbara provided the bulk of the migrant labour force. These movements were essentially inter-rural in that the migrant labour force came and went to work in rural areas where large tracts of land were available for cultivation. This is still the case. Hundreds of migrant labourers from rural areas go every year to work on such estates. With the spread of unemployment throughout the country, migrant labourers have tended to remain in their jobs lest these be taken by new migrants seeking employment.

RURAL-URBAN MIGRATION

An increasingly large number of migrant labourers from rural areas are to be found now in urban centres, of which there are three main concentrations. These are Kampala, Jinja, and the Mbale-Tororo area. This type of migration has tended to attract people from outside Uganda, such as the Ruanda, the Rundi and also the Luo from South-West Kenya. It is reported that already in 1925 the Labour Department alone recruited 11,771 labourers from the south-western area of Uganda, the great majority of whom came from Ruanda and Burundi. The number continued to increase until it was estimated that about 100,000 migrants from Ruanda went to Uganda every year (Dak 1968). The Luo home districts in Kenya are South and Central Nyanza. In 1962, Central Nyanza and South Nyanza had population densities of 366 and 218 persons per square mile, respectively. In certain areas, such as Kisumu, the densities reach over 1,000 and 8,000 per square mile. Because of these pressures due to shortage of cultivable land, the Luo migrate to urban areas in search of jobs and most of them migrate for long periods. In 1959 there were 37,648 Luo residents in Uganda. Illustrating the propensity of Luo to migrate to towns rather than to other rural areas, Dak (1968) says: 'The distribution of Luo contrasted sharply with other migrant tribes in Uganda in 1959. Whereas other mig-

Notes on migration in Uganda

rants were remaining in rural areas, the Luo were concentrated in towns. Thus Kampala (with Mengo) had 5,544 Luo in that year. This was 15·7 per cent of all Luo migrants in the whole of Uganda, and 32·9 per cent of Buganda Luo.'

One of the factors in the Luo preference for work in towns rather than rural areas in southern Uganda may be their linguistic and cultural separateness. Ruanda migrants find it relatively easy to be assimilated among such fellow-Bantu speakers as the Ganda. The Nilotic-speaking Luo apparently do not. But other factors are certainly involved, for the Sudanic-speaking Lugbara from north-west Uganda work in the rural areas of Buganda. Thus, the Luo have very strong ethnic welfare organizations such as the Luo Union, whose function, among others, is to give guidance, assistance and accommodation to new migrants and which are located in urban centres. Again, the Luo, unlike the Ruanda and some other groups tend to go into business such as petty trade, and carpentry, while others go into semi-permanent employment as watchmen, drivers and shop-assistants.

Because of rising expectations and aspirations consequent upon changes in the socio-economic life of the people in general, urban life appears to most rural dwellers, especially the young school-leavers, to hold attractive prospects. Constandse and Hofstee (1968: 29) have characterized the process of rural-urban migration as 'push' and 'pull'. They point out the 'people do not move into towns only because their rural home no longer offers them sufficient means of existence and thus "pushes" them away; they also go because of the "pull" of the town in promising them a better life'. In a society where nearly all the modern amenities that appear to offer a better life are located in urban areas, the stereotype develops that rural life has nothing new to offer, that life is monotonous and unexciting. The stereotype does prompt some to move from rural areas to urban centres to work, even if their earnings are no more than the income they got from the sale of their cash crops. But the available evidence obtained from observation of migrant labourers on rural farms and tea plantations suggests that the large majority of migrants, especially the unskilled, are guided by economic criteria in choosing their place of work. The urban unemployed may not have this choice or may have lived in town sufficiently long to have assimilated urban cultural values which cause them to reject viable economic alternatives in the rural area.

It does seem that rural-urban migration will continue to increase in the absence of significant rural industry, and as more factories, government departments and other kinds of institutional employ-

162 *Special Studies*

ment are located in urban areas and attract the rising number of young school-leavers forced out from their rural areas by population increase and land scarcity.

DURATION OF MIGRANT LABOUR

The time spent away from home by migrant labourers is determined by many factors and motives. Constandse and Hofstee (1968) claim that 'The first to migrate are those who have a better chance to acquire what they want elsewhere and/or the least obligation or desire to stay at home'. This means that the first type of migration consists of those who have a consciously recognized need to fulfil. Batanyisako (1967) points out that young men migrate from Kigezi to Buganda for as long as a whole year trying to raise enough cash for payment of bridewealth; while others migrate for a few months to work for wages so as to be able to pay debts, taxes and to buy land or cows. This group of migrants must be differentiated from those 'who have the least obligation or desire to stay at home', and those who have little, if any, stake in their home society. The point is that social and marital obligations together with psychological attachment in the family or lineage are significant factors in determining the duration of the migrant's absence from home. The more committed he is to his family or lineage, the more unlikely the individual is to migrate permanently, and the shorter the time he will spend away from his domestic circle. On the other hand, the weaker the attachment the more likely he is to migrate either permanently or for protracted periods of time. The weakening of family and filial ties is, therefore, an important factor in determining types of migratory process. Such estranged migrants are still predominantly males who originally came to town as bachelors and who may have since established common law marriages or more casual sexual unions with a more limited number of women similarly unattached. The process of rural estrangement is characterized by a gradual reduction in the number of visits home made by these men, sometimes resulting in their total alienation from rural home ties.

Particular cases suggest that the distance between the place of work and the rural home affect the frequency of visits made there by a migrant, which in turn influences his overall duration in his work-place. The Luo and Ruanda come from outside Uganda and are generally long-term migrants who visit home infrequently. Speedier forms of transport have affected but not significantly. altered this relationship. It is not so long since Ruanda migrants used to make the journey from their country to Kampala by foot,

Notes on migration in Uganda

a distance of over 300 miles which took them several weeks to walk. Modern bus and taxi services enable the journey to be made in one day. Though visits home are in this respect more feasible, the fare needed may be prohibitive. Kiga and Ruanda migrant labourers working in the copper mines at Kilembe in Toro are a special case. They stay for several years before they go back permanently to their homes. But during this period they earn annual paid leave and are given bus fares to and from their homes, which makes it possible for them to visit home at least annually. They tend to stay longer in employment because of the system of regular wage increments. The longer a man stays at his job, the more working experience he tends to acquire, the more useful he becomes to the company, the more he is paid and the more he is likely to stay on. The result is that there are men working at Kilembe who have been there for ten years or more, yet who have been able to visit their homes on public holidays, such as Christmas, and when they take their annual leave.

A different pattern emerges for those migrants who work on farms for private individuals or for small traders, for then the question of formal 'leave' does not arise and it is only those workers whose homes are nearby who are likely to be able to visit them frequently. Hirst (1971: 34) reports of such people in the towns of Bukoba (Tanzania) that 'Visits home were extremely frequent, sometimes as much as once per week'.

We may ask here whether, where agricultural output is the only means of providing a livelihood, absence from home of the male family members may also lead to less production. Among particular culture groups this is not necessarily the case. Batanyisako (1967: 18) reports, for example, that 'customarily one of the most important qualities that a Kiga man looked for in a girl before he married her was whether she was a hard-working woman. This shows how much importance the Kiga attach to a woman's ability to cultivate. . . . A woman often works in her fields from sunrise to sunset and she takes a meal with her in the field. Under these circumstances, therefore, labour migration does not have very serious effects on food production.' Left on her own, a wife is then at least able to provide for herself and her children, though she must make special arrangements for help in clearing land or tending the fields when she is unwell.

There are females from Uganda who migrate independently to urban and trading centres where they work as house-servants, salesgirls, barmaids and prostitutes. Apart from the small number who are skilled or professional workers, women have a much nar-

164   *Special Studies*

rower field of employment choice than men. But the proportion of independent female migrants seems, nevertheless, to be increasing and is largely a movement from rural to urban centres. It is generally supposed that there is already a problem of unemployed, unmarried young women in and around the major cities and trading centres reflecting this increase.

In the rural social systems, discriminatory rules of inheritance, restrictions on the possession and use of property and land may be among the factors stimulating female migration. It should be noted that unemployed women in Uganda are not required to pay the annual graduated tax, formerly the poll tax, nor do they have to raise cash for bridewealth as do men. These, then, are not precipitating factors in their migration.

Though they are still far less numerous, the movements of women are like those of men in converging to a general rural-urban migratory pattern at the expense of inter-rural migration.

CONCLUSION

It is suggested that while inter-rural migration will continue to decline, rural-urban migration is likely to increase as more industries and big businesses are set up and as more people leave school and come to urban areas to seek employment. With population growth leading to land scarcity, urban areas may increasingly become the long term domicile of the 'surplus' population. Unless there is adequate planning of cities and business centres to cater for large numbers of people, we will find that the bulk of those outside the rural areas will be living in areas of sub-standard conditions and amenities and slums will become a major problem.

It is widely accepted that agricultural development programmes could reverse the present trend and draw people back from urban to rural areas. But a more immediately realizable means of promoting a reverse population movement from major to smaller towns and to rural areas might be the decentralization of major business, government and other public concerns.

Inter-rural migration and East African rural development

VICTOR C. UCHENDU

If there is any neglected problem in African development environment, it is not migrant labour. From the early 1920s, and particularly since the end of the Second World War, the implications of migrant labour for the African society, economy and culture have been of practical concern to the administrator and policy maker. For the student of African socio-cultural change, migrant labour has had a particular fascination (Gugler 1968: 463–86; Mabogunje 1972).

Practical problems of labour migration have probably changed faster than our theoretical understanding of the phenomenon. For instance, the 'traditional' concerns of policy on migrant labour formulated by colonial administrators have changed radically in the decade of African Independence (1960–70). Concern about the 'migrant problem' during the post-war decades (1945–60) centred round three 'how' questions:

1. How to equate labour demand with labour supply through administrative action, supplemented by quasi-economic or target incentives.
2. How to maintain the stability of industrial and estates labour.
3. How to minimize the social and economic consequences for the rural society and economy of the heavy outflow of rural manpower into the urban and estates economies.

The changing character of 'migrant behaviour' constitutes a new challenge to development research and practical policy. Only about twenty years ago, the question of how to stabilize African industrial labour dominated policy and research. The impression gained ground in some quarters that Africans were characterologically unsuited to industrial labour. We now face a new reality: African capitals and urban centres are teeming with an army of unemployed and underemployed. The critical question is how to get them away from the cities—even when paradoxically Africa, and certainly Sub-Saharan Africa, is the least urbanized region of the world.

166 *Special Studies*

In retrospect, the history of migrant labour studies in Africa is fascinating for two important reasons. First, it shows how political and administrative imperatives have oriented scholarly research in this field. Second, it reveals the urban-centred approach to the migration question, as seen in the abundance of the literature focusing on rural-urban migration themes and limited efforts on the inter-rural migration trends. The aim of this paper is to redress this balance in migration studies. Specifically, we shall examine conditions under which inter-rural migration makes a net contribution to the rural as well as the national economy and what policy instruments are required to increase this economic contribution.

SOURCE OF DATA

In examining the economic impact of migrant labour on rural African society, we shall draw on two sources of data: material from my recent fieldwork and the general literature on labour migration in East Africa.

Between November 1966 and May 1968, the Food Research Institute, Stanford University, investigated the economic, socio-cultural and technical determinants of change in African agriculture. I was a member of an interdisciplinary team of two economists, an agronomist and an anthropologist in this project. The field studies were aimed at assessing the prevailing agricultural situation and, in particular, the receptivity of the farming population to new techniques, as well as gaining an understanding of the combination of factors fostering innovation at the farm level. Seven district-level case studies were carried out in six countries, four of them in East and Central Africa and three in West Africa.

Although four of the seven study areas fell within the region of this Seminar, I shall concentrate my discussion on the three East African areas—Teso (Uganda), Kisii (Kenya), and Geita (Tanzania). A published report on the Mazabuka study (Zambia) is now available (Anthony and Uchendu 1970). Three other East African studies are now in the press and I have drawn heavily from this project in recent publications (Uchendu 1968: 225–42; 1969: 5–13; and 1970: 447–86).

ECONOMIC CHARACTERISTICS OF THE AREA

Although their general environment is dominated by the Lake Victoria complex, Teso, Kisii and Geita districts have their special geographical characteristics. Their elevations range from about

Inter-rural migration and East African rural development 167

2,000 to 7,000 feet above sea level. Rainfall is unimodal in Geita, but bimodal in Teso and Kisii. The mean annual rainfall varies from 50 inches in Teso and Geita to over 75 inches in Kisii.

Variations in economic achievements of the districts are as marked as the variations in the environmental potentials and population pressure. About 70 per cent to 90 per cent of the available land in Teso and Kisii is cultivable as against 60 per cent in Geita. Practically all the available land in Kisii is under cultivation while the ratio between cropped and cultivable land is over 65 per cent in both Teso and Geita. The density of population reaches 500 to 900 per square mile in Kisii but ranges from only 100 to 200 in Geita and Teso.

Farm sizes vary widely within each district: 5 to 25 acres in Geita and Teso, and 2 to 10 acres in Kisii. Kisii and Geita have practically no land fragmentation problems, but in Teso district, the number of separate holdings per farm averages 1·5.

Millet and sorghum are the chief staples in Teso, while maize has virtually replaced millet and sorghum as co-staples in Kisii. Maize and cassava are the co-staples in Geita. The most important source of farm cash income in Geita and Teso is cotton. However, Kisii has a more diversified economy with coffee, tea, pyrethrum and maize as sources of cash income. As can be expected, the economy of Kisii district is not only the most diversified but the most monetized of the three districts.

DEVELOPMENT EXPERIENCES

Movements of labour in Africa assume major importance within well defined areas. Migratory movements stretch over long distances and have an intricate pattern. To a considerable extent, they represent an adjustment of labour to the unequal distribution of population in relation to economic opportunity, including rights in land. Within a continental frame of reference, we can identify three major migrant streams in Africa. 'Uneven' economic development and the mal-distribution of economic resources have helped to shape this pattern of labour migration.

First is the South African orbit where a mineral dominant economy attracts labour supply from Malawi, Mozambique, and less frequently in recent years from Zambia and southern Tanzania.

The second migrant stream is constituted by the West African region where the cash cropping economies of the forest zone provide opportunities for wage labour to the grain economies of the drier savannah. As Daryll Forde (1953: 206–19) has shown, the cultural

168 *Special Studies*

adaptation in the West African region cannot be divorced from the complementarity which exists between these two contrasting ecologies, the forest and the savannah zones. The current migration trends, which reflect a savannah 'supply push' and a cash-cropping 'demand pull', constitute a continuity in cultural adaptation of this region.

The East African migrant region, our third migrant stream, is like the West African region in one important respect: both are agriculturally based. But unlike the West African region, the developmental process and policy in East Africa had been biased towards agricultural estates. There are notable exceptions to this pattern of development. The coffee-banana zones in Buganda (Uganda), Kilimanjaro and Bukoba (Tanzania) may be cited. Together with agricultural estates, the smallholder cultivators, who are producing export crops combine to influence the direction and the duration of migrant streams in this region. In this respect, there is a large flow from Ruanda and Urundi to Uganda and Tanzania, which also receives workers from Mozambique. More important than the interterritorial migration, is the flow of internal migrants from the regions which have no export capacity to regions which command this capacity.

In addition to these three well-structured migrant streams, ecological factors continue to exert a major influence on the movement of economically productive individuals and social groups. In the submarginal belts of the tropical Savannah, where pastoralism is the dominant economic activity, seasonal movement of population and livestock, in search of pasture and watering points, is a characteristic mode of ecological adaptation. In every country of tropical Africa, there is a growing inter-rural movement of population that is motivated by the opportunity to earn an extra income rather than by the 'bright lights' of the city.

In effect, export capacity, and the characteristics of the economic activities which sustain production for export, have an important bearing on the intensity and duration of inter-rural migration. We shall illustrate this proposition by examining the development experiences of the three East African districts presented here as case studies.

DEVELOPMENT EXPERIENCES IN GEITA, TANZANIA

As late as 1934, the total population of what is now Geita District, was estimated at 55,000 people. The tsetse fly, which is endemic to the area and infects both men and livestock with trypanosomiasis,

Inter-rural migration and East African rural development 169

restricted settlement to the shore of Lake Victoria and the south-western portion of the district. Productive activities were inhibited, and, without understanding the causes, Tour Reports by colonial administrative officers portrayed the Zinza, the native population, as lazy and unresponsive to change.

It was not until 1935 when the Tsetse Research Department helped Chief Bhasama to clear part of Msalala country for settlement that attention began to be paid to the problem of fly control in Geita. Large scale clearing operations, first by the Medical Department, and later by the Tsetse Department, followed the sleeping sickness epidemic of 1938, encouraged settlement and immigration. Immigration, from land-hungry areas of Sukumaland, was at first into the northern part of Geita areas, and continued across Smith Sound into uninhabited areas infested with tsetse fly, which receded as man advanced.

Once obstacles to settlement were removed the three important occupations which influenced the settlement pattern were agriculture, mining and trading, in that order. By 1955, Geita had become one of the most rapidly developing areas in Tanzania. This has been aided by inter-rural population movement—from overpopulated Sukumaland into Geita; the existence of a cash crop (cotton) suited to the environment; government settlement control programme; and, most important, tsetse control through the application of technology.

Inter-rural migration in this area has followed two patterns: first, the colonization of new land by the Sukuma, which is still going on unobtrusively; second, the seasonal movement of migrant labourers from Ruanda and Urundi into Geita district to work on farms growing cotton. The rationalization of the land/man relationship, brought about by land colonization, and the contribution made by agricultural labourers in reducing seasonal bottlenecks, have combined to transform Geita district from tsetse infested bush and *miombo* woodland into a major cash crop and food producing area which supports a population of 371,407 (1970 Population Census).

DEVELOPMENTS IN KISII DISTRICT

Like Geita, the economy of Kisii district has benefited from population movements and technical achievements in agricultural research. But, unlike Geita, Kisii farms no longer attract considerable seasonal agricultural labour, which is largely confined to the tea estates and plantations. Although expenses for wages constitute a large proportion of a Kisii farmer's inputs, the labourer he employs

170 *Special Studies*

is not a migrant, but a Kisii cultivator who hires out his labour from time to time because of shortage of land.

Development of Kisii district represents a pattern of rural change in which the initial 'surplus' factor (land) has undergone pioneer colonization and in which methods of agricultural 'intensification' provide the most economic option for increasing output and productivity.

The two most striking aspects of economic development in Kisii district is the recency of the development effort and its cumulative impact. Technical change in Kisii agriculture started from about 1930, when the extension service of the Department of Agriculture laid emphasis on the value of soil conservation and enclosure, almost as ends in themselves. From 1930 to 1950 the Gusii (the people of Kisii) responded to the economic stimuli around them by exporting their productive man-power to the mines and agricultural plantations. Participation in seasonal labour migration was so general in the district that 80 per cent to 90 per cent of the present generation of farmers have had migrant labour experience.

Labour migration among the Gusii had two important results on Kisii economy. First, most migrants realized for the first time that farming could be a profitable proposition. Second, this realization encouraged migration into the highlands, which had been hitherto an under-populated area reserved for cattle grazing. With rapid colonization of the Kisii highlands, the area became a major exporter of maize which found a ready market among the tea and coffee plantations in Nyanza region.

The real economic achievements which tended to stem the out-flow of migrant labour from the district came in the 1950's when high-value cash crops were introduced. Pyrethrum was introduced in 1952, and was followed in quick succession by tea in 1957, exotic cattle and two different kinds of high-yield maize in 1963 and 1964. A few indications of the rapid diffusion of these farm enterprises may be given. Less than one decade after its introduction, every Gusii farmer in the 'pyrethrum zone' grew a patch or two of pyrethrum. The number of tea growers increased from 90 in 1957 to 3,386 in 1966, while the acreage under tea rose from 16 to 2,390·7 over the same period. The rise in exotic cattle was even more rapid—from 89 in 1962 to over 8,000 in 1966.

Both the Kisii and Geita development experiences demonstrate the familiar proposition that the interaction between man and his environment is an integral part of the process of economic growth. The development process in both areas involved a plentiful supply

Inter-rural migration and East African rural development 171

of resources of land and labour which permitted a considerable expansion of output without any radical changes in agricultural technology. While for the Gusii, the labour force had acquired vicarious experiences through labour migration, the situation was different in Geita where the immigrant Sukuma had had no such exposure and so exerted no such comparable influence on the developing economy.

TESO DEVELOPMENT PATTERN

The pattern of economic development in Teso district contrasts with experiences in Geita and Kisii. Unlike both the latter, planned development in Teso dates back to 1910 when cotton and the ox-plough were introduced as fiscal measures. From the beginning, the Teso were highly receptive to these innovations. The rapid diffusion of the oxplough went hand in hand with increased output of cotton, the main cash crop.

The simultaneous introduction of oxplough and cotton meant that many of the labour bottlenecks in planting were eliminated from the start. It also reduced the Iteso dependence on migrant labour, and their acquisition of a cash crop early in this century— even before they developed any important felt needs that could be met through cash earning—discouraged Iteso from becoming an important migrant labour population.

Although the oxplough solved one important labour bottleneck (land preparation and sowing), it created labour bottlenecks during weeding and harvesting—activities which have not been mechanized. Owing to the short periods involved, this demand for labour has not created a sufficient incentive to retain any migrant stream in the district. Paradoxically, Teso district, which is in close proximity to a migrant labour force provided by the land-deficient West Nile populations (Lugbara, Madi, Lendu), is chronically short of weeding and harvesting labour.

These three case studies represent a range in the impact of migrant agricultural labour on society and economy. The Teso district represents a case in which the early use of an intermediate technology, by stimulating internal development, reduced the demand for immigrant agricultural labour and discouraged the Iteso themselves from leaving the district. Geita district is an example of the sustained use of immigrants, while Kisii district shows the conditions under which a rural economy has capitalized itself from the resources earned from the earlier migrant labour of its own people. All three cases have benefited from internal re-allocation of resources of land and

172　　　　　　　　*Special Studies*

labour, through the colonization of new farm lands. They provide some insights into the nature of the contribution of inter-rural migration to development. These are particularly relevant at this time when the question of appropriate measures to deal with urban unemployment are among the most challenging practical policy issues facing East Africa.

MIGRANT LABOUR AND THE DEVELOPMENT PROCESS

Labour migration cannot be separated from the general problem of economic development. The view of development—particularly economic development—as a socio-cultural and political process whereby a people progress from a static, traditional mode of production toward a modern, dynamic economy and society has led to an emphasis on one aspect of the migration trend: the rural-urban. Guided by this view, labour migration is treated as a transitional but persistent phenomenon which is associated with the early stages of economic growth. In the view of the Commission for Technical Cooperation, Africa South of the Sahara, migrant labour 'will fade out in most areas as development proceeds' (CCTA, 1961: 232). For this to be achieved, the Commission argued, one of two conditions must be satisfied: either the sharp distinction between the subsistence and wage earning sectors of the economy disappears or the manpower effectively available in employment areas becomes adequate to supply local needs. The basis for this was derived from the 'dual economy' model. In this model, it is fashionable to distinguish between two types of labour migrants and to emphasize the urban point of destination. The two types of labour migrants —rural and urban migrants—are associated with distinct socio-economic and occupational statuses and consequently different styles of life and motivations. From this model, we derive the picture of the rural migrant as one who is seeking wage employment in the depressed, low-wage, rural economy and who, over time, shows relatively little change in his life style or his expectations.

In contrast to the rural migrant, the urban migrant operates in an industrial economy characterized by higher wages and longer tenure. We tend to picture him as a migrant whose work and urban environment have combined to bring about considerable and marked changes in his life and life styles, as well as in his expectations. Gulliver, who has helped to give this migrant model an empirical reality, credits the urban migrant with 'the desire, felt with a strong sense of necessity and even urgency, not merely to maintain new,

Inter-rural migration and East African rural development 173

higher standards [of living] but also to follow the idea that there are even higher standards [of living] within reach' (Gulliver 1960: 161).

The point must be emphasized that the model of a dual economy, and the migrant streams and categories associated with it, is inadequate to deal with the complex processes of economic transition. It tends to view the urban environment as the only stimulus to innovation, and the rural environment as an area lacking in innovations and innovators. The empirical evidence suggests that the network of social relations between the urban and the rural society is a strong and mutually-reinforcing one. For a better understanding of the migrant process, we need a network analysis in which the interactions and dynamic processes operating within a total economic environment can be taken into consideration. It is no longer useful, either theoretically or in policy terms, to view rural and urban economies as mutually exclusive units. The fact is that urban economic actors are also often economic actors in the rural sector of the economy. Both the urban economy and the rural economy treat each other, so to speak, as an exploitable environment and the relationship between them must be dynamic if the total economy is to remain buoyant. Besides, policy decisions which affect the various sectors of the national economy are increasingly made by the national élite and economic activities are increasingly mediated by national institutions. In view of this, I suggest that a much more realistic model is one which views African economies as 'incorporated' economies in which many traditionally isolated or institutionally independent or 'self-sufficient' economies are losing their self-sufficiency and regulatory autonomy. The mobility of labour, manifested by various types of population movement, is a process in this trend towards greater economic interpenetration.

MIGRANT LABOUR AND URBAN UNEMPLOYMENT

Population movement, reflecting labour mobility, represents a normal trend in development. It is a well known fact of economic history that material progress has usually been associated with the gradual but continuous transfer of productive agents from the rural to the urban economy. But rising urban unemployment, in an economy where positive marginal products prevail in agriculture, is the result of poor economic policy. A recent review of agricultural policies in Africa (Carl Eicher, *et al.* 1970: 37) identified the following nine common causes of unemployment in African economies:

174 *Special Studies*

(1) Rapid population growth.
(2) Distortion of factor prices which discourages the use of labour-intensive production techniques.
(3) Rising labour productivity as industrial employment levels fall.
(4) Rural-urban income differentials which may be blamed on high export tax on agricultural products and government wage policy.
(5) Urban bias in the provision of social services, leading to out-migration from agriculture into urban areas—migration that is in excess of job opportunities.
(6) Unbalanced educational expansion.
(7) 'Tied Aid' which fosters imports of inappropriate technologies from aid-giving countries.
(8) Political and ethnic barriers to labour migration within and between African nations.
(9) Ecological constraints which limit productive activities to a few months of rain-fed agriculture in a year.

Whatever its causes, unemployment is always a serious economic issue. It is wasteful of human resources. In most African economies where the labour absorption capacity of the industrial sector is severely limited, unemployment poses a political dilemma. The irony of this dilemma is that Africa, the least urbanized of all the continents, is now being described as "over-urbanized."

The simple fact is that Africa is not over-urbanized. Viewed processually, economic development leads to increasing specialization in society and economy. The spatial aspect of this specialization is an ecological transition resulting in the gradual reduction of the proportion of the total population living in rural areas and correspondingly, the dominance of the urban over the rural population. The rate of this transition will depend on (*a*) the rate of increase of the total population, (*b*) the size of the present urban population, and (*c*) the rural population as an initial proportion of the total population. For a continent with less than 10 per cent of its population living in urban areas, the concern should be with why the urban economy has failed to generate adequate employment and how to provide the incentive to the agricultural sector so that it can raise its labour-absorption capacity.

Modern development should be 'guided' development. Growth and development does not occur without vigorous, goal-oriented effort, enormous self-discipline and, as recent experiences show, trial and error and retrial. A laissez faire development policy is an

Inter-rural migration and East African rural development   175

option no longer open to developing societies. The challenge of urban unemployment cannot be met by policies which try to find an 'urban solution' to unemployment. Carl Eicher, (1970: 38) argues that 'an efficient strategy for coping with urban unemployment problems must address itself to employment generation in agriculture.'

How can labour migration contribute to employment generation in agriculture? There is no simple answer to this question. However, our case studies suggest the following conclusions:

(1) Given the structure of Africa's 'incorporated' economies where land surplus areas coexist with land deficit areas, inter-rural migration can make net addition to development through rational allocation of productive resources of land and labour. For this type of result to be achieved, local 'sovereignty' in land rights must be harmonized with development objectives, and where politically feasible a national land tenure policy should be evolved.

(2) Opportunities for rural investment must be created, as a deliberate policy, so that the earnings of the migrant and some of the savings from urban areas can make productive investment possible in the rural areas. The Kisii development experience shows that scarcity of profitable investment opportunity is more limiting than shortage of rural capital.

(3) As Miracle and Berry (1970: 95) point out, 'the most important ways in which returning migrants contribute to the supplying economy are the spread of new techniques, accumulation of capital, and changes in consumption expectations and horizons.'

(4) Development policy must be influenced by the fact that the 'urban' solution to development has had mixed results. A balanced policy, especially for a polity which aspires to socialism, is one which is committed to full employment. The most productive way to go about it lies in paying increasing attention to the rural sector—and this implies that inter-rural migration cannot be ignored.

CONCLUSION

One of the dramatic facts of African culture history which is often ignored is that population movement is not new to the continent. African populations have moved and continue to move in search of better grazing and hunting grounds or better soils to farm. As the

176 *Special Studies*

Geita case study shows, they have fled to avoid tseste fly; or among other populations, to avoid long drought or stronger neighbours. Recent population movements should not be ignored. In Nigeria, Ghana, Zambia and Sudan, for example, large populations have been forced to abandon their homes to make room for man-made lakes and dams. Although accurate statistics are not available, Scudder (1970: 31) estimates that 'well over one per cent of the total rural African population has been relocated during the past fifteen years.' What must be emphasized is that most of this population did not move into towns.

But it is in African towns, particularly the capital cities, that the political implications of labour migration are most felt. The reasons are not far to seek. In modern Africa, development is highly politicized, and government has tended to assume responsibility, not only for social and economic development, but for employment generation. The people who are most likely to cause most political trouble live in towns. In this situation we can appreciate that the close tie between public responsibility for economic welfare, including full employment policy, and political legitimacy, has brought with it a tight interplay between employment and politics.

As African economies face more serious unemployment problems, this interplay between politics and employment will no longer be hidden. Historically, labour migration between African nations has been remarkably open and politically uninhibited. Mining and plantation enterprises have recruited labour without regard for political boundaries. But increasing industrialization and rising unemployment in African countries have led to competition between international migrants and local labour. We expect this problem to generate more conflict, given the trend toward economic nationalism in Africa. Moreover, this conflict is not restricted to international migration. African national economies are increasingly experiencing internal migration conflicts, an inevitable consequence of the effort towards horizontal integration of the economy. The whole process poses a dual challenge—a challenge to economic policy and a challenge to theory of labour migration. The former concerns its ability to reduce ethnic and institutional barriers which might restrain internal migration. East Africa's greatest economic resource today is its people. Given the prevailing level of technology and education, the size of agricultural output still depends on the amount of productive labour. If the mobility of labour between agricultural areas is restricted, it will be difficult to create a national labour market, or to deal with the problem of 'uneven' development which might threaten national unity.

Inter-rural migration and East African rural development 177

There is also a challenge to theory. It is no longer fruitful, in the discussion of migrant labour, to treat ethnic groups in the new African states, as if they constituted 'independent' economies. The fact is that these populations are now part of 'incorporated' national economies and are affected, and often respond to, decisions made for these economies by central agents and institutions. The economic consequences of migrant labour should therefore be viewed in the total context—at national, regional and local levels. We suggest that policies which can maximize the new contribution of migrant labour to society and economy should be developed at the national level.

Controllers in rural Tanzania

H. U. E. THODEN VAN VELZEN

The cornerstone of Andre Gunder Frank's model is the notion that a few metropoles dominate and exploit a vast number of satellites. Relationships within the satellite countries themselves are assumed to mirror the hierarchical and exploitative nature of this mondial pattern: as the metropolis sucks wealth out of the satellites the provincial capitals live off the surrounding countryside. To this should be added the fundamental unity and integration of the whole system. Frank (1969: 6) chose to express this point with these words: 'Furthermore, the provincial capitals, which thus are themselves satellites of the national metropolis—and through the latter of the world metropolis—are in turn provincial centers around which their own local satellites orbit. Thus, a whole chain of constellations of metropoles and satellites relates all parts of the whole system from its metropolitan center in Europe or the United States to the farthest outpost in the Latin American countryside'.[1]

The point of departure of this contribution is that we can profitably use Frank's model but that more empirical data on the processes of exploitation and the extraction of wealth are badly needed. In particular, we often lack detailed knowledge about the various mechanisms which enable the centre to maintain its grip on the periphery and drain off its wealth. If we do not have sufficient information on what is going on at the local level—on the dynamics of the power struggle which is the reality of everyday life in so many of the developing countries—then we will merely repeat and elaborate each other's slogans. In this contribution I will present some case material from Rungwe District in southwestern Tanzania (Mbeya resion) on the process of satellite development.[2]

[1] This model is derived from the systems analysis school of political science: cf. Easton (1965a and 1965b).

[2] Rungwe District is part of Mbeya region. The field work on which this paper is based was conducted between August 1966 and December 1968. The first half of this period was spent in Itumba, the administrative centre of Bulambia, the most western division of the district. I was at that time a member of an interdisciplinary team from the Afrika-Studiecentrum at

THE CONTROLLERS

The units of this analysis are sociological rather than geographical. It is not Tukuyu, the District Capital of Rungwe, which interests us here but rather the elite of administrative and party personnel which represents, or is supposed to represent, the national interest at the local level. Some of these representatives are residents of Tukuyu, while others live in a number of 'outposts', villages which have been selected as rural centres. But wherever they are stationed in the district and whatever their internal disagreements, these controllers form a separate social grouping, occupying a clearly distinct social position vis-à-vis the peasantry. The reasons for this social distance are twofold: the powerful position of the controllers and the vested interests which they attempt to safeguard.

The power assets of the controllers derive from the strategic position which they occupy as gatekeepers. The metaphor used in this connection could be described as follows. Society is conceptualized as a huge flow system: goods are extracted and manpower is mobilized to be put at the disposal of the centre. From there, part of it is redistributed again through certain channels to particular sectors of the periphery. Each channel has its check-points which are manned by what Easton (1965b: 86–96) called the gatekeepers. The gatekeepers regulate the flow and may—to some extent —redirect the stream or shift its projected course, thereby providing privileges to certain sectors of the peasantry. The gatekeepers take their toll as the resources pass them.

Controllers are contestants themselves in the struggle which takes place at the periphery about the distribution of resources. There are a number of reasons for this involvement. Controllers have to defend their own 'class' position and safeguard the various emoluments which are attached to it. Equally important, they cannot be indifferent towards development in rural areas because they—the controllers—have used their advantageous position to develop mutually profitable exchange relationships with the

Leyden (the Netherlands), engaged in investigating social and economic factors hampering or stimulating the development of the rural economy. My colleagues working on this project in other divisions of Rungwe have generously allowed me to make use of their field work data. The responsibility for the conclusions, however, is solely the author's.

This paper essentially covers the same ground as some of the reports which I wrote earlier, in particular *Staff, kulaks and peasants* (1971). However, the emphasis on game analysis as a separate and distinct method for the analysis of micro-political processes is new. Also, the focus of this contribution is now different from those of earlier reports.

180 *Special Studies*

wealthier peasants. This has been observed (Van Hekken and Thoden van Velzen 1972) in one part of Tanzania but it may be the pattern in other parts of East and Central Africa as well. Therefore, it seems justifiable to direct attention to the involvement of the controllers in rural politics and the stake which they appear to have in the status quo.

The elite of controllers forms the centre. Around the centre 'orbit', in Frank's terminology, a number of satellites. The subsequent analysis of the relations between a centre and its periphery is mainly based on fieldwork data from Bulambia division in Rungwe district. Itumba, administrative centre of this division, has a few resident civil servants called 'staff people' (WaSitafu) by the peasants. This group of controllers comprises the Divisional Executive Officer (DEO), his treasurer and messengers but also such functionaries as the agricultural extension officer and the medical dispenser. This élite group of controllers forms the centre. The satellite field is composed of the peasants of Itumba and other villages in Bulambia Division.

EXTRACTION

At first glance, the adjective 'exploitative' seems hardly appropriate to characterize the relationship between controllers and peasants. There is no discernable flow of goods and services from the satellite fields to the controllers. Though some government officials receive goods (vegetables, maize or other agricultural produce, a loan of land and in a few cases a cow) in a clandestine way, their benefactors are wealthy farmers or kulaks, as I prefer to call them.[3] In many parts of the world, the main instrument of extraction is the taxing system. Although a 'local rate' or poll tax of 45 shs existed, this legacy of the colonial epoch was abandoned in 1968. Not only are we in a position to deny that the controllers suck wealth out of the peasantry, but the opposite position can easily be defended. The government of Tanzania is channelling more wealth into the rural hinterland than it gets back, or will ever get back, from direct or indirect forms of revenue. Through the First and Second Five-

[3] The concept of *kulak* has been borrowed from recent Russian history. Dumont (1957) has argued that this is also a significant social category in Africa. The concept should be stripped of most of its emotional connotations of oppression, repression and exploitation which it has acquired in Soviet history. By 'kulaks' I simply mean the better-off farmers whose position in rural areas has become controversial ever since Tanzania committed itself to socialism. Since 'better-off' is a relative concept it has to be operationally defined anew for every rural community.

Controllers in rural Tanzania

Year Plan, the government has greatly expanded both the funds and the manpower which were put at the disposal of agencies promoting local development projects.

This Tanzanian situation is certainly not characteristic of the situation in the Third World. As is well known, Tanzania has for many years accepted and propagated a socialist ideology, which was expounded in the Arusha Declaration of 1967, the 1971 TANU-guidelines and in numerous speeches by President Nyerere. At the national level, the planning agencies of the various Ministries consciously strive to protect the interests of the peasants, and the abolition of the poll tax testifies to the seriousness of their intentions. Thus, in this part of the world, the relationship between centre and periphery cannot be meaningfully characterized as 'exploitative', at least not in the sense that a substantial part of the locally produced surplus of goods and services is drained away and absorbed by the centre.

THE DEVELOPMENT OF SATELLITE STATUS

No matter how beneficial the centre-satellite relationship seems to be for the peasantry, strong pressures are at work which subjugate the satellite field to the centre. To the majority many of the new opportunities created by the processes of development and modernization are denied. This threatens to thwart the projected socialist transformation. Paradoxically, these mechanisms of satellite development operate in a national framework which has created optimal conditions for the growth of socialism. The mechanisms of satellite development apparent in that corner of Tanzania where I conducted field work are the following:

(1) The present position of the controllers in the district capital and at the outposts offers them a vast number of opportunities for the ostentatious demonstration of an élite culture and 'style of life'. In this way, symbolic divisions between controllers and peasants are being sustained. I will not elaborate this point any further as I have done so elsewhere (Thoden van Velzen 1971).

(2) The controllers support the wealthier sectors of the peasantry, thereby encouraging further processes of power accumulation in the satellite fields. This frustrates efforts to introduce programmes for collectivized agriculture (cf. Thoden van Velzen 1970). Moreover, such support tends to discredit the Tanzanian Party, TANU, as an instrument of the happy few. In

182 *Special Studies*

fact, when I first came to Rungwe District TANU was almost a shopkeeper's party; many small retailers occupied functions such as 'ten-house-group' leader and chairman of the Village Development Committee. Elsewhere (Van Hekken and Thoden van Velzen 1972) it was pointed out that the rich farmer is not only overrepresented in TANU's grass-roots machinery, but also occupies most of the salaried positions in the villages. Of 143 such functions available in 1967 in five villages of Rungwe District 72 were filled by the wealthiest 20 per cent of the population.[4]

(3) Though a country such as Tanzania is sparsely populated in comparison with most European or Asian countries, fertile land fit for agriculture is rapidly becoming scarce. The frontier days when good new land could be staked out are coming to an end. The argument then is that Tanzania has now entered a decisive period which, in all likelihood, will not last much longer than a few decades. After that period, new land will only be available at high, and for many, prohibitive costs of reclamation. Nowadays, in many parts of Tanzania there are still some resources as new land can be converted into fertile plots at low costs. The future shape of Tanzania's rural society is to a large extent determined by this crucial distribution process. The relevant questions are: who will dominate this last frontier and what opportunities will those who now find themselves among the landless enjoy in the coming years?

My experience is that, by and large, the controller throws his weight behind the kulak and in that way enables him to expand his landholdings to the detriment of his poorer neighbours.

GAME ANALYSIS

Though more and more lip-service is being paid to the processual study of local-level politics, the development of a method for the systematic analysis of antagonistic interaction lags far behind. Norman Long in 'The local community as an ecology of games' (1967) and F. G. Bailey in 'Stratagems and spoils' (1969) pioneered

---

[4] The five villages concerned are Itumba and Ibala in the western part of Rungwe District and Ilolo, Buloma and Jerusalem in the eastern half. Information on Ilolo was kindly made available by Ir. P. M. van Hekken, while the data on the last two villages were provided by Dr. J. H. Konter.

Controllers in rural Tanzania

new approaches in this field. The authors utilize the concept of 'game' as the centre of their conceptual framework.

A game is a series of antagonistic interactions which can be delineated from other such series and from other forms of interactions. Game analysis attempts to investigate two related subjects. The first one is that of the relative positions of contestants in a political field. Here, attention is devoted to the power base, strategy and arena map of both parties in a dispute. It also investigates the structure of arenas relevant to a competition or struggle.[5] Secondly, game analysis tries to record and understand the processes triggered off by political actors attempting to change the existing distribution of resources and honour. Game analysis is particularly useful when it addresses itself to the study of political dramas, i.e. situations when the status quo is seriously threatened. In *Staff, kulaks and peasants* (1971) I related one such political drama which took place in the village of Itumba in 1966 and 1967. The case study described how one wealthy farmer called Chomo, with the help of some people, maintained his position in the face of mounting opposition from the majority of the population. The fight became particularly bitter when the ownership of a valuable sugar-cane garden was at stake. Chomo received substantial support from the side of the agricultural extension officer (Mwakalinga) and the medical dispenser. From the political drama we extracted the following information on the position of the controllers, and their allies the kulaks.

1. *Power base of the controllers*

(Definition of *power base*: that part of a person's resources which give him the potential to wield power.)

The peasants have an exaggerated view of the extent to which staff members and kulaks co-operate and collude to further their interests and safeguard their privileges. But before dealing with the more distorted perception of field conditions by peasants, I would like to point out the objective basis for at least part of their feelings. This concerns the power base of the controllers:

(*a*) The staff directly control a number of 'legitimate arenas'. Decisions reached in such arenas are recognized by the outside world as authoritative and are backed up by force if necessary. Examples of such arenas are the Primary Court, the investi-

---

[5] An *arena* is here defined as an institutional framework which may serve as a setting for antagonistic interaction, i.e. for restricting and channelling it. By 'institutional framework' I mean rules, procedures and personnel.

G

184   *Special Studies*

gations of the local police commander; the enquiries set up by the Divisional Executive Officer as 'Justice of the Peace'. Indirectly, the staff have an important say in a number of other arenas, the most important of which is the Village Development Committee.

(b) Furthermore, the staff control access to certain material resources such as, for example, medicine and medical treatment, which can be obtained from the medical dispenser and mid-wife. Other valued goods and services which one can obtain through 'staff people' are: employment in a government service as messenger (or other forms of unskilled labour): expertise of government officials; farm implements; sowing-seed; and transport.

(c) Another important power basis of the controllers is their alignment with the kulaks. Objective evidence that such a coalition operates—and that both partners derive considerable benefits from it—is not difficult to procure. In return for information and certain goods, (viz. gardens, food such as vegetables, finger-millet and sugar-cane), the staff help their kulak friends in a number of ways. Not only do they assist them in occupying official functions, they also throw their weight behind their kulak friends in disputes as became apparent when the political drama in Itumba unfolded. From the same drama it appears that the following transactional relations existed between staff member Mwakalinga and kulak Chomo.

. . . Chomo ceded part of his sugar-cane garden to Mwakalinga and gave a river garden on loan to the medical dispenser;

. . . Chomo escorted Mwakalinga to the hospital and took charge of mourning proceedings when his son died;

. . . Chomo regularly received information from his staff contacts which enabled him to forestall his enemies' moves (cf. van Hekken and Thoden van Velzen, 1972);

. . . Mwakalinga assisted Chomo with technical advice and a loan of money in order to make it possible for him to appeal to a higher court after the local Primary Court ruled that one of Chomo's best fields (a sugar-cane garden) would have to be handed over to his enemies. The magistrate appeared to have come to this judgment only after considerable pressure had been exerted by the mass of the peasants in the village.

2. *Arena map of controllers*

The *arena map* comprises the perceptions of a particular participant concerning the position of others in an arena or political field. Thus, it contains estimates of its own and enemy strength and information on the deployment of forces. This is the subjective view of a participant: it is obvious that such 'intelligence' can at times vary greatly from the presumably more objective information gathered by the sociologist.

The staff people know that they occupy a powerful position in rural areas; they feel entitled to the prestige and emoluments of an élite grouping. A basic tenet of these controllers is to relate success and wealth to the innate capacities of the peasants concerned and their (the peasantry's) ideological motivation for furthering the interests of their country. The majority of the staff people believe the poorer peasants to be lazy, ignorant and prone to practise witchcraft, the argument being that as they make no progress while others succeed they would tend to become envious of the more privileged ones. Such opinions are sometimes sincerely held, and sometimes no more than rationalizations of their own interest in aligning with the richer peasants.

3. *Strategy of the controllers*

(A *strategy* is a general plan of action which assesses priorities and indicates to which areas (arenas, other sets of relationships) surplus effort and resources have to be allocated. On the basis of such an overall strategy manœuvres are performed in order to consolidate gains, inflict losses on the enemy or undermine his position.

A strategy contains indications of how these objectives may be achieved with a minimum of losses and a maximum of efficiency. Schelling (1966: 3) emphasized the significance of this concept in the following words: 'The term is intended to focus on the interdependence of the adversaries' decisions and on their expectations about each other's behaviour'.

The controllers follow two important strategic guidelines: (*a*) a 'betting on the strong' strategy and (*b*) concentrating their attacks on weak spots. Wertheim (1964: 262) has formulated the 'betting on the strong' strategy to account for the selective and preferential approach which government personnel use to bring about innovations. He reports the fact that in India and Indonesia government officials rely on the advanced farmer for introducing innovations. The above tendency has also been observed by a number of sociologists working in Tanzania: it has been called the progressive (Saul 1972: 123) or model farmer approach (Cunningham 1968). As mentioned before, official instructions

186 Special Studies

ensure that progressive farmers will represent the peasant population on government committees. Apart from these instructions, however, there is no clear-cut policy of the various government services in this respect. Government personnel work in a climate of laissez-faire which permits them to select their audience according to their own inclinations and interests. It is pertinent to stress here that the tendency to give preferential treatment to a restricted segment of the total peasantry definitely goes against the grain of the national ideology in post-Arusha Tanzania. This acquires an added significance because the category of the advanced farmers seems to overlap considerably with that of the kulaks.

Wertheim rightly assumes that his conclusions are applicable outside the field of innovative behaviour. Basically, he notes that the controllers are likely to choose the wealthy farmers as coalition partners, i.e. to bet on the strong rather than on the weak and the many. This is also the strategic choice controllers opt for in Itumba, since, as we have seen, many exchange relationships have developed between staff people and kulaks. Though this is the most frequently occurring type of coalition, it should not be viewed as the immutable and permanent alliance (Thoden van Velzen 1971).

Another characteristic strategy of the controllers is the tendency to concentrate attacks on weak spots and ask only those peasants to comply with unpopular measures from whom a minimum of resistance is expected.

Many fields in Itumba are cultivated for periods of four to six years continuously, before the field is left to lie fallow for a period of three years. The widow Namatanga let one of her fields lie fallow in 1965. In November 1967—at the beginning of the new agricultural season—Kalinga, one of the more wealthy peasants, visited the Divisional Executive Officer and asked his permission to take over the widow's plot. The official called Namatanga to his office and urged her to start tilling the field immediately. The Divisional Executive Officer warned her that if she did not comply with his request he would regrettably be forced to confiscate her plot and hand it over to others. He pointed out that there were too many people in Itumba who did not have enough land. In vain Namatanga pleaded that the plot had not sufficiently recovered its fertility. In the same year Chomo left unused several acres of river land, which were not undergoing regeneration. These plots could have satisfied the immediate needs of a number of poorer peasants if they had been taken from Chomo and given to them.

Controllers in rural Tanzania 187

We have surveyed the position of the controllers in the political field with the help of some concepts from game analysis. We will now utilize these same concepts to elucidate the position of their counterparts.

4. *Arena map of the peasants*
Peasants are inclined to dramatize the collusion of staff and kulak. Although the suspicions of the peasants are sometimes without any factual basis they are nevertheless important; they influence their actions and mould their strategy and thus form an integral part of the arena map. In the case study the following accusations and suspicions are mentioned.

The medical dispenser was alleged to have kept a stock of medicines reserved for his colleagues and kulak friends in times of scarcity. This, according to the peasants, had resulted in a lower mortality rate among children of this group than among peasant children. Furthermore, the medical dispenser was accused of withholding medicine from the divorced wife of Chomo and thus, indirectly, to have caused her death.

In a law-suit between Chomo and a few poorer peasants concerning the ownership of a valuable sugar-cane garden, the Primary Court magistrate was believed to have come to an impartial judgment only after pressure had been brought to bear on him. In the eyes of the peasants he had relinquished his impartiality by secretively advising Chomo, through his friend the agricultural extension officer Mwakalinga, to appeal.

Chomo was reputed to have supplied the medical dispenser, the Primary Court magistrate, Mwakalinga and two teachers with vegetables, onions and sugar-cane. It was well-known that staff were often among his guests at his beer parties.

The arena map of the peasants contains such information as:

(a) all legitimate arenas are dominated wholly or to a large extent by staff;
(b) staff control access to vital resources;
(c) in case of conflict staff will close ranks;
(d) in case of conflict richer peasants are supported by staff.

5. *Strategy of the peasants*
On the basis of this arena map a strategy evolves which has the following elements:

(a) In case of conflict with a member of staff it is extremely difficult to press a charge against him. A possible course to

188   *Special Studies*

pursue is to enlist the backing of another member of staff before taking action. This happened, for instance, when a farmer from Itumba wanted to protest to Mwakalinga about the alleged sorcery of his son. He succeeded in getting the police officer to escort him to Mwakalinga and deliver his protest.

(*b*) In case of conflict do not enter the 'legitimate arenas' but try another battleground in which more effective manœuvres can be performed.

The medical dispenser at X was alleged to have regularly had affairs with married women in the community. This charge would have resulted in a civil case if the seducer were a peasant. But on the basis of the above stratagem peasants reacted differently: for two years no action was taken, then, in the middle of the night, people set fire to his houses. The dispenser escaped just in time from a blazing house.

More often peasants have recourse to threats which can be as effective as arson. In 1967 some villagers of Itumba bore grudges against the magistrate. Then, on a given day, the wife of the magistrate was advised by a 'helpful' neighbour to leave because 'people' intended to set fire to the thatched roof of her house. Two weeks later they left the village on a transfer. The magistrate who presided over the case of the valuable sugar-cane garden was told by people to pass a judgment favourable to the opponents of Chomo. If he failed to do so, 'things would happen to him'.

This points to the fact that another way of inflicting harm on an opponent is to conduct a 'war of nerves'. Mwakalinga was assailed in this way, mainly because of his support of the unpopular Chomo. This 'war of nerves' consisted of numerous threats, accusations and indications of unpopularity. It turned out to be fairly effective because Mwakalinga considered leaving Itumba, although this entailed considerable losses for him as nobody was prepared to give him a penny for his two houses with corrugated iron roofs. Furthermore, it would have meant giving up fertile river plots which he had on loan from Chomo and another kulak.

CONCLUSION

The controllers in some villages of the Rungwe District occupy a class position in the sense that they form 'an aggregation of persons in a society who stand in a similar position with respect to some

Controllers in rural Tanzania

form of power, privilege or prestige' (Lenski 1966: 75). On the basis of the available evidence it also seems justifiable to conclude that a class consciousness is emerging among the controllers. More significant, the awareness that shared interests require protection has been mentioned as one of the main forces which caused the staff people to cultivate exchange relationships with the more wealthy segments of the peasantry. Evidence for these alliances or coalitions is derived from a number of indicators. For example, it was shown that kulaks are over-represented in official functions. Moreover, game analysis revealed the actual pattern of cooperation between controllers and kulaks in a number of clashes which took place when the ownership of some valuable resources was imperilled. At the same time, game analysis exposed the close weave of interest between controllers and the wealthy peasants.

The coalition of controllers and kulaks is one of the more important mechanisms which—if left unchecked—are bound to transform Tanzania's peasantry into a rural proletariat. Although the cohesion and strength of this coalition should not be overestimated, it is nevertheless a real and potent force at the local level. It denies most of the new opportunities to the poorer majority of the population, and plays a pivotal role in the distribution of the last resources of valuable land. Moreover, it thwarts the spontaneous 'grass-roots' levelling movements aimed at the kulaks.

New economic relationships between the Gwembe Valley and the line of rail

E. COLSON and T. SCUDDER

INTRODUCTION

Villages, like people, respond in idiosyncratic fashion to opportunities made available to them through the presence of natural resources, the growth of towns, the extension of communication and transport systems, and the provision of government services. This paper deals with the difference in response of two villages in the Gwembe Valley in the Southern Province of Zambia. The villages are sited close together. Both are inhabited by Gwembe Tonga. Their people have much the same background. As a result of the Kariba Dam Project, which uprooted 56,000 Gwembe Tonga in Zambia and Rhodesia, both villages were resettled in the Lusitu area of Gwembe District in 1958. (Figure 1).

Planners might be inclined to expect the two villages to accept or reject the same programmes for economic and social development. Yet in recent years they have evolved after two different fashions and now have very different expectations.

One, Mazulu village, has responded to its new environment, which includes access to bus transport to Kafue and Lusaka, by developing urban foci in both towns, which lie approximately fifty and ninety miles away. These foci profoundly affect life within the village as people flow from village to town and back again to work, to shop, or just to visit, assured of supporting kin and a welcome in each place. The Mazulu people see Kafue, Lusaka, and the village as part of the same social field. Their behaviour remains much the same wherever they are in terms of living standards, desires, response to illness and family problems. Since they remain within the same social network they remain responsive to the same kinds of social control and the same kinds of standards. This does not mean that they have encapsulated themselves and retain a purely rural orientation and culture. Ideas originating in the village or the urban foci are easily transferred from one to the other, as witness the flow of town dress, entertainment and curing methods to the village and the flow of possession dances and curing methods to the towns.

Musulumba village, on the other hand, has little to do with towns *per se* and the town is foreign terrain to most of its people. It lies even nearer to bus and taxi services than Mazulu, but it has no town foci and its people do not move between village and town as part of a normal round. Instead they have adapted to what can be called a peri-urban environment within Lusitu. Many of its men work on construction jobs to which they commute on a daily or weekly basis. Wage-work dominates village life and allows many of its people to support an urban standard of living. The same employment base which supports them attracts immigrants from other parts of Zambia with whom they interact on the job, in the shops and beer halls, and sometimes in the village. The immigrants help to support a trading centre near the village which caters for both local and immigrant workers and for passing tourists. Musulumba villagers thus live surrounded by much the same kind of social flux as exists within a town and town standards are familiar to them.

The two villages, close as they are, could be expected to support different government programmes of development. The people of Mazulu would favour a policy which emphasized both urban and rural development, with the latter including wage labour and support for agriculture through loans, technical advice, better marketing arrangements, and the provision of subsidized equipment. The people of Musulumba on the other hand have no interest in urban development and very little in programmes for agricultural development based on cotton or other export crops. They are concerned rather that government encourage large-scale construction or industrial projects in their part of Gwembe District to continue to provide employment to them and the immigrant workers who are the market for locally-grown produce.

Elsewhere in Zambia and throughout Africa a comparable diversification among rural populations appears to be taking place. This suggests that we ought to abandon the old rural-urban dichotomy as a working concept.

We propose in the first portion of this paper to examine the reasons why the two villages have developed their particular modes of life. We will then consider in more detail the adaptive responses of each village since resettlement, as well as the consequences for the villagers of their different modes of attachment to the modern economy. Though it might be assumed that Musulumba villagers

192   *Special Studies*

would be more parochial in their outlook than the people of Mazulu, or represent a more rural point of view, this would be difficult to uphold. Both villages are now closely linked into the wider community of Zambia. Neither could return to the largely self-subsistent and self-sufficient routines they knew and valued before the 1950s.

Ours is a micro-study. We have chosen to concentrate upon these two villages both because they are now within the same general Lusitu community with equal access to Kafue and Lusaka and for practical reasons concerned with our methodology. Since 1956 we have followed members of four Gwembe communities, who represent perhaps 2 per cent of the total population of Gwembe District. We have done this through frequent visits and the up-dating of village censuses begun in 1956 which cover demographic, economic, and social data. We have records for Mazulu and Musulumba for 1956–7, 1962–3, 1965, 1967, 1968, 1970 and 1972. In 1956–7, 1962–3, and 1972 we interviewed every adult resident in Mazulu and Musulumba and some who had left the villages. In the other years we checked basic data either with the individuals concerned or with other villagers who could supply the information. In 1972 Scudder has been able to interview systematically most Mazulu residents in the cities: Colson has not been able to carry out interviews with any of the Musulumba diaspora. This limits some comparisons we would wish to make.[1]

FACTORS THAT ENCOURAGED DIFFERENTIATION

The major differences between Mazulu and Musulumba with which we are concerned in this paper have developed since the 1958 resettlement of Gwembe Tonga in advance of the formation of Lake Kariba. The most important factors leading to the growth of the two different modes of adjustment appear to be the following:

[1] Our studies in 1956–7 and 1962–3 were carried out under the auspices of the Institute for African Studies of the University of Zambia (then the Rhodes-Livingstone Institute). Colson's 1965 visit was supported by the Joint Committee on Africa of the Social Science Research Council and the American Council of Learned Societies. Scudder's visits in 1967 and 1970 were supported by the California Institute of Technology and FAO. Our 1972 research is financed by a grant from the National Science Foundation. Earlier analysis of data has been supported by funds from the University of California, Berkeley; the California Institute of Technology; and the Small Grants Division of the National Institute of Mental Health, Grant 1RO 3MH18528–01. For further information on the research and on Gwembe society and the events of resettlement, see Colson 1960, 1971, Scudder 1962, and Scudder and Colson 1971.

New economic relationships 193

(1) An initial familiarity on the part of Mazulu with a variety of development agencies including a mission and agricultural and extension work.
(2) An initial familiarity by Musulumba men with local construction work under the auspices of one of their own fellows.
(3) Differences in agricultural potential and proximity to wage employment at the two resettlement sites.
(4) A more rapid adjustment to the new area by Mazulu because of the circumstances of resettlement.
(5) Possession of skills and equipment for rapid agricultural expansion on the part of Mazulu.

In 1956–7, when we began the intensive study of the two villages, they were in Chipepo Chieftaincy, about twelve miles apart. Mazulu was one of four villages in a Zambezi river neighbourhood, but it was a late-comer to the area so that residents had little access to the most valued alluvial soils in the deltas of the principal tributaries. It therefore considered itself a poor village by river standards though the gap had been partially closed during the years immediately before resettlement. Starting in 1948 Mazulu men had begun to open up large gardens on Karroo soils several miles back in the bush.[2] By 1956 such gardens comprised approximately two-thirds of the land cultivated during the rainy season. This land was not suitable for tobacco, but it made the village self-sufficient in grain. It had also been possible to introduce cattle in the 1950s, as tsetse fly had begun to withdraw in the 1940s from the thickly settled Zambezi plain. Mazulu was therefore able to buy ploughs and begin the shift to an expansive plough cultivation. By 1956 harvests from bush gardens exceeded those from all other garden types combined. Following relocation, Mazulu farmers continued their expansive agriculture, actively seeking out a wide variety of garden types.

Musulumba was one of two villages occupying a small tributary valley some ten miles inland from the Zambezi. It produced grain and bananas for local consumption, some tobacco for export, and a surplus of groundnuts, a crop favoured by the sandy upland soils found near the village. Unlike Mazulu, Musulumba still lay within the tsetse-belt and could not convert to plough agriculture. It kept such cattle as it possessed in Mazabuka District on the Zambian Plateau or in the higher tsetse-free valleys of Gwembe District, and continued to cultivate with the hoe.

[2] See Scudder (1962: 54–61) for reasons why these bush gardens were not opened up at an earlier date.

194 *Special Studies*

In ordinary years each village was self-sufficient in grain but was also committed to a system of labour migration which had provided much of the cash income for Gwembe District since 1900. In 1956 it was estimated that 42 per cent of the District's able-bodied men were absent at any one time as wage workers. The majority of the older men of each village had worked in Bulawayo in Rhodesia and had formed part of the encapsulated Gwembe community in that city. Mazulu men still commonly went to work in Rhodesia, and preferably in Bulawayo, but Musulumba men were shifting towards a preference for working in the towns of Zambia. This shift was completed throughout Gwembe with the declaration of Zambian Independence in 1964, the unilateral declaration of independence by Rhodesia in 1965, and the partial closing of the frontier in the same year. In 1956 few women from either village reached the towns, although some Musulumba women had lived as children or as young women in progressive Plateau Tonga farming villages in Mazabuka District (Colson 1958). The men, once they returned home, were expected to conform to local standards. Gwembe had its own styles in dress, entertainment and social order until the beginning of the 1950s. Its people did not regard the town and town ways as an appropriate model for behaviour in Gwembe. Few strangers visited the District other than the occasional itinerant trader who came to collect tobacco.

The improvement in transportation with the building of roads in the 1950s began the process of transformation which was accelerated by the Kariba resettlement when the rapid installation of roads, depots and other services brought a great many workers into the area and brought town and country into closer association. In 1949–50 the building of a road from the railway line to the Zambezi River at a point close to Mazulu village created conditions that predisposed Mazulu village to certain lines of development after resettlement. The sixty miles to the railway line could now be covered in a few hours by car instead of three days on foot. The site attracted a large European-owned store and a mission station with a boarding-school and dispensary. Government stationed a veterinary assistant and an agricultural assistant near the mission. Later demonstrations of net fishing appropriate to lake conditions were carried out nearby. Musulumba, on the other hand, was nearly ten miles from the mission and was sited a mile from the road along a seldom used bush track so that most traffic continued to by-pass it. Neither technical assistants nor missionaries were likely to visit it. It had no school. Its people reached the dispensary only after a long walk and for serious illnesses. Its site did favour

New economic relationships

the development of small-scale entrepreneurs, since goods could be imported by road, but conditions were not sufficiently good to attract foreign competitors. One Musulumba man built a small shop before 1956 and another planned to open a shop as soon as he had acquired the capital. Similar ventures were beginning at that time in many Gwembe neighbourhoods as roads spread.

A further characteristic of Musulumba appears to be accidental. A Musulumba man had become a road foreman for the Gwembe Rural Council (then the Gwembe Local Authority) and could recruit labour for work on feeder roads when the Council had funds. He naturally enough recruited first of all in his own village and the other village in his neighbourhood. Although the men were not enthusiastic about the work because of the low wage, married men were likely to choose it in preference to labour migration. Nothing comparable existed at Mazulu.

These circumstances before resettlement had therefore pre-adapted the people of the two villages to seize on different kinds of opportunities. Resettlement provided conditions which re-enforced the initial bias of each village.

The resettlement in 1958 took both villages from Chipepo Chieftaincy to the Lusitu region below Kariba Dam, approximately a hundred miles north-east of their old site. They were settled approximately five miles apart. Both villages violently resented the disruption of their lives, but circumstances made it easier for Mazulu to adjust to its new site and to accept the move as final, thereby releasing its people's energies for exploring the new environment. It had been moved along with the other three villages of its old neighbourhood. Within a year of moving, its people knew that Lake Kariba had flooded the old village site with its fields. It was not only an arbitrary government order which kept them from going home. The old Musulumba site, on the other hand, remained above water for some three years after the move and the associated fields were planted by members of Siabwengo village which was not moved. Musulumba continued to envisage a return home once government became convinced that the resettlement policy was a failure. Its people had therefore little reason to invest in clearing fields or otherwise conquering the new environment. Its men meantime worked for wages on various construction projects as government built schools and other facilities needed by the resettled population. They did not see this work as an investment in their own future in Lusitu, an area which they were prepared to abandon whenever the chance should come.

The sites allocated to the two villages differed in agricultural

196   *Special Studies*

potential and access to local wage labour, a circumstance which further encouraged the bias of each village. Mazulu was resettled overlooking a major bend in the Lusitu river within which there were excellent alluvial and colluvial soils. At the same time it was close enough to the Zambezi to gain access to the extensive alluvia in the Lusitu delta, and to an extensive area of good soil which lay between the village and the Zambezi. This meant among other things access to tobacco soils and tobacco sales could now become for the first time a major source of income for Mazulu cultivators. While some of this land was pre-empted by two other resettled communities it became available to Mazulu people after the former fled following a period of very high mortality in late 1959. Already predisposed towards the pioneering of new land and familiar with the use of oxen for ploughing, Mazulu was quick to gain possession of better soils in greater abundance than it had held before resettlement.

Musulumba, settled further up the Lusitu River, obtained no delta and little tributary land suitable for tobacco, maize, or bananas. It completely abandoned banana cultivation as a result, and only a few elders were able to gain control of enough alluvial land to give them a cash income based on tobacco. While a substantial bush area lay behind the village, this was of lower quality than equivalent Mazulu land. Musulumba people arrived with few oxen and ploughs and little experience in their handling. It took some years for them to equip themselves. Tsetse-fly was controlled as part of the resettlement programme, but Musulumba was more vulnerable than Mazulu to a re-encroachment of fly as long as its hinterland remained uncleared.

On the other hand, Musulumba was sited with a maximum opportunity to take advantage of local employment opportunities for rough labour, the kind of work in which its men had always specialized along with most of the other Gwembe men. Its new site lay above the Kariba Access Road immediately adjacent to what was called Lusitu Township where government was building a boarding-school, a dispensary, an agricultural research substation, a PWD camp, and a number of less permanent ventures. Such a concentration of services also meant that the location attracted a number of shops. Musulumba therefore found a large amount of immediate employment on its doorstep, while relatively little building went on in the immediate vicinity of Mazulu.

While their Musulumba fellows were slow to invest in agriculture, Mazulu senior men rapidly appropriated and exploited the good soils available to them, which they were equipped to cultivate.

New economic relationships 197

Younger men also had an immediate interest in equipping themselves as farmers. Many entered the fishing industry developing on Lake Kariba as a quick source of cash for this and other purposes. Twelve Mazulu men became fishermen, while only two Musulumba men diverted into fishing from wage labour. When fishing profits fell in the mid 1960s, the Mazulu fishermen either turned to agriculture or to the towns which provided them with an alternative means of acquiring the capital for farming. Musulumba, in the absence of a sufficient supply of tobacco soils, was unable to find a cash crop which might have reconciled the older men to their new site. Those too old to find employment chose instead to return to Old Chipepo once the government ban on return movement was lifted, taking some of their younger kinsmen with them. Young men moved between Lusitu and Old Chipepo in response to job opportunities in one area or the other. As Mazulu developed town foci, so did Musulumba develop an alternative focus in Old Chipepo where its people visited, settled down, and felt at home. Mazulu had the agricultural resources to hold its people, even though they spent part of their time in the towns, and investment in the village economy was accepted as desirable by town workers. Musulumba lacked this resource. As a result, over the years Musulumba has lost more residents than has Mazulu. At the same

Table 1

1972 residence of members of Mazulu and Musulumba adult samples

	MAZULU		MUSULUMBA	
Current residence	*Men*	*Women*	*Men*	*Women*
Village	30	58	54	54
Matongo[1]	0	0	16	28
Elsewhere in Gwembe District[2]	13	26	2	22
Lusaka	8[3]	4	2	1
Kafue	5	4	3	5
Other line of rail towns and cities	1	0	3	3
Other	0	2	6	9
Totals	57	94	86	122

[1] *Matongo* is the term used for an abandoned village site and here is used to refer specifically to the neighbourhood from which people were resettled, which is current Lusitu usage. Mazulu now has no *matongo* in Old Chipepo since all villages in the neighbourhood were resettled in Lusitu and all the area once exploited by the neighbourhood is now under Lake Kariba.

[2] The discrepancy between men and women is largely explicable in terms of virilocal residence after marriage.

[3] This figure plays down the importance of Lusaka for Mazulu sample since it omits 7 males who left for the town before their nineteenth birthday. Today at least three of these still consider themselves as Mazulu people and are so considered by resident villagers.

198 *Special Studies*

time it has attracted a larger number of immigrants who share with its men an interest in employment and settle for a short time in the village to exploit the local opportunities.

Table 1 shows the 1972 residence of members of Mazulu and Musulumba adult samples. If people in town or elsewhere in Gwembe continue to maintain a house or send personal belongings to the village for safe-keeping, they are counted as members of the village. The adult sample includes all adults resident in the two villages at the time of the original 1956–7 census, any immigrant adults who have lived in the villages for one year or more since 1956–7, and any children who have reached the apparent age of eighteen and lived at least one year as an adult in either village since 1956–7. The table also reflects the differential ability of the two villages to hold their members since those in the Musulumba sample who were resident outside the village are no longer considered Musulumba people. In contrast only six of the Mazulu sample no longer consider themselves Mazulu people.

CASH CROPS AND CITY JOBS: THE MAZULU ADAPTATION

Since 1957 a systematic attempt has been made to keep in contact with all adult males who have lived in Mazulu for at least one year. The large majority have been re-interviewed at several year intervals irrespective of their current residence. The total number in the sample was 23 in 1957; today it is 57.

Fifty-one of these we consider to be Mazulu people, even though twenty-one currently live outside the village. They are so defined simply because they still consider Mazulu their home. Three-fourths of married men maintain liveable houses within the village and only one has no house site at all. As with village residents, most houses owned by absentees are made from sun-dried brick. Increasingly they are furnished with iron beds sent from the line of rail even though the owner sleeps on the ground or on a makeshift bed at his place of work. On visits to Lusaka and Kafue, Scudder is invariably asked to transport a wide range of materials to the village including timber, cement and door frames, 44 gallon water drums, iron beds and mattresses, cupboards, tables and chairs.

The sample has more than doubled over fifteen years primarily because of Mazulu's growth from a village of less than 150 people to one of over 300. Augmented by immigration, this growth is primarily due to Mazulu's favourable agricultural position relative to other Gwembe villages. In contrast to Musulumba, a large

New economic relationships 199

majority of Mazulu residents are farmers. Six of the twenty-nine married resident men grow cotton as a cash-crop, while the principal source of cash for others comes from such agricultural sources as the sale of brewing sorghum, tobacco, livestock and scotch-cart rental (see Table 2).

In part because Mazulu has better land and more livestock than Musulumba, there has been less turnover in membership. Within the adult sample only six men no longer consider themselves Mazulu people. They fall into three general categories. The first consists of three older men who have moved to neighbouring villages with roughly equivalent agricultural resources. Two were not born in Mazulu but rather settled temporarily with Mazulu kin between 1967 and 1971. Though born locally, the third moved with his family several years after relocation because of intra-village tensions.

The second category consists of young transients who use Mazulu as a temporary convenience while trying to better themselves. Of the young men in this category only one was old enough to fall into our adult sample. Like the majority of his fellows he came to the village for educational purposes—so that he could attend the local Upper Primary School after exhausting educational opportunities near his own village. Today he is attending secondary school in Lusaka as a night student. The third category consists of two young men who were born in the village but who now consider themselves mobile Zambians. One has received his Form V certificate and teaches in a Gwembe primary school. The other, though only educated through Form II, has recently returned to Zambia after completing a nine month course in England. While the emigrants in category one retain the town and country orientation described in this paper, those in the second two categories are attempting to pioneer new life styles. Typically primary or secondary school leavers, they no longer see the village as an acceptable locale in which to live and work. Upwardly mobile, their preferred life style is that of urban middle class Zambians. While their departure has had little influence on the village itself, this situation could change rapidly should a majority of future school leavers attempt to follow their lead.

In spite of its favourable agricultural resources, Mazulu is not just another rural village. Rather it is part of a much wider system which includes all of Southern Province and the line of rail as far north as Lusaka. Within this area there is a steadily increasing mobility between four principal foci. These are Mazulu itself, the District (Gwembe) of which Mazulu is a part, Kafue (which the government is developing as an industrial centre), and Lusaka (see Figure 1).

Following relocation, Mazulu was rebuilt close to the Kariba Access Road with vastly improved communication with the outside world. When the local school adjourns, those Grade 6 and 7 school boys who have the money leave for the towns to visit and assist kin with small urban businesses. Whereas elderly women prior to relocation frequently had never seen a train or ridden in a car, now they travel to Lusaka by bus and taxi to visit married daughters and other kin. As for young men, today they elope to the cities with their wives whereas formerly the pattern was for single men to seek urban employment as a means of obtaining marriage payments while their usually pregnant wives remained at home.

Most Mazulu people irrespective of residence move freely back and forth between the village and the urbanized portions of the line

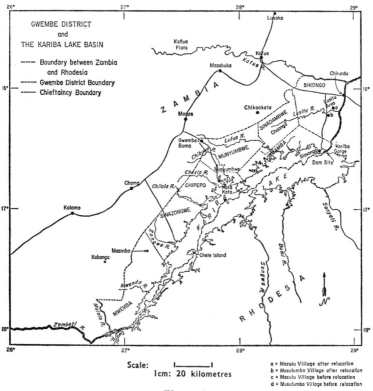

Figure 1

New economic relationships 201

of rail. Although young wives prefer to live in town where conveniently sited tap water, charcoal and maize meal cut their labour load immensely and make life far less tedious, they regularly return to the village. All go back to have their first baby at their mother's house and most go back to cultivate village gardens during the rainy season. While some young wives will be found living in towns during the rains, there is no clear cut distinction between those who return to cultivate and those who do not. Rather the wife who cultivates a small maize garden outside a Lusaka township one year, returns to the village to cultivate the next. As for those six older men who have chosen to cash crop cotton, they too are at home in town. Though the government marketing organization (NAMBOARD) has a depot within two miles of the village, these cotton-growers obtain empty bales direct from the Lusaka ginnery. Then they arrange with a Lusaka trucker to carry their harvest to the ginnery, hence halving their transportation and service charges. Subsequently they travel to town to pick up their earnings. Dressed in their town clothes, some of these men are indistinguishable from government civil servants.

Though Mazulu people are at home within a town and country context, they are caught up within a much wider interaction field with all its concomitant tensions. Life *is* more difficult than before resettlement; people *do* have to choose between a wider range of alternatives. Recently we brought one village woman in her late thirties to Lusaka to visit kin. She sought a ride because of her fear of buses—because she had been in a bus accident that resulted in two deaths. Another Mazulu woman was struck and killed by a car while crossing a street en route to Lusaka's General Hospital to visit her ailing mother. As for other types of modern trauma, those too impinge upon the sample. One constant reminder is a man who sustained permanent injury when systematically beaten while on the job as a Lusaka night watchman. The only other Mazulu man to have worked as a watchman lost his job when the furniture factory which he was guarding burnt down. Though both men now farm in the village, they still travel to Lusaka several times a year to buy supplies for the construction of sieves that they make for sale within the Lusitu, and, in the case of the injured man, to seek therapy at the hospital and draw monthly compensation payments.

Though the increasing complexity of life has a number of interesting implications, the main purpose of this section is to stress the commonality of belief and behaviour shared by the people of Mazulu irrespective of residence. For them there is no rural-urban

Special Studies

continuum, nor do sample members behave differently when living in town as opposed to when living in the village. Rather town and country are part of a single habitat in which the same mechanisms for coping are used.

While the older men, without exception, live in the village today, there are few differences between the young marrieds who live in town and those who live in the village. Young married men tend to disdain the cult of the ancestral shades by refusing to join beer-pouring rituals in the homes of participating kin. But in most cases this aloofness is a temporary product of primary school emulation of teacher disdain for village life. When a crisis occurs, such as the illness of one's wife or wives, or of one's children, most young men find themselves caught up in the same system of diagnosis and treatment that has characterized the Gwembe Tonga for generations. While they also take their children to free Government services and to the private doctor, this behaviour is no different from that of village elders who seek out government clinics and hospitals.

While these examples show that both villager and townsman have widened the range of ways for dealing with misfortune in a similar fashion, they also illustrate the increased complexity of decision-making that follows incorporation within a wider frame of reference. With more alternatives from which to choose, stress presumably increases in times of crisis since there is no easy way to select between different forms of treatment. Certainly there are ailments which people categorize as best treated in the village as opposed to the hospital. We suspect, however, that these are in the minority. Rather in most cases, both townsmen and villagers cover their bets by trying the whole range of available treatments. The one that works is the one followed most immediately by a cure.

Another factor breaking down village isolation and linking Mazulu to Lusaka and the line of rail as part of a single system with both rural and urban foci is occupational specialization. Before the Kariba resettlement, everyone farmed, the goal of each adult male being to found and support his own independent homestead. Farming was supplemented by labour migration. While few women and children joined their male kin at that time, nonetheless a form of pre-socialization towards urban life had already begun since women and children were constantly in contact with men who had returned recently from town.

Though the majority of Mazulu people still farm to some extent, they can be divided into two broad categories—those who have intensified cash cropping and those who have not. In addition there are those such as school leavers who have left farming entirely or,

New economic relationships 203

like one fisherman, relegated it to secondary importance. Unlike Musulumba, Mazulu had access to primary school education before relocation. This is one reason why today Mazulu has more than double the number of Grade 7 students. Like their predecessors, some of these will become teachers, skilled and semi-skilled artisans, and clerks and small businessmen. Few will choose voluntarily to remain in Mazulu although most can be expected to remain in close contact with the village. (See Table 2).

In spite of increasing specialization, there is little clearcut distinction between those in rural as opposed to urban occupations. Consider, for example, small traders and hawkers. Some prefer to live in the village where they buy up fish, chickens, smallstock and cattle for retailing elsewhere. Though recently their sales have been local this is largely a response to the presence of a large labour force connected with the tarring of the Kariba Access Road. Several years ago, when there was less cash and fewer buyers for local produce, village-based traders took the bus to Lusaka to sell chickens in lots of 15 and more. They are equally familiar with trading in the country and in the town. On a District scale, the same applies to the better Lake Kariba fishermen. Because of an unsatisfactory local marketing system, these men are largely fishermen-traders who dry their product and then journey to the plateau to sell it there. Such was not always the case; rather their current practice is a careful evaluation of the relative merits of local versus line of rail marketing. In contrast to the situation in 1962 when the largest profit fell to the full-time fisherman who sold his fish fresh at the lake side, today the balance has shifted to those who carefully dry their product and then market it themselves in urban centres.

If we compare the behaviour of these rural based people with their urban counterparts, differences are hard to perceive. Currently a number of small-scale Mazulu businessmen make a good income as produce hawkers on the streets of Lusaka. Some work alone; others periodically employ fellow villagers including school-boys on vacation. Like other urban residents, those who are married almost all have substantial rectangular houses of sun-dried brick in the village which they furnish with iron bedsteads and other urban purchases. Indeed, if we take the time factor into account, the same man often alternates between rural and urban occupations.

The town and country network of Mazulu people is in flux and the tendency of an increasing proportion of new family units to spend more time in town has significant implications. This is especially true of those few who plan to build or purchase substantial urban houses. While contemporary house owners continue to visit

204 *Special Studies*

the village, and to take in country kin during their Lusaka visits, their children are being reared in the city. It is unlikely that this generation, on reaching adulthood, will maintain close contact with their parents' village, or any other village for that matter.

RURAL WAGE LABOUR AND SUBSISTENCE AGRICULTURE: THE MUSULUMBA ADAPTATION

Musulumba men think of themselves as construction workers responsible for most of the visible improvements in Lusitu. 'We built that' is a common theme. Originally they worked on Lusitu Township and when that was built they moved on. A few found jobs in the services the Township provided. The one shopkeeper re-established himself as a shopkeeper in the Township and began to branch out into other businesses. The rest who were young enough got construction jobs elsewhere, either in Lusitu or in nearby areas from which they could visit their homes at weekends. Characteristically as they have moved from job to job, they have gone as individuals rather than as an organized gang. As one project has ended, another has become available, until Musulumba men assume that this is the natural order of things. They also expect rural wages to be comparable to or better than wages they could earn in town. In August 1972 local wages, with overtime, had median and modal ranges between K31 and K40, with a total range from K30 to K100.[3] Since the men lived at home, paid no rent, and ate from fields planted by themselves and their wives, the real value of their wages was higher than it would have been in town. They were also able to increase their incomes by other transactions such as the sale of beer and agricultural produce.

Children and women also share in the Musulumba adaptation. Youngsters begin to experiment with wage labour early in life as house servants for construction workers, shopkeepers and others employed about Lusitu Township. Children also sell produce. Women are rarely employed for wages but they profit from the presence of immigrant workers and the monthly wages of local men through the sale of beer and produce. Wives of employed men also expect to receive a monthly allowance, which currently appears to be of the order of K12, of which K2 are to be spent on relish. The rest is for the woman's clothing or other wants. The husband expects to provide clothing and blankets for the children, who have earned their reward by working in the fields, herding stock, and preparing and carrying his meals. The balance belongs to him to spend as he

[3] In 1972 the Kwacha was worth approximately 60p or $1.40.

New economic relationships

sees fit. As in town, most men appear to use a good part of their earnings for beer, but they also invest in stock and marriage payments in the old village fashion. In Musulumba at least very little is spent on improved housing and comparatively little is spent on purchasing agricultural equipment, though some money may be spent on the hire of ploughing.

Table 2 is an indication of how Musulumba and Mazulu men spend their incomes. Each of those resident in 1972 was asked if he had certain items. The importance of the bicycle, which allows men to move to and from work easily, is apparent, as well as the willingness to invest in personal comfort shown by the number who claim to have purchased one or more metal beds. The greater investment of Mazulu men in agriculture is also evident.

Table 2

Major items of property reported by Musulumba and Mazulu men

Item	Number of men claiming to own one or more	
	Musulumba (44 men)	*Mazulu (43 men)*[1]
Metal bed	21	31
Plough	17	23
Bicycle	15 (2 broken)	24
Wireless	4 (1 broken)	8
Sewing machine	2	0
Cultivator	1	4
Harrow	1	1
Scotch cart	1	3
Lorry	1	0

[1] Unlike Musulumba, the Mazulu sample includes both resident and non-resident married men.

Life in Musulumba, in the dry season at least, is subject to rhythms stemming from wage-work. Some workers said they would leave the job for the period of intensive cultivation when most help is needed in the fields. Work histories of men seemed to reflect this pattern of seasonal employment and underscored the continued importance of subsistence agriculture. But during much of the year, the day is dominated by the work routine of men who leave early in the morning for the job, expect to have food carried to them at the noon break, and return at a regular time each evening if they do not stop at the beerhall or a beer drink en route. The week is dominated by its division into working days and weekend. Musulumba women, like most Gwembe women, get much of their cash income through the sale of beer. Beer is usually available every day in the week, but they brew in largest quantities for Saturday and Sunday when workers feel free to drink deeply and are most apt

206   *Special Studies*

to spend their money. The month is dominated by the magic 'Thirty', the day on which men are paid. Then they settle their debts, give wives their allowance, buy clothing for their children, and themselves drink heavily and sing loudly.

In agricultural villages, families expect to make major expenditures after the sale of crops. In the old days of labour migration, it was the return of the migrant which brought an influx of goods and an occasion for display. The local wage régime alters rhythms of expenditure and receipts to one that resembles that of the town. It also sets a standard of consumption difficult for families of unemployed men to contemplate. It has become more difficult to be 'poor' in a village such as Musulumba when the families of workers have so many occasions to be 'rich'.

Only two Musulumba men cultivate on anything like the scale common in Mazulu or in other nearby villages which have concentrated on cash crops. Elders who are able to grow and sell tobacco or deal in stock may handle at any one time as much cash as the wage workers in the village, but the wage workers look forward to as much again the next month and have yearly incomes well above that of the vast majority of elders, most of whom take in less than K100 per year. Table 3 shows the source of cash income for Musulumba and Mazulu men. It indicates how heavily the earnings of young men dominate the scene at Musulumba, and in contrast to

Table 3

Sources of cash income of Musulumba and Mazulu men
Mazulu figures (for married residents only) shown in brackets.
Marriage payments, beer, and minor items omitted

Income source	Men born before 1938		Men born in 1938 or later	
Wage labour	3	(0)	11	(3)
Temporarily unemployed	1	(0)	2	(0)
Wage labour and stock sales	1	(0)	4	(1)
Wage labour and sale of produce other than stock	0	(0)	1	(0)
Wage labour, stock sales, and sale of other produce	3	(4)	0	(1)
Business plus stock sales plus sales other produce	1	(1)	0	(0)
Business and other produce	0	(1)	0	(0)
Stock sales and sale of other produce	5	(7)	0	(1)
Stock sales only	5	(2)	1[1]	(0)
Sale of other produce only	5	(3)	0	(0)
No source (other than gifts, sale of beer, marriage payments)	4	(3)	5[2]	(0)
Other	0	(1)	0	(1)

[1] Includes one young man who sold chickens as his only source of cash.

[2] Includes school boys supported by parents and young men working for kin who were not paid a wage.

New economic relationships 207

the Mazulu situation, how little most Musulumba men have to expect once they are no longer able to find employment.

Musulumba people have acquired town standards of expenditure without visiting the town. Unlike the people of Mazulu, they rarely visit the towns of the railway. Only sixteen of the forty-six men asked about visiting the towns replied that they had been to town in 1972, as opposed to eighteen of twenty-nine Mazulu men who are married residents. Only seventeen out of forty-six Musulumba men had been to town the year before. Only nine of fifty-seven Musulumba women, as opposed to sixteen of sixty-three resident Mazulu women, had been to town in 1972, and only fifteen out of sixty Musulumba women had been to town in 1971 versus 22 out of 63 in the Mazulu case. Mazulu people typically visit Lusaka and deliberately choose to visit the towns. Musulumba people are most likely to reach a town when they pass through one of the railway townships en route to Old Chipepo. Though Musulumba people are convinced that prices are lower and quality higher in shops in Lusaka and Kafue, they do not use the convenient bus service to enable them to do their shopping in town. Only four persons, including the shop keeper, claimed to shop in the city; the rest rely upon local shops.

This does not mean that Musulumba people are less subject to town standards than Mazulu people. Urban standards are transmitted to them by intermediaries who are regarded as exemplars of town life. School teachers and other elite employed locally, as well as migrants returning to other villages from town, are watched and emulated. Villagers expect local shops to carry stocks which enable them to be in fashion. Their clothing is therefore indistinguishable in pattern, colours, and cut from that worn by townsmen, and Musulumba taste in this respect is no less sophisticated than that of Mazulu. Nor has Musulumba been laggard in acquiring a taste for new kinds of food, and its women, like those of Mazulu, depend on shops for supplies. More and more village diet approximates to that of the town: this is what people want, and they expect somehow to find the money that makes it possible.

Only in its standard of housing does Musulumba lag behind Mazulu. This is not due to a lack of familiarity with town styles. Its men helped to build the improved housing occupied by school teachers and other élite employed nearby. Both men and women have examples of such housing available in the immediate vicinity of the village. Nevertheless in 1972, only one family, which had recently joined the village, occupied a house with a metal roof and cement-plastered walls. Most families occupy old style pole and

Special Studies

dagga huts; only a few have built in sun-dried brick as is now the common practice at Mazulu. Men who might want better housing are either fully employed and have neither time nor energy to build as they would like, or they are reluctant to invest in improvements that would hold them permanently to one site.

Few older Musulumba men and women have any schooling, and villagers for the most part have been reluctant to keep their children in school. Two young men who completed Form V in 1970 have left the village for employment elsewhere in Zambia and are not expected to return. The only others from the village to reach secondary school were three young men still in Forms I and II in 1972. Few children expected to move past primary school and many dropped out after a year or two. Nevertheless, despite the differences in appreciation of the value of schooling, Musulumba shares much the same view of the nature of human ills as Mazulu and follows much the same procedures in dealing with them. In both villages, people regard it as one of the responsibilities of Government to ensure that they have medical facilities readily available to them. From both people go to hospital and they have become equally sophisticated about the merits of the various hospitals available to them. In both villages, moreover, people make use of diviners, herbalists, and local medicines, and they continue to make the annual offerings to the shades of the dead to ensure good health and prosperity.

Although Musulumba villagers seem to shun the towns, they are no more parochial in their outlook than Mazulu villagers. They are accustomed to mixing with strangers who come to work in Lusitu. They trade with them, shop with them, work with them, visit with them, drink with them, quarrel with them, and marry them. Their children attend school together. They may find themselves in the same ward at the Lusitu Dispensary. Interaction with the immigrants on their own ground, together with their appreciation of the ease of movement by bus and taxi, enables them to greet with equanimity the prospect that they or their children might live elsewhere. In 1956–7, Musulumba villagers, like other Gwembe villagers, were reluctant to allow their daughters to marry men who would take them more than one neighbourhood away. By 1972, even marriages with immigrant workers who would take the women to other parts of Zambia apparently aroused little concern. Elderly women, who have never before visited a town, are prepared to set forth on a visit to kin in Old Chipepo, though it may mean that they must take a bus, transfer to a train, transfer to another bus, and have long intervals of waiting at the transfer points.

New economic relationships 209

Familiarity with strangers on their own ground predisposes Musulumba people to believe that they can cope with comparable people wherever they may find them. Though the majority of them are unwilling to face the violence they believe to be endemic to urban life, if they are willing to risk the town, then they see no special advantage in seeking out kin or fellow villagers to give them protection. Unlike the Mazulu villagers who move between their town foci and the village, Musulumba villagers who have moved to the railway line are scattered here and there, one family to a town, each making its own way (see Table 1).

Musulumba then has become accustomed to many of the amenities of the town and has expectations of life comparable to those of the town dweller. It is dependent, like the town, upon a market for labour and continued finance for industrial development. This makes its people vulnerable in two respects: local employment may not always be available, and the men who offer themselves for employment grow old and have no retirement pensions. Subsistence agriculture with sale of minor amounts of produce, which they now combine with wage labour, offers them no alternative economic base. Government programmes to develop agriculture and thereby encourage people to remain on the land do not interest them. Fewer than at Mazulu have applied for government loans for agricultural purposes or shown any interest in the new cash crops such as cotton or brewing sorghum. While some Mazulu men make substantial sums from cotton, only one Musulumba man has grown cotton and that on a small scale. Most of his fellows are interested in agricultural programmes only if these call for the recruitment of labourers at wages comparable to those they are now accustomed to receive on construction projects. Mazulu villagers with their alternation between town and country are more open to agricultural extension work and government assistance in agriculture since its people see rural development as based on cash cropping as well as wage labour. They are therefore developing some long-term agricultural investments that provide support in old age.

Musulumba men have a wasting asset in their labour. Men in employment have little opportunity to secure their future since the only good investment open to them, which does not demand a further heavy investment of labour, is in stock. This, however, is hazardous at Musulumba, and more so than at Mazulu. Twice since the 1958 resettlement, men have lost heavily through the death of cattle infected with trypanosomiasis. Every few years large numbers of goats and chickens die in an epidemic. In 1972, all chickens in Musulumba and Mazulu were wiped out by Newcastle's Disease.

210 *Special Studies*

A few men can look forward to the inheritance or gift of tobacco land, but only a little land available to Musulumba is suitable for tobacco. Men can expand into cotton or other cash crops only by a large-scale clearance of new land. Such clearance competes with wage labour, and men will probably contemplate it only when they can no longer find employment at what they regard as reasonable wages; for they now prefer the regular rhythm of the monthly wage to the old uncertainties of the agricultural year. Indeed, given the frequent bad harvests of Gwembe, when grain has to be purchased to ward off famine, it is not surprising that they spend so little time developing a farm against the future.

Sons for the most part have followed their fathers into rough labour, attracted by the wages which reward physical strength rather than school attainments. Musulumba has lost some of its younger people, but only a very few have gone because they have finished primary school and have ambitions beyond the village. In this again, Musulumba differs from Mazulu, whose boys have chosen school to agricultural work and then gone on to the towns from which now some at least will not return. They form a bridge over which more and more of their younger kinsmen are likely to pass as they move out from the rural area. Musulumba has not established its bridgeheads in the towns or given its children the opportunity to try town life and find it to their liking.

Local wage labour attracts and then traps Musulumba youngsters in the rural area and encourages them to continue the style of life Musulumba began to develop with resettlement: one based on wage work for men supplemented by subsistence agriculture largely carried on by women and children.

THE RURAL-URBAN FLOW OF
LANGUAGE, BELIEF, AND
EDUCATIONAL OPPORTUNITY

Continuity and change in Kiganda religion in urban and peri-urban Kampala[1]

PETER RIGBY and FRED D. LULE

The study of traditional religious beliefs and practices, and developments of them, in modern African urban areas has been largely ignored in the considerable number of otherwise excellent and comprehensive monographs on African cities. This is now being rectified to some extent as urban studies in Africa shift back from a straightforward emphasis upon quantitative survey-type studies which predominated in the decade 1950–60 (see Mitchell 1966: 39–43), to more sophisticated combinations of intensive and survey methods.

The role of the 'world religions' in urban social, political, and economic processes has always received attention, but statements upon traditional religious beliefs in African towns are often at best very brief, and at worst highly impressionistic. Thus Banton, in his study of Freetown, devotes a whole chapter to 'Tribal Groups and Religious Alignments' (1957: 121–41), which tells us something of the role of Islam in urban social structure; but he confines his remarks on traditional religious beliefs mainly to the difficulties of collecting sufficient reliable data on this topic. The relative importance in Freetown of traditional religious beliefs and practices, including 'magic' and 'witchcraft', are recognized, but little systematic information is given on them.

Such difficulties do indeed beset the student of 'traditional' religion in urban Africa. The study upon which this paper is based was a specific attempt to overcome these problems and penetrate an area of African urban life which has long been recognized as critically important.[2]

---

[1] The term *Kiganda* denotes custom or the form and 'style' of the culture of the Baganda people. I have retained the prefix *Ki-* here, despite international usage, since the concept *Kiganda* lies at the very heart of the material presented here.

[2] See Rigby and Lule 1971; a short monograph is in preparation on aspects of traditional Kiganda religion, divination, and healing in and around the city of Kampala.

214 *Special Studies*

A few West African scholars have concentrated their studies upon this topic, demonstrating clearly that the methodological problems stated by Banton can be overcome. For example, Fiawoo (1959a, 1959b, 1961) contributes a great deal to our understanding of urban African religion.

The analysis of traditional African religions in towns cannot easily be separated from a consideration of attitudes to disease, psychiatric disturbances, and their cure; a large proportion of urban religious beliefs and practices with strongly traditional elements are concerned with healing and the alleviation of personal crises in the lives of African townsmen. The urban emphasis is upon those aspects of traditional African religion which have been called the 'rituals of affliction' (cf. Turner 1969). Such studies as Field's *The Search for Security* (1960), while not concerned primarily with urban problems, illustrate the dynamic aspects of traditional religions, and their considerable degree of flexibility and adaptability to new structural situations, including the urban. The work of Jahoda (e.g. 1966, 1969, 1970) also provides a number of important insights on the analytical problems encountered in the study of African religions in a changing society, as does that of Maclean (1965, 1966, 1969, 1971).

From the point of view of comparative religion, studies such as that of Parrinder (1953) are useful for comparative material. Little (1965: 38), drawing mainly upon Fiawoo, sums up the West African material on what he calls 'syncretist cults' which:

> . . . attract many devotees, largely because they claim to cure and protect against sickness of both natural and supernatural causation. Illness may sometimes be traced to the displeasure of the lineal ancestors, and in this case the appropriate propitiatory rites pacify the spiritual agents and restore the patient to health. . . . (The cult) also claims to offer complete protection against jealous rivals and the machination of bad spirits. . . .

Much of this could apply, *mutatis mutandis*, to the situation of traditional Kiganda religion in the city of Kampala and also, for example, to traditional religion in the city of Kinshasa (La Fontaine, 1970). After an excellent description of the role of Christianity, Islam, and the syncretistic Kimbanguist religious movement, La Fontaine also discusses the relevance of traditional religious beliefs and rituals. Apart from some of the *rites de passage* which can still be carried out in the urban milieu, she also emphasizes the importance of the curative and protective aspects of traditional religious observance in Kinshasa. She describes, for instance, a woman diviner ('practitioner of magic') who cures illness and provides fertility medicines. She charges a fee of nearly Shs 100/-, she has a reputa-

Continuity and change in Kiganda religion

tion for success, 'and has cured the wife of a member of Parliament' (La Fontaine 1970: 182). There are others 'who specialize in good-luck charms and magic for ensuring success in work, financial enterprise, or love affairs'.

But none of these writers proceed beyond a basically descriptive level; there is little attempt at any kind of analysis, even of an elementary structural kind. It often seems that merely to label such religious developments as 'syncretistic' is enough.[3] In this paper I try to go beyond this; although effectively to do so must await the fuller analysis in our forthcoming book.

I

In their pioneering study of Kampala, Southall and Gutkind (1957) mention the importance of traditional, particularly Kiganda, religion in the lives of many Kampala townsmen, even for the non-Baganda. But again, they do not provide any detailed analysis of the context of such beliefs and their associated rituals. Although the great majority of the people included in their survey claimed affiliation to one or other of the Christian denominations or Islam,[4] this did not mean that these people did not take part in 'traditional' religious activities. The authors show clearly that, in their attitudes to sickness and success, a large number of urban dwellers have a strong commitment to traditional religion and the 'efficacy' of its symbolic manipulation (Southall and Gutkind 1957: 110–12).[5] They also describe (1957: 149 fn. 2) the widespread belief in the power of the *mayembe* ('speaking horns'); an element of traditional belief whose importance is amply demonstrated in what follows.

This statement of the importance of traditional belief in Kampala, which is situated in the heart of Buganda, is in contrast with much of what has been said about religious change in Buganda as a whole. Because of the rapid adoption of Christianity and Islam in Buganda, and their involvement in the political system and political change, it has often been assumed that traditional Kiganda religion virtually disappeared. Certainly the Christian missionaries and their converts spared no pains to destroy what they considered, and still often

[3] Although we have used the term elsewhere (see Rigby and Lule, 1971), I would no longer apply it to the Kiganda case. Professor T. O. Ranger, in a comment on the paper cited, has pointed out to us the possible dangers of using the concept of syncretism in analysing such religious phenomena.

[4] Only 5 per cent of respondents in Kisenyi classified themselves as 'pagan' and only 6 per cent in Mulago (Southall and Gutkind 1957: 29, 110), the two areas described in this study.

[5] cf. Levi-Strauss 1963: *passim.*

H

216 *Special Studies*

consider, to be 'heathen superstitution'. Welbourn states (1965: 42):

> The Christian leaders of the new Buganda believed by 1900 that they had suppressed the old gods; but as late as 1916 the *Omulamuzi* (Chief Justice) circulated to chiefs a memorandum directing them to take more severe measures to 'suppress *lubaale* worship[6] and witchcraft'.

Insofar as Kiganda religion was a 'state religion', this interpretation is partly correct. In fact, Apter links directly the diminution in importance of traditional religion in the public domain with changes in the political structure of Buganda (1961: 106):

> The shift both to instrumental values and to hierarchical authority would have left a structural lacuna had not the role of the Kabaka (King) emerged sharply and strongly as central in the Kiganda system. The vacuum left by the shift away from consummatory values brought about the quick demise of the traditional religious system and the pervasive spread of Christianity....

Welbourn (1965: 42–6) also describes admirably the 'resurgence' of traditional religion in Buganda, upon the deportation of the Kabaka in 1953, implying that traditional religion had been in abeyance. This resurgence applies only to the public and political aspects of Kiganda religion; it is the contention of this paper that, as far as the general population of Buganda is concerned, their religion never died, although its practice had to be largely secret at one time.

For the 'man in the street' in Kampala, whether he be Christian or Muslim, traditional religious beliefs and practices have always been a part of his everyday life and 'world view', even if considerably modified in form. There is for the urban dweller a strong continuity of religious belief with the past and with the present rural society of Buganda. In fact it could be maintained that with its removal from the public and political sphere, Kiganda religion has become *more* important to the average individual, especially in the towns. In many ways, Kiganda society and culture are unique in their ability to adapt to new conditions and still retain 'Kigandaness' (see Rigby 1971). Gutkind, although not referring specifically to religion, puts this point succinctly in his historical study of the *Kibuga*, the 'traditional' part of the city of Kampala, when he says (1963: 258):

> No doubt Africans *are* townsmen the moment they enter a *modern* urban setting. But in other situations, such as in Buganda, where the

[6] *Lubaale* are the most important hero-gods amongst the large variety of supernatural beings and spirits of Kiganda religion (see below).

Continuity and change in Kiganda religion 217

force of tradition is still strong . . . even the townsman continues to live and work in many respects in the context of a tribal rather than an urban setting.

This rather lengthy introduction has been necessary to indicate that, however transformed it may be, the Kiganda religion which is contemporarily of such importance in the lives of many Kampala townsmen, it is not a 'resurgence'. It has been a continual feature of the growth of urban society, and forms one of the many strong bonds which still link Kampala townsmen to their traditional past and the rural present. The comparative evidence adduced shows that this general picture is probably true of many African cities, whatever the formal religious affiliations of their inhabitants may be.

I I

A good deal has been written about the formal features of traditional Kiganda religion (e.g. Kagwa 1901, 1905: 209–37 *et passim* 1908; Roscoe 1911: 271–364; Nsimbi 1956: 119–48 *et passim*; Mair 1934: 223–65 *et passim*; Gorju 1920; Welbourn 1962; and many others). But it is necessary to give a brief outline to make intelligible what follows.

In traditional Kiganda belief, the most important spiritual entities are the *lubaale* and *misambwa*. Some are clearly one or the other; many are ambiguous in status (cf. Welbourn 1962: 174–5). All the gods of Buganda have anthropomorphic attributes, including Katonda, the 'Creator God', whose name is taken to translate the Christian God. They may, however, manifest themselves in non-human ways and forms. For example, Ggulu, the Sky-God, can also be *Ggulu*, the 'power of the heavens', The two manifestations are different, but related. They are two *significata* of the same symbol.

For our present purposes, it is the *lubaale* who are the most important. They are both gods and mythical heroes; all *lubaale* are heroes of the past, but not all mythical heroes are *lubaale*. The founder of the Buganda Kingdom, Kintu, is not a *lubaale*, although all the kings (*basekabaka*) of Buganda are said to be descended from him.

Only about one quarter or one third of the seventy-three *lubaale* listed by Kagwa (1905: 209–28) are generally known, and the average modern townsman seldom knows the names of more than a dozen or so. All *lubaale* are divided into 'those of the lake' (*abalunnyanja*) and the Ssese islands (*abasese*), and 'those of the dry land' (*abalukalu*), sometimes referred to as 'the princes'

218 *Special Studies*

(*abalangira*). *Lubaale* Mukasa of the lake, for example, is the senior *lubaale* who is shown greater respect than all the others (*Naye lubaale oyo Mukasa yali wakitiibwa okusingako kubalubaale banne abalala*, Kagwa 1905: 213). His great shrine (*ekiggwa*) is on Bubembe island, Ssese.[7] *Lubaale* Wanga who 'fixed' the earth and the sky, the sun and the moon in their places (cf. Nsimbi 1956: 123–4), was the son of Bukulu who came to the mainland with Kintu. Muwanga who vies for place as the greatest *lubaale*, was the son of Wanga, and his great shrine is at Kiwanga in Kyaggwe county. Other famous *lubaale* are Musisi ('earthquake'), Wannema ('the lame'), Musoke ('rainbow'), Kibuka ('War'), Ndawula ('smallpox'), and several female ones such as Nagaddya, Nalwoga, and Nanziri. Rather confusingly, these days, many of these *lubaale* appear as *mayembe* ('speaking horns').

Traditionally, only a few of the many *lubaale* were nationally recognized and had shrines of political importance. The priests of their shrines were sometimes appointed by the king, although the mediumship was often hereditary. In all probability, the vast number of lesser *lubaale* were relevant only to divination (*okulagula*) in the everyday lives of ordinary people in their local areas. At any rate, that a chief function of the *lubaale* was to divine through possession (*okusamira*) is clearly established, and this is still true of the urban context.

The *misambwa* (singular *musambwa*), on the other hand, are practically irrelevant to the practice of Kiganda religion in the urban areas. *Misambwa* are associated with the natural features of Buganda, such as hills, trees, rivers, animals, reptiles, clumps of forest, and so on. Although many urban dwellers know stories about various places in Buganda associated with *misambwa*, and some of them are in or near present-day Kampala, they hardly ever appear in contemporary Kiganda ritual. If they do, it is usually through a confusion of categories; as I have stated, the dividing line between them and *lubaale* is by no means clear. *Misambwa* are conceived of as having been people once, and they are thought to be able to cure disease as well. Some were closely associated with kin groups or clan sections. (See Nsimbi 1956: 119; Welbourn 1962: 175). Their association with place and kin groups diminishes their significance in the urban areas.

A category of spirits which have perhaps assumed in the urban context greater importance than they had before are the *mayembe*

---

[7] For some reason, the correct statement by Kagwa (1905: 212) on the location of Mukasa's shrine is changed to Bukasa in Kalibala's translation (1934: 114).

Continuity and change in Kiganda religion 219

(singular, *jjembe*). There are some *mayembe* which were of national importance (Kagwa 1905: 234), and again, there is frequently a considerable vagueness about the distinction between them and the *lubaale* (cf. Orley 1970: 18, 64; cf. Kagwa 1905: 44). Although *mayembe* literally means 'horns', and some of these spirits are said to reside in cow, rhinoceros, or buffalo horns, or calabashes and pots, they are thought to be highly 'mobile' and play a very important role in modern Kiganda religion, particularly in the context of divination and healing. They are basically of two kinds: clan *mayembe* (*ag'ekika*) which are inherited, and other *mayembe* which can be bought and sold. Most *mayembe* are morally neutral, but they are potentially dangerous. Even if a person turns to them for help, he is always a little afraid of the powers he may be unleashing. And they can be 'sent' to kill, maim, and destroy, whence they are called *mayembe agakifaalu* (cf. Rigby and Lule 1971: 18; Orley 1970: 18; Ssekamwa 1967: 32; etc).

Although there are other categories of spirits, the final one that concerns us here are the *mizimu* (singular, *muzimu*). These are the spirits of the 'recently dead', whose names and graves are remembered. The ghosts of parents, grandparents, and 'father's sister' (*ssenga*) are the most usually identified.

The *mizimu* do not provide the basis for an ancestor cult as they do in some African societies, since the relationships between them and the living are of an entirely different character to those which existed when they were still alive (Mair 1934: 224–9; but cf. Welbourn 1962: 177). In the abstract, the *mizimu* are upholders of clan and kinship solidarity and morality. Welbourn (1965: 177) maintains that the cult of the *mizimu* was more important in the past, and that it was eroded by the increasing centralization of political power and authority at the expense of clan, lineage, and kinship groups. He provides little evidence for this contention. Mair (1934: 225), Richards (1955), and Southwold all seem to agree that the Baganda did *not* have ancestor worship, and this is certainly true today. However much the *mizimu* are theoretically revered by their descendants, they interfere in the world of the living only for ill. This is because any particular intervention by a *muzimu* is only identified *ex post facto*; that is, after a series of unfortunate events among his descendants. The *mizimu* certainly do not now reflect a continuation of lineage relationships with the 'world of the dead', and this fact is entirely consistent with the structure of Kiganda kinship.

At any rate, most Baganda now think of *mizimu* mainly in times of trouble, although children are named for them and they are

220 *Special Studies*

supposed to be present at mourning and inheritance ceremonies. For example, a *muzimu* of a wronged woman may attack a man, his wife, his children, and his home. A diviner with strong *mayembe* can catch the *muzimu*, force it to identify itself through possession of its victim, and then 'tie it up'. A large proportion of the more complex urban ceremonies revolve around such situations.

There are other categories of spirits and their mediums, but I cannot go into detail here. I now turn to the cultural setting of modern, urban, Kiganda religion.

III

If one were to take a map of the area which constitutes the modern City of Kampala,[8] and were to plot upon it every *ssabo* (shrine; plural *amasabo*) used in Kiganda religion and divination, it would be covered by a high density of dots. Some priests and diviners, away from the city where they have large banana gardens, hide their *amasabo* in among the trees. But with increasing frequency, the shrines stand proudly near the dwelling house, sometimes taking up a good deal of room on very small residential plots.

Most *amasabo* present a mixture of traditional Kiganda and modern architecture. They are round, with conical thatch roofs; but instead of the thatch sweeping down to the ground as in the traditional building, it usually rests upon a mud-and-wattle wall about five or six feet high. The entrance to the *ssabo* is sometimes approached through a passageway of reeds, which features in some rituals.

The word *ssabo* has the special connotation of a shrine dedicated to specific *lubaale* who manifest themselves in spirit possession, are dedicated to 'good', socially acceptable, ends, and who are also propitiated by their mediums and clients. In the urban context, however, *ssabo* is also used to describe any room, often rectangular and with a metal roof, that can be completely darkened in preparation for consultation with the *mayembe* horns. *Ssabo* therefore must be distinguished from *ekiggwa*, a shrine of a 'national' *lubaale* such as that of Mukasa on Bubembe island, or a shrine dedicated to clan ancestors and used for divination and propitiation by clan members. Both of those are again different from *ekiggya*, the clan burial tombs in which all Baganda wish to be buried at their own *butaka* (sacred clan land). The tombs of Kings are called *amasiro* (singular: *essiro*), such as that of the last four kings of Buganda at

[8] Greater Kampala, as presently defined, includes urban, periurban, and almost rural, areas. At the 1969 census, it contained 330,700 individuals.

Continuity and change in Kiganda religion   221

Kasubi, three miles from the centre of Kampala. Constant parallels are drawn in urban ritual between the sometimes humble *ssabo* and the tombs of Kings and notables, I have frequently heard the *ssabo* shrine of a diviner being referred to as 'Kasubi'.

The modern, round *ssabo* for the *lubaale* usually has only one entrance, or at the most two. More or less opposite the main entrance is a raised earth platform, covered with animal skins (*amaliba*, singular: *eddiba*) and barkcloth (*embugo*, singular: *olubugo*), called *ekiwu*. The word *ekiwu* usually refers to a sewn carpet of animal skins, normally confined to the palace and houses of politically important people. The King's throne is placed upon *ekiwu* (cf. Lugira 1970: plate 19). Here again, as with the word 'Kasubi', ritual connections are established with the Kingship.[9]

The diviner, or 'doctor priest', usually sits upon the *ekiwu* when in a state of possession; but this is not essential. During the ceremony itself, the *ekiwu* is separated from the rest of the shrine and its congregation by a barrier of spears (*amafumu*) stuck into the earthen floor. The floor of the *ssabo* is covered with lemon-grass (*essubi*), upon which mats (*emikeeka*) and hides are placed. A client or patient is asked to kneel upon a hide or mat when consulting the *lubaale*.

Almost all the contents and architectural features of the *ssabo* have important symbolic connotations. For example, a 'proper' shrine should not have a centre-pole, despite its conical roof. The 'centre ring' of the roof should be supported on four closely-spaced poles, as is the case with the King's shrine at Kasubi. Medicines and ritual objects are then hung from the centre of the roof, symbolizing the various *lubaale* who enter the shrine, protecting it, and transmitting their efficacy to the clients who are enjoined to sit directly under them.

Again, a fire should be kept burning in the *ssabo* at all times when it is being used regularly for divination. There is also a symbolic opposition between 'centre' and the 'periphery' of the shrine, as there is between 'inside' and 'outside'. When the congregation assembles, almost invariably the women sit on the right facing the diviner or doctor-priest, the men on the left. This is an explicit 'reversal' of what would be expected, and symbolizes the 'sacred' rather than the 'profane' nature of the ceremony.

All these symbols are manipulated to generate new meanings and emotional states during rituals. Most urban priests and diviners try

[9] The common term for a platform of earth is *ekituuti*, now used by extension to denote the pulpit in Christian churches (cf. Ssekamwa 1967: 33).

222 *Special Studies*

to incorporate as many as possible, but they do not always succeed; sometimes the *ssabo* is too small, at others the diviner himself forgets the significance of particular objects and procedures, and they disappear from his ceremonies. But despite the changing and sometimes ephemeral content, the general form of the ritual remains essentially Kiganda. For example, a universally observed traditional prohibition is that on 'looking back over the shoulders' (*okutunula emabega*) when leaving a traditional ceremony of any kind.[10] If one does so, the whole efficacy of the ritual, and any medicines one has obtained, is lost and the ceremony must be performed again.

Lubaale possession ceremonies take place in 'normal light', either the daylight coming through the doorway, or by lamp or fire-light during the night. There is no 'secrecy' about them; people come and go during the possession itself, and the atmosphere is highly 'informal'. Visual symbols play a very important part.

Ceremonies involving the *mayembe* ('speaking horns') take place in total darkness, are much more mysterious and, perhaps, more dramatic and awe-inspiring than *lubaale* rituals. The *lubaale* are always upholders of the 'good'; the *mayembe*, though morally neutral, can be used for both good and evil.

Apart from the clan and national *mayembe*, which can be inherited and controlled by clan and political officials, 'horns' are normally 'bought'. *Lubaale* 'possess' people who become their mediums; *mayembe* (singular, *jjembe*) are normally 'possessed' by people who become their 'masters', and they do as he bids them. This distinction, however, is not clear-cut. Sometimes it is very difficult to tell the difference between a *jjembe* and a *lubaale*, and priests often confuse the two categories themselves. The same diviner or priest may possess, or be possessed, by both *lubaale* and *mayembe*. For instance, King (1970: 34–8) recounts a possession ritual identical to a normal *jjembe* consultation, but one of the officiants later tells him that the spirits who came were *lubaale*, one being the famous *lubaale* Wanga. A *mayembe* diviner (*omusawo ow' amayembe*) well known to me also has a senior *jjembe* called Wanga. But despite this confusion and overlap, the rituals and beliefs associated with *mayembe* are distinct in many respects from those concerning other spirits.

The *mayembe* ceremonies begin with loud singing, led by the priest, which eventually induces the *jjembe* to enter the darkened *ssabo* with tremendous bangs on the door, loud rattling of bells (*endege*), and the flashing of tiny lights in the darkness. The

[10] This prohibition is widespread in traditional African religious observance.

Continuity and change in Kiganda religion 223

mayembe insist upon being 'introduced' to all the clients and on-lookers present, and often 'greet' them by clashing bells all over their bodies. Different kinds of problems are best treated by different *mayembe*, and several may appear in succession during the same ceremony. They are both male and female, and are thought to be able to move vast distances at incredible speed to investigate the root causes of a client's troubles. They frequently 'catch' offending *mizimu* ancestor ghosts, bring them back to the *ssabo* and force them to reveal themselves and their motivations for interfering in the affairs of the living.

Most *masabo* for the *mayembe* horns are just ordinary rectangu-lar rooms attached to the densely-clustered houses of Kampala's low-income areas and peri-urban villages. There are no paraphernalia other than what the diviner brings in his bag: bells, a small lamp for the preliminaries, and perhaps a hippo-hide cane (*embooko*). The only condition is that the room must be capable of being completely blacked-out, the doorway draped with heavy barkcloth for this purpose. But almost any room will do at night.

Some famous *mayembe* diviners in Kampala, however, have establishments that look like modern medical doctors' private clinics; although they are usually constructed of more 'traditional' materials, with mud-and-wattle walls. In some cases, rooms are provided for 'in-patients' who have to remain overnight or longer, either to give time to the *jjembe* to 'travel' and find out what is wrong, or for the more lengthy cures which may take months (cf. Orley 1970: 27). On an average day, one may often find twenty or thirty people waiting to see such a practitioner, while the same number of people, clients and their relatives, may attend a single consulation in a large *ssabo*.

IV

The consultation, propitiation, and possession of *lubaale* and *mayembe* spirits dominate modern Kiganda religion in urban and peri-urban Kampala. The same situation exists in most of rural Buganda, and there is a good deal of interchange and travelling back and forth from urban area to village by the diviners and priests themselves, as well as their clients. Some of the more com-plex rituals, such as those concerning particularly difficult cases of infertility, cannot be carried out satisfactorily in the urban context. Sometimes a diviner in the urban area will arrange for the client to go out to a village to consult a colleague or perhaps the priest who 'taught' him before he came to town.

224   *Special Studies*

But most everyday problems are settled on the spot, with one or two visits to an urban priest, diviner, or doctor. A large number of them live within five miles of the city centre. For example, one quite successful 'horn' diviner (*omusawo ow'amayembe*) has a faithful following and regular rituals half a mile from the Kampala Protestant Cathedral at Namirembe. He himself is a regular church-goer and active member of the Catholic community of Kampala, centred on nearby Rubaga Cathedral. He also has a part-time job in the City Council, and was once destined to become a Catholic priest. The diviner who taught, or 'revealed', his profession to him lives some thirty miles from Kampala, and is a Muslim. They frequently visit each other's homes and *amasabo*, and conduct ceremonies together when they do.

Another quite famous *lubaale* priest has a *ssabo* some three and a half miles from the city centre. She has many *lubaale*, both 'of the lake' and 'of the mainland', but she is best known for her possession by a Christian *lubaale*, named Matayo after the Biblical Saint Matthew (see Rigby and Lule 1971: 22–37). Such instances could be repeated a great many times.

Before I conclude, a final word must be said about the variety of priests, diviners, doctors, and their 'congregations' or clients who are responsible for keeping alive and developing Kiganda religion in Buganda's urban and rural areas. Priests and diviners of both *lubaale* and *mayembe*, as well as other spirits, are some-times referred to by the same terms, or different terms in different contexts. *Omusamize* (plural: *abasamize*) literally means 'one who is possessed', from the verb *okusamira*, 'possession', or 'medium-ship'. However, an *omusamize* may equally well be called *omulaguzi* (literally: 'diviner' or 'seer') and, in some contexts, *omusawo* ('doctor'). The latter word is used for 'European trained' doctors, and the two kinds may be distinguished adjectively.

A medium possessed by any kind of spirit, or even possessing *mayembe*, may be called *emmandwa* (cf. Runyoro *mbandwa*: Beattie 1961; 1964; 1966; *et passim*). A *lubaale* priest or keeper of a shrine, when not in a state of possession, may be referred to as *omukongozzi*, 'one who bears another on his shoulders', from the verb *kukongojja*, 'to carry a person on one's shoulders'. Even the term currently used for a Christian priest, *kabona* (plural: *baka-bona*), can be used for a priest of Kiganda religion, as Kagwa (1905: 209–26) consistently does for the priests of the various *lubaale* shrines.[11]

---

[11] Curiously, the Oxford Luganda-English Dictionary (Snoxall 1967) defines *kabona* as 'heathen priest'!

Continuity and change in Kiganda religion

Individual specialisms may lead to a particular person being referred to predominantly by one of these many terms; but there is no clear classification of the *practitioners* of traditional religion by them, only of their *functions* in particular contexts.

As for the congregations or 'clients', all I can say here is that they come from all age categories, all socio-economic levels, all religions, and even from different ethnic groups (cf. Rigby and Lule 1971; *passim*). This problem must await fuller analysis in our forthcoming monograph. Suffice to say here that probably between seventy or eighty per cent of them are women, although priestly functions and the power of divination and healing are equally distributed between the sexes; which is more than can be said for the situation in the practice of Christianity or Islam!

V

Although no detailed analysis is possible here, a few generalizations and preliminary structural observations may be made.

I have not been able to trace the evidence in detail in this short paper, but it can be stated that, despite the continuity of belief between modern, urban Kiganda religion, its traditional past, and the rest of rural Buganda, there are different emphases in the three situations.

On the time dimension, Christianity and Islam have ousted traditional religion from the public, political domain, except for minor periods of 'resurgence', and in times of crisis for the whole Baganda people. The 'national' *lubaale* have been removed from the political centre to the 'periphery' of the mass of the village and urban population of Buganda. There is also evidence to show that this process began long before the intrusion of foreign religions and the growth of modern urban centres (Apter 1961: *passim*).

In both the space and time dimensions, the earlier importance of *misambwa* spirits, linked as it was to clans and the topography, flora, and fauna of rural Buganda, has virtually disappeared. So too will have entities such as the *ebitaambo* and the clan *mayembe*, which they closely resemble (cf. Orley 1970: 19). Kinship and descent ties of some depth or extent are still important in rural Buganda, and link townsmen more with the village than with each other. Thus the spiritual entities related to them are still of relative importance to the many townsmen who intermittently maintain their rural links, but they are largely irrelevant in the urban context itself.

Instead, the now 'peripheral' but still powerful *lubaale*, and the

226 *Special Studies*

much more manipulable and effective *mayembe*, take pride of place. The *lubaale* are only partly specialized by *function*, not by clan or lineage ties, and they can easily be ascribed new functions in the urban context. Failing that, new 'syncretistic' *lubaale* can be recruited from the ranks of Christian and Islamic saints and prophets. The *mayembe*, on the other hand, having severed all connections with political power and the throne, could become even more powerful, free-floating entities, to be bought and sold, used for good or evil, individual gain, or the explanation of personal loss and failure.

At the family level, the ghosts of the recently dead (*mizimu*) still operate in towns much as they do in the rural areas and as they did in the past, although they too may have lost some of their significance with the attenuation of some categories of kinship bonds.

Finally, two interrelated factors may be established. The first is general, but significant for our discussion of urban Kiganda religion. Science does not necessarily eliminate religious, or 'magical' belief (cf. Jahoda 1966; 1969; 1970, *et passim*; Maclean 1971: 135). In crisis, most human beings appeal to forces other than those in the realms of science, and Kampala townsmen are no exception. Secondly, Christianity and Islam in their modern forms do not in themselves provide either sufficient or immediate enough relief from sickness and failure; neither do they offer familiar and manipulable enough symbols with which to take action against 'the slings and arrows of outrageous fortune'. Traditional Kiganda religion provides all of these, and exciting and intelligible drama to boot. Its ritual action is immediate and intimate, its symbolism satisfyingly efficacious (cf. Lévi-Strauss 1963: *passim*).

There is no reason to invoke the concept of syncretism to understand why a Kampala *mayembe* diviner can attend Mass in the morning, and in the afternoon take off his suit and shoes, put on a piece of barkcloth, and perform a ceremony to protect a house and its occupants from the malevolent *muzimu* (ghost) of a rejected wife's mother's brother. The logic of his changing conception of a live and thriving, 'traditional' religion is perfectly compatible with the tenets, if not the specific injunctions, of the Catholic faith. And there is equally no incompatibility between his easy integration of what others may consider as two distinct kinds of religious belief, and the belief and practice of his Muslim professional tutor, living some miles away in rural Buganda. It is just that one set is more effective than another in specific contexts, and therefore is the logically more applicable.

Continuity and change in Kiganda religion 227

Hence it may be said that, although a large proportion of the citizens of Kampala City are committed 'townsmen', and will probably never really live in the rural areas again, the religions they profess, and many of the rituals they attend, are derived from traditional Kiganda culture and a still predominantly rural society, but easily adapted to some of the specific constraints of modern urban life. Although constantly changing, Kiganda religion is still Kiganda religion, and there is no reason why it should not survive indefinitely in both urban and rural Buganda.

Migration and language change: The inter-action of town and country

MUBANGA E. KASHOKI

INTRODUCTION

In a short but highly interesting article published in 1951,[1] White examined the interaction of languages where speakers of different but related languages were living in close proximity in their villages in two districts of Zambia, Zambezi (then Balovale) and Kabompo. He was particularly concerned with 'the effects of contact with other Bantu languages through migrant labour or trade, and the effect of contact with European languages' (p. 66).

White considered that '[one] of the outstanding features of modern Africa is the great impact which it has experienced from contact with the outer world' (p. 66), and so far as this affected Central Africa, he isolated two causes—the advent of the European, and, concomitantly, industrialization—as being of the greatest significance. Industrialization in particular set in train a number of social factors which could not but have far-reaching effects on the linguistic situation in the area. Among these, White singled out migrant labour (the immediate consequence of the high demand for cheap labour that the various mines in South Africa and Rhodesia, and later the copper mines in Zambia, generated), as one of the most interesting phenomena. He also mentioned 'an extensive demand for labour on account of railways, building, motor transport, urban settlement, and farming' (p. 66). A somewhat independent factor— colonial administration based on the Westminster model, while incorporating indigenous forms—is also mentioned by him. As a crowning factor he cites the introduction of what he calls the 'moneyed economy' (p. 66).

Thus, all in all, White identified migrant labour, trade, the geographical proximity of communities speaking various if related

---

[1] Readers interested in the details of the article should consult C. M. N. White, 'Modern influences upon an African language group', *Rhodes-Livingstone Journal*, No. 11, 1951, pp. 66–71.

The inter-action of town and country 229

languages, the Western type of administration, and the moneyed economy, as the factors which most immediately and most significantly impinged on the adaptation of the languages he was considering to 'modern influences', to adopt his terminology. One should, however, at this time also add education, which has been an important factor in the social and linguistic changes that have occurred in much of present Africa, no less so Zambia.

In this paper I set out merely and very tentatively to explore the extent to which two factors mentioned by White—migrant labour and British administration—and two others not mentioned by him —Christianity and education—have affected the development of one of the major languages of Zambia—Bemba. As a primary premise, I am concerned to demonstrate that the migration of people from the rural to the urban area, and *vice versa*, has had a sort of 'double-edged' diffusional effect on the language in that, to a considerable extent, word borrowing in Bemba has not been uni-directional. It is the central argument of this paper that the borrowing of foreign words into Bemba is not the result of contact of the Bemba speakers with Western culture in urban areas only, but that more correctly, because of the constant movement of people from the rural to the urban area and *vice versa*, borrowing manifests itself in criss-crossing patterns in the sense that words borrowed by people living in rural villages are transmitted to those living in urban centres by immigrants to these areas. Similarly, words borrowed by those living or working in urban centres are transmitted to the rural areas by those going on short or long visits to their original homes in the rural areas. White makes much the same point when he says that 'it must be remembered that, despite a growing tendency to urban stabilization, the basic feature of migrant labour at the moment is that it is migrant, and that whatever trends evolve in the urban centres are therefore taken back to the rural areas to influence conditions there' (p. 67).

A complete study of the linguistic changes taking place in any language should take into account the whole grammar (i.e., the lexicon, syntax, and phonology) of that language. This, however, is a major undertaking requiring time and a great deal of effort, and is clearly beyond the scope of this preliminary work. In the following discussion, which aims at correlating migration and language change, I intend, for purposes of simplicity and brevity, to confine myself to the lexical aspect only, and to draw for examples on one specific Zambian language, Bemba, with which I am most familiar.

230 *Special Studies*

THE PROBLEM

In the main, it is safe for one to assume that word borrowing follows certain patterns or trends which can be categorized to some extent. As indicated by White, we have already seen that the two major cultural forces which may be said to impinge most directly on language change in central Africa are the arrival of the European in the area, and industrialization. To these may be added other socio-historical (or partially socio-historical) forces such as conquest, colonization, and trade. Literature, where literate communities are involved, is another force to consider, but not in central Africa, where for the most part literature in indigenous languages is a relatively recent phenomenon.

Word borrowing is a consequence of one or the other, or a combination, of these forces. For example, in studying word borrowing in English one may find that conquest has played a part in contributing a certain category of foreign words to the language. Indeed, Serjeantson (1935, p. 11) has observed that 'from the time of Julius Caesar onwards we have evidence from the Roman historians of contact between the Germanic and Latin people, which led to the adoption of Germanic words into Latin and of Latin into Germanic. The Roman armies included northern cohorts, and their familarity with Latin military terminology and with the names of every-day objects in use in camp and town, served to introduce Latin terms into the native dialects of these soldiers from Nordic tribes.'[2] Words borrowed into English after the Norman Conquest were of a somewhat different kind: they seem to relate predominantly to culinary, court, judicial and political objects or concepts. Thus within these trends one may distinguish the different types of loan-words that have, over the years, found their place in the English language, in themselves helpful indices to the main areas or categories of borrowing.

The documentation of such trends, including the attendant description of observable types of borrowed words, is a comparatively easy task in cases where a long tradition of recorded history exists, such as is the case with English. Where, however, there are no written records, or where such sources are scant, the task, it seems to me, must involve the use of bits of oral and written history that are available, plus a bit of 'guess-work' (or extrapolation), based on the known corpus of loan-words, to explain

[2] For a fuller reading of how the English language has grown as a result of borrowing, see Mary S. Serjeantson's *A History of Foreign Words in English*, 1935 (third impression 1962).

The inter-action of town and country 231

the patterns and types of borrowing. This is the approach adopted in this paper.

A different difficulty also deserves mention. In the study already cited, White was primarily concerned with the effects the inter-action of geographically contiguous linguistic communities had upon each other's language. This aspect is not explored in this paper. There are two reasons, the first being that, without the aid of recorded sources, it is difficult at this time to establish what are essentially 'true' Bemba words, as opposed to words the Bemba may have borrowed and incorporated into their language during their contact with the people whom they conquered, or who were their neighbours, in their present region of residence. The second reason is that the languages spoken all round the Bemba country are all of Bantu origin, and it is, therefore, not always easy to distinguish between Bemba and non-Bemba words. For these reasons the primary emphasis in this paper will be on foreign words borrowed from non-Zambian and especially non-Bantu (European, etc.) languages.

Key to abbreviations. In subsequent sections, the following abbreviations will be employed:

Afrikaans	Afr.	Nyanja	Ny.
English	E.	Portuguese	Port.
Kabanga	K.	Swahili	Sw.
Latin	L.	Zulu	Z.

MAIN TRENDS OF BORROWING

It is not necessary for our present purposes to discuss in any great detail the factors most responsible for the migration of rural people during the first half of this century to the areas of Zambia now collectively referred to as the 'line of rail', this being a corridor of urban centres which stretches from the Copperbelt in the north-west, to Livingstone at the southernmost tip of Zambia. However, several salient points about migration deserve brief comment. Ohadike (1969, p. 1) attributes what he considers to be the beginning of a really significant outflow, within Zambia, of the rural population to the line of rail (mainly the Copperbelt) to the increased activity in copper mining after 1925. Before that, he does not consider migration, within Zambia, to have been of any real consequence, and describes the situation thus: 'the total internal flows of labour were mere trickles, and many Zambians went as labour recruits to

232   *Special Studies*

Rhodesia, South Africa or the Congo, which by then had well-developed mining and agricultural industries' (p. 1).

In relating labour migration (or population shifts generally, either within Zambia or to areas outside Zambia) to language change, account will be taken, where this is possible, of the two periods as delineated by Ohadike: that is, we shall consider language changes that may have taken place before 1925 as well as those which occurred later.

It is perhaps in order to mention at this point some of the factors that seem to have given impetus to the migration of the Zambian population to urban centres, whose end does not appear to be in sight even at the present moment. Mitchell (1958, pp. 12–18) after considering several factors (personal, psychological, political, sociological, etc.) concludes that while the *incidence* of labour migration may depend on psychological conditions, the *rate* is determined by economic conditions (p. 18). Writing specifically about the Bemba of the Northern Province, Meebelo (1971, p. 122) records that the 'introduction of the hut tax in 1901 and, not unnaturally, the desire to earn more money and acquire wealth drove hundreds of young men to places of employment outside their home areas'. Whatever factor or factors that initiated, and precipitated the resultant labour migration, one thing seems clear. The Northern and Luapula provinces, whose population, for the most part is Bemba-speaking, provided, as Ohadike (*op. cit.*, pp. 5–8) has been able to demonstrate, the lion's share of labour migrants to the Copperbelt between 1940 and 1946[3] This point needs to be borne in mind throughout the present discussion.

Swahili loan-words in Bemba

Prior to the arrival of the missionaries during the 1880s and of the British colonial officials during the 1890s, the Bemba of the Northern Province of Zambia had only two other contacts of some significance with peoples of a dissimilar culture, viz., the Portuguese and the Arabs. Of these, Bemba contact with the Arabs seems to be of more importance. On arrival, the missionaries and the British colonial officials found a lively, flourishing trade (in military hardware, commercial goods, slaves and ivory) between the Bemba and the Arabs, the latter having, according to Meebelo, in some instances exerted considerable political and personal influence on a number of important Bemba chiefs (cf. Meebelo, 1971, pp. 1–21). In return for 'guns, gunpowder and various items of merchandise',

[3] This factor is largely responsible for the establishment of Bemba as a *lingua franca* on the Copperbelt.

The inter-action of town and country 233

(Meebelo, p. 3) the Bemba sold to the Arabs mostly ivory and slaves (captured in war for the most part).[4]

Thus it is not surprising that, owing to this early Bemba–Arab cultural contact, there is today in the taxonomy of borrowed words in Bemba a considerable number of Arabic origin, mostly borrowed through Swahili.

What is of crucial importance here is not so much the precise time at which these words were assimilated into Bemba—this in any case would be very difficult to establish for the reasons given already—or the precise manner in which they were borrowed.[5] What is far more important is that, whatever the subsequent diffusion elsewhere of the words so borrowed, it is possible to trace them back to the rural area as the original point of contact. This would, therefore, establish the rural area, in this case, as the source. That these loan-words of Swahili (and originally, in most cases, of Arabic) origin can be ascribed to the rural and not to the urban areas as the source is strengthened by the fact that their early incorporation into Bemba tends to make them be regarded today as 'typical' or 'traditional' Bemba words, in contrast to subsequent loan-words of the same meaning from the urban area.[6]

While attributing most Swahili loan-words in Bemba to Bemba–Arab contact, it must be remembered that not all such loan-words were due to this contact. As we shall see later, some of these Swahili loan-words may have come into Bemba through missionaries acting as agents. Moreover, there are many loan-words of this type which, while having a similar shape and meaning in Swahili, may in fact have been borrowed directly into Bemba from Portu-

[4] For a more detailed account of this period, see Andrew Roberts, *A History of the Bemba* (1973), especially chapters 5 and 6 for Arab–Bemba contact and chapters 7 and 8 for early European–Bemba contact.

[5] Dr Harry Langworthy, for example, has pointed out that, in some cases, it is probable that words were transmitted by intermediate agents, e.g. Bisa, Luunda, Nyamwezi, or 'Nyanja' middlemen, who had much earlier contact with Arab or Swahili-speaking traders (personal communication). Similarly, Dr Roberts questions whether there is sufficient evidence to suggest direct Portuguese–Bemba contact, and points out that the only example he is aware of is of traders from the Zambezi visiting Chief Chikwanda in the late 1880s (personal communication). See also his *A History of the Bemba*, pp. 221–2.

[6] Here as elsewhere in this paper, I shall be using 'rural' and 'urban' in the conventional sense that they have been used in Zambia, i.e., the former to mean areas away from the line of rail, and the latter to include only major urban centres along the line of rail. In other words, small towns or bomas, such as Chipata, Kasama, Mongu, etc., away from the line of rail, will be regarded as part of the rural area in which they are situated, although it may be argued that rural towns in their turn have had some influence on linguistic change at the village level.

234 *Special Studies*

guese, perhaps as the result of Portuguese–Bemba contact, or at least through agents with direct contact with the Portuguese.

Swahili loan-words: military terms[7]

Mention has already been made of a lively trade towards the close of the last century in guns and ammunition between the Bemba and the Arabs (or their agents). One would, therefore, expect a considerable number of loan-words in this area. Indeed, some of the oldest loan-words of Swahili origin in Bemba are military terms, as shown in the table below.

Again, what is of significance here is that all these terms were first incorporated into the language through rural speech, and appear to have been transmitted to other areas, especially the urban area, by people leaving the rural area. But subsequently, as will become apparent later, some of these words began to be seriously challenged by a reverse counter-wave of new loan-words, so that we now begin to hear increasingly of *gaanipaauda* or even *kaanipaauta*, rather than of *amaluti* 'gunpowder'.

Bemba	*Swahili*	*Meaning*
imfwataaki	fataki (*from Arabic*)	percussion cap (on gun as a firing mechanism)
amalisaawa	marisawa *or* marisaa *or* marisao (*from Arabic*)	(small) shot, lead
amaluti	barudi *or* baruti (*from Turkish*)	gunpowder
umushikaale	askari *or* asikari (*from Arabic*)	soldier

Swahili loan-words: commercial terms

Before the rural Bemba population was exposed to the now more familiar European commercial products (mainly as a result of migrant labourers coming back to their villages with goods acquired in the urban centres), it is reasonable to assume that they would already be acquainted with certain goods, such as bales of cloth, with which the Arabs were wont to entice their trading counterparts. As would be expected, units of currency, as a necessary part of the trade transactions, are high on the list of borrowed words. In point of fact, we do find that such words as *ulupiya* 'money'

[7] The term 'military' as used here should be understood to refer to items, or concepts, associated with firearms.

The inter-action of town and country 235

(Swahili *rupia*, apparently derived from the Indian *rupee*), and *ipeesa* (plural *amapeesa*) 'penny' (Swahili *pesa*, originally a Portuguese word meaning 'money'), have a long history of usage in Bemba, to the extent that in some cases (for example, that of *ulupiya* and *amapeesa*), many Bemba speakers would argue that these are indeed 'traditional' Bemba words. Quite often the argument centres on the fact that *ulupiya*, and *amapeesa* have as synonyms what appear to be relatively more recent incorporations into the language, viz., *indalama* (from Greek *drachma*?), and *amapeni*, from English 'penny', the latter less frequently heard now since the introduction of new units of currency in the country in 1968.

As further elaborations on this point will make clear, it is relatively much later that we begin to hear of other newer terms for money, the result, no doubt, of increased contact with British units of currency, so that as the cultural contact in this direction grows, and as, in consequence, a much more differentiated vocabulary connected with money develops, the language accommodates such terms as *peni* or *ikoobili* (from 'copper') 'penny', *tiki* 'tickey', *susu* 'sixpence' (source unknown), *shiliini* 'shilling' or *boobo* 'bob', *ikolooni* 'half-crown' (from 'crown'), and *paaundi* (from 'pound') or *immondo* (source obscure) 'pound'.

In addition to the loan-words just discussed, the following borrowings may be regarded as having come into Bemba from Swahili either during the Arab–Bemba contact or some time subsequently, perhaps as a consequence of some Bemba-speaking migrant labourers going to work for a while in Tanganyika:[8]

Bemba	Swahili	Meaning
ici-biliiti/ifi-	kibiriti *or* kibriti *(from Arabic)*	match-box
kolobooi/ba-	koroboi *(from Arabic)*	small lamp (now also used to refer to a home-made, paraffin, 'bottle-wick' lamp)
makashi/ba-	makasi *(from Arabic*	pair of scissors

[8] On this point I am informed by Dr Roberts that 'by 1935 there may have been as many as 20,000 Northern Rhodesia [i.e. Zambian] Africans at work there, about 15,000 of whom were on the Lupa goldfields. These were a major employer between about 1930 and 1940.' Moreover, 'the sisal plantations near the coast (especially around Tanga) employed 'thousands' of Northern Rhodesia Africans by 1924, and at least 5,000 in 1937. Since these Northern Rhodesia migrants came from the areas closest to Tanganyika, many would have been Bemba speakers.' (Personal communication).

236   *Special Studies*

Bemba	Swahili	Meaning
in-sa/in-	saa (*from Arabic*)	clock, watch, hour, (period of) time.
i-tepe/ama-	debe (*of Indian origin*)	four-gallon petrol can (of a square shape)
i-tuuka/ama-	duka (*from Arabic*)	shop, store.

Many words of this kind, as most of the others already considered, have a relatively long history of establishment in Bemba,
and it is interesting to note that they were regarded as worth including in the dictionary by the compilers of the only dictionary of the
language, the White Fathers' *Bemba–English Dictionary*. On the
whole, the compilers appear to have been averse to the inclusion
of loan-words of insufficient permanence, or at least of words not
considered by them as part of a 'true' Bemba vocabulary.

Swahili loan-words: miscellaneous

There are other loan-words in Bemba of Swahili origin which,
in the absence of factual evidence to the contrary, one could attribute
directly to Bemba–Arab contact. Among these are words referring
to beasts of burden, e.g. *ingamiya* or *ingamila* (Sw. *ngamia*, from
Arabic) 'camel', and *imfwalaashi* (Sw. *farasi*, from Arabic) 'horse'.
In recent years, English terms have tended to replace these Swahili
loan-words in the speech of many, especially as regards 'horse'
which one now frequently hears being referred to as *iyaaci* (from
Zulu *ihhashi* through Kabanga[9] *hashi*) or even *iooshi* or *ioosi*,
from English.

Swahili loan-words of Portuguese origin

A number of Swahili loan-words may have been borrowed either
directly from Portuguese (through Portuguese–Bemba contact or
intermediaries), or indirectly through Swahili (a more likely explanation). Whatever the agents whom one may pinpoint as the
actual transmitters, one thing seems certain: the loan-words were
borrowed through rural speech, and subsequent transmission elsewhere began from there.

The best known examples are:

Bemba	Swahili	Meaning
i-peela/ama-	pera	guava
i-peesa/ama-	pesa	penny
ici-kopo/ifi-	kopo	tin, can

[9] For a definition and the origins of Kabanga (Fanagalo), see pp. 244–5.

The inter-action of town and country 237

Bemba	Swahili	Meaning
im-mendeela/im-	bendera	flag
kabaalwe/ba-	(Port. *cavalo*)	donkey, mount

Swahili loan-words through missionaries as agents

One of the largest groups of loan-words which appear to have originated from Swahili is that associated with Christian missionaries, notably the Roman Catholic White Fathers. From the very beginning of missionary activity, Catholicism has remained the most influential Christian religion in the Northern and Luapula provinces, and many of the religious terms which have been borrowed into Bemba either from Latin, or from Portuguese or Swahili can be attributed mainly to the presence of the White Fathers in the area.

The White Fathers' penetration of Bemba country began around 1893, according to Meebelo (p. 34), whose main source of information on this point is Andrew Roberts's doctoral dissertation, 'A political history of the Bemba'. This penetration was considerably consolidated during the first four decades of this century, for by the 1950s the White Fathers had greatly extended their influence throughout the Northern and Luapula provinces, and had established mission stations in strategic localities throughout the area.

Three other relevant points need stating. Firstly, the White Fathers, coming as they did in the twilight of Arab prominence, usurped the influence, prestige and status that the Arabs before them had enjoyed, so that, not only because of the special position the imported religion accorded them among the local population but also because of the unusually high social esteem in which they were held, it is reasonable to assume that the Bemba looked up to these new arrivals as the reference group for emulation, a factor which is often of considerable consequence in the spread of loan-words.

Secondly, before deployment in the field, many of the White Fathers had been trained, or had gained some practical field experience, at their Carthage headquarters in Algeria. As a result of this, many, if not all, had come in contact with Arab culture, or had a fair knowledge of Arabic or at least of religious terms in Arabic.

Thirdly, Zambia being situated far inland, the White Fathers had in many instances necessarily to pass through East Africa before taking up their pastoral posts. In so doing, it would seem that they became acquainted with Swahili religious terms, or that through their use of Swahili-speaking carriers and/or catechists they came to know of these terms.[10]

[10] In elaborating on this point, Brian Garvey has stated that the 'first mission helpers at Mambwe [the first mission station to be established just on

238 *Special Studies*

These last two points in particular would seem to provide the explanation for the proliferation of religious terms of Arabic origin (through Swahili) in Bemba:

Bemba	Swahili	Meaning
shikoofu/ba-	askofu, askafu (*Arabic*)	bishop
umu-takatiifu/aba-	mtakatifu	saint
in-neema/in-	neema (*Arabic*)	grace
ibalaka	baraka (*Arabic*)	benediction (i.e., the ceremony)
ubu-baani[11]	ubani (*Arabic*)	frankincense
i-saali/ama-	sali (*Islamic*)	prayer

Some of these words have already been challenged by relatively new incorporations, the result either of increased urbanisation or of more widespread education in Zambia. For example, the word *shikoofu*, traditionally regarded as a 'proper' Bemba word, is currently having continual skirmishes with an upstart, *bishoopo*! On present evidence, the outcome looks decidedly in favour of *bishoopo* and words like it.

The other group of Swahili loan-words which appear to have been introduced by missionaries refers to various types of fruit or fruit trees. In the early days of missionary activity, almost all the mission stations had to be self-sufficient in the matter of foodstuffs, as supplies could not easily reach these outposts (from nearby urban centres when these developed). We thus find growing even today at most mission stations the following types of fruit tree: *imi-peela* 'guava trees', *imi-ndimu* 'lemon (lime) trees' (Sw. *dimu*, *ndimu*, of Indian origin), *imi-cungwa* 'orange trees' (Sw. *michungwa*) and *imi-embe* 'mango trees' (Sw. *embe*, of Indian origin).

It is worth noting that in most major urban centres of Zambia today, especially along the line of rail, newer alternatives to these terms are heard much more frequently: *leemooni* for *indimu*, *ioolenji* or *ioolinji* for *icungwa*, and *mango* for *embe*. It is also

the outskirts of Bemba country], who afterwards moved to Kayambi . . ., were former East African slaves, redeemed in Mpala or Karema and sent to Mambwe to provide the nucleus of a Christian community in the new mission. They acted as overseers (*nyampara* in the mission documents, replaced by *kapitao* in later years) and ambassadors.' (Personal communication).

[11] The word *ububaani* 'frankincense' may have already been incorporated into the Bemba language by the time Christian Catholic missionaries arrived among the Bemba. *Ububaani* is said to have been sold by the Arabs or their intermediaries and used by the Bemba for medicinal purposes, sorcery, or for communication with spirits (Moses Musonda, personal communication).

The inter-action of town and country

worthy of note that invariably *indimu, icungwa* and *embe* are associated with traditional rural speech, whereas *leemooni, oolenji* and *mango* have immediate associations with urban speech.

Swahili loan-words: educational terms

Another group of words to be considered under Swahili loan-words is that associated with the earliest educational efforts in the country. It is widely recognized that, in Zambia, as in many other parts of Africa, the provision of education at the initial stages was almost exclusively the attribute of missionary activity (cf. Mwanakatwe, 1968, pp. 8–16). Mwanakatwe (p. 10) states that 'During the period 1882 to 1905 there was intense missionary activity which led to the establishment of several mission stations throughout Zambia', and that 'In spite of the early difficulties and problems of educational development, a fairly widespread education system had been established in Zambia by 1924 when the British Government assumed direct responsibility for the administration of the Protectorate', i.e., Northern Rhodesia. What Mwanakatwe omitted to stress—a point of particular pertinence to our argument—is that most of the schools established at that time were in the rural areas, and came into being well before there were any government schools.

As in the case of religious terms, some of the terms relating to education which were introduced at that early stage were of Swahili origin: *ici-tabo/ifi-* (Sw. *kitabu*, from Arabic) 'book', *umu-shitaale/imi* (Sw. *mstari*, from Arabic) 'line', and *aalufu* 'thousand' (Sw. *alfu, alaf*, etc., from Arabic). Increasingly today one hears in their place *i-buuku, umu-laaini* and *saausande* respectively.

Swahili loan-words associated with early colonial administration

These are very few, and it cannot be established reliably that they were in fact borrowed as a result of the introduction of colonial administration and not through some other means. They are recorded under this heading merely because this is one possible theory to pursue, and because these words relate more immediately to administration:

Bemba	Swahili	Meaning
i-booma/ama-	boma (*from Persian*)	administrative centre
in-tepa/in-	tepe (*from English* 'tape'?)	chevrons on uniforms
uku-peleka	peleka	deliver, send, transmit (message, letter, etc.)

We have so far attempted to establish that some of the earliest loan-words in Bemba are of Swahili origin, and that before spread-

240 *Special Studies*

ing elsewhere these words were first introduced into the language through rural speech. We now turn to what may be considered as another important source of loan-words, viz. European languages.

LOAN-WORDS FROM EUROPEAN LANGUAGES

The migrant worker who leaves his village and spouse (*umukashi*) behind in search of employment (*imilimo*) and money (*ulupiya*) or clothing (*ifyakufwala*), carrying *ulupu lwampao* 'a bark-cloth bag of provisions', after a brief or protracted stint in the mines, or on the road or railway gang, comes back *kukombooni* (to his village, from 'compound') on leave (*liifi*), and if a soldier, *cuuti*, ('off-duty'?). This time he asks his *doona* or *toona* (from 'dona'), instead of *umukashi*, for a bag of *iposo* (source unknown) or even *icikaafu* (from South African English 'scoff', but through Kabanga *isikafu*), instead of *impao*, so that he can return to *incito* (from Nyanja?), instead of *imilimo*, to earn more money, *indalama*, (from Greek *drachma*? through Kabanga?) instead of *ulupiya*, by means of which to acquire more *impasha* 'clothing' (from Kabanga *mpashle*), instead of *ifyakufwala*!

We thus are now confronted with a new trend in loan-words from the opposite direction—the line of rail—a trend which at present appears to have had the most far-reaching consequences on the growth of Bemba. As more and more migrant workers shunt between their temporary places of work and their original homes, on *liifi* or *cuuti* of varying lengths, or return to stay permanently, they bring back with them the foreign vocabulary to which they have been exposed and which in due course they have internalized. In time, an ever-increasing foreign vocabularly is imported to the rural areas, and is subsequently widely diffused throughout the region. With diffusion and frequent enough usage, the new vocabulary gradually gains general acceptance and reasonable permanence in rural speech. The net result is that the rural population, who initially, it will be remembered, had exported mostly Swahili loan-words to the line of rail themselves begin, in a reversal of earlier trends, to sprinkle foreign expressions, derived from European languages, in their rural speech so that in place of the earlier (Swahili) loan-words we now increasingly encounter:

maacisa	*for*	icibiliiti	match-box (matches)
aka-lilampi	*for*	kolobooi	small lamp
shiisala	*for*	makashi	scissors
in-kolooko	*for*	insa	clock
ici-tini	*for*	itepe	tin (can)
i-shitoolo	*for*	ituuka	store

The inter-action of town and country   241

Loan-words from European languages: from village to town

However, before considering the different categories of loan-words in Bemba which have been borrowed from European languages, with the line of rail as the main point of primary contact, it might be of interest to examine first those which have come into the language through rural speech. These consist mainly of religious terms and were borrowed, as might be expected, as the direct consequence of Christian evangelization in the rural areas, and, like the Swahili loan-words preceding them, they were only much later exported to the line of rail (mainly the Copperbelt) by labour recruits who were (most of them) by this time converted to Christianity.

Bemba	*European language*	*Meaning*
in-sakalamenta	sacramenta (*Latin*)	sacrament(s)
kwaleshima	quadragessima (*Latin*)	**Lent**
im-minsa	missa (*Latin*)	**mass**
ulukalishitiya	eucharis (*Greek through Latin*)	Eucharist
katoolika/ba-eekeleesha	catholica (*Latin*) ecclesia (*Latin from Greek*)	Catholic church

These examples should give some indication of the nature, perhaps not so much the range, of the loan-words which Christian evangelization in the Northern and Luapula provinces seems to have bequeathed to Bemba. But by far the largest, and best known, group of loan-words coming into the language from European languages, through the rural areas initially, but subsequently exported to the line of rail, relates to what are generally referred to today as 'Christian' names. As indicated earlier, most of the labour recruits from the Northern and Luapula provinces who went to work in the copper mines on the Copperbelt had already been converted to Christianity, to Catholicism principally, and in accordance with Roman Catholic practice then, they had assumed Christian names (i.e., had been named after Catholic saints) upon baptism. This fact alone would seem to account for the predominance on the Copperbelt of Christian (or more correctly European or Europeanized) names of Latin origin among the African urban population. It will suffice to give only a few examples here for illustration: *Maliya* (Maria) 'Mary', *Yusufu* (Josephus) 'Joseph', *Peetelo* (Peterus) 'Peter', *Paaulo* (Paulus) 'Paul', *Andele* (Andre) 'Andrew', etc.

It should be observed that, perhaps as the result of greater contact

242   *Special Studies*

with the culture of English-speaking peoples having taken place, the earlier Latin-sounding names began to give way, so that at some point in this contact—exactly when it is hard to pinpoint—one begins to notice a palpable swing to English-influenced pronunciations: *Meli* or *Meeli* instead of *Maliya, Piita* instead of *Peetelo, Andulu* or *Andulo* instead of *Andele*, etc.

Loan-words from European languages: from town to village

The trends described above were significantly reversed when increasing numbers of rural people left their areas to look for work, or were conscripted to work, on European farms in Rhodesia, on the mines (in and outside Zambia), on road or railway construction, in the army (during the First and Second World Wars), or at government or missionary administrative centres. Each of these occupations entailed a great deal of cultural interaction, not only between Africans in general on the one hand and Europeans on the other, but also between Africans from one region and Africans from another region. In this interaction, a considerable degree of linguistic exchange occurred, with one or the other party gaining to varying degrees from the experience.

For the Bemba-speaking Africans from the provinces under discussion, the linguistic experience which was gained in these varied working situations was to be a source of considerable importance and significance in the word-borrowing process. The Bemba-speaking labour recruit brought back with him to his home the words which he had encountered in distant lands, words which perhaps had never before formed part of his native experience. On his arrival in the village, the returning migrant worker was often a centre of attraction, an object of admiration and envy, and the man to be emulated. As such, he was without doubt an effective tool for disseminating loan-words from European languages throughout the rural area.

Loan-words from European languages: commercial terms

Whether his wanderings took him to the Rand mines in South Africa, or to the gold or coal mines of Southern Rhodesia, or the copper mines of Zambia, the labour recruit seems to have been motivated chiefly by two things: (*a*) to amass material wealth, and (*b*) to bring back some money. Material wealth and money in the rural areas, at that time (as at this), were important for a variety of social reasons. Money, for example, was required to meet one's tax obligations, and material wealth could be used for paying one's *lobola*, for distribution to relatives, or purely for ostentation.

The inter-action of town and country 243

Thus, as more and more migrant workers, or army recruits, returned home burdened with an assortment of European commercial products, we begin to notice an accelerated growth of loan-words in this area. This growth is particularly striking as regards items relating to clothing, cooking utensils, bedding, etc.

Bemba	Meaning	Source
(a) *utensils*		
im-pooto/im-	pot (European)	E.
im-beketi/im-	bucket	E.
akeetulo/utwetulo	kettle	E.
(b) *clothing*		
i-tolooshi/ama-	trousers	E.
in-sapato/in-	shoe(s)	Port. (*sapato*)
in-sookoshi/in-	socks, stockings	E.
i-shaati/ama-	shirt	E.
in-deleeshi/in-	dress(es)	E.
(c) *furniture, household fixtures*		
i-teebulo/ama-	table	E.
i-windo/ama-	window	E.
aka-abati/utu-	cupboard	E.
(d) *bedding*		
ubu-langeeti/ama-	blanket	E. (through K. *buranget*)
piilo/ba-	pillow	E.
beeti/ba-	bed (European)	E.
umu-shiishibeeti/imi-	bed-sheet(s)	E.

Swear words

In tracing the different categories of loan-words that seem to have originated from European languages, one cannot fail to remark the interesting variety of swear (i.e., obscene or insulting) words that the European source has contributed to Bemba. On their return, virtually all the various types of migrant labourers brought back with them these swear words, perhaps as the result of contact with the more brusque, uncouth, and race-conscious type of European on the farm, road construction, in the army, and occasionally in the colonial administration. Their acceptance by rural people, and the consequent permanent incorporation in the language, was greatly facilitated by the fact that the obscene and swear words being borrowed did not have the same social or functional significance in the recipient as in the donor language. In many cases, words considered obscene, and not to be treated lightly in English, came to acquire a 'light' or innocuous meaning in Bemba. For this reason we find today the following types of swear word in the language:

244   *Special Studies*

Bemba	*Meaning*	*Source*
saanamabiici(ki)	son of a bitch	E.
mbulalishiiti	bloody shit	E.
mbulalifuu (fuulu)	bloody fool	E.
fwakiyo	fuck you	E.
kontaelo	go to hell	E.
konteemiti	God damn it	E.
fuseeke	get away! (as to a dog)	Afr. *voetsak* (K. *fuzek*)
paashiteeti	bastard	E.

On the Rand mines, the gold mines of Southern Rhodesia and the Zambian copper mines, because very often the 'native' (borrowed into Bemba as *umu-tifi/aba-*) was held in low esteem, if not in contempt, by his white *kapitaao* 'overseer', it is to be expected that the word 'kaffir' would be used rather liberally to accompany most of the instructions that are given. It is, at any rate, understandable that when the migrant worker returned home, he on his part resorted, perhaps in a conscious ostentation of urbanity, to the use of *kaafa* or *kaafula* when putting what he must have regarded as 'country bumpkins', *bakaamushi*, in their place.

In time, *kaafula* and *umutifi*, like the other swear words borrowed in a like manner, came to acquire a certain harmless 'respectability' in the recipient language, and the rural speakers who finally also internalized them were entirely unaware of their inherent self-damning connotations. In any case, in this way the two words were added to the repertoire of borrowed swear words in Bemba.

European loan-words through Kabanga (Fanagalo)

Desmond T. Cole (1953),[12] in an attempt to trace the origin of the workers' language known by various names in various parts of southern Africa,[13] states that 'Concerning the place and date of origin of Fanagalo there seems to be no definite information available', but concludes after reviewing some literature extant on the subject that 'Fanagalo developed primarily out of the interaction

[12] Cole's article first appeared in the *Tydskrif vir volkskunde en Volkstaal* in 1953 and was reprinted in 1964 in Del Hymes's *Language in Culture and Society* (ed.) under the title 'Fanagalo and the Bantu languages of South Africa'. The references in this paper are to the reprint.

[13] In South Africa alone, for example, besides Fanagalo, Cole enumerates such other names as 'Kitchen-Kafir, Mine-Kafir, Pidgin Bantu, Isilolo (because of the extensive use of the 'article' *lo*), Basic Bantu, Basic Nguni, Basic Zulu, Silunguboi (the type of *Isilungu* [Zulu for 'European language'] which is used for speaking to the 'boys'), Conversational Zulu, Isikula. . . .' (p. 547).

The inter-action of town and country   245

of English and Zulu, and this must have happened in Natal, some time after 1823, when the settlement of that territory took place, mainly by English-speaking people' (p. 548).

For our purposes, what is of immediate relevance is that, drawn as they were from many parts of Africa, and even as far afield as Asia (viz., India, East Africa, including Abyssinia and Somalia, Central Africa, and countries south of the Zambezi), the migrant workers' principal vehicle of communication, at least at the place of work, whether in the Rand mines, on the Rhodesian farms, or on the copper mines of Zambia, was Fanagalo or Kitchen Kaffir in South Africa, and Chilapalapa or Kabanga in Zambia.

In the course of its development, although minimally Bantu in grammatical structure, Kabanga drew continually for its ever-adaptive vocabulary from many languages, notably English, Zulu, Xhosa and Afrikaans in South Africa, Ndebele in Rhodesia, and Bemba and Nyanja in Zambia. It is to be expected that the Bemba-speaking migrant worker, upon coming in contact with this language, would acquire an extensive vocabulary in it, and would subsequently transmit some of this vocabulary to his home area. This in fact is what seems to have happened on a rather significant scale as the following examples indicate:

Bemba	Kabanga	Meaning and source
(a) English loan-words through Kabanga		
i-loofwa/ama-	lofa	absentee, loafer (E. *loafer*)
kontalaaki	kontolaki	contract (E. *contract*)
uku-pikita	pikita	search (E. *picket*, i.e. search)
ama-lekeeni	ma leggin	leggings; rubber strings for a catapult (E. *leggings*)
(b) Loan-words from Afrikaans through Kabanga		
shiteleke	sterek	very much (Afr. *sterek*)
pasoopo	basopa	beware! (Afr. *pas op*)
bululu	blulu	relative, relation (Afr. *broer*, meaning 'brother')
ninkishi	nikisi	no, nothing, not at all (Afr. *niks*)
uku-lopa	lopa	to be timid, slink off in fear (Afr. *loop* 'be off')
icikaafu	skafu	food, meal (from South African E. 'scoff', Dutch *schoft*, meaning quarter of a day, hence meal; cf. Cole *op. cit.*, p. 550).

246   *Special Studies*

(*c*) It is interesting to note that while giving Bemba words of European origin, Kabanga has also contributed loan-words of Zulu (mostly), and (only occasionally) of Xhosa or Ndebele origin:

aikoona	no, not at all	Zulu (*ayikhona*)
kaashe	wait a minute	Zulu (through K. *kahle* 'gently')
fuuti	moreover, again	Zulu (through K. *futhi*)
uku-fwakasha	to visit	Ndebele (*vakatsha*)
i-fontiini/ama-	ignoramus	Zulu (*umfo-ndini* 'worthless')

(*d*) Sometimes Kabanga loan-words in Bemba are derivatives from a combination of European and Bantu languages:

mbicaana	a little, slightly	K. *mbitshana* (Afr. *bitjie* 'a little bit' + diminutive Zulu suffix *-ana*)
uku-cipisha	to reduce price	K. *tshipisa* (E. *cheap* plus Zulu causative suffix *-isa*)
uku-laisha	to load (soil, coal, etc.) with shovel; to shovel, lash	K. *layisha* (Afr. *laai* + Zulu? verb-formative suffix *-sha*)

Loan-words related to mining

The main industrial activity in Zambia from the very beginning has been, and still is, copper mining, and urbanization has always been most noticeable on the Copperbelt where thousands of Zambians and non-Zambians have been brought to live together in a compact complex of urban centres, notably Kitwe, Mufulira, Luanshya and Chingola. Apart from this fact, most of the labour migrants who went to work outside Zambia, whether in South Africa, Rhodesia, or Zaire (formerly the Congo), were recruited to work on mines of various types. It is understandable, therefore, that owing to this association with mining and ancillary activities, the Bemba-speaking migrant worker would in due course introduce into his native vocabulary mining terms which he had necessarily to use in the course of his duties. Indeed, we find today a proliferation of mining terms in Bemba, a clear indication of the importance of mining in the lives of the migrant workers, on the Copperbelt particularly, and elsewhere:

Bemba	Meaning	Source
i-ola/ama-	hole(s) (i.e. feet dug)	E. (*hole*, through K.)
pande/ba-	conveyor, belt	K. bande*
ici-kweepe/ifi-	cage, skip (small cage)	K. cikwepe*
umu-kooti/imi-	mine	Z. *mgodi*, meaning 'hole' (through K.)

The inter-action of town and country

Bemba	Swahili	Meaning
i-lela/ama-	ladder, mainway	K. *manela**
in-shimbi/in-	piece of iron, steel	K. *simbi**
shimata	smelter	E. *smelter* (through K. *simata*)
i-lasha/ama-	coal	K. *malasha**
aka-pata/utu-	dynamite, detonator explosive	K. *kapata**

* These words can perhaps ultimately be traced to some African languages as the initial source, although this has not been attempted here.

Some of these words have not proceeded beyond localized significance and have remained the specialized vocabulary of the miners, or at best, of the larger population affected more immediately by mining operations. Several tens of these, however, have in time gained wider currency, and it is these chiefly that have been accepted in rural speech and have in many cases achieved permanence now in Bemba. Notable examples are: *amalasha* 'coal', 'charcoal' or 'stone for cleaning body'; *aka-pata/utu-* 'dynamite, explosive'; *aka-mpompo/utu-* 'hard helmet', *ici-kwepe/ifi-* 'cage, automatic lift'; *umu-kooti/imi-* 'mine(s), urban area'; *in-shimbi* 'piece of iron; iron (noun)'; *uku-ciisa* 'to blast; to iron clothing', (from Zulu through Kabanga *tshisa* 'burn').

Loan-words of military origin

One more important group of loan-words in Bemba, that, as far as can be determined, of military origin, needs to be considered in this paper. During the First World War the Bemba-speaking communities of the Luapula, but more especially of the Northern Province, were affected one way or the other, and to varying extents, by the war activities of that period. Many hundreds of the young men from these areas were employed either as military porters or, in some instances, as actual combatants. (Cf. Meebelo, *op. cit.*, pp. 133–5).

When the Second World War broke out a little more than two decades later, even greater numbers of young men were directly involved in the war effort, since many of them were pressed into the army, and subsequently saw action in such distant areas as Abyssinia, the Middle East, and Burma. An example of the experience gained in the army by some of these Bemba-speaking conscripts is told in Stephen Mpashi's entertaining novel (no date), *Cekesoni Aingila Ubusoja* 'Jackson Becomes a Soldier' (Zambia Publications Bureau).

248 *Special Studies*

As will be evident from the examples, many of the military terms borrowed into Bemba pertain to ranks in the army, military operations, different types of troop division, tools, accoutrements, etc.:

Bemba	Meaning	Source
koopolo	corporal	E.
saacenti	serjeant	E.
peleeti	parade	E.
taputapu	quickly, fast	E. *double-double*
umu-nshinga/imi-	machine gun	E.
mantiini/ba-	type of rifle	E. (from Martini-Henry, a brand name)
i-patuuni/ama-	platoon	E.
i-bataalyeni/ama-	battalion	E.

The linguistic experience gained in the army seems also, in some instances, to have given rise to borrowed words of a non-European nature. Of these, those of Nyanja origin are of the greatest significance:

Bemba	Nyanja	Meaning
ama-lamuno	malamulo	instructions, orders
ukucimwa	ku-cimwa	to make a mistake, error
inde	inde	yes
icandamaali	candamale	shooting range, shooting competition
katundu	katundu	luggage
uku-patika	ku-pathika	to load on vehicle

In speculating about the manner and period of incorporation into Bemba of these Nyanja-derived words, it must be borne in mind that some of them may have been borrowed under circumstances of a non-military nature. For example, *katundu* 'luggage' may just as well have come into Bemba during the period when porters from Nyasaland (now Malawi) were used to transport provisions and supplies for the early British colonial administrators. However, the justification for attributing such words as *katundu* to a military origin lies in the fact that their presence in the language began to be felt particularly after the demobilization of soldiers, *aba-sooca*, after World War II. It is then, at any rate, that the rural speakers of Bemba seem to have become familiar with them.

CONCLUSION

In this preliminary sketch of the main types of loan-words that one may find in the Bemba language today, an attempt has been

The inter-action of town and country 249

made to trace, and then to suggest, the main trends of borrowing. There are two main conclusions that could be drawn from the evidence so far presented. The first is that the main group of loan-words in Bemba appear to be the result, on the one hand, pre-dominantly of Arab–Bemba, and, on the other, predominantly of European–Bemba, contact. The first type of contact occurred primarily in the rural areas, and the second primarily on the line of rail.

The second conclusion to be drawn is that once borrowing had taken place, the subsequent transmission of the words so borrowed indicates a process which is not exclusively the prerequisite of one socio-geographical environ. In other words, the transmission of borrowed words across the rural–urban gap is the function of both the rural and the urban sector, though, no doubt, in unequal degrees. The transmission of borrowed words in Bemba can best be described as a two-way traffic, with some words being borrowed into the language through the rural sector and then transmitted to the line of rail, and others borrowed through the urban area and subsequently transmitted to and diffused throughout the rural area. This process is indicative of the constant migration of people that has taken place in the past, and continues to do so at present, from the rural to the urban area, and vice versa.

ACKNOWLEDGEMENTS

This paper is based on data still being gathered by the writer for a larger study tentatively entitled 'Language adaptation: a study of loan-words in four Zambian languages'. The writer is grateful to the University of Zambia which, through its Research and Higher Degrees Committee, provided the financial support which has facilitated the gathering of the data included in this paper. The writer has benefited from comments and criticisms made by Professor Donald J. Bowen, Mr Moses Musonda, Dr Andrew Roberts, Dr Brian Garvey, and Dr Harry Langworthy, to whom he owes a special debt of gratitude.

Movements of schoolchildren and provision of secondary schools in Uganda

W. T. S. GOULD

It has been the stated aim of virtually every African government to engineer the development effort so that existing imbalances, whether social, tribal, regional or rural/urban, are reduced or even eliminated altogether. The zeal with which policies to achieve this have been formulated and implemented may have varied from country to country, but allocation of resources has aimed to ensure a more equitable social and geographical distribution of the national income. Since the largest single item of development expenditure is in education, policies concerning access to and provision of schools have been formulated to further the general aim. Problems of inequalities in access to education have been considered in studies in West Africa (Foster 1965; Clignet and Foster 1966), but much more work needs to be done on the important questions raised by the known social inequalities. More direct control can be exercised over geographical inequalities in education, and it is to this aspect that Government policies have been directed.

Inequalities in the regional and rural/urban distribution of enrolments are the inevitable consequences of low enrolment ratios and a combination of historical and political factors associated with the colonial period and the introduction of the formal education system (Gould 1970). Post-Independence policies have tried to spread opportunity more equitably by providing more schools in under-provided areas, but such policies are not always successful. This paper considers the case of expansion of secondary education in Uganda since Independence in 1962. It illustrates how administrative and financial constraints have affected adversely policies designed to reduce imbalances in provision of schools, and, in particular, how the rural/urban imbalance has altered to the extent that an increasing proportion of secondary school places for African students is found in urban areas.

Uganda, like most countries of Africa, is educationally underdeveloped, but the education system has expanded rapidly in recent

Movements of schoolchildren 251

years and particularly since Independence in 1962. In that year there were 7,400[1] pupils in aided secondary schools but by 1970 this figure had risen to over 40,000. This enrolment, however, represents less than 5 per cent of the relevant age group. Only about 50 per cent of the relevant age group attend aided primary schools (it is likely however that a further 25 per cent attend unaided primary schools, mostly at the lower levels). The present school system consists of a 7-year primary course, P.1–7, then selection on the basis of a national primary leaving examination for a 4-year secondary school course, S.1–4, which leads to 'O' level (before 1966 there was a 3-tier system of P.1–6, then 2 years of junior secondary before the 4–year senior secondary course). After 'O' level there is further selection for a 2-year Higher School Certificate course which is a preliminary to University entrance (Chesswas 1966).

Flows of schoolchildren from home to school are inevitable, but in this highly selective system there is very considerable variation in the distance and periodicity of individual movements. Despite the spatial restriction imposed by the absence of a satisfactory system of rural public transport necessitating children walking to school, and despite a dispersed rural settlement pattern in most parts of the country, the majority of P.1 pupils can live at home and be within daily walking distance of school. As one ascends the educational ladder to higher primary schools, the percentage of children attending school declines and there are fewer schools. Average home-school distance is greater. Flows of school pupils will therefore be over longer distances and of longer duration, with more pupils living away from home while attending school. Living away from home is even more necessary for secondary school pupils, for it is inevitable that where less than 5 per cent of the age-group go to school, the family home of most pupils will be beyond daily travelling distance of any school.

Performance in the national primary leaving examination is the sole criterion for admission to a government secondary school in Uganda. All students sitting the examination indicate a preference of six schools, in the order that they would wish to attend, from the national list. There is no restriction except that students are *advised* not to name a day-school unless they can be assured of accommodation near that school. Students choose schools in all districts, with

[1] Unless otherwise stated all statistics are taken from the volume of education statistics published annually by the Ministry of Education, 1965–1967. Figures for 1970 remain unpublished but the author was given access to them.

first choice very often an old-established school with a national reputation, second choice a regional school and third and subsequent choices local schools. The top 14,000 or so in the examination are distributed according to the pattern of choice.

THE PRESENT PATTERN OF SECONDARY SCHOOL PROVISION

The distribution of the 73 aided secondary schools in Uganda in 1970 is shown in map 1. In table 1 this distribution is compared with

Movements of schoolchildren

Table 1.

Schools and population by region, 1970

Region	% total population	% schools	% S.1 places
Buganda	27·9	30·1	36·4
Eastern	29·5	28·9	30·7
Northern	17·1	19·1	14·2
Western	25·5	21·9	18·7

the distribution of total population in each of the four regions[2] and the national pattern is clearly one of a relatively even spread of schools to the extent that there are no overwhelming regional discrepancies between the two distributions. There are, however, greater discrepancies within the regions than between them. The distribution of schools obscures the distribution of total enrolments for not all schools are the same size. It is clear from column 3 of table 1 that there is a concentration of S.1 places in Buganda and that the Northern and Western regions are under-provided. More particularly, the four lake shore districts of Masaka, West Mengo (including Kampala) East Mengo and Busoga with 34 per cent of the total population have 49 per cent of the S.1 places.

Since all schools have national catchments and students are under no obligation to attend the school nearest their home, the distribution of schools need not indicate the distribution of access, i.e. the geographical origins of students within the schools. The Ministry of Education does not collect data on the precise geographical origins of students but can provide a breakdown for each school by region in which students took the primary leaving examination (summarised by region in table 2); 76 per cent of boys and 73 per cent of girls were in P.7 in the same region as they were in secondary school and this allows for considerable inter-regional movement. As would be expected from table 1, the dominant flows are from the relatively under-provided North and West into Buganda and Eastern region, which have an excess of capacity over population.

The map shows that secondary schools are a feature of the urban or peri-urban landscape, for many schools are located in or near a town or district headquarters. This is particularly marked for the largest towns with ten schools in Kampala and seven within five

---

[2] The administrative structure is that of 1970. Buganda region includes the districts of East and West Mengo, Masaka, and Mubende; Eastern region includes Bugisu, Bukedi, Busoga, Karamoja, Sebei and Teso; Northern region includes Acholi, Lango, Madi and West Nile; Western region includes Ankole, Bunyoro, Kigezi and Toro. Several boundary and name changes have been made since then.

254 *Special Studies*

Table 2

Inter-regional flows of secondary school students, 1970

Region of Secondary School	Buganda	Eastern	Northern	Western	Outside Uganda	Total
Boys						
Buganda	5,785	1,005	924	2,442	215	10,373
Eastern[1]	325	8,046	898	284	49	9,602
Northern	49	199	4,265	94	5	4,612
Western[1]	217	160	413	4,496	46	5,350
Total	6,378	9,410	6,518	7,316	315	29,937
Girls						
Buganda	2,806	917	137	624	54	4,540
Eastern[1]	184	1,893	220	105	9	2,411
Northern	59	177	952	91	1	1,280
Western[1]	73	12	17	1,300	1	1,403
Total	3,124	2,999	1,326	2,120	65	9,634

[1]Incomplete; one school in each region did not provide a regional breakdown of students.

miles of Jinja, the second largest town in Uganda. However, over 95 per cent of the population of Uganda live in rural areas, and although a disproportionately large percentage of secondary school pupils come from urban areas there is inevitably a large rural-urban component in the movements of secondary school pupils.

The predominant north-south and rural-urban flows have evolved out of the location policies of three decision-making groups—the religious, ethnic and official, i.e. the Missions, the Asian community and the Government respectively. Each of these three factors has operated independently for the most part and with varying relative importance at various stages in the evolution of formal education in Uganda over the last 70 years.

EFFECTS OF MISSION SCHOOL LOCATIONS ON HOME/SCHOOL MOVEMENT

The first schools in Uganda were established by the main missionary groups in the Buganda heartland near Lake Victoria. Each of the groups had established its main educational focus by the first decade of this century—the Church Missionary Society at Budo and Gayaza, the White Fathers at Rubaga and Kisubi and the Mill Hill Fathers at Namilyango, all located within 15 miles of Mengo, the royal capital. Mission schools were subsequently established in other districts but the main focus of educational effort, as with mission effort in general, continued to be in Buganda.

Movements of schoolchildren

From the beginning the boarding school was characteristic of the mission school. This was very necessary when so few children attended school, but as the number of pupils grew it became possible to have more and more day primary schools. Some schools became junior secondary schools, fed by several primary schools; senior secondary schools were established, fed by junior secondary schools. These senior secondary schools have generally remained as boarding schools. This is not only a logical response to low enrolment ratios and the majority of pupils living at a distance from the school, but also it was considered by the mission authorities to have important advantages for the education of the pupil. He or she does not have to cope with the physical difficulties of finding accommodation and food that are problems for day-school pupils living away from home, and the impact of education on the pupil was considered to be more effective.

The mission boarding school in Uganda is essentially an urban institution. Although the majority of such schools are not within towns they are usually within a few miles of town in peri-urban locations, sufficiently far from the town to be removed from its direct influence on pupils but sufficiently near to be conveniently reached from the town and for the town to be easily reached from the school. Most district headquarters have mission boarding schools within a few miles, and often there are two such schools, one Catholic and one Protestant. The location of mission stations in general and of mission boarding schools in particular has been much affected by proximity to towns. The legacy of the policies of the missions is to generate what are essentially rural-urban rather than rural-rural flows of pupils.

THE EFFECT OF ASIAN SCHOOL LOCATIONS ON HOME/SCHOOL MOVEMENT

Non-Africans were 1·3 per cent of the population of Uganda in 1970 but occupied 14 per cent of the secondary school places. These were mostly Asians and the Asian population was highly urbanized. Inevitably, therefore, urban day-schools were established to cater for the Asian population and there are urban day schools in Kampala, Jinja, Mbale, Soroti and Masaka. These were initially for Asian pupils exclusively, or even for one community of Asians (e.g. Ismailis), but since the late 1950s all schools have become racially mixed, and many of the 'Asian' schools had a majority of African students by the mid-1960s. However the contrast between the pattern of urban day-schools with large numbers of non-African

256   *Special Studies*

pupils and of peri-urban boarding schools with an almost wholly
African population remained until the expulsion of most of the
Asians during 1972.

THE EFFECT OF GOVERNMENT POLICY ON HOME / SCHOOL MOVEMENT

Until 1925 control and administration of education in Uganda was
entirely in the hands of the missions and the Asian community. In
that year the Government Department of Education was established,
and since then the influence of Government has grown to the present
level where all aided schools are controlled by the Government. The
voluntary agencies, especially the Churches, continue to supply staff
and nominate members of the Boards of Governors of schools they
established. Direct Government initiative in the establishment of
secondary schools began with Makerere College in the 1930s and
in the 1950s a few Government secondary schools were established
(Ntare School in Ankole, Butobere S.S. in Kigezi, Kabarega S.S. in
Bunyoro and Sir Samuel Baker S.S. in Acholi). These differed little
in character from the mission model, being boarding schools and
situated near the chief town (or in the case of Kabarega one of the
twin foci) of the district. These schools in the Western and Northern
regions had the effect of reducing disparities in the provision of
secondary education, for until 1950 all secondary schools except one
were in Buganda or Eastern Province.

The reduction of regional disparities was continued in the very
large expansion of secondary education during the 1960s. In 1962
at the time of Independence there were 39 aided secondary schools;
by 1970 there were 73, the main expansion being in 1965 when 25
new schools were opened. Map 1 indicates the distribution of the
34 new schools established between 1962 and 1970. Only 5 of these
schools are in Buganda, with 6 in the Northern Region, 13 in the
Eastern Region and 10 in the Western Region. Furthermore, some
of these new schools were located away from district headquarters
but near other centres in a downward diffusion to levels of the
urban hierarchy below the district centres. In Ankole, for example,
Bushenyi, Rwashamaire and Ibanda, all county centres, now have
secondary schools nearby. The creation of new schools apparently
generated centrifugal tendencies in the areal pattern of provision
both within individual districts and in Uganda as a whole and these
would be expected to reduce spatial inequalities in the provision
of secondary education.

The effect of new schools on gross patterns of provision needs to

Movements of schoolchildren 257

be balanced against the expansion of existing schools during this period. Immediately after Independence the emphasis was on establishing new schools, largely for political reasons. Since 1966 however, expansion has followed the policy laid down in the National Development Plan that 'the expansion of secondary education will

Table 3

Secondary schools by district, 1962 and 1970

	Schools				Capacity in S.1 as % of Uganda S.1 capacity		% of total population
	1962		1970				
	No.	%	No.	%	1962	1970	
East Mengo	3		4		7	5·2	8·9
West Mengo	4		4		10	6·0	5·4
Masaka	3		4		6	6·6	6·7
Mubende	0		0		0	0	3·5
Kampala	7		10		5	18·6	3·5
BUGANDA	17	44	22	30	48	36·4	28·0
Bugisu	2		4		8	7·6	4·4
Bukedi	1		4		8	4·6	5·5
Busoga	3		8		11	12·7	9·9
Karamoja	0		1		0	0·4	3·0
Sebei	0		1		0	1·1	0·7
Teso	2		3		5	4·3	6·0
EASTERN	8	21	21	29	28	30·7	29·5
Acholi	3		5		5	5·8	4·9
Lango	2		4		3	3·5	5·3
Madi	0		1		0	2·2	0·9
West Nile	3		4		5	2·7	6·0
NORTHERN	8	21	14	19	13	14·2	17·1
Ankole	2		6		4	7·3	9·0
Bunyoro	1		3		1	3·5	3·7
Kigezi	1		4		1	4·8	6·8
Toro	2		3		5	3·1	6·0
WESTERN	6	15	16	22	11	18·7	25·5
UGANDA	39	100	73	100	100	100	100

concentrate on enlarging existing schools as there are significant economies in larger schools' (Uganda Government 1966: 138). The main economies in large schools are to be derived primarily from a more intensive use of capital. In boarding schools this has meant a more realistic standard of accommodation, for many of the older schools have standards similar to, or even better than, those in many boarding schools in developed countries. The provision of, for example, double bunks instead of beds, has enabled greater intake without greatly increasing capital expenditure, so that cost per pupil is reduced. Expansion in day-schools has been made possible by

258   *Special Studies*

operating a double shift system, one section from the early morning until mid-day, the other in the afternoon. This has, understandably, been severely criticized by educationalists, but the shift system is thought to reduce costs per student by as much as 20 per cent (Jolly 1969: 94). The implementation of a policy of expanding existing schools has raised enrolments up to (and beyond in many cases) the recommended optimum size of 480 students in S.1–4.

From table 3, a comparison of the number and size of schools in each district in 1962 and 1970, it is clear that there has been a reduction of regional disparities, but that the extent of the reduction of disparities in capacity is less than those in the number of schools. The effect of Government expansion policy since 1962 would appear to have been to reduce the *relative* importance of flows of pupils from the North and West into Buganda, for the proportion of S.1 capacity in Buganda fell from 48 per cent to 36 per cent. However, with the expansion of primary education in the less well provided districts and the rapidly increasing total enrolments in secondary schools, *total* flows into Buganda have increased. Weeks (1967) found that the parental home of 48·8 per cent of a sample of African students in one Kampala school in 1963 was more than 15 miles from the school, but this percentage had risen to 67·3 by 1965 (p. 372), and the evidence of table 2 confirms movement into Buganda in particular continues on a large scale.

URBAN DAY-SCHOOLS IN UGANDA

The provision of new schools in peripheral districts and overall expansion of secondary education obscures an increasing rural-urban component of the flows of secondary school pupils. The urban day-school constitutes a major element in the secondary systems with 30 per cent of school places in 1970, though this is less than the 38 per cent in 1962 and 35 per cent in 1967, but the proportion of national S.1 capacity in Kampala rose from 5 per cent in 1962 to 18·6 per cent in 1970. Kampala with seven exclusively day schools is the main centre, but there are also two such schools in Jinja and in Mbale and one each in Masaka and Soroti. The number of non-African students fell absolutely between 1967 and 1970 (table 4) so that there was a relative as well as an absolute increase in the number of Africans in day schools. That this should have happened was more a result of many more Africans taking and passing the primary leaving examination than of any direct government initiative in regulating admission of non-citizens to

Movements of schoolchildren

Table 4

Enrolment in aided urban day schools

	1967		1970	
Town	Africans	Non-Africans	Africans	Non-Africans
Kampala	3,154	2,667	4,258	2,601
Jinja	588	1,297	1,770	923
Mbale	678	778	1,358	551
Masaka	145	314	504	238
Soroti	218	216	264	256
Total	4,783	5,272	8,154	4,569
% national enrolment	21·9	96·2	22·9	90·0

government schools. The expulsion of most of the Asians during the latter part of 1972 clearly had an enormous impact on the rural/urban balance of school places. Since many teachers in urban day schools were Asians, total enrolments in the short term will not match those of 1970, but many more places became available for African students. The rate of movement from rural to urban areas to find a school place has increased.

Expansion of day schools has the extremely important advantage over expansion of boarding schools of savings in costs per student. Since there is no need to provide accommodation and food there is a saving to the Government of 30 per cent in capital and recurrent costs (Chesswas 1966: 49–50). Expansion of day-schools by double-shifting enables, in addition, quick short-term results for there is no delay while new premises are being built. Day-schools are in urban areas since enrolment ratios in rural areas have not been sufficiently high to enable secondary schools to operate above an efficiency threshold even where rural population densities are very high. There is one rural day-school, at Mukono about 15 miles east of Kampala, but the majority of students at this school come from beyond daily commuting distance and find accommodation in the school hostel or locally. Some boarding schools have taken in day pupils in recent expansions, and this trend is likely to continue.

Although the continuing and growing rural/urban imbalance offers an attractive solution to the Government of reducing per capita cost and increasing total enrolments, it presents serious difficulties for the individual student. If he or she is lucky enough to find a place in a boarding school, then the transition from the home environment to the usually very different school environment is eased. Not only are the physical needs of accommodation, food, light, etc. provided, but the social context of the boarding school is less difficult

260 *Special Studies*

than it is in the urban school. Furthermore, there is a belief inherited from the colonial period that boarding school education is somehow 'better' than day-school education and the most prestigious schools are all boarding schools. Even if their homes are in urban areas and within easy walking distance of a day-school, African students will usually prefer to go to a boarding school.[3] Thus, while most Asians opted for day-schools and lived at home and since the best African pupils found places in boarding schools, the Africans who attended day-schools were in general less able academically. This presented problems and exacerbated racial tensions within the day schools.

The main problems for the African student are, however, in the urban environment outside the school. If he or she is lucky, accommodation can be provided with a friend or relative, if not parents, or in one of the few Government hostels, but generally pupils have great difficulty in a town such as Kampala where accommodation is in very short supply. People in paid employment will be able to pay rent but non-earners, such as students, are as badly off as the unemployed. The economic position of the student is very weak indeed. Weeks' (1967) study of African students in Kampala day-schools from 1963 to 1965 presents a very depressing picture of the difficulties that have to be faced both in terms of physical conditions and in terms of study facilities. There is clearly a need for more hostel accommodation. His work indicated that the gross cost of providing a hostel place is lower than the living costs incurred by the individual student; furthermore, the cost of providing a boarding-school place is lower than the overall cost of providing hostel accommodation and a place in an urban school. Thus the *gross* cost of a secondary school place would appear to be minimised at a boarding school. But the public cost, i.e. cost borne by the Government, is at its lowest when day-school places are provided and students are left to find their own accommodation and other facilities. Planning thus encounters one of the classic dilemmas of social policy—who gains and who pays; how can public and private costs and benefits be assessed and differentiated?

PRIVATE SCHOOLS

This public/private costs dilemma is not relevant to consideration of the important and growing private sector. Since the Government

[3] There is a tendency for some pupils in newer, very poorly endowed boarding schools to want to transfer to another school, even a large urban day-school, to take advantage of the better facilities and supposed better chance of success in examinations.

Movements of schoolchildren 261

has little or no control over private schools data are very difficult to gather, but it is known that there were over 300 private secondary schools in the country in 1971 (Uganda Government 1972: 336). These schools receive no government financial support, though they are obliged to register with the Ministry of Education (only 74 were registered in 1970). Some of these schools are seminaries or other mission foundations and others, the majority, are individually sponsored commercial enterprises with all costs met from students' fees. A large number of these schools, especially the larger and better organized ones, are in towns and in Kampala in particular. These were established by individual entrepreneurs, often Asians, and charge high fees, though facilities are less good than in government schools and many teachers are unqualified.

In 1967 over 70 per cent of the 9,000 students in registered private secondary schools were day-students and over 4,000 of these, of whom 3,000 were Africans, attended the ten day schools in Kampala.[4] This pattern of provision in private schools inevitably swells the numbers of people who come to Kampala in search of education. The economic position of students in the private schools is even weaker than that of students in government schools, for not only is there no chance of their finding a place in a government hostel, but with much higher fees to pay they will be less able to afford adequate accommodation and food.

CONCLUSION

Expansion of secondary education in Uganda has affected both the volume and direction of flows of students from home to school. Government initiative between 1962 and 1966 in the establishment of new schools in less well provided districts reduced the regional imbalances that existed at the time of Independence, but policy since 1966, necessitated by severe financial constraint, of concentrating expansion in the larger urban schools has strengthened the role of towns in general and the capital in particular as foci of educational provision. The rural/urban imbalance in provision, though not necessarily access, has increased rather than decreased, and a growing number of secondary students leave home to live in towns, often in very difficult conditions. They constitute a considerable proportion of the immigrant population of Kampala in particu-

---

[4] It is difficult to be more precise about enrolments since some registered private schools made no statistical return to the Ministry of Education in 1967. These included two large private schools in Kampala. The 1967 figures are the most recently available.

262 *Special Studies*

lar, attracted by the educational opportunities the capital offers as labour migrants are attracted by the employment opportunities it offers. Government policy in school expansion in Uganda has accelerated the rate of urban growth.

The presence of schools in urban areas raises the question of their effect on the overall growth of towns in the long term. Are students who move to town to go to school any more likely to seek urban employment than those who have been at school in a rural area? Would the rate of growth of towns be reduced by providing secondary school places in rural areas and these schools being more integrated socially and economically with the rural system than is presently the case? A physical separation of schools and urban areas would probably have a similar, negligible effect as attempts to have a rural based rather than an urban based curriculum have had, for the education system mirrors rather than engineers society. So long as the distribution of opportunities for people with 'O' levels and above remains in urban areas, the location of a secondary school will have relatively little direct impact on the subsequent migration history of its students.

THE RURAL LINKS IN URBAN SETTLEMENT

Forms of ethnic linkage between town and country

AIDAN SOUTHALL

Ethnicity, though frequently given a false emphasis, remains the paramount problem of Africa. Intense feelings and contentions about its presence or absence feed into all situations, especially those of the national scene, where with a few notable exceptions, more and more autocratic leaders are drifting by a seemingly ineluctable process in the direction of military dictatorships.[1] They all publicly denounce what they call tribalism in the most stringent terms, while privately forced to foster it by giving special privileges to their own local group on whom they come to rely more desperately for their core support and ultimate loyalty. Happy are those few who like the late Tom Mboya transcend ethnicity through the sheer depth and intensity of their urban occupational involvement, or who like the Presidents of Tanzania and Zambia both profess the principles which transcend ethnicity and themselves come from groups which in fact offer them little temptation to practice it.

I feel that anthropologists have in the past exacerbated this problem and that we have an obligation to contribute in however small a way to setting the matter straight. I have found in the case of Uganda, and any other country which I examine closely—as I am sure many others have done—that practically all the groups which we long aquiesced in calling tribes are not in fact what they have been taken to be. They are popularly taken, with little effective correction by anthropologists, to be clearly distinct local and cultural groups whose origins are so primeval that their identity is virtually impossible to modify. Whereas, on the contrary, most of these identities are of recent origin, moulded and defined by the exigencies of the colonial situation. The so-called tribes were either states and should be considered as such, or they were essentially segmentary not unitary entities, with multiple identities at a number of different levels equally meaningful in different contexts.[2] From the point of

[1] Aidan Southall (1974 and 1975c).
[2] Frederik Barth's deservedly popular formulations of subjective ethnicity are deficient in this respect, that they do not appear to recognize the

266   *Special Studies*

view of the primeval aura which usually invests them they are false and fabricated entities, but of course this in no way affects their current political relevance.[3] However, it may perhaps mean that a more correct understanding of their nature and origins might render them a little less dangerous and tend to diffuse their influence more innocuously at a number of different levels. This assumes that ideas have some influence on action. Thus, in Kenya, the Luyia came into existence in the 1940s, the Kalenjin in the early fifties and the Mijikenda in the late fifties. Yet most people seem to regard them as primeval tribes. The explorers of the 1860s found no Acholi tribe in Uganda, the Lugbara did not exist until so named after the small northern clan first met with by the Arabs, the Batoro came into existence in about 1830, the Bakiga are simply 'highlanders' so defined by the first colonial administrators, in Burton's day Nyamwezi and Sukuma simply meant people of the west and north, with a very variable contextual definition—and so on *ad infinitum*.

When it comes to the urban situation the confusion is worse confounded. It would not matter so much if tribalism and ethnicity were understood in their largely recent and essentially colonial sense, but even so, many aspects of urban behaviour are better understood when organizations such as the Ibo or Luo Unions are not related as tribal associations to a falsely imagined primeval past, but as ethnic associations to a relevant contemporary category of phenomena to which the activities of Poles and Italians in American cities, of Irish in Liverpool or Flemings and Walloons in Brussels obviously in various ways belong. All cases show the effect of migration and the problem of national identity in differing degrees, as is the case throughout Africa. I have therefore expunged the term tribe from my anthropological lexicon and use the concept of ethnicity in reference to all differentiations based on a sense of common ancestry and culture between individuals and groups at a number of different levels. This avoids absurdities such as the current references to both nepotism, or favouritism towards brothers or other kin, and caste differences between Tutsi and Hutu in Rwanda or Burundi as tribalism. The utility of the concept of ethnicity is, as Raymond Firth once remarked of such terms, to cover a rather wide and varied range of phenomena, with a great deal in common but a rather indistinct boundary.

multiple levels of ethnic identity (quite apart from other levels of identity such as lineage or age set) that may be relevant for the same person in different situations (1969: 13 et seq.).

[8] Aidan Southall (1970) and (forthcoming 1975a).

Forms of ethnic linkage between town and country 267

The recent anti-structural emphasis on micro-behavioural process has produced some excellent empirical studies but few effective generalizations. One of the promising ones, though not quite adequate in its original form, was Parkin's distinction between Hosts and Migrants in Kampala.[4] All such dichotomous labels are bound to embrace a number of factors, whose incidence is somewhat diverse and whose distributions do not coincide. Labels are a matter of convenience, but here I do not think it is convenient thus to blur the distinction between Host and Migrant and that between Centralized and Non-centralized societies, both of which are fundamental, but quite independent of one another, a point now accepted by Parkin (*infra:* 36).

Host status is significant, for example, in that a Host group never forms an ethnic association as such. Innumerable examples bear this out: Ganda in Kampala, Kikuyu in Nairobi, Luyia in Kitale, Zaramo in Dar-es-Salaam, Yoruba in Ibadan or Lagos. But a group which is Host in one town may form an ethnic association in another far away, as the Yoruba do in Niamey. In the case of the Ibo and the Luo their ethnic associations were formed in foreign towns and generated home branches later. The combination of localized segmentary lineage organization with massive labour migration to cities generates a particular type of many tiered ethnic association which does not appear otherwise. The Luo, Luyia and Ibo cases, though incompletely studied, are sufficiently documented to demonstrate this, on the strength of which I had predicted that Tiv, having the same type of social structure, would generate the same type of urban ethnic association if heavily involved in migrant labour to cities[5] I now have some evidence to suggest that this is in fact the case. In all these examples the Host/Migrant factors are combined with the localized segmentary lineage factor. Other contrasts appear in the literature such as that of the Kru and Vai in Monrovia, the Temne and Mende in Freetown and the Lokele and Babua in Kisangani (the former Stanleyville).[6] The relevant factors and features are not sufficiently well unscrambled in any of these latter cases to make adequate comparative analysis possible.

The activities of the various Ibo Union branches in welfare and development for their home areas have often been described. Though on a smaller scale, the Luo Union has demonstrated a similar function, most recently in mobilizing the collection of

---

[4] David Parkin (1969a).
[5] Aidan Southall (forthcoming 1975b).
[6] Merran Fraenkel (1964), Michael Banton (1957), and Valdo Pons (1969).

268 *Special Studies*

resources for building and establishing the Ramogi Institute of Advanced Technology.[7]

I have cited this brief instance of a rather formal kind of generalization to suggest that generalizations for the field of urban studies in Africa or beyond will require greater depth as well as breadth than we have yet achieved. The variety of urban situations in Africa does provide an approximation to an experimental situation in which first one and then another variable can be held constant while the rest are studied in detail, by selecting appropriate cases with a clear experimental end in view. The attempt to do this with other people's data, collected with other ends in view, inevitably finds vital data lacking. Nor is it feasible for one research worker to cover the necessary field, nor is there any experience to suggest that grandiose team projects can succeed here, rather it should be the cumulative unfolding of the collective efforts of individual fieldworkers directed to well thought out ends.

The variables involved in the Host/Migrant and Centralized/Uncentralized dichotomies are just one case in point. Their utility could be better assessed as well as empirical situations better understood if they could be used with sufficient depth in a larger number of cases. Centralized political structure and *laisser faire* policy towards the growth of a modern city out of a traditional capital are factors favouring the development of Host characteristics, as in the case of the Ganda in Kampala, Amhara in Addis Ababa, or Yoruba in Ibadan. Does it apply to the Mossi in Ouagadougou,[8] or the Ashanti in Kumasi? We presume so but have no adequate data. Such further exploration would greatly refine the categories, since the assumed familial and marital implications of these two dichotomies in Kampala might not follow in the case of Ouagadougou and Kumasi with differing domestic and kinship institutions. The Kikuyu hardly had the status or the feelings of Hosts in Nairobi. The city was only on the edge of their country and not being

[7] Information from Dr. David Parkin. During the last few years there has been a great resurgence of ethnic activity in Kenya, with every major ethnic group organizing to collect funds to start its own college of technology. This movement has sanitized ethnic organization for the most élite and urban based persons who might otherwise have disapproved or disdained such involvement. With such a goal, calculated to foster nation building, economic development, productivity, education and modernization, as well as helping fellow ethnics to compete more effectively in the ever more bitter battle for employment, ethnic organization seems to have become positively virtuous despite its separatist dangers.

[8] Elliott Skinner (1974: 204, 212) in fact confirms that the Mossi, like other centralized and host people, do not form ethnic associations as such, while other stranger groups such as the Fulani do.

Forms of ethnic linkage between town and country   269

centralized they had no traditional focus to attract the grafting of a city on it. Furthermore, they were oppressed by a settler dominated colonial régime, so that although they were the urban majority they were there on sufferance, like the Xhosa in East London and Cape Town or the Ndebele in Bulawayo.[9] However, the increasingly effective political dominance of the Kikuyu in Nairobi during the post-Independence period has given them much more of the status and attitudes of Hosts.

Another instance of the general atrophy of promising hypotheses is Mayer's well known contrast between Red Xhosa and School Xhosa in East London. What are the effective determinants of such a situation? Is it the combination of proximity between rural and urban residence with the results of reaction to the oppressive racial régime of South Africa? Proximity permits the Red Xhosa to draw moral strength and purpose for their urban living from a persistent rural based traditionalism, in a way that might otherwise be difficult. At the same time, it is hard to believe that such attitudes would persist if it were not for the harsh deterrents and bitter discouragements to participation in the westernized sector of South African society. Brandel-Syrier's study of a 'Reeftown Elite' has shown that full participation in urban life and status produces a brain-washed condition in which respectable urban Africans, who are outcasts in relation to white society, none the less concentrate their efforts on a pathetic mimicry of white social ceremonial.[10] Are we to assume that all Black élites in South Africa who eschew political involvement because of its heavy risks and penalties approximate to this condition? The School/Red dichotomy can be

[9] Philip Mayer (1961); Monica Wilson and Archie Mafeje (1963).

[10] Mia Brandel-Syrier (1971). It is pathetic because it represents an acting out of the superficial trappings of a status from which the players are excluded. Mimicry may be in ridicule or in fantasy and aspiration, where the miming is permissible but the reality is prohibited. In another context, Okot p'Bitek (1973) pillories the 'apemanship' of post-colonial Africa, blond wigs on the heads of black Ugandan youths, meaningless names, the desire to sing exactly like some foreign pop star; leaders who wear tailed coats and striped trousers for their weddings, African bishops blessing black congregations in Latin, and medieval costumes in African universities. 'There is no creativity in "aping".' During her field work in the summer of 1974, Christine Obbo noticed in Ombeyi village, West Kano, Kenya, how Luo servants from European houses in Nairobi bought and kept special suits to wear on their return to the village. One even varied this by carrying a rucksack to reflect the more informal style of his Swedish employer. They and their wives also dress up in the same way to receive their relatives when they come to town and to show them round. Audrey Richards (1954: 59) also noted that Rwanda migrants returning home from Kampala saved their better clothes to put on when they approached their homes.

270 *Special Studies*

perceived in many other parts of Africa as an aspect of different degrees of urban development, but without the persistent discontinuity between the two categories which is implied for the East London situation. Why is the School/Red dichotomy not found in Cape Town (as one must conclude from the Langa Study)—or is it present but unreported? If it is not present, is this due to the greater distances of the Langa Africans from their rural homes? Correspondingly, why are the 'Oo-scuse me/Oo-Mac' categories of Langa not reproduced in East London—or are they again present but unreported? Surely the determinants could be pinned down with much greater precision by comparative research in Salisbury, Bulawayo or Gwelo, with their slightly different blend of social and industrial apartheid, and in Lusaka or Livingstone, Luanshya or Ndola, where the results of a similar past but a changed present could be studied. Or are the answers to such questions still lying hidden in the field notes of those who have conducted research in all these and other places?

The extreme discontinuity suggested by Mayer's study seems to result from the combination of several factors. In the neighbouring areas of the Ciskei from which most of them come, there is already a longstanding rural distinction between pagan villages and Christian villages—such as those dominated by the Presbyterian Church. Thus 'Reds' coming to East London from pagan villages and 'School' Xhosa coming from Christian villages simply carry over into the urban situation a dichotomy which is already present in the countryside. Furthermore, the conditions of East London facilitate this perpetuation because they are able to rent houses for themselves so that Red and School continue to live separately from one another. The urban network here is therefore a direct extension of the rural one. On the other hand, in the conditions of Langa in Cape Town, the Africans have to accept what accommodation they can get in the barrack rooms of the compounds. There is no possibility of maintaining such distinctions and in any case the Red and School categories are more locally mixed in the areas from which they come, not separate village communities such as those which feed East London. However, there are some similarities which can be traced in the two situations.

The inhabitants of the barrack compounds in Cape Town do behave rather like 'Reds' in keeping to themselves and not attending cinemas and dance halls like the more settled townsfolk of Cape Town, who in this resemble the 'School' people of East London. Since the African population of both cities is so predominantly Xhosa, ethnic differences are objectively slight and are not in fact

Forms of ethnic linkage between town and country   271

manipulated for mobilizing support or expressing cleavages. Mayer exaggerated the division between Red and School by restricting his study to a rather narrow aspect of their lives and omitting the many occasions which bring Red and School together, in place of work, in labour disputes and in reaction to common emergencies, when being raided by the police, when linked by clanship to the same funerals and mourning ceremonies, or when assisting one another to send money home. There are also cases of intermarriage between Red and School, and both are brought together in some of the separatist sects such as the Bhengu Church. However, a comparable distinction to Red and School appears between those who do or do not belong to the mutual aid associations of home boys from the same neighbourhood. These are the ones who can trust one another and who can always trace and bring pressure on anyone who defaults or absconds. Although technically voluntary, you are in effect obliged to join as long as you identify yourself with this category, for to refuse is really to assert that you are 'Town' and can bear responsibility for yourself. The poor migrant cannot afford to do this; he needs his credit association and he does not abrogate his home boy ties.[11]

To judge from the East London and Langa studies, ethnic factors are unimportant in these African populations. Is this because ethnic differences are indeed so slight among them, or because the overarching White–Black confrontation overwhelms lesser differences of identity? Studies of Sotho, Tswana, Nguni and other ethnic identities in Johannesburg should throw light on this very easily, since the White–Black confrontation is obviously in evidence there, while ethnicity is also the basis of some important group activities within the African population. Presumably those who select the Red Xhosa type of option must stress ethnic differences within the African population when they are present. The matter could be much further illuminated, if sports activities and organizations, which have been quite considerably studied in South Africa, could be more fully and reliably interpreted in relation to the paramount need for escapist outlets and for the generation of some satisfyingly status-giving roles in an oppressive situation of deprivation,[12] and on the other hand the inevitability of the emergence of such activities and organizations when certain levels of education and urban involvement have been reached, as evidenced in other African countries where racist oppression is not a relevant factor. (I specify racist oppression, because, of course, other forms of social and

[11] Information from Dr. Archie Mafeje.
[12] Leo Kuper (1965) and Monica Wilson and Archie Mafeje *op. cit.*

272 *Special Studies*

political oppression have also become highly relevant determinants of the urban process.)

In the areas round Johannesburg it appears that the differences in the situation correlate quite clearly with the different factors involved, mainly the presence of distinct ethnic groups and the exploitation of these by the White authorities in the township and compound system. There are Pondo, Tswana, Sotho, Nguni, Shangaan and Venda sections of townships. You have to declare your 'tribe' and are allocated to compounds in these specific groups accordingly.[13] In these circumstances the Red–School type of identity distinction is unworkable and useless. The fellow ethnics compulsorily concentrated in the same compounds have their own language, perform their own rituals and are only very tenuously linked to Johannesburg. The ethnic rivalry imposed upon them is carried into other fields, so that Nguni compete with Sotho for position in the Johannesburg traders' associations, as Kikuyu and Luo might in Nairobi. But in South Africa they cannot move on to the next stage of opulence by investing in land and property.

On the Zambian Copperbelt the mines provided coffins, truck transport and graves in case of death so one of the main motivations for mutual benefit associations was thereby removed and ethnic associations were correspondingly weak. However, certain distinctly situated ethnic groups tended to keep to themselves, especially the Nyakyusa from southwestern Tanzania, constituting 8 per cent of the mines labour force, particularly concentrated in certain mining towns such as Kitwe and specializing in certain kinds of hazardous work such as lashing. They left their wives at home and often lived in tight little groups, sharing the same single quarters, with their own kind of food and of course their own language which no one else understood. They participated very little with other ethnic groups in sports and leisure activities. They even came close to forming their own trade union, but finally threw in their lot with the rest.[14] Epstein's account of how in the labour organization of the Copperbelt generally, occupational interests triumphed over the ethnic structure favoured by the mine authorities is very well known.[15] Although strong ethnic associations were not formed, home boy groups comparable to those described for Langa were important and they provided the basic cells which were transformed into the structure of the United National Independence Party.

Elsewhere in Zambia there was more need for ethnic associa-

[13] Information from Dr. Archie Mafeje.
[14] Information from Professor J. Clyde Mitchell.
[15] A. L. Epstein (1958).

Forms of ethnic linkage between town and country 273

tions, where the employment structure was less monolithic and fewer services were provided. Thus there was a 'Sons of Barotse' organization in the city of Livingstone. Other activities which provide the strength of ethnic organizations elsewhere were discouraged or forbidden by the colonial government. When the Mazabuka people organized to tax themselves to build more schools at home, the Government prevented them and required them to support only government approved schools. Schapera described how Tswana chiefs actually ordered men to go to work in the mines and send back money for schools. Another factor which partly substituted for ethnic associations in Zambia was that as in Tanzania many peoples had clan and cross cousin joking relationships which they were able to extend to general interethnic patterns of reciprocity and mutual aid in the urban situation.[16] The Host-Migrant distinction was irrelevant in Zambia, and in the rest of Southern Africa, because the urban areas were white dominated and no African ethnic group could achieve the status of Hosts.

Another influence upon the strength or weakness of the ethnic factor in African urban life is government policy, past and present, whether colonial or independent. Thus, it would appear that in Windhoek (Namibia) ethnic organization was definitely imposed upon the African population by the early German administration. But even in the absence of such imposition, ethnic organization in some form seems to have been an inevitable product of the early urban migrant labour situation, and to have been so regarded by both its African participants and White colonial administrators (and even Black also in the case of Monrovia). It was thus treated as a matter of convenience in Dar-es-Salaam, the Copperbelt Towns, Monrovia, Freetown and many other places. Anglo-Saxon colonialism regarded urban ethnic organization either neutrally as a convenience, or, in the case of settler countries, more positively as a proper element maintaining and perpetuating the inferior life of Africans in the city, helping them not to be confused or spoilt by new western institutions. Epstein's analysis demonstrated the contradictions and ultimate failure of this attitude on the Copperbelt. Was there any comparable sequence of events on the Rand? If not, how is this to be explained? Especially as the outlook shows itself strongly in South Africa in the promotion of ethnic dance teams by White companies as a subtle attempt to emphasize to the White world the unchanging primitive tribal culture of the happy African in the White-ruled city. By contrast, there was an intrinsic bias against any official recognition or countenancing of ethnic differences

[16] Information from Professor Elizabeth Colson.

274 *Special Studies*

in French colonial theory, although the exigencies of local situations led to plenty of variation in practice. It would appear that this contrast of the colonial era has naturally been reversed during the period of independence, in which it is the independent governments of Anglophone Africa which have shown much the greatest sensitivity about organizations and activities based on ethnicity, often amounting to official prohibition. The paradox is, of course, that while the potential contribution of permitted ethnic organization to political separatism is justifiably feared, there is a great yearning to return to the indigenous sources of African culture, which are felt to have been disparaged during the colonial era, and to drink fresh draughts of inspiration from them.

A different aspect of the relation between urban and rural living, which is becoming increasingly important in the independent countries of tropical Africa, is the growth of middle-class families, living in their own houses on their own land, within reach of a town by bicycle, motor cycle, bus, or car, growing most of their own food as well as cash crops for extra income, while the husband (and, increasingly, even the wife as well) works in town daily at a clerical or administrative job. This process began some decades ago in the case of Kampala (where it has been studied by Gugler) and many others where the situation was similarly favourable, but it could not develop in the White settler countries of Southern Africa where the system of land distribution prohibited it, since Africans could not usually acquire their own residential and agricultural land within easy reach of the White-dominated urban areas. The African élites of the independent countries are combining urban and rural resources in the opposite way, by living in the city where both husband and wife may have professional jobs, but acquiring farms and ranches in the countryside, even at some distance since they can afford to maintain easy contact by car. In a formal sense this recalls the ancient practice of the urban Yoruba, who controlled their agricultural land from residences in the city. Ethnicity also remains very important here, since very few people outside the local ethnic group are prepared to risk investment in agricultural land, even if they have permanent jobs in the nearby city. However, in Kampala during the last two or three years, members of the political, administrative, professional and business élite of all ethnic groups (though Ganda are still in the majority), have begun very actively to buy up small building plots within the urban area and to construct buildings ranging from mud and wattle to permanent houses and even office blocks for the sake of rental income. In fact, at the moment, the rate of return on mud and wattle lodging houses

Forms of ethnic linkage between town and country 275

(capitalized at about two years' purchase) is more rapid than on any other form of local investment. The prevailing political climate is also an important factor, since, with more frequent changes of régime, the top élite have come to feel extremely insecure in their careers, and this has acted as a very powerful stimulus to energetic entrepreneurship on the part of both men and women. There is a growing number of independent professional and business women, while many of the wives of men in the ruling élite feel that their husbands' future careers and income are uncertain, so they wisely exploit their current income and their privileged access to loans, permits and controlled property to form profitable investments in businesses and real estate as an insurance for the future.

What I have tried to show is that in this field of urban and ethnic social relationships and organization the apparent diversity of different African cities and countries can be shown to vary according to quite intelligible, orderly and consistent principles if the relevant variables are carefully sorted out, thus demonstrating that apparently unlike situations arise mainly from the same sets of factors differently combined and operating at different strengths. If space permitted, this could be demonstrated more convincingly, by detailed comparative studies of neighbouring situations and countries, of different cities and towns within the same country, illustrating how contrasting situations arise predictably from variations in the component factor combinations.

Three styles of ethnic migration in Kisenyi, Kampala

PHILIP HALPENNY

INTRODUCTION

Studies of migration in Africa seem to have shifted in the last few years from social anthropological analyses to demographic analyses of regional flows. Internally this has meant that ethnicity as a factor in migration has been stressed less than have regional economic disparities, while internationally attention is placed on flows of labour and refugees (e.g. Langlands 1972: 352).

The ethnic factor can be significant even here however. For example, there has been a constant inflow of population into Uganda from Rwanda for a long time, but the earlier flow of labour (described in Richards n.d.) differed ethnically from the refugees who entered Uganda in the early 1960s. For urban specialists ethnicity is often the most significant variable, although not perhaps for demographers—thus Ravenstein defended his original formulation of the concept of step-migration by the claim that the presence of the 'floating element' often obscured this significant demographic pattern. As an example he gave the case of the United States, where the universal step-migration pattern had been hidden under the massive influx of ethnic immigration (Ravenstein 1885: 235).

On the one hand the description of a single ethnic community in an urban area perhaps over-emphasizes the 'urban-village' aspect of urban structure (e.g. Gans 1962). On the other hand many studies in African cities of small areas which contain much ethnic diversity did not include all of that present in the city, very often such studies described 'African' residential areas only (there were some exceptions, e.g. Sofer and Sofer 1955). In another paper I have attempted to show that the distinctiveness of 'European', 'African' and 'Asian' in economic and class terms is less than exact in Kampala, particularly for an entrepreneurial bourgeoisie composed primarily of Africans, Arabs, Somalis and Indians (Halpenny 1972).

The only way by which an ecologically diverse area can be

Three styles of ethnic migration in Kisenyi, Kampala 277

analysed sociologically is to consider, following the methodology of regional demographic studies, that residence in an area defines the population to be sampled. The synthesis of this concept of aggregate studies with the delineation of patterns usually described in micro-studies (the ethnic variable) is attempted below.

KISENYI

Even the name of the densely populated Kampala area called Kisenyi reinforces its local image as a 'slum', for in Luganda *kisenyi* means a swamp margin, the low flat which lies between the hill and the edge of the papyrus mat.[1] As in other cities of the world the characterization of an area as a slum simply indicates a failure to comprehend and order its diversity.

The gross mobility of the Kisenyi population is apparent, as 32 per cent of the adults in the sample have come to Kisenyi within a year.[2] 68 per cent of the adults were born in an agricultural area, but only 23 per cent of them came directly from their birthplaces (and 35 per cent came directly from agricultural areas). Some 71 per cent have lived in an intervening residence between their parents' home and the time when they came more or less permanently to Kisenyi. Three ethnic groups, the Ganda, the Luo/Luhya and the Arabs, Somalis, Indians and Mixed (ASIM) show significant differences in the pattern of intervening residences.

Table 1

Three ethnic groups by last residence

	Rural area	Town	Total
Ganda	144 (47·2%)	161 (52·8%)	305
ASIM	8 (5·1%)	150 (94·9%)	158
Luo/Luhya	42 (68·9%)	19 (31·1%)	61
			N = 524

[1] The area has been completely described in Southall and Gutkind (1957). The current sampling in 1971–2 is part of a research project sponsored by the Rockefeller Foundation by a grant made to Professor A. W. Southall, but the interpretations and uses of the data here are my own. The sample included 163 residential structures from a frame of 803. This is a 20 per cent sample of the structures, but only the most complete interviews were used in this paper; a demographic analysis of the area will be made elsewhere. Figures in this paper are hand-counted and may differ from later machine counts. The work of John Muwonge was vital to the project, and Patrick Mulindwa provided useful criticisms of the draft.

[2] An adult is defined here as a male over 18 and a female over 16, although wives under 16 were also counted as adults, except in male–female ratios, where the count is of all males and females over 16.

278 *Special Studies*

The Luo/Luhya pattern is a familiar one of long-term circular migration (Elkan 1972) where wives join their husbands in Kampala during slack agricultural periods, but return to their husbands' land to plant and harvest. Some Luo women have moved completely to Kampala with their husbands, and so there is an important difference between the Luo and Luhya populations; the male–female sex ratio for the Luo is 1·778, while the Luhya figure is 3·50. Luo women at the least seem to come more often and for longer periods.

The Luo/Luhya tendency to maintain the rural tie might be skewed however, because a man may have returned to his home after working in a city and before he came to Kisenyi—his last residence is rural but he has wide urban experience. Thus 45 per cent of the Luo/Luhya men had experienced urban living before they came on their last move to Kisenyi. The urban network of the Luo has been well-described by Parkin (1969a: 146–7), while Dak also noted a great difference between the Luo and other migrants in their spatial distribution, caused by the significant urban concentration of Luo in Uganda (Dak 1968: 39–40). This Kisenyi case provides an illustration of prior urban residence. He was counted as coming from an agricultural area.

> Onyango, a Luo about 48, left his home in 1941 and went to Karamoja in Uganda where he lived in the small administrative (and only) town of that District. He worked as a tailor for an Indian who owned a tailoring shop. After nine years the 'town council' (i.e. the town administration) produced a regulation requiring the 'upgrading' of some business premises, but the Indian did nothing so the shop was condemned and destroyed. Onyango had no other place to go so he went back to his home in Nyanza. After three years at home he returned to Uganda and lived in the administrative town of the neighbouring district of Teso. He again worked for an Indian as a tailor and stayed there for some time, three years or so. He then went back to the first town, where he worked this time for an Arab, once again as a tailor. About 1959 he moved to Kisenyi after a home interlude of six or eight months—a friend was living in this room and had a business as a launderer, so Onyango put a leased sewing machine on the veranda and thus began his own business (November 1971).

It should be emphasized that the political factor does not account entirely for the maintenance of the link with rural areas of Kenya, nor with the lack of investment in rural holdings in Uganda by so many in this group. Some Luo do obtain rights to cultivate in rural Uganda, just as one Kikuyu shopkeeper of Kisenyi had an agricultural holding 10 miles from Kampala. Many Luo have not hesitated

Three styles of ethnic migration in Kisenyi, Kampala 279

to invest in businesses and housing in Kampala, and some have actually purchased land in both urban and rural areas.[3] They are not forced by political factors into maintaining the link with Kenya, especially as many have now learned to live with political commotions such as occurred in February 1973.

Citizenship can be a confusing factor. For example, Onyango's son was born in one district capital in Uganda and began primary school in another. He did his secondary schooling in Kampala up to the GCE level. The Government of Uganda wants him to do his Higher School Certificate (sponsored by the government) in Kenya, but he feels he has a right to an education in Uganda. Perhaps the confusion faced both by governments and people over the citizenship issue was illustrated once again in February 1973 when the Uganda Government threatened to deport all Luo in Uganda. One prominent Luo in Kisumu responded that 'Luos are subjects of the Kenya Government' (*Daily Nation*, 13 February 1973), but a Luo refugee from Uganda said 'We told them that we were citizens of Uganda and showed them our trade licences, which are valid up to the end of 1973' (*East African Standard*, 16 February 1973).

The ASIM urban pattern is quite different—the urban network in Uganda was synonymous with the spatial distribution of the Asian community (Larimore 1958: 154). This pattern was produced again, to some extent, by political factors since non-Africans in general were prohibited from investing in land in Uganda. The complexity of the citizenship issue faced by the Luo also affects the ASIM, but on a deeper and often discriminatory level.

The ASIM were prevented from investing in land from as early as 1906. The colonial policy was clearly to prevent land from falling into the hands of those who did not have a customary claim to it. In one case land could not even be alienated to 'a person not a native of the *district*' (Uganda Protectorate 1957: 27, my italics).

The definition of African and non-African has continued to be vague up to the present, but even now current land law restricts ownership to an 'African citizen of Uganda' (Public Lands Act, 1969; sec. 19d). The Trade (Licensing) Act, 1969 applied all of the restrictions against carrying on trade by non-Africans outside gazetted areas to non-citizens. This move to restrict commerce on the basis of citizenship (used as an euphemism for ethnicity) was less than successful, so when non-citizen Asians were expelled from Uganda a move was made to extend this policy to force the expulsion of Ugandan Asian citizens as well. This move was rescinded two days later (*Uganda Argus*, 21 August 1972, 23 August 1972).

[3] Information from C. Obbo.

K

280 *Special Studies*

The final solution to the Asian urban presence seemed to be a reversal of the old policy of urban containment by the announcement that Asian citizens would be resettled in agricultural areas as peasant farmers (*Uganda Argus,* 13 November 1972).

Arabs and Somalis are often thought to be in a separate category from Indians and they were not expelled along with them; the history of whether they were considered to be Africans or not is long and complex, but often they were not (as in Legal Notice 65/1958).

Some few ASIM could occasionally obtain access to land despite the legal prohibitions if they had kinship ties with Africans—this applies not only to those called Mixed (the *Bakyotara*) but also to some of those classified as Arab or Indian, although even here the land would be put to particularly 'urban' uses. An example follows.

> He is 33 and an Ismaili (Indian) whose mother's father had come from India and married a Musoga—his other relatives were Indian. After four years of secondary school he worked in a number of skilled jobs, teaching for a few years in Kenya towns, making his own transport business for a year at his home in a small town in eastern Uganda, and working for a few years for a medicine dispenser in Kampala. He quit a job as an accountant at a large Indian factory in Kampala a year ago and established his own transport business again; he has a large lorry and carries dry-goods among the towns lying on the highway which passes through his town. Most of his business comes from smaller towns where competition is less and he is more well-known. The transport business is too competitive however, so he wants to build a poultry farm on the eight acres still held by his grandmother (June 1972).

This example delineates part of the urban network of the ASIM, which stretches without pause into Kenya and extends down to the smallest rural trading centres.

The ASIM usually make their living either as skilled employed artisans, as owners of construction companies or carpentry shops and furniture manufacturing operations, in the long-distance transport business as either owners or drivers, or are in the restaurant business (commerce in the form of shop-keeping was much less common among Kisenyi ASIM). Many Africans are involved in all of these as well. The urban character of these occupations is obvious.

This urban life-style is possibly produced by factors at several levels. On the deepest is a cultural orientation by Arabs and Indians to urban living: even 'villages' in north India are nucleated settlements with populations of more than a thousand, and Islam in Uganda was introduced by urban populations.

Three styles of ethnic migration in Kisenyi, Kampala 281

There were two streams of Islamic penetration into Uganda, a military intrusion by soldiers from the Sudan at the end of the nineteenth century, and a slower, constant flow of traders from the east coast which began about the middle of that century. The descendants of the soldiers are the Nubi (eight households in the Kisenyi sample) who have a different pattern of migration into Kisenyi from that of the ASIM in that most Nubi in Kisenyi have rural backgrounds. Wanji (1971) explains why this is so for an otherwise urban Muslim population.

DEPENDENT AND INDEPENDENT WOMEN

Because Freetown was located in the Temne area, Banton noted that they had many different reasons for coming into the city, while the Mende and other populations came mainly for work (Banton 1957: 133). Similarly the Ganda in Kampala, who, like the Temne are also Hosts, exhibit much more variation in their migration paths to Kisenyi than is found in other populations. This is clear from the percentages in Table 1.

Some regularity in the pattern of migration of the Ganda into Kisenyi is provided by a measure which distinguishes the marital condition of females when they last entered Kisenyi.

The striking figure is the number of Ganda women who have undergone rural separations before they came, 81 cases or 39 per cent. Four Ganda women had had more than one *rural* separation (cf. Gutkind 1962: 199).

Table 2

Ethnic group by marital condition of adult female's first marriage at time of entry into Kisenyi

	Ganda		ASIM		Luo/Luhya	
Came by marriage	51	(24·8%)	41	(54·7%)	17	(77·3%)
Came alone	29	(14·1%)	1	(1·3%)	2	(9·1%)
Rural separation/ came by marriage	12	(5·8%)	0		0	
Rural separation/ came alone	69	(33·5%)	1	(1·3%)	0	
Urban separation/ came by marriage	8	(3·9%)	1	(1·3%)	0	
Urban separation/ came alone	20	(9·7%)	5	(6·7%)	1	(4·5%)
Came with parents	8	(3·9%)	12	(16·0%)	2	(9·1%)
Born in Kisenyi (may have moved in and out)	6	(2·9%)	13	(17·3%)	0	
Not stated	3	(1·4%)	1	(1·3%)	0	
Total	206		75		22	

282   *Special Studies*

A high proportion of Ganda women are household heads in Kisenyi, 100 or 48 per cent of all Ganda household heads (while 33 per cent of all household heads in the sample were women).

A high incidence of female household heads is also found in the rural areas of Buganda and in other Interlacustrine Bantu districts. In one sample of four villages, all, in part, selected for isolation from urban influences, 22 per cent of Ganda household heads were women (Southwold 1959: 208, 309, 338–42); in one of the most isolated of these the figure was 27 per cent (*ibid* 341–2). In another of these villages 50 per cent of the adult Ganda women were un-married or separated (*ibid* 309–10). Taylor found, in two villages in the same area as one of Southwold's villages, that 23 per cent of Ganda household heads were women (1958: 123). Richards and Reining found that 28 per cent of 299 Ganda households were headed by women, and this was in a village only 12 miles from Kampala (1952: 5).

Female household heads in rural areas are not necessarily new; Mair found seven women out of 58 households (12 per cent) living alone in Bowa in 1932–3 (1940: 23) (compare with another of Southwold's villages which had 13 per cent; 1959: 208). Of these seven women three (43 per cent) were widows, two had left their husbands to come to Bowa and two had been left there by husbands (Mair 1940: 23).

In contrast to these figures for females, Southwold found in two of the four villages that 18 per cent of Ganda household heads were single men (1959: 336); Taylor found exactly the same number of single male householders as female (1958: 123), and Mair found 33 per cent of the householders to be single men (1940: 23). Nine of these men in Bowa were married but their wives were elsewhere.

The presence of widows, of course, can be expected as a neces-sary phase of the developmental cycle of the rural household. Other single women also have a well-defined position in the rural social structure. Obbo mentions one of these, the *nakyeyombekedde* (1973: 17ff). The term is interesting. It denotes a woman who lives alone, a female household head who is not dependent on a man (cf. Perlman 1963: 190–1, 202, 239–40).

In the town as well a woman who is not economically dependent on men because of her income from economic activities or from her investments is a kind of *nakyeyombekedde*. These women are often the female houseowners found in urban areas (cf. Southall 1961: 223–4). Her economic independence gives the *nakyeyombe-kedde* the right to choose her lovers, and she may support them (see Obbo 1973: 85). On the other hand, and perhaps more usually,

Three styles of ethnic migration in Kisenyi, Kampala 283

she may have rich boy-friends (who are also influential political and economic contacts) who appreciate the company of a mature, successful and non-dependent woman. She may appreciate their gifts which leave her even more basically independent of men, while other *banakyeyombekedde*, usually older, may have little or nothing to do with men.

The *nakyeyombekedde* may visit men in their rooms or men may come to stay with her, but her economic independence is always uppermost in determining her place of residence and whatever arrangement exists with her lover. The *malaaya* (often but inaccurately glossed as 'prostitute') on the other hand is economically dependent on the man, and this alone determines her choices of lovers and residences.

The Ziba women of Kisenyi are true prostitutes who live in a specific area and receive men in their rooms (see Southall and Gutkind 1957: 79). They are spatially stable in that they do not 'roam' about, moving in with men, but their total income is dependent on sexual relations with innumerable men in rapid succession. Most Ziba utilize their high incomes by making investments in their home areas—and so these Kampala *bamalaaya* may become *banakyeyombekedde* (often rural) when they retire home.

The usual *malaaya* on the other hand may rent a room and return to it every few days or so, spending the time in between in her current lover's room; alternatively she may remain in her room but the rent is paid by one lover, the food bill by another, and so on. This arrangement contrasts with the flat fee per occasion charged by the Muziba. This *malaaya* may sometimes think of herself, and be thought of, as having multiple 'husbands', a kind of polyandry.

The term *nakyeyombekedde* can only be applied to an older woman, one who is at least 28 or 30. This is obvious from the economic component, for a woman rarely if ever can establish her economic independence before such an age. The *nakyeyombekedde* therefore is a figure of some stability. She is often a house-owner if she is in the city (but she may only rent, usually in the same room for many years while she continues her established business). If she is in the village she usually owns an agricultural holding with a house on it. She must of course be distinguished from women who live alone on their husband's holding while he lives either in the town or on another holding with another wife, just as some women in Kisenyi live alone but carry on a business while the husband pays the rent and is involved in financing the business (see Kabwegyere 1972: 153, 156; Obbo 1973: 18, 38).

In rural areas women are either attached to others or are

284 *Special Studies*

banakyeyombekedde, although some few floating *bamalaaya* and barmaids are probably found everywhere. Young girls are residentially attached to their parents—but they may in practice be sleeping with men in exchange for cash or gifts. Since they are *attached* residentially however they are not strictly *bamalaaya* until they start staying out at night.

If a girl is sleeping around her parents may try to get her married. She may run away from her husband and with accumulated capital (particularly if she has saved for some years) she may establish herself as a rural *nakyeyombekedde.* It can be seen here that the crucial factor in both rural and urban areas is to what degree the married woman is able to accumulate a separate source of capital (see Obbo 1973: 38). She may go directly to the city, or may join another man. Often she goes back to her parents' home for a time. While living with her parents she may have comparatively great independence and her behaviour may resemble that of the *nakyeyombekedde* (Perlman 1963: 288), but she is probably still considered to be married, particularly if the payment has not been refunded. Her behaviour therefore must be discreet or her husband could sue for adultery, while her economic possibilities may be limited. She may accumulate enough capital to establish her own household, or she may inherit a plot (many widows become *banakyeyombekedde* by remaining on the deceased husband's plot).

If she does not become a rural *nakyeyombekedde* a woman may go from her parents' home into another marriage, or she may go directly to the city. If the latter and particularly if she is young she may get a job working in the *munanansi* (pineapple beer) business or as a barmaid, where salaries are so low that they must be supplemented by sex.

These polarities of *malaaya* and *nakyeyombekedde* are ideal types; many *bamalaaya* have some kind of residual job, often of a kind which brings them into contact with men. Many claim to even have 'husbands', men with whom they feel they have some slightly more stable relationship (also cf. Obbo 1973: 27, 30). As time passes the *malaaya* may accumulate enough to establish her own business and so become a *nakyeyombekedde.* If the woman comes into the city older and with a little capital she may become a *nakyeyombekedde* directly. The *malaaya* may establish a stable relationship with a man as she grows older, or perhaps has a succession of stable relationships. If she does not, and does not become a *nakyeyombekedde* then as she gets older and becomes less competitive she becomes derelict. Stability of course is a relative term and so a stable relationship may be one which lasts

Three styles of ethnic migration in Kisenyi, Kampala 285

more than three weeks (Perlman 1963: 14), or more than a year.

It is becoming increasingly clear that the decision to migrate is primarily cognitive (Hutton 1968: 37ff.; Todaro 1969: 138), and a person will migrate if his view is that by doing so his situation is improved. Female migrants may indeed be escaping from the drudgery of rural life (Southall 1961: 221), but other unattached women in similar situations do find rural life viable.

It may be that those who decide to migrate find themselves enmeshed in a slightly less viable matrix of social and economic situations, but on the other hand it is also reasonable to suppose that those who migrate are more adventurous and competent and already possess some of the entrepreneurial qualities of aggressiveness and risk-taking which predisposes some of them to success in the Kisenyi economic arena. Not all of them succeed and many go from Kisenyi to rural areas, which are not necessarily those they left; town-born girls may even seek positions in rural bars.

But while many women do remain in the villages others go to Kisenyi and in more than proportional numbers—about double the number of female household heads are found there, if the rural data are valid. Perhaps in part this difference is produced by the greater economic opportunities available to women in such places as Kisenyi (see Halpenny 1972; Obbo 1972, 1973; Southall and Gutkind 1957), although it is important to remember that, however restricted, economic opportunities for women do exist in rural areas.

The rural–urban difference here is real and relatively important (cf. Dewey 1960) and can be measured quantitatively (another statistic is the low number of widows among Kisenyi Ganda women, 16 per cent of female household heads instead of the rural figure of about 50 per cent), but the difference between urban residence and rural is often arbitrary, as should be expected in a population which is highly mobile residentially (Richards 1966; Southwold 1959: 127). The movements of Nalwoga's mother's sister's daughter show that if we had come at an earlier date she would have been in the village —and before that would have been found in another area of Kampala. There are no data available on the number of women in villages who have lived in Kampala or other towns but many *banakyeyombekedde* must have done so.

Nalwoga, who makes a living brewing *munanansi* on a low-income scale, says she is 30 and she may be 40. She was married in 1954 and moved to the next village where she cultivated her husband's

286   *Special Studies*

fields until she left him in 1969. She went back to her parents for six months, and was not allowed to leave until her family was satisfied that she had refunded the marriage payment of Shs. 370/-, which she raised by cultivating coffee on her father's land. She then came to Kampala and got a room with another woman in Kisenyi for a few months. Her MZD joined them from her room in Kisenyi. After two months Nalwoga and her MZD came to this room, as the three of them had been crowded in the other room.

Her MZD had moved to her husband's holding when she married in 1953. When she left her husband in 1965 she went back to her father's holding for a year (her parents are separated and her mother has her own purchased holding in a rural area 80 miles from that of the father). She then came to Kampala and lived in another dense area for four years. She then went back to her father's holding for another year, then came to Kisenyi last year and lived in her own room until she moved in with the others.

Nalwoga's MZD had not refunded the marriage payment; she was terrified that her husband would find her by some fluke and force her to go back. Nalwoga said that the reason she left her husband was that he never bought her anything, never any new clothes. Husbands are really terrible; they use your labour to dig coffee (a labour-intensive cash-crop which requires three to four years of labour input before producing), then when enough is planted they make your life miserable so that you have to leave. (January 1972).

CONCLUSION

Three patterns of movement into Kisenyi have been described. With the exception of the ASIM pattern these are not characteristic of ethnic 'supertribes', groups which are geographically, linguistically and culturally close (Parkin 1969b: 282). For example the Toro, who are geographically, linguistically and culturally rather close to the Ganda, particularly in the forms of female roles (see Hoover 1972: 7; Perlman 1963: 241), differ in the sample on the male–female household head ratio, 5·00 to the Ganda 1·10, the overall male–female ratio of 1·375 to the Ganda 0·665, and especially in the number of women who came married into Kisenyi, 74 per cent, a figure closer to the Luo proportion than to that of the Ganda.

The Host-Migrant and Centralized-Noncentralized distinctions do not of course necessarily distinguish groups which are geographically, linguistically or culturally close. These two conceptual dichotomies, so useful in other contexts, are less than satisfactory in explaining why the migrant groups, Luo and Luhya, have highly divergent sex ratios or why the Kiga, a noncentralized migrant group, have a Kisenyi male–female ratio of 1·625 (despite a 1959 ratio of 0·926

Three styles of ethnic migration in Kisenyi, Kampala 287

for Kiga nationally), and a household head male–female ratio of 2·667. These figures for the Kiga so far indicate a great difference from the Ganda, but only 44 per cent of the Kiga females came by marriage while 56 per cent came alone, a figure near that of the Ganda. Only the ASIM pattern can, to some degree, be explained by the Host-Migrant dichotomy, and then only if modified so that the Hosts are thought to be Ugandan Africans in this situation, while both the ASIM and Luo conditions can be partially explained if the Hosts are thought to be Ugandan citizens. It should also not be forgotten that Africans thought Asians to be the Hosts in urban areas because of Asian urban dominance.

Political factors do not fully explain these patterns either, and economic, occupational and cultural factors are also significant and operate in combination. Thus, Luo women may adopt Kiganda ways of behaving, as occurs particularly in other areas of Kampala (see Obbo 1972). The single Luo woman who came alone to Kisenyi (Table 2) is a woman who first moved to another dense area of Kampala with her husband, then separated and moved into Kisenyi where she sold illegal spirits. On the other hand, Luo and Ganda men may follow Somali patterns of involvement in the urban-centred transport business. Southall, for example, gives a case of Luo in the goat trade (in the early 1950s) which involves a spatial network similar to that of several Somali, although these Somali in Kisenyi now have their own lorries (Southall and Gutkind 1957: 56).

This inter-relation of factors suggests two main conclusions. First, this paper has dealt with a sample area within Kampala which is highly multi-racial: so what has been said here may apply still more strongly to urban areas in even more heavily multi-racial societies such as Kenya, Zambia and Tanzania, in which, for example, Europeans and Asians constitute a large and influential component of the 'host' communities. Second, the distinction produced by the data between the *malaaya* or male-dependent single woman and the *nakyeyombekedde*, the economically independent single woman may be extremely common throughout urban Africa, although the rural *nakyeyombekedde* may or may not be characteristic only of Ganda social structure. As an urban role it may be found in cities outside Africa. A role identity economically independent of men and 'emotionally' autonomous seems to be desired by increasing numbers of women, but unlike the situation in Kampala the *nakyeyombekedde* role does not exist fully in Europe or America, and is not yet named.

Women's careers in low income areas as indicators of country and town dynamics

CHRISTINE OBBO

The first aim of this paper is to shed some more light on the 1920s Chicago school views usually persistently articulated by R. Redfield as the folk–urban ideal types. This ideal model hypothesis pictured the movement from a folk culture to an urban culture as involving secularization, individualism, and disorganization; (Redfield 1941: 342). The paper is concerned only with the last two characteristics. Secondly, the paper is a modest proposal that unskilled migrant women should be recognized as a legitimate category for study.

The rural–urban dichotomy has tended to obscure planning strategy, policies and academic theory. As long as villages (scattered houses each surrounded with a garden) and cities (closely built houses with well planned roads) were seen to exist empirically, urban planners emphasized life styles as either 'traditional' or 'modern'. Even when Africans started settling in cities in large numbers, rural and urban sectors were not treated as aspects of the same social field. Thus an African is a miner when he is at the mines and a tribesman when he returns to the country (Gluckman, 1961). The circulatory migrants shuttling periodically between town and country in search of employment on the other hand, and culturally satisfying life styles on the other; target labourers responding to the requirements of a cash economy and working for specific economic requirements, for example bridewealth, bicycles, taxes, school fees, etc., and commuters whose homes are near enough to town so that they can use public transport (buses, taxis, etc) or private means such as bicycles, cars, lorries, or by going on foot; (see Elkan 1959) convinced some planners further that Africans preferred rural to urban life. The fact remains that the urban areas were not planned to accommodate migrants and their families. Either the rents were too high in relation to the wages, or the houses were one-roomed and not designed for family living. In East Africa, already by the late 1930s many thousands of itinerant traders appear to have been moving in and out of Nairobi, Kampala, and Dar-es-Salaam, but

Women's careers in low income areas 289

before long they had started settling there. They settled in the so-called slums where the city authorities did not have control. (Southall 1957). The significance of the growth of East African slums is due to the fact that the people who lived in them during the colonial period constituted the majority of the city population; also that the development of these urban slums was directly related to the character of economic development in East African society as a whole.

Perhaps this is the point to specify the type of urbanization this paper is concerned with. It is not the most common one—the growth of modern cities which are well planned, serviced, essentially western, and which need educated people to operate them. We are concerned with what has often been called 'subsistance urbanization'. But since it involves the majority of town dwellers, we feel that special attention should be paid to it. In East Africa it is growing faster than the modern urban sector. Akin L. Mabogunje has shown that between 1950 and 1970 the population of large urban centres in Africa has been increasing at the rate of 7 per cent a year while the total population itself is only growing by 2·3 per cent a year. (Mabogunje 1971). We also know that the cities have large bureaucracies and busy markets but few industries (Muthiora 1970: 226). This means that all the migrants cannot be absorbed in the urban formal job structure and therefore there must be a lot of people coming to the cities to look for work that does not exist—and who in government statistics fall into the category of the unemployed poor. They are treated as undesirables in the urban areas by planners and policy makers (see Van Velsen *infra*). Not only are they ignored in educational, health, and housing policies but they are constantly urged to go 'back to the land'. In Uganda, co-operative 'Young Farmers' clubs'; in Kenya rural centred industries; and in Tanzania Ujamaa villages have been attempts to relieve the urban areas of the burden of supporting the poor.

Perhaps it should be pointed out that East African urbanization has often been looked at from the standpoint of the minority élites whose life styles are perhaps not so radically different from the élites in other cities of the world; and the role of the common people in skewing the direction of urbanization has either been underestimated or regarded as deviant and therefore unimportant. It is the contention of this paper that the future Eastern African city will be shaped by the fate of the common people, the so-called urban poor. At present the poor are not wanted in the city and women are treated as prohibited immigrants. And although it is often assumed that low income people are recent immigrants to the city, in most cases

290 *Special Studies*

they have been there for more than 5 years—longer perhaps than the élite or policy makers who see themselves as urbanites. In East Africa, the Vagrancy Acts and Prevention of Prostitution Acts seem to have been used specifically to harass women, and the poor in general. Take for instance Kampala, where throughout the 1950s the City Council and Kibuga officials periodically arrested single women who were found in low income areas of the city (Southall 1957, Parkin 1969a: 95). The prostitute hunts were in accordance with the 1941 law to prevent prostitution. The law defined a prostitute as 'any woman who habitually gives her body indiscriminately for profit or gain, or *who persistently indulges in promiscuous intercourse with men though she derives no gain or profit thereby*' (emphasis mine, Argus 1957: 6). With such an ambiguously broad law any women could be guilty of prostitution. The law seems to have been aimed at controlling the movement of women to town so that female migrants were inevitably regarded as prostitutes.

The case history that will be sketched later is illustrative of the different strategies open to female unskilled migrants in the urban areas. The data were collected from Namuwongo-Wabigalo, one of the low income areas of Kampala in 1971–2. This is an official classification based on the fact that the residents employed in the formal sector of the economy do not earn more than shs 500/- a month. However, residents who are in self-employment may earn from a little less to twice that amount. The area attracts many categories of people, the first includes students, school leavers, and civil servants who stay in the area because it is good for saving. For example, the area is 2 miles from the city centre and people can easily walk instead of spending shs 4/- on taxis and buses every day. Food is cheap and plentiful: for example, a plateful of potatoes and fish or *matooke* (steamed bananas) and meat cost shs 2/50 and a cup of tea or coffee 20 cents: thanks to the female food vendors and *hotelis* (shack restaurants). The second group of residents in the area are people in the self-employment business. In Namuwongo-Wabigalo (population 2,006) alone there were 100 carpenters, 87 tailors, 58 female food vendors, 20 small '*hotelis*', 20 hawkers, 20 water vendors, 10 taxi owner/drivers, approximately 100 *enguli* brewers (20 of whom have licences to supply the Uganda Waragi distilleries), 60 market sellers, 37 fishmongers, 58 charcoal sellers, 40 firewood sellers, 120 shopkeepers, 4 tin smiths (making pails, drinking water containers, oil candles and lamps), 6 blacksmiths producing charcoal stoves and coil pipes for distilling *enguli* (crude waragi or gin), 3 bicycle repairers, 2 paraffin stove repairers, 12 cement building block makers, and 10 cobblers.

Women's careers in low income areas   291

The third category of people in the area are shopowners and houseowners. These people are relatively well off and the capital invested in the businesses has either been accumulated from activities of residents in the above second category or generated outside Namuwongo-Wabigalo. Most people aim at eventually owning houses because it is one of the most profitable activities which guarantees the owner a regular monthly income.

Because of the large number of shops in the area and the high casualty rate of shops, it is not clear that shopowning is a very profitable activity except for a few individuals who make at least shs 320/- a month. But owning houses is profitable because the demand for housing is most pressing as migrants flood into Kampala. The old leaking mud and wattle houses have rooms that can be rented for shs 15/- or 20/-, but rooms in modern brick, iron-roofed houses fetch from shs 35/- to 140/- each. So the average house owner with, say, 5 rooms can hope to have an income of shs 500/- a month (after taxation).

The life history below of Fatuma Mukasa is not untypical and illustrates generally the fates and fortunes of the migrant women found in Namuwongo-Wabigalo.

In 1971, Fatuma was aged 38. Her father had been a Muslim religious leader in Soroti (he had gone to Soroti during the Kakunguru campaigns in Eastern Province at the beginning of the century). According to Islamic custom, so Fatuma says, a marriage was arranged for her at the age of 15 years.

'At first I was unhappy but then learnt to love Hussein, my husband, who was twice my age. His first three wives hated me because I was his favourite. After about six months, however, I found that I could not stand him and his wives. He begged me to stay with him but I went home to my parents. I became tired of my father's nagging, and encouragement of Hussein to issue threats against my lover, Mukasa, who was about my age. We eloped and came to Wabigalo in 1952. We worked hard and by 1962 we had saved enough money to build a house. We have four children aged 18, 16, 12, and 8 years. They are with my father in Soroti because I feel that children reared here are wild, disrespectful towards their parents and turn into useless citizens. We send money every month for their upkeep and school fees. Depending on how they perform, we now hope to send all of them to boarding schools next year. I know that my husband spends a lot of money on other women but it does not bother me. I also have male friends but what I celebrate most is having an independent source of income.'

Fatuma sells cooked food at lunch time to workers in the indus-

292 *Special Studies*

trial area, and in the evenings she sells *enguli* at home. Her husband owns a coffee and pancake 'box' (stall), also in the industrial area. Not only does Fatuma make up to shs 800/- a month from her food and *enguli* sales, but she supplements it by gifts of clothes and money from two influential boyfriends (one a business man, the other a top civil servant). Currently she has built a ten-roomed house for renting. Given the current high rents in the area she will probably get shs 750/- or more a month. But it is interesting to note that her husband is ignorant of her real income and investments although he suspects that Fatuma's income is probably more than the shs 200/- she claims to earn.

Among 164 respondents eight reasons were commonly given by women for coming to town. These were as follows:

63 accompanied husbands.

10 were tired of rural life and desired to share urban life with the husbands or alone.

30 were tired of marriage and came to seek a more satisfying alternative.

5 had run away from polygynous marriages and the associated jealousy and sorcery.

5 were barren and migrated to escape the stigma.

4 were widows—second or third wives of the deceased.

5 were adventurers looking for something more in life than village life offered.

20 were pregnant and needed to get away from self-righteous village morality.

To return to Redfield, there does not seem to be evidence to support the hypothesis of disorganization in family institutions. A large number of women migrated with their husbands and the rest migrated alone. The significant features of these latter is that they were likely to have been involved in inter-rural migration anyway, with the town just offering a better alternative. There is evidence to show that women are individualistic in that they are saving and investing independently of male control; but we need more evidence to ascertain whether this is purely urban behaviour. In addition the economic activities that women engage in do not require many skills and are in most cases a continuation of the activities they performed in the rural areas, the only difference being that in the urban areas their labour is rewarded by cash payments. For example, cultivation, brewing, distilling, cooking food, house-owning, are rural activities; whereas only prostitution, bar-tending and shop-owning are predominantly urban activities.

Having arrived in the city women employ different strategies in

Women's careers in low income areas 293

order to stay. They usually engage in some economic activity but to avoid starvation or eviction from the rooms or to save for 'a rainy day', their different strategies include befriending influential businessmen or civil servants 'of means', who become patrons and clients. These latter enjoy the company of these women and at the same time can help them secure jobs or trade licenses in the formal sector. This strategy is very important. Normally women will operate illicitly and hope for the best but when that fails, they must be prepared to pay the fines or bribes to the city council officials. In conclusion it should be acknowledged that the strategies work for some women and not for others.

Urban squatters: Problem or solution

J. VAN VELSEN

INTRODUCTION

The systematic analysis of squatters, shanty towns or slums receives scant attention in general textbooks; but in the world of political and social affairs these 'irregular' residential areas figure prominently. Indeed, mention of them tends to be in terms of 'problems' which need 'solutions'. Yet it is not always clear for whom the squatters constitute problems: for urban administrators, for politicians, or even for themselves? This is the main point I want to discuss in this paper. I will restrict myself to urban squatters and most of my material comes from Zambia.[1]

It might be useful to start with some quotations from published opinions about the squatters in Zambia which are representative of the views held by many, both official and non-official.

On the 30th May, 1970, 571 houses were demolished in Nguluwe squatter compound in Lusaka. According to one newspaper report it was 'the biggest ever anti-squatter operation by Government squatter controllers and police.' (*Zambia News* 31/5/1970). This operation affected some 2,000 people. An editorial comment in the same issue expressed the following views on the squatter problem. After pointing out that the previous day's operation 'might seem very inhumanistic, in that it deprives many of a roof over their heads', the article continued that it was a necessary exercise for two reasons:

> The first is that our cities, and more particularly our capital, must rid themselves of the scars of such settlements, thus removing the

[1] I owe much of my understanding of the squatters' issue in Zambia to the following students from the University of Zambia who I supervised when they were doing their field work in Chipata from February until the end of May, 1972: Mr. E. N. Chidumayo; Mr. M. M. Gondwe; Mr. G. C. Kaluba; Miss E. D. Lungu; Miss J. J. Ngalande. I will refer to their field notes as Chipata Reports. I am grateful for their permission to quote from these notes. Another important source, apart from newspaper reports, is a series of roneo'd reports on surveys (CD/Res/2) carried out by the Department of Community Development of the Ministry of Co-operatives, Youth and Social Development.

Urban squatters: problem or solution   295

liability from the municipal authorities who are doing their best to plan the most effective future building schemes.

The squatters themselves must realize that the day of living in unauthorized areas and expecting councils to provide for them—without offering anything in return—are well and truly over. The sooner more of these demolition projects are carried out in other parts of the country the better.

It isn't as if these people had not been given a chance. There have been many opportunities for them to take part in self-help housing schemes. But they have ignored all the offers and warnings put forward presumably because they have been basically too lazy to help themselves . . . without expecting the state to do it for them, and there can be no sympathy for those who are now homeless. It is entirely their own fault.

Yet there is an acute housing shortage not just in Lusaka. But allowing the squatter compounds to remain until more accommodation is available is not going to solve the problem at all. They are just going to get bigger and bigger and a large source of headaches for the councils and, of course, perfect havens for the criminal element.

If the people living in these terrible areas used more initiative instead of sponging from a community to which they are contributing nothing, they need not suffer in any way by being moved away from their hovels. . . .

. . . Councils where possible up and down the country have been only too willing to provide assistance to . . . self-help housing schemes. This is . . . contributing towards a particular area's housing development. In a growing city or town there is no place for the lay-about. Either he helps himself or gets out and goes back to his home area where he will have to do something useful if he is to survive at all.'

It so happened that about three years previously the Department of Community Development had carried out a survey of Nguluwe. Significantly in the present context the survey's report was entitled: *Ground Floor to Development: A Survey of Nguluwe Compound* (Okada 1967). This report refutes almost every allegation against the settlement's inhabitants: being idle layabouts not prepared to help themselves but instead 'sponging, from a community to which they are contributing nothing', etc. In fact, these allegations were refuted in a subsequent letter to the editor of the same newspaper (*Zambia News* 14/6/1970) which quoted some of the findings of the Nguluwe survey. Presently I will return to the points raised in the editorial article and the survey.

In 1971 a then prominent Cabinet Minister referred in a public

296 *Special Studies*

speech to '90,000 uninvited guests'.[2] The figure refers to the number of people who were believed to have arrived in the towns from the rural areas.

The phrase implies some interesting views which have frequently been stated explicitly by others. 'Uninvited' seems to suggest that people in the rural areas should only move to the urban areas when they are called, i.e. when they are needed as workers. Otherwise the urban areas should remain the preserves of those who are there already. A further implication is that all those 90,000 arrivals from the rural areas were not needed and thus presumably unemployed. Hence squatter settlements and rural-urban migrants are not infrequently associated with 'loafers'.

The term 'guests' reinforces the analysis of the preceding paragraph: towns are not really for the rural people whose 'home' is and should remain the village—as, in fact, the last sentence of the quoted editorial states explicitly.

These and many similar opinions imply a peculiar and I would say an unhistorical view of the growth of towns, *viz.* that normally all towns should be planned. When the houses have been built and all necessary urban amenities have been provided, only then should people be allowed to come and live there. In fact, of course, very few towns have ever come into being in this fashion.

These implications and assumptions are part of a stereotype of squatter areas. They are 'dens of vice' (*Zambia Daily Mail*, 4/5/1972) where drunkenness and prostitution are rife. This is where the unemployed and the loafers (these two words are often treated as synonyms), and most newcomers not only to a specific town but to urban life in general, are found.

In this paper I want to examine some of these assumed characteristics of squatter areas. I will try to show that, firstly, the squatter far from being typically a loafer who sponges on a community to which he contributes nothing, is engaged in useful economic activities. From this it follows, secondly, that it would be unwise (even if it were possible) to stop this flow into the towns. Not only is the squatters' labour needed for the economic life of the towns but as long as the standard of living in the rural areas is so glaringly inferior to that of the towns, very strong oppressive measures would be needed (e.g. the introduction of influx control passes along South

[2] This person has since resigned from the Government and the ruling party after a serious political disagreement. However, his remark cannot therefore be dismissed as coming from a potential opponent because many similar views have been expressed by others and, indeed, the editorial comment quoted earlier is in the same vein.

I am quoting the Minister's phrase from memory as I cannot trace the newspaper report.

Urban squatters: problem or solution 297

African lines) to halt the rural-urban migration. Finally, the squatters' economic activity must be assessed in terms not only of their gainful employment but also of their considerable contribution to the national capital. They have invested much labour and other resources in the provision of houses without which the urban housing problem would be far worse than it is.

UNAUTHORIZED SETTLEMENTS

Among the variety of definitions of the term 'squatter' one finds one common element, *viz.* a reference to the squatter's lack of legal title to the land or even the dwelling he occupies. The latter category of squatters is not usually found in Zambia or for that matter elsewhere in Africa but rather in the older towns in the more industrialized nations where squatters have moved into empty buildings. In this essay I will be concerned only with squatters who occupy land—and have built houses—without title.

A further difference between the squatter 'problem' in Zambia (and apparently in other African countries) and elsewhere is that the illegal occupation of *private* land is a minor aspect of the definition of a squatter in Zambia. It is not, in my view, a conflict with private landed interests that characterizes the Zambian squatter. This is in marked contrast with the Latin American situation. From the literature on Latin America it is clear that the illegal occupation of private land is an important element in the definition (and solution) of the squatter problem.[3]

Apart from his illegal occupation of land another legal aspect of the squatter is his infringement of a variety of building, planning, sanitation and other regulations. These formal, legal, aspects of the status of the squatter explain why he cannot get building loans from public financial institutions. They are also contributory factors to the squatters' lack of security: the instance of the Nguluwe squatter settlement shows how with the backing of legal sanction a whole community may be deprived of a roof over their heads. However, for every squatter removed many more have been left undisturbed. Indeed, it would be socially and politically impracticable forcibly to remove the literally untold thousands of squatters in Zambia. I would therefore argue that it is the uncontrolled, and seemingly uncontrollable urban expansion which is the principal concern of administrators, politicians and others. It is this that makes squatters a 'problem'. In other words the main parameters of this 'problem' are social, political and administrative rather than legal. I will return to this point below when I try to answer the question why squatters,

[3] See for instance the various papers in United Nations (1968).

298 *Special Studies*

in spite of their considerable economic contribution, are persistently referred to as a 'problem'. The distinctly unfavourable stereotype of squatters is in conflict with available evidence. This stereotype frequently also has a historical dimension which is equally contrary to the facts. There is a belief, often publicly stated, that squatters (and 'loafers') are a post-Independence phenomenon; that in the colonial era administrative control over the urban areas (through the 'pass system') was so tight that 'illegal' entry into and settlement in the towns in Northern Rhodesia (as it then was) was practically impossible (cf. *Zambia Daily Mail* 4/5/1972). The implication is that under the more generous conditions of the Zambian government all the constraints disappeared and that this allowed an uncontrolled inflow into the towns with all its attendant problems of squatters, loafers, crime, etc. The fact of the matter is that the squatter 'problem' goes back several decades and is likely to have come into existence with (or to have been created by) the first Ordinances. Indeed, some of the present squatter settlements predate Independence in 1964. Thus the Eccles Report of 1944 lists the various types of urban settlements and among them we find: 'Unauthorized Settlements: Settlements which have been established by African Squatters on Crown land in the vicinity of municipalities or townships', (p. 4) and in 1955 Mr. E. Tikili reported that the Kanyama 'unauthorized settlement' (which still exists) had a population of between 1,600 and 2,000 people.[4]

The older term 'unauthorized settlement' seems more appropriate: it sums up the position better than 'squatter settlement' (or 'compound') with its dominant connotation of illegal occupation of land. The term can also serve as my definition: *viz.* a settlement without planning and building permission. The illegal occupation of land is in Zambia at least a minor aspect of the problem. As most squatters live on public land it is largely a matter of central government legislating for 'a simplified system of land tenure' in order to give self-help housing schemes proper security of tenure.[5] In other words, apart from passing laws the legalizing of squatter compounds should not involve the extensive buying out of private landlords.

There are some squatters on private land although the indications are that they form a small minority. The owners of the land may either build pole-and-dagga houses themselves and rent them out or

[4] Tikili (1955).

[5] This would also seem to be the view of Government. See the Ministry of Local Government and Housing Circular 'Housing Policy. . . .' The general tenor of this document is that the legal obstacles to the new housing policy, which includes the 'legalizing' of squatter areas, should not be too difficult to overcome through legislation.

Urban squatters: problem or solution 299

charge rent for the land only and leave it to the renter to build his own house. This means that in fact the landowner is establishing a housing estate without the necessary planning permission or the provision of adequate services such as water, sewerage etc. Thus whilst the house-owner is not illegally occupying land *vis-à-vis* the landowner he is still considered a squatter. This, again, indicates that the essential aspect of the squatter 'problem' is that it is effectively beyond the control of the authorities rather than a matter of illegally occupying land. The landowners, though breaking the law, collect their rents quite openly.

Another category of squatters paying rent are those who rent a house from the owner who is himself a 'squatter' in that he has built the house without proper permission, generally on public land. Finally, a squatter may buy a house in an unauthorized settlement.[6] Although there is no conclusive evidence, the indications are that the majority of the squatters have not bought their houses and live rent-free. Indeed, this is one of the compensations for, if not attractions of, life in an unauthorized settlement with its insecurity and lack of services.[7] At the same time squatters falling within certain income categories receive a legally stipulated housing allowance irrespective of whether they actually have to pay for their housing.

Although it is mainly the unauthorized settlements in or around the bigger towns which tend to attract public attention, it should be noted that they are ubiquitous. They can be found near almost any town, however small, including small District Headquarters (Bomas).[8]

Finally, after this brief summary of some of the administrative and other general features of *un*authorized settlements, I just want to mention the *authorized* residential areas. These are, principally,

(*a*) the ordinary municipal housing estates, such as Matero and Liballa in Lusaka, where the houses are for rent or sale;

(*b*) the various 'site and service' and 'resettlement' schemes where individuals can build their own houses on planned and serviced sites.

[6] See for instance Lundgren *et al.* 1969: 21; Okada 1967: 5; Chidumayo *et al.* 1972.

[7] See for instance Zelter and Witola (1967: 36).

[8] E .G. Kamwengo (1971). This is a particularly interesting example of the administrative creation of an unauthorized settlement. When the township boundaries of Mongu, the Provincial Headquarters of the Western Province, were extended, they came to include a considerable number of village homesteads on the edge of the Barotse Plain which had been there for a considerable time, possibly generations. The villagers thus became overnight 'squatters'.

300 *Special Studies*

THE SQUATTERS

As mentioned earlier I shall be mainly concerned with the unauthorized settlements of the major towns in Zambia. That means in fact the towns which lie along the 'line-of-rail', that uniquely Zambian socio-economic geographical concept that so often leads to confusion. Zambia's main railway runs from Livingstone north through the capital Lusaka and on to the Copperbelt from where it continues into Zaire. The 'line-of-rail' is the belt of land on either side of the railway, some forty or fifty miles wide. This is where the main urban and industrial development has taken place. Indeed, in common parlance 'the urban population' is frequently equated with the entire 'line-of-rail' although in fact there is a considerable farming population in this belt. That is one confusion. Another one is linguistic: because of the equation of 'urban' with 'line-of-rail', 'rural' refers to that part of Zambia that lies beyond the 'line-of-rail'. Hence a 'rural' farmer or village is not the counterpart of an 'urban' farmer or village but refers to farmers and villages in the rest of Zambia, generally with the connotation of 'subsistence' or 'less developed'.

Another fact which inflates the figure for the urban population is the tendency to quote the figures for a district as a whole rather than the size of the population of the town only when this town is the headquarters for a district.

With these provisos in mind the published results of the 1963 and the 1969 censuses can give us at least some idea of the trend in the growth of Zambia's ten major towns, *viz.* Chililabombwe, Chingola, Kalulushi, Kitwe, Luanshya, Mufulira, Ndola, Lusaka, Kabwe and Livingstone. In 1963 the ten major urban areas (including their Districts) had a population of approximately 649,000 out of a total population of 3,405,788, or about one-fifth of the total population.[9] According to the preliminary report of the 1969 census[10] and presumably using roughly the same criteria for determining the urban population, it had grown in six years to approximately 1,146,000 or about 28 per cent of a total population of 4,055,995. Thus the urban population had by 1969 increased by about three-quarters since 1963. Whilst these calculations are rather rough and ready, more refined calculations regarding the growth of

[9] The 1963 Census was a census of Africans so that only figures for the African urban population are available. However, following the census report I have added the figures of the 1961 non-African urban population to those of the 1963 African population. See Central Statistical Office (1968: 9–10).

[10] See Central Statistical Office (1970: A9; and table A7–A8).

Urban squatters: problem or solution

301

Lusaka can be found in a recent town-planning report on Lusaka. According to this report the annual rate of growth of Lusaka was 5·3 per cent in the period 1953–8, 10·9 per cent for 1958–63 and 11·8 per cent (or an absolute increase of 94,000) for the years 1963–8.[11] Final mention must be made of the growth rate of Chipata (Fort Jameson of the colonial days)—a town not on the 'line-of-rail' to which I will refer again later. According to the 1963 census report (p. 37) the population of Fort Jameson (Chipata) Township was 7,602. The research team of the students mentioned earlier reported that in May 1972 the Chipata municipal housing area had about 13,470 inhabitants; that means an increase of some 75 per cent. The inhabitants of the unauthorized settlements numbered some 5,000. It would seem most unlikely that in 1963 there were no squatters in Chipata. However, their numbers are not known.

Whatever the accuracy of the urban population figures, it is clear that the rate of urban growth is considerable. What is equally clear is that the provision of authorized housing has not been able to keep pace with the population increase. It is thus inevitable that all towns should have unauthorized settlements. But, as in the case of urban growth, it is far from easy to find data on the numbers of squatters. In the published census data no distinction is made between authorized and unauthorized settlements. Nor can one use the criterion of the payment of rent: whilst the majority of the squatters do not pay rent, either for a house or for the land, some do. Moreover, a significant category of the lower paid Government employees do not pay rent, but they are not squatters. I will, therefore, accept the opinion held by many who are familiar with the squatter situation, *viz.* that some 40 per cent of Zambia's urban population are squatters.

In the light of the negative stereotype of the squatters I now want to consider some of their social and economic characteristics. What contribution do they make to the towns in which there is no housing for them?

The following four tables have been derived from sources of uneven quality but they are the best I have so far been able to find. They should be considered as indicators rather than as precise statements. The main variables I am concerned with are the age and sex ratio; employment; length of residence; and where possible the last place of residence before the current one.

The data refute the general notion that squatter areas are largely inhabited by bachelors who have recently arrived in the urban areas for the first time and tend to be unemployed. There is not only a broad correspondence between the employment patterns of the

[11] Doxiadis (1969: 90–1 quoted in Ohadike in this volume).

302   *Special Studies*

Table 1

'High density' municipal housing area: Copperbelt

Married Persons	182	(92·4%)
Unmarried Adults	15	(7·5%)
	197	(99·9%)
Employed	162	(82·2%)
Self-employed	24	(12·1%)
Unemployed	8	(4·0%)
Not Stated	3	(1·5%)
	197	(99·8%)

Source: Okada (1968).

Table 2

Unauthorised settlements in the Kafue Township area

Males	
Under 15 years	37·6%
15 years and over	62·4%
	100%
Females	
Under 15 years	40·5%
15 years and over	59·5%
	100%
Heads of Households*	
Employed	79·5%
Self-employed	14·5%
Casually Employed	2·0%
Unemployed	6·5%
	102·5%
Previous Residence	
Village of Birth	10·1%
Other Rural	26·9%
Line-of-Rail Urban	56·5%
Outside Zambia	5·4%
Not Stated	0·6%
	99·5%

Most of these unauthorised settlements are of comparatively recent origin, but in the two oldest ones the majority of the heads of households had by the end of 1968 lived there for over five years.

*The excess over 100% is accounted for by persons who worked for wages and also had a business of their own.

Source: American Friends (1970).

Urban squatters: problem or solution

Table 3

Nguluwe: an unauthorised settlement in Lusaka

Males	Number		Employed	
Under 18 years	98	(23%)	5	(5·1% of males under 18)
18 years and over	141	(33%)	115	(81·5% of males over 18)
Females				
Under 18 years	83	(19·6%)	0	
18 years and over	101	(24·8%)	4	(3·9% of females over 18)
	423	(100·4%)		
Heads of Households				
Employed	98	(87·5%)		
Self-employed	6	(5·3%)		
Unemployed	6	(5·3%)		
No answer	2	(1·7%)		
	112	(99·8%)		

Previous residence
Practically all people had come from elsewhere in Lusaka, mostly from other unauthorised settlements.

Source: Okada (1967).

Table 4

Kalingalinga: an unauthorised settlement in Lusaka

Males		
Under 15 years	1,276	(22%)
15 years and over	1,787	(31%)
Females		
Under 15 years	1,456	(25%)
15 years and over	1,287	(22%)
	5,806	(100%)
Heads of Households		
Employed	134	(77%)
Self-employed	30	(17%)
Unemployed	10	(5·7%)
	174	(99·7%)

(Taking all males over 15 years, it was found that 48 out of 249 or 19·3% were unemployed)

Previous Residence
Out of 174 heads of households, 97 had lived in Kalingalinga ever since they came to Lusaka, while 77 had moved there from residence elsewhere in Lusaka. 36·21% had lived in Kalingalinga for five years or more.

Source: Zelter and Witola (1967).

304 *Special Studies*

unauthorized settlements but also between them and the municipal housing area.[12]

There is no evidence of squatter areas being overrun by rural migrants who keep flowing in irrespective of whether there are jobs for them. What is also striking is the generally small percentage of self-employed: a high rate of self-employment might have been an indication of large-scale disguised unemployment. Taking the generally high percentage of men in wage-employment and considering the large number of squatters in Zambia, one can only conclude that the unauthorized settlements harbour not so much a large 'loafing' element but rather a significant proportion of the country's urban labour force. This leads one to wonder how the country's economic life would be affected if indeed all the squatters were to 'return to their villages' as they are so often publicly exhorted to do.

THE URBAN COMPLEX

The unauthorized settlements are part of the town but do not share with it the usual urban services: piped water; a sewage system; properly maintained roads; clinics; schools; or even the routine services of the police. The inhabitants of the settlements have to go to the municipal area for some of these services: schools, clinics and even shops. The Chipata research team report that the landowner of one of the unauthorized settlements refuses to allow anybody to open a shop on her land.[13]

Many of the functions of local government are performed by a branch of the ruling party (UNIP: United National Independence Party).[14] It is the party which allocates (or denies) a plot to newcomers. It is the local party leadership that acts in many situations as a law-enforcement agency, protecting life and property. However, the leaders are not concerned with the more technical details of statute or bye-laws. Thus it is they who issue 'licences' to women for 'illegal' brewing: this is a source of patronage and a sanction. Indeed, it is exactly in the provision of these shebeens that most unauthorized settlements play an important role *vis-à-vis* the municipal (including the mining) townships. In the latter, with a closer surveillance by the police, the shebeen trade is exposed to much greater risks. And when the licensed bars in the municipal

[12] See also Pandawa (1970: 9–10).
[13] See Chidumayo *et al.* (1970).
[14] I am aware only of UNIP playing this role but I presume that in areas where the African National Congress (ANC) has a stronghold, it is the local ANC leadership which fulfils this role. (But see reference to Kapipi in Introduction (p. 34) *ed.*)

Urban squatters: problem or solution 305

areas are closed, people can and do continue their drinking in the shebeens. Pandawa (1971) gives a graphic description of the important role of the shebeens, and the squatter areas in general, in the field of entertainment. Similarly, illegal butcheries (slaughtering and selling meat without a licence) frequently operate from unauthorized areas. Their cheaper meat attracts customers also from the municipal areas.

I have already discussed what is undoubtedly the most important function of the unauthorized settlements not only in the national economy but also in relation to individual towns: they provide housing for a large proportion of the labour force for whom there is no alternative provision in the municipal areas. Thus the squatter areas rather than constituting a 'problem' play an essential part in the process of urbanization. And insofar as a person who needs a house in a particular town has any options, the unauthorized areas offer some important attractions. One I mentioned earlier: housing is cheaper. Even where rent has to be paid, it is less than that generally demanded for housing in the municipal areas.

Possibly another advantage in settling outside a municipal area with its building regulations, is that a prospective home-owner has greater freedom to choose a site and erect a building to suit his own specific purpose. For instance I have been told that people in the unauthorized areas of Kafue expressed the desire to select a plot which would be able to accommodate houses for kinsmen who want to live close together and thus create their own neighbourhood.[15]

However, whatever advantages may be attached to unauthorized housing areas their disadvantages are keenly felt. The lack of clean water is a common complaint and so is the absence of a proper sewage system and reasonable roads. Considering the absence of these services it is not unreasonable to assume that life in unauthorized areas is likely to have greater health hazards than in the municipal areas.

This was the assumption underlying a recent study of the effect of town life on child health. In presenting her preliminary results the author came to the conclusion that in this respect the difference between Mwaziona, an unauthorized housing area in Lusaka and the adjacent municipal area, Matero, was minimal if any.[16]

[15] Personal communication from Mr. H. van Doorne who did a study of the unauthorized areas around Kafue Township. Mangin (1967) reports a similar observation from Peru.

[16] Savage (1972). In the course of the discussion of that paper some preliminary results of a similar study in some rural areas were presented. These appeared to show that the hazards for child health might be greater in the rural areas. It would appear therefore, that life in a housing area without clean water, sewage and other forms of sanitation might be no more un-

306 *Special Studies*

I have argued that the squatter and the municipal areas are complementary. The squatters have to be near a municipally serviced area on whose services they have to draw. Conversely, the municipal part of a town would be severely handicapped, at least under present conditions in Zambia, if it could not rely on the labour and some specialist services of the squatter areas. This may seem a truism but in fact these two complementary parts of an urban complex are not infrequently treated as if separable. Indeed, the unauthorized areas are sometimes considered pathological phenomena.

THE PROBLEM OF THE SQUATTERS

I have already mentioned some of the problems of the unauthorized areas as the squatters see them.[17] But these problems are not likely to be solved unless the officially designated 'problem' of the squatters ceases to be perceived as such. The latter 'problem' is basically different from that perceived by the squatters themselves. This problem is summed up in the editorial article which I quoted at the start of this paper. The 'problem' would seem to be that squatters are a threat. Certainly, the stereotype of the squatters contains all those elements that would make any other category a 'problem' and a threat: parasitism ('scrounging'), crime, prostitution, laziness and general unproductiveness; and, indeed, an abuse of and threat to Zambia's newly won Independence. This latter element is represented by the historical dimension of the stereotype: *viz.* there were no squatters and 'loafers' under the tough colonial rule but they are a consequence (an abuse) of the greater scruples of a national (independent) government.

Other arguments against the squatters are part of a broader attack on the rural-urban drift and rapid urbanization. It has been stated in public that as the village is the repository of Zambia's traditional culture, the exodus from the rural areas may destroy it.[18] The drift to the towns also denudes the rural areas of their strongest men who should stay in order to contribute to the development of the rural areas.

The squatter 'problem' then is seen as a consequence of the 'exodus' from the rural areas. In order to solve this 'problem' the

healthy than in an urban area with these services or even in the rural area. After a long discussion the seminar was no nearer to isolating the crucial variables in this apparent paradox.

[17] For brief summaries of these problems see Okada (1967: 13 *seq.*) and Zelter and Witola (1967: 35 *seq.*).

[18] cf. *Zambia News*, 2/8/1970; *Times of Zambia*, 5/7/1972.

Urban squatters: problem or solution 307

'exodus' must be stopped. Hence the concern to make the rural areas more viable economically, to reverse the trend of the deterioration of the terms of trade between the rural and the urban section.[19] Other suggestions have not been so reasoned. There have been suggestions to introduce a 'pass system'. This has been one prong of the attack: to stem the flow at source.

Another prong is at the urban end. This is more difficult: to remove the squatters physically would be a gigantic task, as well as politically dangerous. However, the unfavourable stereotype of the squatter which seems to have gained wide acceptance is certainly not making his position easier and might well make it worse by causing a great deal of prejudice.

One final point: it is worth looking into what groups have expressed anxiety about the presence of squatters. Amongst them are politicians. It is not difficult to see that large, sprawling, poorly constructed and serviced, and densely packed suburbs are likely to be thought politically volatile.

Trade Unionists, too, have involved themselves in this 'problem' and one of the most senior leaders is reported to have made the following interesting statement: '. . . the exodus from the rural areas to our towns . . . has caused a serious threat to the stability of trade union members, since not all the rural migrants coming to towns can be given jobs. Unemployment, and under-employment, and the offer of cheap labour, *weakened* the bargaining position of trade unions' (*Times of Zambia* 15/4/1971). Clearly at least this trade union leader sees the newcomers to town as potential competitors with his members. It may well be that the rank-and-file think the same. The use of the damaging stereotype against the squatters has certainly not been confined to the trade union and political leaders. The Chipata research team came across a surprising number of occasions when people of roughly the same social stratum, but living in an authorized area expressed contempt for people living in the same town but in an unauthorized housing area.

Would one be correct to conclude that under present conditions with a tight job market, all those who are in the towns already do not want too many people to join them from the rural areas and compete with them for scarce jobs? If this helps to explain the apparent, and wide-spread, antagonism towards squatters, could one then argue that attaching an unfavourable stereotype to the opponent is a way of *legitimizing* opposition?

[19] See Young (1971).

The ecology of social types in Blantyre

A. B. CHILIVUMBO

In considering problems of urbanization in Central Africa, social scientists have identified various emerging patterns of social relationships and urban personality. From these studies some views have emerged which present urban and rural as dichotomized phenomena; African personality in an urban setting is defined situationally with ethnicity a major radix in the definition (Epstein 1958).

This analysis is less concerned with the process by which rural emigrants become urbanized but more with the consequences of this process: it looks synchronically at the inter-relations of components of the contemporary social structure of Blantyre. Various socially identified urban areas are treated as indices of stratification in order to analyse differential patterns of social relations, rural–urban contact, economic power and urban behaviour patterns. No statistical data are used; material is derived from discussions, observations and unpublished seminar papers of students and staff of the University of Malawi. The paper is essentially suggestive rather than conclusive.

As Pirenne observed, with reference to social change several hundred years ago, urbanization restructures rural and traditional social relations and creates new personality types (Pirenne 1956). More precisely, both rate and level of urbanization have generally been regarded as responsible for such change (Hauser 1965). Both these causal factors operate in Blantyre City, but because of its current rapid growth the factor of the rate is more prominent. Over the past five years some estimates have put this growth at not less than 10 per cent per annum. Other estimates based on comparison of dwellings appearing on two sets of air photographs taken several years apart put the rate at 22 per cent per annum!

Though the level of urbanization is still low by world standards, coupled with the rate, it is already causing serious social strain especially in housing, employment, the provision of social services and other facilities. The employment sector and the available housing are unable to absorb the rapidly growing urban population. The

The ecology of social types in Blantyre 309

1968 Household and Expenditure Survey and 1970 Estimates (Government of Malawi) provide some confirmation. In 1968, out of an enumerated 30,492 heads of households, 27,984 were employed and 2,508 were not. Two years later, the unemployed figures more than doubled and rose proportionately, 5,500 out of 38,000 heads of households.

Not all people who come to Blantyre City can be accommodated. Houses are already overcrowded and the 'squatter' colonies on the periphery of this city and several other urban centres in recent years provide a visual confirmation of the housing situation. The distribution in the country of this urban population is uneven. Blantyre alone accounts for 54 per cent (107,461) of the enumerated 203,303 urban population. The rest is scattered in a number of small urban centres, the largest being Zomba Town and Lilongwe Town with just about 20,000 people in each (Malawi Population Census 1966).

There appear to be two main causes of the rapid growth of urbanization in Malawi; the political policies of the neighbouring countries, and the process of internal economic development. Before independence, Zambia, Rhodesia and South Africa drew on Malawi for migratory labour, employing more persons than Malawi itself. Since independence, Zambia has not only closed off the labour migration from Malawi but has embarked on a process of Zambianization. Since Rhodesia's unilateral declaration of independence, a number of Malawians have been returning home with offspring, most of whom are urban-orientated. Though substantial numbers of unskilled labourers still find their way to South Africa through the Witwatersrand Native Labour Association the previous massive and free exodus to South Africa is at a standstill.

From all these three areas migration home is steady and sizeable. The returning population, unused to rural life, seek employment in the urban centres, but are not always successful, and so add to the growing urban population.

Rural economic development is another factor. One effect has been to create aspirations towards a cash economy and consequently urban wage employment. An attempted solution by Government to stabilize the rural population and slow down the rate of urbanization has been through agricultural development and settlement schemes, seen as ways of raising earnings in rural areas and achieving a desirable quality of life. The major projects are the Lilongwe Land Development Project, in the Central Region; the Chikwawa Cotton Development Project; and the Kasinthulo Rice Project in the Lower Shire, Southern Region. There are also several other

310 *Special Studies*

schemes. All are intended to be sources of high income for the rural population and many farmers are already receiving an annual income per capita much higher than some urban white-collar workers. But these measures of rural stabilization have so far only reduced the influx to town. They have not stopped it. Consequently, the urban level continues to grow and to mould urban social structures in contemporary Malawi, thus having an impact on patterns of emerging social relations and personality types. To investigate these patterns, using established social areas as a point of departure is the basic aim of this paper.

Blantyre City has well defined social areas or ecological zones, which can be classified into four groups. Lacking terminology we designate them as residential area types, one, two, three and four. Each type demonstrates relatively distinct socio-cultural and socio-economic characteristics. Since independence the constraints put on urban centres as non-African areas have been removed and choice of residential area is determined largely by socio-economic status factors, especially type of occupation and income.

In Blantyre City, type one is an exclusive, formerly European, residential area, but now Europeans live alongside Africans who hold high-ranking jobs such as Government ministers, permanent secretaries, under-secretaries, company directors and managers of companies and firms. It is a low density area, with multi-room, fully furnished, detached houses, large gardens, domestic workers' quarters, hedge fences, telephones, and a few have swimming pools. This type is found in Nyambadwe, Namiwawa, Mount Pleasant, Sunnyside and Mpingwe. African residents here fall within the same occupational statuses and enjoy relatively equal incomes and position but display considerable educational and age discrepancies. A large proportion is fairly old and has achieved its occupational position through long service and promotion. A few younger men have achieved the position through a combination of good luck, education or commendable service. Type one is the most expensive land area. The monthly rent for land is extremely high, ranging from £400 to £1,000 per acre, as is the value of the houses with rents of £50 to over £100 per house. The high rents are off-set by institutional subsidies. The African residents pay $12\frac{1}{2}$ per cent of their salary while the expatriates pay either 7 per cent of their salary or £12, whichever is the lower, as their contribution to house rent (as at 1972).

Type two residential area has less elaborate housing and facilities. It includes New Ndirande Lines, Soche East, Soche South and Zingwangwa West. It is a high density area with tarred roads and good sanitation. The semi-detached or detached two to three

The ecology of social types in Blantyre 311

bedroom houses have paraffin stoves, inside cold showers, asbestos roofs without ceilings, garages and water closets, but no garden facilities or domestic workers' quarters and rooms are generally small. The residents are mostly young, holders of university degrees and diplomas, in second-ranking occupational statuses: principal administrative officers, senior assistant secretaries, professionals, administrative officers and related jobs. They occupy their positions largely through educational achievement and aspire to the top posts. A few are single but those who are married have young children. However, as in type one, there are in this category a proportion of men who have no university education but have advanced through promotion; here also African residents pay rents of $12\frac{1}{2}$ per cent of their salary for houses of about £20 to £30 per month.

The third type is found in Kanjedza, Soche and D. C. Line. The houses are fairly old and comprise one to three bedrooms without ceilings, a firewood kitchen only moderately ventilated, a small sitting room and a water closet and shower. The area is highly congested with no garages; roads are untarred and badly eroded. Occupants of type three are not easily identified. A large proportion are white-collar workers and skilled blue-collar workers with secondary or primary school education but there is a sprinkling of university graduates or holders of diplomas working in firms, companies or parastatal organizations who are not given firm or company houses but must find them on the open market and pay non-subsidized rents. For these lower rents are an attraction. Consequently there are more varied socio-economic characteristics, in amount of income, educational level and occupational statuses.

The fourth type is peri-urban. It is found in Zingwangwa, Ndirande, Makbeta, Chilomoni and Chilobwe, where the land rent is quite cheap. Houses do not conform to any set standard quality, ranging from the well-built to semi-shacks, often in juxtaposition to each other. House-owners may buy or lease land on which to build houses, which are put up at random and haphazardly, creating an unplanned appearance. Sanitation is a problem with no sewage system, pit latrines, shack-like baths and scattered public water taps, either owned by the municipality or individuals who sell water to others at one Malawi *tambala* per pail. Roads are untarred, eroded, sometimes impassable to cars. The occupants are largely unskilled labourers, semi-skilled workers, messengers, market-sellers and the unemployed. The good houses vary in quality, and are largely multi-roomed, with inside water closets, baths, electricity and even a ceiling. Owners are mainly persons living in type two or three areas, who have saved enough money to buy a plot and build a house. A

L

312 *Special Studies*

few live in their own houses but this is considered uneconomical. Residents in the good quality houses in type four area work in private firms, companies, other non-government organizations and range from blue-collar workers to executives who cannot find houses in type two or type three areas.

These four ecological types adequately depict the existing residential pattern, which is important for analysing the emerging pattern of new social relations, urban–rural links, life styles, life chances, cultural patterns, occupational groups, tribal orientations, types of emerging personality and urban–rural modes of communication. The rest of this paper attempts to establish links between these factors and residential patterns.

THE ECOLOGICAL BASIS OF SOCIAL PERSONALITY TYPES

In its composition the type one area is pluralistic (Kuper and Smith 1969). Europeans, a few Asians and Africans live side by side, but physical nearness is not accompanied by social closeness. Interacial interaction is minimal, social interaction is largely along racial lines with the Asians being the most secluded and least integrated with others. A large proportion of them live in the centre of the city behind their shops.

The Africans share similar occupational statuses, come from various parts of the country, belong to many different ethnic groups and exhibit a wide range of educational levels. Since employment is their chief source of income they have similar earnings, power and life chances (Mills 1963: 305–23). In their mode and style of life they resemble the European middle class. The houses are fully furnished with wall-to-wall carpeting, one car or two, a pool of domestic workers, a gardener, a cook and a nanny. The nuclear family of man, wife and her children is the norm, though there are a few with more than one wife. Relations with kinsmen are selective and manipulative; poor relations are commonly shunned and regarded as a source of shame and embarrassment. Assistance to close relatives, when it comes, is in the form of money or clothes normally sent to kinsmen either at home or elsewhere. Accommodation is not readily given to kinsmen or home people. When a visitor from home comes, he will be accommodated for a couple of days but will not be welcome to stay for a long period. On arrival he is mostly likely asked for how long he intends to stay and what the purpose of the visit is. Overcrowding is disliked and poor relatives who visit are often sent home almost immediately.

The ecology of social types in Blantyre 313

Nevertheless the group visits the natal home often, but only for short periods; even over long holidays for no more than a few days. Basically the link with home is functional. Home is where one runs a business such as shops, farms and other money-making ventures. It is also an important part of one's 'biography' to be able to claim 'I come from such and such a home'. It provides free land; it is an area of economic security. The predominant philosophy of the country supports utilitarian ties with one's home. For this group the rural link has become relatively de-personalized and is less dependent on the warmth of existing personal social relationships but is more a source of nostalgia and old memories of childhood. But in pragmatic terms to one with political ambitions and aspirations, the rural link provides a cushion and a base. Here he is an important figure, whose success makes him a source of pride to many, a model and an idol and the object of envy. He is a pace-setter and thereby a standard for parents and youth. His personal success enables him to exert a degree of influence on the rural population.

Occupational position rather than tribal values is manifestly the chief basis of emerging social relations among this group. Executive meetings, official dinners, cocktail parties, constant presence at public events and meetings foster and mould informal relationships among them and these constant contacts provide a foundation for the new forms of social relations. These are the people with power over others. Their decisions not only affect those who work directly under them, but have far-reaching consequences. Awareness of the extent of their power in decision-making leads them to avoid mixing freely with the 'powerless'. Professional concerns extend into and become inextricably involved in their private lives, drawing them away from those who do not belong to their 'in-group'. In their leisure activities they frequent the most expensive and prestigious places such as Mounth Soche and Ryall's Hotels, the Chinese Restaurant or Maxims. Material success seems to have been a factor in the unattractiveness of religion for them. Sunday mornings are often for late sleeping after a busy Saturday evening at cocktail parties, drinking or chatting with friends. Normally a cold beer before breakfast wakes them up. To meet the dictates of this new style of life a literate wife is often sought. Those who originally married humbly may have found themselves a new wife who is much younger and better educated than themselves. It is often frankly accepted that new wives may enter into such marriages more for material gain than for emotional attachment. Uneasy marital relationships may develop, but in other cases there may be acceptable marriages of convenience.

314 *Special Studies*

Ethnic affiliation is selective; in general people of similar positions are drawn into one another's social network. Such ethnic cliques as exist in the top group are weak and secondary to the pulls of the occupational statuses; ethnicity here is neither a necessary nor sufficient factor though it may be an intervening variable for the development of informal groups and personal friendships. In line with this, traditional norms and cultures are often shunned and children brought up according to the values of the European middle class. Individualism, personal success and achievement are stressed and English is spoken at home. Music is Western from records made in the United States and the United Kingdom and traditional dancing is replaced by ballroom and popular dances. The home approximates to that of a middle-class European family. Children play with European toys and call each other by first names rather than relational terms of younger brother, elder brother, sister, brother, as in the rural areas, which indicate respect and ascribed status and differences. Equally, parents address each other by their first names, which is almost unheard of in rural areas.

Personal relationships with the nuclear family are emphasized to the detriment of those of the extended family. The need to maintain a high standard of living underlies this de-emphasis, for the household budget does not allow the fulfilment of wider obligations to many kinsmen.

The situation in a type four residential area is the polar opposite of that in a type one area. The semi-slum houses occupied by unskilled and semi-skilled labourers are small, built of wattle and daub with corrugated-iron roof, uncemented floor and a tiny hut which serves as a kitchen. Taps, baths and toilets are often communal. The houses are close to each other. The whole environmental setting resembles that of a rural village and provides conditions very much like a village setting. As is well known, in the rural context helping each other is a predominant norm. The rich are constrained to use their wealth for the welfare of kinsmen, the sick and the disabled, a philosophy which is extended to the urban setting. In the tiny urban rooms kinsmen must be helped, even at the cost of comfort. The arrival of a kinsman or a home person is ostensibly a welcome event. Scarcity of food is no barrier to entertaining and playing host to visitors who are expected to share it happily. To supplement household incomes many wives return for most of the rainy period to the village, where singly or with the help of kinsmen or employed labour they produce food from the gardens which is then sent to town. Where wives remain in town they may earn money through beer-brewing, baking cakes, knitting, etc,

The ecology of social types in Blantyre   315

Social interaction between neighbours is high. They visit and help each other in times of trouble. The women may find time to sit around and gossip, chat and sing, while their husbands are at work. The communal water taps also provide a venue for interpersonal contacts. As the same people constantly meet they come to know each other and so a strong neighbourhood sentiment develops in these areas. Whenever people quarrel neighbours gather round to settle their differences in the rural style. As the rooms are small, the children play outside in groups as in the villages and older people do not complain of the noise. On the whole people are indeed more at home and relaxed.

Incomes are low, yet money is sent home to help kinsmen. The rationale behind such expenditure stresses the maintenance of satisfactory relationships with kin. Acquiring money is seen not as an end in itself but as a means of sustaining good social relationships. With no provision for occupational pension or gratuity, the working situation offers no security in old age, and so it is to kinsmen and the village that a person must turn in retirement.

There are, of course, exceptions to this general rule. A number invest their income in the urban setting by buying plots and building houses for rent. They become entrepreneurs and tend to regard kinship ties as detrimental to their business aspirations. The entrepreneurial spirit guides their behaviour and more often than not leads them to wish to escape traditional obligations. Though not large, this type is growing.

To many in these areas traditional values remain strong factors in their daily behaviour. Having absorbed few western values through formal education, their likes and dislikes are dictated by values which are in content essentially traditional. Not surprisingly they seek the company of home people and fellow ethnics. However, though they do not know English, they do tend to know Chichewa, the official language and most effective trans-ethnic *lingua franca*, and this helps to extend the span of friendship beyond ethnic groups. Both Christianity and Islam are strongly followed. One explanation for such dual support may be that religion offers two layers of comfort to people living in such precarious conditions. Additionally, such activities as church services provide both spiritual satisfaction and a social venue for meeting friends and home people. The pastor wields a strong local influence and people come to him for both social and spiritual guidance. It is interesting to note that the most active participants in religious organizations, the political party branches of the Malawi Congress Party, and dancing groups come from this fourth and lowest ranked type of area. People here hold

316 *Special Studies*

most of the official positions in the local political party branches and are genuinely active at party meetings. Their wives constitute a spearhead of the party. It is from them that the party draws its dancers on national days and at public meetings and the welcoming and sending off of dignitaries. At national and local conventions they provide the voluntary workers. The Party is not rich and so its day-to-day running at the crucially important grassroots level relies on the self-help and abundant support of such voluntary workers.

Yet, in spite of this nationalistic orientation, local values governing behaviour and conduct remain largely based on ethnic standards. Residents in Blantyre belong to more than fifteen different ethnic groups, each proclaiming a distinct value system though the differences between them may, in fact, be very small. In contrast to the type one area, ethnicity in type four is a strong factor in residents' orientations and inclinations, together with a largely rural world-view, and it is this which gives an ideological basis to the persistence of strong urban–rural ties.

Residents of type two and three areas are in many respects marginal. In type two a large proportion are university-educated young men who are ambitious and aspiring and who look at their academic achievements, which are the basis of their middle-range administrative and professional occupations, as entitling them to even higher positions. It is only the few older among them who have no more than primary or secondary school certificate education.

The wives of type two men also have substantial education and many of them work. Where both partners work, a nanny is employed to look after the children and someone else to do housework and cooking. As well as addressing each other by first names, husbands and wives have a relatively egalitarian relationship and are likely to regard their marriage as based on the modern concept of 'romantic love' and not as one of 'convenience'. This is very different, it may be recalled, from the situation in families of type one in which there may be considerable age and/or education discrepancies between spouses, with an older or at least mature man having a younger but more educated wife and/or an uneducated wife of the same generation as himself.

The type two nuclear families are generally small, and obligations to kin continue to be regarded as an unavoidable necessity, for, as young aspirants not yet fully secure in their jobs, most residents have themselves only recently benefited from the help of kinsmen. However, their salaries are not large enough to meet all kinship obligations. Though bachelors are better placed, the married fulfil

The ecology of social types in Blantyre 317

such obligations at the risk of straining marital relations as wives also wish help to be extended to their relatives in return for their own past education. The very egalitarian nature of the conjugal relationship highlights the dilemma created by the conflicting interests and demands of spouses and kin.

Though the third type of area includes some public and private sector executive officers with university- or diploma-level education, most household heads are white-collar workers who hold primary or secondary school certificates. The older among them may have accumulated enough money to build 'respectable' houses in the area, either for renting or for living in. In this area there is a wide span of socio-economic characteristics and educational attainment as well as of house types, and it is difficult to identify a common cultural pattern beyond the simple generalization that the mix and range of traditional and western values are here at their greatest. Correspondingly, the sense of 'community' is least developed.

SUMMARY

These impressions of some salient features of the social ecology of Blantyre city indicate that ethnicity varies considerably in the four areas as a radix of social personality. In the type one social area there is a de-emphasis on ethnicity and a strong stress on high occupational position and the European middle-class life style as governing family structure, personal relations and outlook. The biggest contrast is with type four, where residents behave in most situations in a manner not very different from that in rural areas, perceiving no sharp cleavage between urban and rural contexts, and emphasizing their respective ethnic values in behaviour and world-view.

It is likely that in the third type of area the wide and complicated differences of socio-economic and educational levels produce the kind of selective and manipulative behaviour which can only be explained through intensive situational analysis (Epstein 1958), for residents seem to appeal almost indiscriminately to both traditional and western values. By contrast, the socially aspiring residents of the second type of area consistently hold to an idealized concept of 'modernized', educated man. Many of them have studied abroad and see themselves as having absorbed much western culture through their education. They consider that their outlook and world-view differ but little from university counterparts in the west, and in Blantyre they mix freely with westerners with whom they may share many common interests. They are relatively young but, unlike the

318 *Special Studies*

older élite in the type one area, they are sure of where they stand as individuals in relation to whites, regarding their academic achievement as a measure of their personal worth and excellence and demanding to be treated and judged on this.

Though impressionistic this description throws light on the contemporary situation in Blantyre city. The broad features described here are found in different magnitude in all urban centres of Malawi. Though the features have been presented as static they are in fact dynamic. The problem has been to isolate the structure while leaving out the process which can only be understood after systematic investigation. The aim has been to outline the contemporary urban social structure and its possible implications. The situation may not be the same a few years from now.

The distribution of migrants in Kampala, Uganda[1]

M. A. HIRST

When a migrant enters a town or city for the first time, the most urgent and fundamental decision is where to live. Leslie (1963: 32), describes an apparently typical situation for Dar-es-Salaam which probably has wider application:

> 'It would be difficult to find a single African who arrived in Dar-es-Salaam knowing not a soul. . . . Almost every African who decides to come to Dar-es-Salaam comes to a known address, where lives a known relation; this relation will meet him, take him in and feed him and show him the ropes, help him to seek a job, for months if necessary until he considers himself able to launch out for himself and take a room of his own.'

Mayer (1961: 101) writes in identical vein about the arrival of migrants in East London:

> 'The migrant newcomer has to find somebody in town to take care of him, that is, receive, house, and feed him. He cannot pay until he gets a job and some money; he must find someone who feels sufficient sense of moral obligation to help him for nothing. This means finding either a kinsman or a man from home.'

Thus, if institutionally or officially provided housing is limited or unavailable, the migrant will usually live initially with a relative or friend from his home area who is already living in the town. In a survey of rural–urban migration in Ghana, Caldwell (1969: 129–30), estimates that:

> 'Over half the potential migrants in the rural areas expected to stay at first with relatives or fellow villagers. If to these are added those joining their nuclear families, mostly wives going to husbands

---

[1] The author wishes to express his gratitude to Mr. K. Hill, for making available the Kampala birthplace data; and Dr. L. J. Wood, for reading and offering comments upon part of the original typescript. The Population Council, New York, gave financial assistance.

320 *Special Studies*

and children going to parents, the proportion exceeds two thirds.'

'If migrants do not know any specific person in the town, they often seek out the most important persons among their own ethnic group, frequently a kind of elective chief of the specific immigrant community. It is usually one of his tasks to provide personally the necessary initial accommodation or to suggest someone who can do so. The system is made easier by the tendency for the various ethnic groups to settle in clusters.'

Once wage employment is found and the migrant is able to support himself, there will be some relocation of residence and this is likely to be determined by both the characteristics of the available housing, for example rent/price, number of rooms, location, and the attributes of the individual, for example, income, number of dependents, place of work. Where the great majority of migrants are in unskilled, and often initially, casual employment, the residential location decision is probably largely constrained by a low income-level, an incapacity for home ownership, and the need to live near to the place of work in order to minimize the cost of the journey to work. Other housing needs, for example the desire for more space to accommodate dependents, or a preference for particular types of neighbours, may not be satisfied.

The new residential location is likely to be near to the initial residential location because individuals are more aware of their immediate environs, particularly in a large urban centre, and will be in a better position to evaluate information referring to their adjacent neighbourhoods. Short-distance moves are likely to predominate in urban areas (Simmons 1968), especially if the new residence is obtained through the same kinship and ethnic assistance that provided the initial accommodation. Wage employment is often found through such relationships and this may again reinforce the choice of a residence being near to the initial residential location. If this behavioural pattern of searching for a residence is dependent upon the decisions made by earlier migrants from the same place of origin, then migrants from the same rural areas are likely to become associated with particular urban neighbourhoods. This is especially probable if there is an acute housing shortage: in such a situation, the migrant, if he moves at all from his initial location, is likely to move to the residence of another friend or relative in the city.

The network of social contacts developed prior to moving to the town and maintained by the sending back of information concerning urban life, will therefore tend to conserve a bias in the urban residential patterns in a cumulative or feedback process as successful migrants help those who decide to join them in the city to find

The distribution of migrants in Kampala 321

accommodation and employment. Residential separation and the spatial clustering of migrant groups is a natural consequence of this process of chain migration, which is probably the major mechanism in African rural–urban migration (Caldwell 1969: 81–2). In addition, the degree of residential separation will be partly maintained by the strength of kinship ties and community bonds which will result in the choice of a migrant group to continue to live together. Segregation may also be forced upon the migrant group by the discriminatory tendencies of the host society, especially when the former deviates from the latter in culture, behaviour or appearance. Clearly, a variety of reasons will account for the residential clustering of migrants groups, but in Africa where urban growth has been recent and rapid and where rural-urban migration is still largely of a transient nature, current urban residential patterns may reflect to a large extent the initial residential location of dependence upon pre-migration social contacts.

Inevitably with time, several forces contribute to a continued net decline in the segregation of each migrant group: urban neighbourhoods become more mixed and the original patterns of migrant settlement become blurred. As familiarity with urban life increases and socio-economic status improves, the successful migrant becomes less dependent upon kinship and ethnic ties for social and economic security, and tends to move away socially and spatially. Individuals will gradually become assimilated into the wider urban society reinforcing, and reinforced by, the spatial process of gradual dispersion through the urban neighbourhoods. However, if the mixing of migrants in particular neighbourhoods is itself a selective process, then new residential patterns of several migrant groups being associated in particular neighbourhoods may emerge on the basis of similar socio-economic characteristics and similar modes of living.

The purpose of the subsequent analysis is to examine the residential pattern of twenty-four migrant African groups within Kampala in order to determine the nature and degree of residential segregation by migrant origin. Between 1959 and 1969, Kampala more than doubled its population and this was largely due to in-migration: over two-thirds of the African population in 1969 were born outside the city (Table 1). Migrants are not a typical cross-section of any population group because they are largely pre-selected according to various propensities to migrate, and in large numbers they are likely to have a marked influence upon the ecological structure of an urban area. The following analysis is therefore a preliminary exercise to characterize the distribution of migrant groups in Kampala prior to assessing their impact upon the city's human ecology.

322 *Special Studies*

Table 1

Indices of residential segregation

District or country of birth	Index of segregation	Index of concentration	Percentage in areas of overlap	Total numbers
West Buganda[1]	29	33	23	104,469
East Buganda	20	39	31	36,804
Masaka	21	41	29	11,392
Mubende	25	41	32	6,856
Teso	44	59	39	4,202
Bugisu	30	52	33	4,235
Bukedi	33	53	35	7,226
Busoga	23	48	36	6,013
Sebei	52	65	38	250
Karamoja	55	71	36	288
Kigezi	31	50	30	13,650
Ankole	23	41	31	7,528
Toro	33	55	32	10,065
Bunyoro	29	51	38	3,448
West Nile	35	52	37	8,981
Madi	45	65	42	1,007
Acholi	46	61	44	7,591
Lango	47	62	35	3,152
Kenya	43	61	46	34,420
Tanzania	32	48	39	5,234
Rwanda	25	43	36	5,349
Burundi	31	41	31	847
Zaire	35	55	43	3,348
Sudan	40	66	46	2,469

[1] Kampala is situated in West Buganda and it is not possible to separate those who were born in the city from those who were born in the district but outside the city.

THE MEASUREMENT OF RESIDENTIAL SEGREGATION

Migrant residential neighbourhoods within African urban areas are frequently identified on the basis of ethnic affiliation: for example,

'In Greater Kampala there are many tribal quarters . . . associated with Toro, Rwanda, Luo, Nyambo, Haya, Acholi and other tribes. They are in no sense exclusive and have no formal basis. The same tribe has several small clusters in different places' (Southall 1961: 40).

The following analysis is itself based upon persons classified by place of birth. Ethnic affiliation and place of birth are of course not

The distribution of migrants in Kampala 323

synonymous and the former is certainly the more relevant in the maintenance of social contacts and the feedback of information, which have been postulated as the processes giving rise to residential segregation by migrant origin. Unfortunately, ethnic data were not collected in the 1969 Uganda census enumeration and are not available for intra-urban areas from the 1959 census. However, the use of birthplace data imparts a degree of comparability with similar studies in other parts of the world (e.g. the emergence of migrant clusters in the cities of the United States during the nineteenth century), and avoids the problem of a circular proof when ethnic affiliation is used both to identify and to explain patterns of urban residential segregation. It seems more appropriate to invoke ethnic affiliation as a summary variable of a whole range of social, linguistic, economic, demographic and cultural factors, in explaining patterns of segregation identified according to place of birth.

From the 1969 Uganda census enumeration, data are available on the place of birth of the African population, by district if born in Uganda and by country if born outside Uganda. One hesitates to be critical of the census data available for Kampala because few cities of tropical Africa could boast of having data available on age, sex, and place of birth for eighty-seven census divisions (Uganda 1971). The disadvantages in using information on persons classified by place of birth, referring as it does to lifetime migration, are well known, but perhaps the most serious deficiency in the present context is that such data provide no clue as to when an individual made his first visit, and the number of subsequent visits to Kampala. As noted earlier, the length of a migrant's urban experience may have considerable bearing upon his residential location decision, if he depends upon his pre-migration social contacts for only his initial urban residence. Ideally, one would wish to differentiate migrants in terms of the recency of their move to Kampala and to examine the postulated process that the residential segregation of migrants decreases over time as their length of urban residence increases.

Another major deficiency in the census data is that they are only available in aggregate form for eighty-seven census divisions which have an average size of approximately 0·75 square miles. The measurement of segregation is of necessity directly related to this system of areal units but if residential segregation occurs on a smaller areal scale, this would not be revealed by the measures employed. There is indeed some evidence that residential segregation by place of origin occurs within some census divisions: for example, in 1954, seven settlements varying in size from four to thirteen huts

324 *Special Studies*

were occupied by members of individual tribes in Mulago parish, which is equivalent to one of the 1969 census divisions (Gutkind 1961: 22). To an unknown extent therefore, the available birthplace data are incompatible with the process and scale at which residential segregation apparently takes place and measurement will tend to underestimate the degree and extent of segregation. The analysis is thus limited to an examination of the varying tendency for different migrant groups to be associated with particular neighbourhoods or census divisions. This is essentially a preliminary statistical exercise: more adequate information should permit greater progress to be made in research on the segregation of migrant and minority communities in African urban areas.

Detailed mapping and analysis of the birthplace data followed two complementary lines of approach: the comparison between one group's distribution and that of the rest of the population, and the comparison between the distributions of two component groups of the population. This confirmed respectively the importance of two basic characteristics of the residential distribution of migrants in Kampala.

INDIVIDUAL PATTERNS

The spatial patterning of migrants by place of birth was characterized by a multi-modal or poly-nucleated distribution rather than a single locational cluster, and it was not uncommon to find migrants from a given origin having three or four foci of settlement within the city separated by two or more miles. This feature made redundant an initial attempt to characterize the spatial pattern of each group by the two areal statistics of central tendency and dispersion which may only meaningfully be applied to unimodal distributions (Neft 1966). The evolution of spatially non-contiguous entities may be attributed to variations in the characteristics (e.g. income, stage in the life cycle, number of dependents, place of work) of segments of the given migrant group which result in some being constrained to live in one area and others being found in alternative locations. The absence of spatial contiguity might also reflect the location of officially or institutionally provided housing and the availability of private housing for rent. Finally, district of birth may be too gross a measure of origin and the apparently fragmented residential pattern of migrants in Kampala may reflect significant variations in origin within individual districts which will channel urban–rural links to more circumscribed areas.

In order to identify migrant communities, two criteria have been

The distribution of migrants in Kampala 325

combined to map the residential patterns of each group by census divisions:

(a) density, or the number of persons in a given group per square mile;
(b) intensity, or the percentage of a given group in the total African population (cf. Hart 1960: 246).

For each birthplace group, the census divisions were arrayed in descending order of both their density and intensity, and for each array the cumulative per cent of the population belonging to each group was computed. Those census divisions which together con-

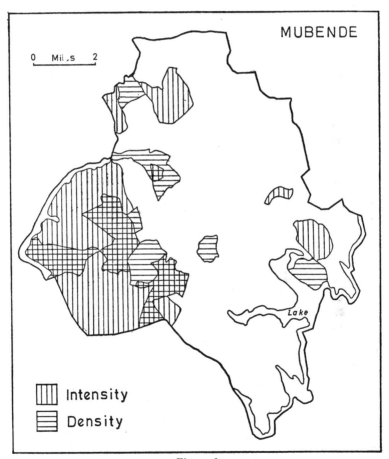

Figure 1

tained an arbitrary fifty per cent of a group's total population were marked on a map and the spatial overlap of the two criteria, shown by cross-hatching, identified the principal residential foci of each group. The resulting maps illustrate in a simple way the spatial expression of a population concentration curve and a population segregation curve for each birthplace group (Duncan 1957; Duncan and Duncan, 1955). Table 1 summarizes the results for all birthplace groups and the distribution of Africans born in Mubende and Acholi districts are illustrated as exemplary cases (Figures 1 and 2).

Persons born in Mubende district form two main clusters centred upon Mengo (Mengo-Nakulabye-Kasubi-Natete) and Entebbe Road

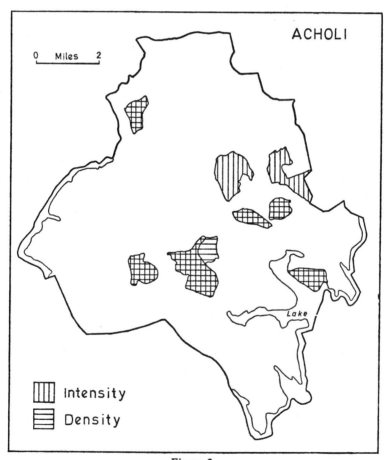

Figure 2

The distribution of migrants in Kampala 327

(Katwe-Kibuye) plus an isolated focus at Mulago. Overall, and in common with others born in the Buganda province, they display little tendency towards clustering and only 32 per cent are found in the areas of overlap between the two distributional criteria, out of a possible maximum of 50 per cent. Almost the whole of the former Mengo township has an important intensity by Mubende-born and this area of Kampala is dominated by those born in Buganda, reflecting their traditional association with the former Buganda capital.

Persons born in Acholi district display a stronger tendency towards clustering and are characterized by six distinct foci at Kawempe, Kiswa, Lubiri, Nsambya, Mbuya, and Luzira. This residential pattern is similar to that of others born in the Northern province and reflects segregation by occupation coupled with the provision of official housing quarters by the police, armed forces, prisons and railways in the last four neighbourhoods, as well as the more voluntary choice to live together in Kawempe and Kiswa. Occupational stratification of migrants is reportedly important in Kampala and will have an important bearing upon the degree of residential segregation. In the case of Northerners this has led to a marked residential clustering, but in other instances it may lead to dispersal as in the case of those born in Toro district: the latter are apparently often found in domestic service and will therefore usually reside adjacent to their employer's residence. Toro-born are in fact not only one of the more dispersed migrant groups but are also the group which displays least residential dissimilarity with Kampala's non-African population. Unfortunately, census data on economic activity were not collected in 1969 and the absence of this important variable clearly limits the present analysis. Socio-economic status and migrant status are probably the major dimensions of African urban society.

Further generalization on the relative variation in group segregation is likewise limited but some gross relationships, partly confirmed by correlation analysis, were examined. The indices of segregation and concentration for the eighteen groups born in Uganda (Table 1), displayed a direct relationship with their proportion of males, an indirect relationship with their proportion of Kampala's population, a direct relationship with the distance from Kampala of their place of birth, and an indirect relationship with the proportion born in that district who were living in Kampala. In other words, the more distant the place of birth, the fewer the number of migrants to Kampala, the greater the proportion of males, the smaller the proportion they form of Kampala's population, the more residentially clustered they are within Kampala. These relationships

Table 2

Indices of residential dissimilarity

District or country of birth	1	2	3	4	5	6	7	8	9	10	11	12	13	14	15	16	17	18	19	20	21	22	23	24
1. West Buganda	—	14	17	15	55	43	48	35	62	63	42	33	39	38	46	59	60	57	52	36	30	34	45	51
2. East Buganda		—	21	21	53	40	45	33	61	62	40	31	37	35	43	58	58	55	52	34	29	35	45	52
3. Masaka			—	16	51	42	46	33	61	60	43	33	39	38	45	58	59	54	53	34	29	38	47	49
4. Mubende				—	58	48	53	39	66	64	47	39	41	38	51	64	65	61	57	39	31	38	47	55
5. Teso					—	32	28	29	45	42	48	39	45	36	33	32	29	23	50	53	49	53	55	53
6. Bugisu						—	22	20	42	51	35	28	34	29	25	34	35	30	39	40	37	48	43	42
7. Bukedi							—	21	44	52	39	31	44	31	25	25	23	28	37	43	42	44	45	41
8. Busoga								—	47	48	34	22	32	21	25	35	36	32	41	35	33	41	43	44
9. Sebei									—	51	54	46	56	50	41	49	43	44	56	58	57	64	60	53
10. Karamoja										—	58	53	50	51	46	48	47	42	65	61	56	61	60	60
11. Kigezi											—	32	34	36	41	46	47	50	43	43	31	40	37	41
12. Ankole												—	35	28	29	45	41	42	43	35	29	37	41	44
13. Toro													—	24	43	53	56	48	45	39	35	46	38	47
14. Bunyoro														—	30	43	43	40	49	41	38	44	44	47
15. West Nile															—	30	23	27	42	44	43	49	49	44
16. Madi																—	21	27	45	56	54	56	55	47
17. Acholi																	—	24	44	57	55	56	53	47
18. Lango																		—	50	56	52	56	57	55
19. Kenya																			—	47	49	54	32	30
20. Tanzania																				—	32	37	44	47
21. Rwanda																					—	32	35	47
22. Burundi																						—	41	55
23. Zaire																							—	32
24. Sudan																								—

The distribution of migrants in Kampala 329

do not reveal anything novel but confirm a largely expected pattern. They do emphasize however, that variations in the process and pattern of migration will have an impact upon the ecological structure of Kampala.

MULTIPLE PATTERNS

Some of the non-contiguous settlement foci coincided for different groups of migrants and this suggested that it might be more appropriate to examine the associations between various birthplace groups rather than emphasize particular differences. Some similarities in the residential pattern of different migrant groups have already been alluded to and Table 2 indicates the percentage differences between the distributions of pairs of migrant groups. Adopting an arbitrary threshold of 25, two groups readily emerge: a Buganda group containing West Buganda, East Buganda, Masaka, and Mubende and a larger group containing all the remaining districts of Uganda except Sebei, Karamoja, and Kigezi. These last three groups and the six groups born outside Uganda do not join any group. Clearly, there is some selective neighbourhood mixing of migrants and in order to identify those spatially associated groups more precisely, the taxonomic procedure outlined by Berry (1967) was employed. Principal components analysis was used to reduce and identify the basic patterns of variation of the original twenty-four variables and distance-scaling of the orthogonal loadings of the 'significant' components was followed by a complete linkage analysis which provided groups of birthplace categories. This procedure was completed three times: when the original observations on each birthplace category for each census division referred respectively to their absolute numbers, their density, and their intensity. The groups of birthplaces derived from each analysis were not identical in every detail but there was sufficient similarity to be able to identify four groups which showed, more or less, a consistent pattern of linkages:

Group I	West Buganda	Group IV	Teso
	East Buganda		Bugisu
	Masaka		Bukedi
	Mubende		Busoga
			. . . .
			West Nile
Group II	Kigezi		Madi
	Kenya		Acholi
	Zaire		Lango
	Sudan		

330 *Special Studies*

Group III   Tanzania
               Rwanda
               Burundi

Group IV may be subdivided because it was noted that the four districts of the Eastern and Northern provinces respectively, tended to have stronger links with each other than with the districts of the other province. Migrants from five districts, Sebei, Karamoja, Ankole, Toro, and Bunyoro, displayed no consistent pattern of linkages with other birthplace groups. Very few residents in Kampala were born in Sebei and Karamoja and it was not surprising to find that they showed no consistent residential association with other migrants. Similarly, those born in the three districts of the Western province could not be placed satisfactorily in any one of the identified groups because they are found in the main foci of both Groups I and IV. Tables III and IV summarize the residential distribution of each of the four groups which will now be briefly discussed in turn (Figures 3 to 6).

Table 3

Indices of residential segregation
(Four groups)

Birthplace group	Index of segregation	Index of concentration	Percentage in areas of overlap	Total numbers
Group I	38	35	21	159,521
Group II	36	57	41	53,887
Group III	22	43	36	11,430
Group IV	38	52	34	42,407

Table 4

Indices of residential dissimilarity
(Four groups)

Birthplace group	I	II	III	IV
Group I	—	44	26	46
Group II	44	—	37	35
Group III	26	37	—	39
Group IV	46	35	39	—

Those born in Buganda province formed the most strongly and closely linked group; Kampala is located in Buganda which is dominated by one ethnic group, the Ganda. Although many of the latter are themselves migrants to the city, there is a clear residential distinction between Ganda and non-Ganda confirming an earlier

The distribution of migrants in Kampala   331

simple characterization of Kampala's population into Ganda Hosts and Migrant Strangers (Parkin 1969a). The residential pattern of the Ganda encircles the pre-1968 city limits of present-day central Kampala and the contiguous Nakawa township to the east, to form three distinct zones. Along the pre-1968 city boundary, a zone of high density from Mulago through Namirembe and Kisenyi to Kibuli largely reflects the general high density zone of these so-called peri-urban areas. In general, Africans were largely discouraged from living in the mainly non-African city centre by the absence of suitable housing but tended to live just over the line to be near their city employment. The second zone is broken into four foci at Bwaise, Kasubi, Mengo, and Entebbe Road, characterized by both a high density and a high intensity of Buganda-born residents. Finally, there is an outer zone of high intensity in the semi-rural areas of north and south Kampala which were only designated as urban in 1968, and the former Mengo township to the west.

Group IV, the largest group in terms of the variety of different origins and the group which is most distinguishable from Group I, is made up of most of the remainder of those born in Uganda and includes those born in the Northern and Eastern provinces. Their only apparent common basis is that they are all aliens in the territory of the Ganda and this has produced a tendency to associate with one another despite differences in language, diet, etc., rather than associate with the Ganda group. The residential pattern of Group IV is more fragmented than that of the Ganda group. Most parts of the central city and the former Nakawa township have a high intensity of northerners and easterners and surrounding this are pockets of high density at Mulago, parts of Mengo, Katwe and Kibuli comparable to the similar high density inner zone of Ganda. Then there are pockets of both high density and high intensity at Kawempe, Lubiri, Nsambya, Kiswa, Mbuya, and Luzira, identical to, and for the same reasons as, the individual pattern of those born in Acholi (Figure 2).

Those born in the three districts of Western Province, Ankole, Toro and Bunyoro, have weak links with the members of both Groups I and IV, while Kigezi is linked, inexplicably, with the non-Ugandan Group II. The westerners neither display any clear residential preferences for each other, nor for any of the derived groups of migrants.

The non-Ugandan migrants form themselves into two groups. Group II is dominated by Kenyans who comprise almost two-thirds of the total: they have been a distinctive feature of Kampala's residential pattern since the 1930s and the map confirms their localization in Namuwongo and Kibuli. Two smaller foci occur at Kiswa and Kamwokya. Group II also display a high intensity in the industrial and commercial areas where they are presumably employed, and also in the high status areas of Kololo and Mbuya: although this may indicate employment in domestic service, it is more probable that in these latter areas, the members of Group II and particularly the Kenyans, are themselves of a high socio-economic status, e.g. East African Community employees. The high intensity at Port Bell may well reflect the arrival of Kenyans by Lake Steamer from Kisumu who settle at this point of entry and take up industrial employment in the factories nearby.

Group III, the smallest group is formed almost equally of those

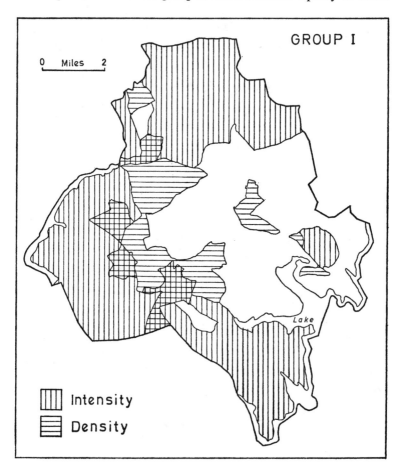

The distribution of migrants in Kampala

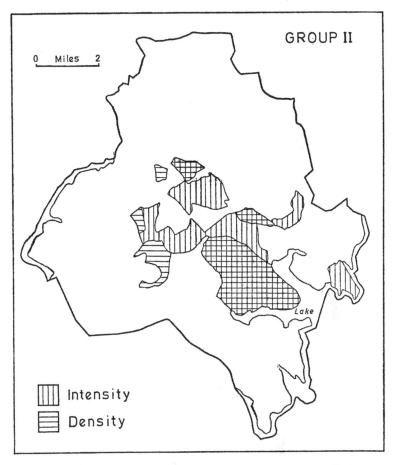

born in Tanzania and Rwanda, plus a few hundred born in Burundi. They enter Uganda by four main routes which converge at Masaka for the final eighty miles to Kampala and some also come by Lake Steamer from Bukoba (Richards 1954: 53ff.). It is somewhat surprising therefore that those born in Kigezi and Ankole are not members of Group III, but the latter in fact display a closer association with the Buganda-born than with anyone else: many Rwandans particularly are employed by the Ganda. Their residential focus is consequently found in the Mengo, Katwe and Kisenyi area and other foci are found at Mulago, Nakawa, and Luzira. Large areas of southern and eastern Kampala as well as the commercial and industrial areas, have a high intensity of Rwandans and Tanzanians.

334 *Special Studies*

CONCLUSION

It has not been easy to describe and generalize the residential pattern of migrant communities because, unlike many cities of the world, the residential patterns in Kampala are not characterized by the simple zone and sector models (Johnston 1971: *passim*). Migrant groups in Kampala do not live in the relevant zones of relevant sectors but, either through necessity or choice, the aggregate of their residential location decisions has given rise to the development of several separate residential nuclei. The multi-nucleated residential character of Kampala is probably the city's most distinctive ecological feature and is reflected in other aspects of its population

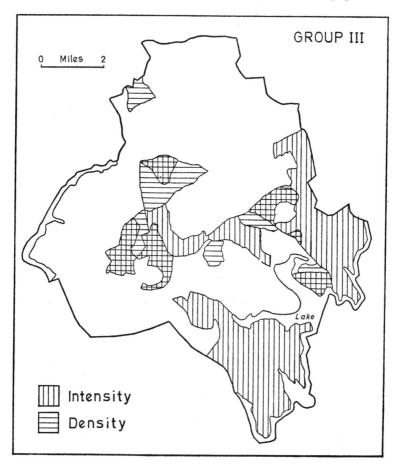

The distribution of migrants in Kampala

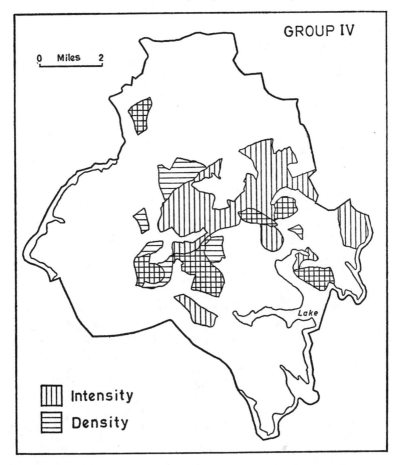

structure such as the distribution of population density, age-structure, fertility indices and sex ratios. It is not unlikely that Kampala is similar in this respect to other, former colonial, cities of tropical Africa.

Although complicated, the residential mosaic portrayed on the maps confirms some known general impressions about the residential location of migrants within Kampala, and the derived groups of birthplaces confirm some popularly-held notions about the social, economic and political relationships between the different groups of migrants. However, these relationships remain to be explored in detail and the results presented here should more properly form a basis for further research rather than provide a definitive statement.

336   *Special Studies*

With the exception of Group II and accepting the subdivision of Group IV, the members of each group or sub-group originate from the same relative location and probably share the same route to Kampala. Clearly, the mixing of migrants in given urban neighbourhoods is a selective process biased to a discernible extent by the geographical origin of the migrants. But a migrant's place of origin is not the most important factor in determining his residential location decision. The statistical indices presented in Tables I–IV betray the existence of other important factors in differentiating the residential pattern, and ideally one would wish to have the birthplace data stratified by at least occupation and place of work: if these variables could be held constant then migrant origin might be shown to be of greater importance. All that may be concluded at present is that a migrant's place of origin does have a bearing, sometimes small and not invariant, upon his residential location decision at the scale of measurement employed here.

Spatial patterns and spatial processes are circularly causal: each is a determinant of the other, but spatial patterns in themselves tell us very little about the processes at work. Basically, we do not know whether the migrant communities identified in Kampala represent an intermediary stage of a tendency towards continuing segregation, or ghetto formation; or, of a spatial assimilation process paralleling social and economic assimilation of the migrants in which the residential patterns may or may not be relatively stable. The latter process was favoured in the introductory discussion but both ghetto models and assimilation models cover a variety of different spatial processes and the study of migrant residential patterns alone do not help to discriminate between the various possibilities since the same spatial pattern could be produced by a number of processes (Johnston 1971: 242ff.). In the rapidly growing cities of tropical Africa, a clearer theoretical understanding of migrant settlement in urban areas and the subsequent role of intra-urban migration is presumably vital if planners wish to intervene and effectively control and direct urban growth towards some desirable objective; or at least, to prevent some of the worst excesses of accelerating rural-urban migration and urban growth. But migrant status is only one dimension of African urban society and socio-economic status is at least of equal or greater importance. Most probably these two dimensions are not independent of each other but to date, few generalizations on the ecological structure of African cities have been tested and this is clearly a major research area in which all social scientists can make valuable contributions.

Bibliography

Abrahams, R.
1961. 'Kahama Township, Western Province, Tanganyika', in A. W. Southall (ed.) q.v.

Alker, Hayward R. Jr.
1969. 'A Typology of Ecological Fallacies' in Dogan, Mattei and Rokkan, Stein (eds.) *Quantitative Ecological Analysis in the Social Sciences*. Cambridge, Mass.: The M.I.T. Press, pp. 69–86.

Alvarez, J. Hernandez
1967. *The Return Migration to Puerto Rico*. Berkeley: University Press.

American Friends Services Committee
1970. *A View of the Kafue Squatters*. Kafue.

Amin, S. (ed.)
1974. *Modern Migrations in Western Africa*, Oxford University Press for the International African Institute.

Anthony, K. R. M. and Uchendu, V. C.
1970. 'Agricultural Change in Mazabuka District, Zambia', *Food Research Institute Studies*, XIV, 3, pp. 215–67.

Appleyard, R. T.
1962. 'Determinants of Return Movement . . .' *The Economic Record*, No. 38 (September), pp. 352–68.

Apter, D.
1961. *The Political Kingdom in Uganda*. Princeton: Princeton University Press.

Apthorpe, R. (ed.)
undated *c*. 1969. *Land Settlement and Rural Development in Eastern Africa*, Nkanga No. 3, MISR, Kampala.
c. 1969. 'Planned Social Change and Land Settlement' in Apthorpe (ed.) q.v.

Aquina, Sister Mary
1964. 'The Social Background of Agriculture in Chilemanzi Reserve', *Rhodes-Livingstone Journal*, No. 36, pp. 7–39.

Argus, Uganda
1957. Native Laws of Buganda (revised edition).

Arrighi, G.
1967. *The Political Economy of Rhodesia*. The Hague: Mouton.

Bailey, F. G.
1968. 'Parapolitical Systems' in M. J. Swartz (ed.) *Local-Level Politics*. Chicago: Aldine, pp. 281–94.
1969. *Stratagems and Spoils*. Oxford: Blackwell.

338 *Cumulative Bibliography*

Banton, M.
1957. *West African City: A Study of Tribal Life in Freetown*. London: Oxford University Press for the International African Institute.

Barber, W. J.
1960. 'Economic Rationality and Behavior Patterns in an Underdeveloped Area: A Case Study of African Economic Behavior in the Rhodesias', *Economic Development and Cultural Change*, VIII, pp. 237–51.
1961. *The Economy of British Central Africa: A Case Study of Economic Development in a Dualistic Society*. London: Oxford University Press.

Barth, Frederik
1966. *Models of Social Organisation*. Occasional Paper No. 23, Royal Anthropological Institute.
1969. *Ethnic Groups and Boundaries: The Social Organization of Cultural Differences*. Boston: Little, Brown.

Batanyisako, M. N.
1967. *Labour Migration and the Family Structure in Ruhonwa, Kigezi*. Sociology Paper No. 50, Makerere University College.

Beattie, J.
1961. 'Group Aspects of the Nyoro Spirit Mediumship Cult', *Rhodes-Livingstone Journal*, 30, 11–38.
1964. 'Divination in Bunyoro', *Sociologus*, 14, 1, 44–62.
1966. 'Consulting a Diviner in Bunyoro: A Text', *Ethnology*, 5, 2, 202–17.

Beidelman, T. O.
1974. 'Social Theory and the Study of Christian Missions', *Africa* XLIV, 3, pp. 235–49.

Bell, E. M.
1963. *Polygons: Part Two: A Study of Turnover*. Occasional Paper No. 3, Department of African Studies, University College of Rhodesia and Nyasaland.

Bernard, J.
1954. 'The Theory of Games as a Modern Sociology of Conflict', *The American Journal of Sociology*, LIX, 5, pp. 411–24.

Berry, B. J. L.
1967. 'Grouping and Regionalizing: An Approach to the Problem Using Multivariate Analysis' in W. L. Garrison and D. F. Marble (eds.) *Quantitative Geography*, Studies in Geography No. 13, Northwestern University, Evanston, Illinois, pp. 219–51.

Blau, P.
1964. *Exchange and Power in Social Life*. New York: Wiley.

Blau, Peter M., Gustand, John W., Jessor, Richard, Parnes, Herbert S., Wilcock, Richard C.
n.d. 'Occupational Choice: A Conceptual Framework', *Industrial and Labour Relations Review*, pp. 531–43.

Cumulative Bibliography

Böhning, W. R.
1970. 'Foreign Workers in Post-War Germany', *The New Atlantis*, II, 1, pp. 12–38.

Boswell, D.
1974. 'Kinship, friendship and the concept of a social network' in C. Kiliff and W. Pendleton (eds.) *Urban Man in Southern Africa*, Gwelo, Rhodesia: Mambo Press.
(unpublished paper). 'Self-built: the social organization of an African urban slum' (Lusaka, Zambia).

Bott, E.
1957. *Family and Social Network*. London: Tavistock Publications.

Boulding, K.
1963. *Conflict and Defence*. New York: Harper.

Brandel-Syrier, Mia
1971. *Reeftown Elite: A Study of Social Mobility in a Modern African Community on the Reef*. London: Routledge & Kegan Paul.

Breese, G.
1966. Urbanisation in Newly Developing Countries. Englewood Cliffs, N.J.: Prentice Hall

British South Africa Company
1899. Reports on the Administration of Rhodesia.

Brokensha, D. and Pearsall, M. (eds.)
The Anthropology of Development in Sub-Saharan Africa, Society for Applied Anthropology, Monograph 10, Lexington: University Press of Kentucky.

Bujra, J.
(forthcoming.) *The social organization of Pumwani*, (?) Eagle Press, Nairobi.
c. 1973. 'Women entrepreneurs of early Nairobi', paper circulated by the Department of Sociology, University of Dar es Salaam.
1974. 'Language use in an urban Muslim Community' in W. H. Whiteley (ed.) q.v.

Caldwell, J. C.
1969. *African Rural-Urban Migration: The Movement to Ghana's Towns*. Canberra: Australian National University Press; London: Hurst.

Cartwright, Desmond S.
1969. 'Ecological Variables' in Edgar F. Borgatta (ed.) *Sociological Methodology 1969*. San Francisco: Jossey-Bass, pp. 155–218.

C.C.T.A. (Commission for Technical Cooperation)
1961. Report of a Conference on Labour Migration.

Census of Employees, 1961
1965. *Final Report of the September 1961 Census of Employees*. Salisbury: Government Printer.

Central Statistical Office
1964. *Final Report of the April/May 1962 Census of Africans in Southern Rhodesia*. Salisbury: Central Statistical Office.

340 *Cumulative Bibliography*

1965. *Final Report on the September 1961 Census of Employees.* Salisbury: Central Statistical Office.

1968. *Final Report of the May/June 1963 Census of Africans.* Lusaka.

1970. *Census of Population and Housing 1969.* Lusaka.

Chambers, R.

1969. *Settlement Schemes in Tropical Africa.* London: Routledge & Kegan Paul.

Chesswas, J. D.

1966. *Educational Planning and Development in Uganda.* UNESCO, International Institute for Educational Planning.

Chidumayu, E. H. *et al.*

1972. Research Reports from Chipata. (Unpublished.)

Clark, D.

1973. 'Kibera: Social Dynamics of a Low-Income Neighbourhood in Nairobi', MA thesis, Makerere University, Kampala.

Clignet, R. and Foster, P.

1966. *The Fortunate Few: A Study of Secondary Schools and Students in the Ivory Coast.* Evanston, Illinois: Northwestern University Press.

Coale, Ansley and Demeny, Paul

1966. *Regional Model Life Tables and Stable Populations.* Princeton N.J.: Princeton University Press.

Cohen, A.

1969. *Custom and Politics in Urban Africa.* Routledge & Kegan Paul.

1974. *Two Dimensional Man.* London: Routledge & Kegan Paul.

Cole, D. T.

1953. 'Fanagalo and the Bantu Languages in South Africa' reprinted in *Language in Culture and Society.* New York: Harper and Row, 1964, pp. 547–54.

Colson, Elizabeth

1958. *Marriage and the Family among the Plateau Tongo.* Manchester University Press.

1960. *The Social Organization of the Gwembe Tonga.* Manchester University Press.

1971. *The Social Consequences of Resettlement.* Manchester University Press.

Constandse, A. K. and Hofstee, E. W.

1968. *Rural Sociology in Action.* Agricultural Development Paper No. 79 Food and Agricultural Organization, Geneva.

Copper Industries Services Bureau

n.d. *Glossary of Chikabanga.* (A publication of the Nchanga Consolidated Copper Mines.)

Cunningham, Griffiths

1968. *Socialism and Rural Development.* Dar es Salaam: Kivukoni College (mimeo.).

Cumulative Bibliography

Daily Nation
13 July 1970. 'Kenya shocked by Uganda move to "sack" workers.'
13 February 1973. 'Luos are being made scapegoats for lack of security in Uganda.'

Dak, O.
1968. *A Geographical Analysis of the Distribution of Migrants in Uganda*. Occasional Paper No. 11, Department of Geography, Makerere University College (mimeo.).

Davies, D. H.
1969. *Lusaka, Zambia: Some Town Planning Problems in an African Capital City at Independence*. Lusaka, I.S.R., University of Zambia.

Dewey, Richard
1960. 'The Rural-Urban Continuum: Real but Relatively Unimportant', *American Journal of Sociology*, LXVI, pp. 60–66.

Doxiadis Associates
1961. *Report on the Development of Greater Lusaka*. Lusaka.

Dumont, René
1957. *Types of Rural Economy*. London.

Duncan, O. D.
1957. 'The Measurement of Population Distribution', *Population Studies*, Vol. II, pp. 27–45.

Duncan, O. D. and Duncan, B.
1955. 'A Methodological Analysis of Segregation Indexes', *American Sociological Review*, XX, pp. 210–17.

East African Standard
16 February 1973. 'Kenyans arrive by busload after expulsion.'

Easton, David
1965a. *A Framework for Political Analysis*. Englewood Cliffs: Prentice Hall.
1965b. *A Systems Analysis of Political Life*. New York: Wiley.

Eicher, Carl *et al.*
1970. *Employment Generation in African Agriculture*. East Lansing: Michigan State University.

Elkan, W.
1959. 'The Persistence of Migrant Labour'. *Bulletin of the International Labor Institute*, VI, 5, pp. 36–43.
1960. *Migrants and Proletarians: Urban Labour in the Economic Development of Uganda*. London: Oxford University Press for East African Institute of Social Research.
1969. 'Economists and African Towns'. (Paper given at the Institute of Commonwealth Studies, London University.)
1972. 'Is a proletariat emerging in Nairobi?', Paper presented to the 8th Annual Conference of the East African University Social Science Council, Nairobi.

Emmet, D. and MacIntyre, A.
1970. *Sociological Theory and Philosophical Analysis*. London: Macmillan.

342 *Cumulative Bibliography*

Epstein, A. L.
1958. *Politics in an Urban African Community.* Manchester University Press.
1959. 'Linguistic innovation and culture on the Copperbelt of Northern Rhodesia' *Southwestern Journal of Anthropology* XV, 3.

Epstein, T. S.
1962. *Economic Development and Social Change in South India.* Manchester University Press.

Fiawoo, D. K.
1959a. 'Urbanization and Religion in Eastern Ghana', *Sociological Review*, 7, I, pp. 83–97.
1959b. 'The Influence of Contemporary Social Changes on the Magico-Religious Concepts and Organization of the Southern Ewe-speaking People of Ghana', unpublished Ph.D. dissertation, University of Edinburgh.

Field, M. J.
1960. *The Search for Security: an Ethno-Psychiatric Study of Rural Ghana.* London: Faber.

Floyd, B.
1961. *Changing Patterns of African Land-Use in Southern Rhodesia.* Lusaka: Rhodes-Livingston Institute.

Forde, C. Daryll
1953. 'The Cultural Map of West Africa: Successive Adaptations to Tropical Forests and Grasslands', *Transactions of New York Academy of Science*, Series 2, XV, 6, pp. 206–19.

Foster, P.
1965. *Education and Social Change in Ghana.* London: Routledge & Kegan Paul.

Fraenkel, Merran
1964. *Tribe and Class in Monrovia.* London: Oxford University Press for the International African Institute.

Frank, Andre Gunder
1969. *Latin America: Underdevelopment or Revolution.* New York: Monthly Review Press.

Frank, C. R. Jr.
1968. 'Urban Unemployment and Economic Growth in Africa', *Oxford Economic Papers*, July.

Fry, J.
1975. 'Rural-Urban Terms of Trade 1960–1973'. *African Social Research*, No. 19.

Gans, Herbert J.
1962. *The Urban Villagers: Group and Class in the Life of Italian-Americans.* New York: Free Press.

Garbett, G. K.
1960. *Growth and Change in a Shona Ward.* Occasional Paper No. 1,

Cumulative Bibliography

343

Department of African Studies, University College of Rhodesia and Nyasaland.

1963. 'The Land Husbandry Act of Southern Rhodesia' in D. Biebuyck (ed.) *African Agrarian Systems*. London: Oxford University Press for the International African Institute, pp. 185–202.

1967. 'Prestige, Status and Power in a Modern Valley Korekore Chiefdom, Rhodesia', *Africa*, XXXVII, 3, pp. 307–26.

1970. 'The Analysis of Social Situations', *Man*, V, 2, pp. 214–27 (The Malinowski Memorial Lecture).

Garbett, G. K. and Kapferer, B.

1970. 'Theoretical Orientations in the Study of Labour Migration', *The New Atlantis*, II, 1, pp. 179–97.

Ghai, Dharam P.

1970. 'The Buganda Trade Boycott: A Study of Tribal, Political, and Economic Nationalism' in Robert I. Rotberg and Ali A. Mazrui (eds.) *Protest and Power in Black Africa*. New York: Oxford University Press, pp. 755–70.

Gluckman, Max

1940. 'Analysis of a Social Situation in Modern Zululand', *Bantu Studies*, No. 14, pp. 1–30, 147–74.

1947. 'Malinowski's "Functional" Analysis of Social Change', *Africa*, XVII, 2, pp. 103–21. (Republished in Max Gluckman *Order and Rebellion in Tribal Africa*. London: Cohen and West, 1963, pp. 207–34.)

1960. 'Tribalism in Modern British Central Africa', *Cahiers d'Etudes Africaines*, 1, pp. 55–70. (Republished in P. Van den Berghe (ed.) *Africa: Social Problems of Change and Conflict*. San Francisco: Chandler, 1971.)

1961. 'Anthropological Problems Arising from the African Industrial Revolution' in Southall (ed.) *Social Change in Modern Africa*. Oxford University Press for International African Institute.

Goffman, I.

1970. *Strategic Interaction*. Oxford: Blackwell.

Gorju, J.

1920. *Entre le Victoria, l'Albert et l'Edouard*, Rennes: Oberthür.

Gould, W. T. S.

1970. 'Geography and Educational Support in Tropical Africa', *Tijdschrift voor economische en sociale geografie*, 62, pp. 82–9.

Gower, R. H.

1952. 'Swahili Borrowings from English', *Africa*, XXII, 2, pp. 154–6.

Graves, Theodore G.

1966. 'Alternative Models for the Study of Urban Migrations', *Human Organisation*, XXV, 4, pp. 295–9.

Greenberg, Joseph H.

1962. 'The Study of Languages in Contact' in *Symposium on Multilingualism*. Brazzaville: CSA/CCTA, pp. 167–75.

M

344 *Cumulative Bibliography*

Grillo, R. D.
1969. 'Anthropology, Industrial Development and Labour Migration in Uganda' in D. Brokensha and M. Pearsall (eds.) *The Anthropology of Development in Sub-Saharan Africa*. Kentucky University Press. Monograph No. 10. The Society for Applied Anthropology.
1973. *African Railwaymen*, Cambridge University Press.
1974. *Race, Class and Militancy*, New York and London: Chandler.
Grohs, G.
1972. 'Slum Clearance in Dar es Salaam' in J. Hutton (ed.) q.v.
Gugler, J.
1968. 'The Impact of Labour Migration on Society and Economy in Sub-Saharan Africa: Empirical Findings and Theoretical Considerations', *African Social Research*, VI, pp. 463–86.
1972. 'Urbanization in East Africa' in J. Hutton (ed.) q.v.
Gulliver, P. H.
1955. *Labour Migration in a Rural Economy. A Study of the Ngoni and Ndendeuli of Southern Tanganyika*. East African Studies No. 6, Kampala.
1960. 'Incentives in Labour Migration', *Human Organization*, 19, pp. 159–63.
Gutkind, Peter C. W.
1961. 'Urban Conditions in Africa', *Town Planning Review*, 32, pp. 20–32.
1962. 'African Urban Family Life', *Cahiers d'Etudes Africaines*, 3, pp. 149–217.
1963. *The Royal Capital of Buganda*. Mouton: The Hague.
1967. 'The Energy of Despair: Social organization of the unemployed in two African cities, Lagos and Nairobi', *Civilisations* XVII, Nos. 3 and 4.
1968. 'Urbanization and Unemployment' *Manpower and Unemployment Research in Africa* I, 1.
1969. 'The Small Town in African Urban Studies', *African Urban Notes* Vol. 3, No. 1, 5–10.
Halpenny, Philip
1972. 'Getting Rich by being "Unemployable": Some Political Implications of "Informal" Economic Activities in Urban Areas not usually represented in Official Indices'. East African Universities Social Sciences Council Conference (mimeo.).
Harries Jones, P.
1965. 'The Tribes in Towns' in W. V. Brelsford (ed.) *The Tribes of Zambia*. Lusaka: Government Printer.
Hart, J. F.
1960. 'The Changing Distribution of the American Negro'. *Annals, Association of American Geographers*, L, pp. 242–66.
Hauser, P. M. and Schnore, Leo F.
1965. *The Study of Urbanization*. New York: John Wiley and Sons.

Cumulative Bibliography

Heisel, H.
1974. *Urbanisation and the Government of Migration: the Inter-Relation of Urban and Rural Life in Zambia.* London: Hurst.

Hekken, P. M. van and Thoden van Velzen, H. U. E.
1972. *Land Scarcity and Rural Inequality in Tanzania.* The Hague: Mouton.

Hirst, M. A.
1971. *A Migration Survey in Bukoba Town, Tanzania.* Occasional Paper No. 44, Department of Geography, Makerere University College.

Holleman, J. F.
1969. *Chief, Council and Commissioner: Some Problems of Government in Rhodesia.* Assen: Royal Van Gorem for Afrika Studiecentrum.

Hoover, Sandra
1972. *Aspects of Village Structure and Mobility in Toro.* Sociology Working Paper No. 130, Department of Sociology, Makerere University (mimeo.).

Hutton, Caroline
1966. 'Aspects of Unemployment in Uganda'. EAISR Conference paper, Kampala.
1968. Unemployment and Labour Migration in Uganda. Kampala: University of East Africa, Ph.D. dissertation.
1973. *Reluctant Farmers: A study of unemployment and planned rural development in Uganda.* Nairobi: East African Publishing House. East African Studies No. 33. For Makerere Institute of Social Research.

Hutton, J.
1972. *The Urban Challenge in East Africa.* Nairobi: East African Publishing House.

Hyden, G.
1969. *Political Development in Rural Tanzania.* Nairobi: East African Publishing House.

International Labour Office.
1972. *Employment, Incomes and Equality: a strategy for increasing productive employment in Kenya.* Geneva.

Jackson, J. A. (ed.)
1969. 'Migration', *Sociological Studies 2.* Cambridge University Press.

Jacobson, D.
1973. *Itinerant Townsmen: Friendship and Social Order in Urban Uganda.* California: Cummings.

Jahoda, G.
1966. 'Social Aspirations, Magic and Witchcraft in Ghana: A Psychological Interpretation', in Lloyd, P. C. (ed.) *The New Elites of Tropical Africa*, London: Oxford University Press for International African Institute.

M*

346 *Cumulative Bibliography*

1969. *The Psychology of Superstition*, London: Allen Lane, The Penguin Press.

1970. 'Supernatural Beliefs and Changing Cognitive Structures among Ghanaian University Students', *Journal of Cross-Cultural Psychology*, 1, 2, 115–130.

Johnston, R. J.

1971. *Urban Residential Patterns.* London: Bell.

Johnston, R. W. M.

1964. *Notes on Rural African Population Statistics S. Rhodesia.* Technical Paper in Agricultural Economics No. 3, Department of Economics, University College of Rhodesia and Nyasaland.

1964a. 'Introduction', *Rhodes-Livingstone Journal*, 36, pp. 1–6.

1964b. 'An Economic Survey of Chiweshe Reserve', *Rhodes-Livingstone Journal*, 36, pp. 82–108.

1964c. *The Labour Economy of the Reserve.* Occasional Paper No. 4, Department of Economics, University College of Rhodesia and Nyasaland.

Jolly, R. (ed.)

1969. *Education in Africa: research and action.* Nairobi: East African Publishing House.

1969. *Planning Education for African Development.* Nairobi: East African Publishing House for Makerere Institute of Social Research. East African Studies No. 25.

Jordan, J. D.

1965. 'Kimutu Reserve: A Land Use Appreciation', *Rhodes-Livingstone Journal*, 36, pp. 59–81.

Kabwegyere, Tarsis B.

1972. 'Family Life and Economic Change in Uganda' in M. B. Sussman and B. L. Cogswell (eds.) *Cross-National Family Research.* Leiden: Brill, pp. 147–59.

Kagwa, A.

1901. *Ekitabo Kya Basekabaka be Buganda*, Kampala; Reprinted 1927 and 1971: Nairobi: East African Publishing House, and Uganda Bookshop.

1905. *Ekitabo Kye Mpisa za Baganda*, London and Kampala: Uganda Bookshop. Reprinted 1934 and 1952; London: Macmillan and Co. Ltd.

1908. *Ekitabo Kye Bika Bya Baganda*, Kampala: Uganda Bookshop, reprinted 1949.

Kamwengo, M. M.

1971. 'A Preliminary Analysis of the Life, Background and Settlement of Limulunga Squatter Township, Mongu' in *A Nation-Wide Study of Life in Squatter Townships: Preliminary Reports.* Research Project No. 17, University of Zambia Sociological Association (roneo.).

Kapferer, B.

1969. 'Norms and the Manipulation of Relationships in a Work

Cumulative Bibliography

Context', in J. C. Mitchell (ed.) 1969b *q.v.*

1972. *Strategy and Transactions in an African Factory*. Manchester University Press.

Kashoki, Mubanga E.
1972. 'Town Bemba: A Sketch of its Main Characteristics', *African Social Research*, No. 13, June, pp. 161–86.

Keesing, Roger M.
1967. 'Statistical Models and Decision Models of Social Structure: a Kwaio Case', *Ethnology*, 6, pp. 1–15.

Kerr, Madeline
1958. *The People of Ship Street*. London: Routledge & Kegan Paul.

King, N. Q.
1970. *Religions of Africa*. New York, Evanston, London: Harper & Row.

Kuper, Leo
1965. *An African Bourgeoisie: Race, Class and Politics in South Africa*. New Haven: Yale.

La Fontaine, J. S.
1970. *City Politics: A Study of Léopoldville*. Cambridge University Press.

Lamb, G.
1974. *Peasant Politics*. Lewes, Sussex: Julian Freedman.

Lang, B.
1974. Migrants, Commuters and Townsmen: Aspects of Urbanization in a Small Town in Kenya. Ph.D. Thesis, University of Edinburgh.

Langlands, B. W.
1972. 'Demographic Statistics—Uganda Needs' in S. E. Ominde and G. N. Ejiogu (eds.) *Population Growth and Economic Development in Africa*. London: Heineman, pp. 351–8.

Larimore, Ann Evans
1958. *The Alien Town: Patterns of Settlement in Busoga, Uganda: An Essay in Cultural Geography*. Research Paper No. 55, Department of Geography, University of Chicago.

Leach, E. R.
1960. 'The Sinhalese of the Dry Zone of N. Ceylon' in G. P. Murdock (ed.) *Social Structures in Southeast Asia*. Viking Fund Publications in Anthropology, 29.
1961. *Pul Eliya, a Village in Ceylon*. Cambridge University Press.

Lenski, Gerhard
1966. *Power and Privilege*. New York: McGraw Hill.

Leslie, J. A. K.
1963. *A Survey of Dar es Salaam*. London: Oxford University Press.

Levi-Strauss, C.
1963. *Structural Anthropology*. New York: Basic Books Inc.

Lewin, L.
1951. *Field Theory in Social Science*. New York: Harper and Row.

348 *Cumulative Bibliography*

Leys, C.
1971. 'Politics in Kenya: the development of peasant society'. *British Journal of Political Science* I, pp. 307–37.

Little, K.
1965. *West African Urbanisation*. Cambridge University Press.
1973. *African Women in Towns*. Cambridge University Press.

Long, Norton E.
1966. 'The Local Community as an Ecology of Games' in Lewis A. Coser (ed.) *Political Sociology*. New York: Harper and Row.

Longmore, L.
1959. *The Dispossessed: A Study of the Sex-Life of Bantu Women in Urban Areas in and around Johannesburg*. London: Cape.

Lugira, A. M.
1970. *Ganda Art*. Kampala: Osasa Publication.

Lundgren, Thomas, Schlyter, Ann, Schlyter, Thomas
1969. *Zambia: Kapwepwe Compound: A Study of an Unauthorised Settlement*. University of London (roneo.).
1971: Urbanisation Problems in Africa: Paper presented at Conference on Urbanisation and Development in Developing Countries. Israel.

Mabogunje, Akin L.
1972. *Regional Mobility and Resource Development in West Africa*. Montreal: McGill University, Centre for Developing Studies.

Maclean, Una
1965. 'Traditional Medicine and its Practitioners in Ibadan', *Journal of Tropical Medicine*, 68, 237–44.
1966. 'Hospitals or Healers? An Attitude Survey in Ibadan', *Human Organization*, 25.
1969. 'Traditional Healers and Their Female Clients: An Aspect of Nigerian Sickness Behaviour', *Journal of Health and Social Behaviour*, 10, 3, 172–186.
1971. *Magical Medicine: A Nigerian Case Study*. Allen Lane, The Penguin Press.

Mair, Lucy
1934. *An African People in the Twentieth Century*. London: Routledge & Kegan Paul.
1940. *Native Marriage in Buganda*. London: Oxford University Press. (Memorandum No. 19, International Institute of African Language and Cultures.)
1969. *African Marriage and Social Change*. London: Cass.

Malawi
1966. *Malawi Population Census 1966*. Zomba: Government Printer.
1968. *The 1968 Household and Expenditure Survey*. Zomba Government Printer.

Mangin, William
1967. 'Squatter Settlements', *Scientific American*, CCXVII, 4.

Cumulative Bibliography

349

Marris, P.
1961. *Family and Social Change in an African City*. London: Routledge & Kegan Paul.
Mayer, Philip
1961. *Townsmen or Tribesmen*. Cape Town: Oxford University Press.
Meebelo, Henry S.
1971. *Reaction to Colonialism*. Manchester University Press for the Institute of African Studies, University of Zambia.
Meillassoux, C. (ed.)
1971. *The Development of Indigenous Trade and Markets in West Africa*. Oxford University Press for International African Institute.
Middleton, J.
1966. *The Effects of Economic Development on Traditional Political Systems in Africa South of the Sahara*. The Hague: Mouton.
1969. 'Labour Migration and Associations in Africa: Two Case Studies', *Civilisations*, XVIII, pp. 42–9.
1970 (ed.). *Black Africa*. Toronto: Macmillan.
Ministry of Local Government and Housing
1972. 'Housing Policy under the Second National Development Plan', circular LGH/54/7/3 of 20th July, 1972, Lusaka.
Miracle, M. P. and Berry, S. S.
1970. 'Migrant Labour and Economic Development', *Oxford Economic Papers*, XXII, 1, pp. 86–108.
Mitchell, Hilary Flegg
1967. 'Sociological Aspects of Cancer Rate Surveys in Africa', *National Cancer Institute Monographs* No. 25, Bethesda: Maryland National Institutes of Health.
Mitchell, J. C.
1942. 'The Distribution of African Labour by Area of Origin on the Copper Mines of Northern Rhodesia'. *Rhodes-Livingstone Journal*, 14, 30–36.
1956a. *The Kalela Dance*.
Manchester University Press for the Rhodes-Livingstone Institute. (Rhodes-Livingstone Institute Papers No. 37).
1956b. 'Urbanisation, Detribalisation and Stabilisation in Southern Africa: A Problem of Definition of Measurement' in D. Forde (ed.) *Social Implications of Industrialisation and Urbanisation in Africa South of the Sahara*. UNESCO, Tensions and Technology Series, pp. 693–711.
1958. 'Factors Motivating Migration from Rural Areas' in *Present Interrelations in Central African Rural and Urban Life*. Lusaka: Rhodes-Livingstone Institute.
1959. 'Labour Migration in Africa South of the Sahara: The Causes of Labour Migration', *Bulletin of the Inter-African Labour Institute*, VI, 1, pp. 12–46. (Reprinted in Middleton, 1970).
1961. 'Wage Labour and African Population Movements in Central Africa' in K. M. Barbour and R. M. Prothero (eds.) *Essays on African*

350 *Cumulative Bibliography*

1965. 'The Meaning in Misfortune for Urban Africans' in M. Fortes and G. Dieterlen (eds.) *African Systems of Thought.* Oxford University Press for International African Institute.
Population. London: Routledge & Kegan-Paul, pp. 193–248.
1966. 'Theoretical Orientations in African Urban Studies' in Banton, M. (ed.) The Social Anthropology of Complex Societies. ASA Monographs No. 4 London: Tavistock.
1969a. 'Structure Plurality, Urbanisation and Labour Circulation in Southern Rhodesia' in J. A. Jackson (ed.) 'Migration', *Sociological Studies 2.* Cambridge University Press.
1969b. 'Introduction' to his edition *Social Networks in Urban Situations.* Manchester University Press, for Institute for African Studies, University of Zambia.
Moore, S. F.
(forthcoming). 'Political Meetings and the Simulation of Unanimity: Kilimanjaro' (Chagga, Tanzania).
Moris, J.
undated *c.* 1969. 'The evaluation of settlement schemes performance: a sociological appraisal', in R. Apthorpe (ed.) q.v.
undated *c.* 1969. 'The impact of secondary education upon student attitudes towards agriculture: some preliminary considerations' in P. Rigby (ed.) q.v.
Muthiora, J.
1968. The human element in city, town and village planning'. Paper presented at University Social Science Conference on 'The Urban Challenge in Africa'. Makerere.
Mwanakatwe, J. M.
1968. *The Growth of Education in Zambia since Independence.* Lusaka: Oxford University Press, pp. 8–35.
Neft, D. S.
1966. *Statistical Analysis of Areal Distributions.* Philadelphia: Regional Science Research Institute.
Nichols, Ralph W.
1968. 'Rules, Resources and Political Activity' in Marc J. Swartz (ed.) *Local Level Politics.* Chicago: Aldine, pp. 295–321.
Nsimbi, M.
1956. *Amannya Amaganda N'emnono zaago,* Kampala: East African Literature Bureau.
Obbo, Christine
1972. 'The Myth of Female Submission: Economic Activities of Luo Women in Namuwongo-Wabigalo, Kampala.' East African Universities Social Sciences Council Conference (mimeo.).
1973. Women in a Low Income Situation—Namuwongo—Wabigalo, Kampala. Makerere University, M.A. thesis.
O.E.C.D.
1967. *Emigrant Workers Returning to their Home Country.* Final Report and Supplement. Paris: O.E.C.D.

Cumulative Bibliography

Ohadike, Patrick O.

1969a. *The Development of and Factors in the Development of African Migrants in the Copper Mines of Zambia 1940–66.* Zambian Papers No. 4. Manchester University Press for the Institute of Social Research, University of Zambia.

1969b. *Some Demographic Measurements for Africans in Zambia.* Lusaka: Communication No. 5, ISR, University of Zambia.

1972. 'Urbanization, Migration and Migrants in Zambia: A Survey of Patterns, Variation and Change in Lusaka.'

Okada, F. E.

1967. 'Ground Floor to Development: A Survey of Nguluwe Compound'. The Research Unit, Department of Community Development, Ministry of Co-operative Youth and Social Development, Lusaka (roneo.).

1968. 'Notes on Drinking Patterns in a Municipal Housing Area'. The Department of Community Development, Ministry of Co-operatives, Youth and Social Development (roneo.).

Okumu, J. J.

1969. 'The By-election in Gem: an Assessment', *East Africa Journal,* June.

Orley, J.

1972. *Culture and Mental Illness,* Nairobi: East African Publishing House for Makerere Institure for Social Research.

Pain, D. R.

1975. Incorporation, Participation and Division in Northern Uganda. Ph.D. Thesis. University of Cambridge.

Pandawa, Abel

1971. Life in a Squatter Community: An Analysis of the Life, Background and Resettlement of the Residents of Chibili Township. Project No. 8, University of Zambia Sociological Association (roneo.).

Parkin, David J.

1966. 'Voluntary Associations as Institutions of Adaptation: *Man* (n.s.) 1: 1.

1969a. *Neighbours and Nationals in an African City Ward.* London: Routledge & Kegan Paul.

1969b. 'Tribe as Fact and Fiction in an East African City' in P. H. Gulliver, *Tradition and Transition in East Africa: Studies of the Tribal Element in the Modern Era.* London: Routledge & Kegan Paul, pp. 273–96.

1971. 'Language Choice in Two Kampala Housing Estates', in W. H. Whiteley (ed.) q.v.

1972. *Palms, Wine and Witnesses.* San Francisco and London: Chandler.

1974. Chapters 5–8 on language use in Nairobi, in W. H. Whiteley (ed.) q.v.

1974. 'Congregational and Interpersonal Ideologies in Political

352 *Cumulative Bibliography*

Ethnicity' in A. Cohen (ed.) *Urban Ethnicity.* A.S.A. Monograph No. 12. London: Tavistock.

Parsons, F. W.
1962. 'Some Observations on the Contact between Hausa and English' in *Symposium on Multilingualism.* Brazzaville: CSA/CCTA, pp. 197–203.

Parrinder, G.
1953. *Religion in an African City.* Oxford University Press

p'Bitek, Okot
1973. *Africa's Cultural Revolution.* Nairobi: Macmillan Books for Africa.

Perlman, M. L.
1963. Toro Marriage: A Study of Changing Conjugal Institutions. Oxford University D.Phil. thesis.

Phillips, J.
1962. *Report of the Agro-Ecological Survey of Southern Rhodesia.* Salisbury: Government Printer.

Pirenne, Henri
1956. *Medieval City.* New York: Doubleday and Company Inc.

Plowman Report, 1956
Report of the Urban African Affairs Commission. Salisbury: Government Printer.

Polomé, E. G.
1971. 'Multilingualism in an African urban centre: the Lubumbashi case', in W. H. Whiteley (ed.) *q.v.*

Pons, Valdo
1969. *Stanleyville: An African Urban Community under Belgian Administration.* London: Oxford University Press for the International African Institute.

Powesland, P. G.
1954. 'History of Migration in Uganda' in A. I. Richards (ed.) *Economic Development and Social Change.* Cambridge: Heffer for East African Institute of Social Research.

Prothero, R. M.
1957. Migratory Labour from North-Western Nigeria. *Africa,* XXXVII, 251–61.

Rado, E., and Wells, J.
1972. 'The Building Industry in Kenya', in J. Hutton (ed.) q.v.

Ravenstein, E. G.
1885. Discussion of E. G. Ravenstein, 'The Laws of Migration', *Journal of the (Royal) Statistical Society,* 48, pp. 228–35.

Rechenbach, Charles W.
1968. *Swahili-English Dictionary.* Washington D.C.: The Catholic University of America Press Inc.

Richards, A. I.
1952. Report on Fertility Surveys in Buganda and Buhaya. East African Institute of Social Research (mimeo.).

Cumulative Bibliography 353

(ed.) 1954. *Economic Development and Tribal Change: A Study of Immigrant Labour in Buganda.* Cambridge: Heffer for East African Institute of Social Research.

1955. 'Ganda Clan Structure', *E.A.I.S.R. Conference Proceedings,* Kampala: East African Institute for Social Research.

Richards, A. I. and Reining, Priscilla
1966. *The Changing Structure of a Ganda Village.* East African Studies 24, East African Institute of Social Research.

Richards, A. I., Sturrock, F. and Fortt, J. M.
1973. *Subsistence to Commercial Farming in Present Day Buganda.* Cambridge University Press.

Richardson, Irvine
1961. 'Some Observations on the Status of Town Bemba in Northern Rhodesia', *African Language Studies,* Vol. 2.
1963. 'Examples of Deviation and Innovation in Bemba', *African Language Studies, IV,* pp. 128–45.

Richmond, A. H.
1967. *Post-Immigrants in Canada.* Toronto University Press.

Rigby, P.
undated *c.* 1969. 'Pastoralism and Prejudice: ideology and rural development in East Africa', in P. Rigby (ed.) q.v.

Rigby, P. (*ed.*)
undated *c.* 1969. *Society and Social Change in East Africa,* Nkanga No. 4. Kampala: Makerere Institute of Social Research.
1972. 'The Relevance of the Traditional in Social Change', *The African Review,* II, 2, pp. 309–21.

Rigby, Peter and Fred Lule
1973. 'Divination and Healing in Peri-Urban Kampala', in F. J. Bennett (ed.) *Medicine and the Social Sciences in East and West Africa,* Nkanga Ed. No. 7, Kampala: Makerere Institute for Social Research.

Roberts, A.
1973. *A History of the Bemba.* London: Longmans.

Robinson, W. S.
1950. 'Ecological Correlations and the Behaviour of Individuals', *American Sociological Review,* XV, pp. 351–7.

Ross, A. M.
1969. *Migrants in Europe: Problems of Acceptance and Adjustment.* Minneapolis.

Ross, M.
1968. Politics and Urbanization: Two Communities in Nairobi. Northwestern University, Ph.D. dissertation.
1973. *The Political Integration of Urban Squatters.* Evanston: Northwestern University Press.

Safier, M.
1972. 'Urban Problems, planning possibilities and housing policies', in J. Hutton (ed.) q.v.

354 *Cumulative Bibliography*

Salisbury: Final (1962) Census Report
1964. *Final Report of the April/May 1962 Census of Africans in Southern Rhodesia.* Salisbury: Government Printer.
Salisbury: Interim (1969) Census Report
1971. *1969 Population Census. Interim Report. Volume II.* Salisbury: Central Statistical Office.
Saul, John S.
1972. 'Class and Penetration in Tanzania' in Lionel Cliffe and John Saul (eds.) *Socialism in Tanzania*, Vol. I. Nairobi: East African Publishing House.
Savage, Felicity M. A.
1972. 'The effect of town life on child health: A study from Matero and Mwaziona, Lusaka'. Paper delivered at the Institute for African Studies, University of Zambia.
Schelling, T. C.
1963. *The Strategy of Conflict.* New York: Oxford University Press.
Schumacher, E. F.
1974 *Small is Beautiful. London*: Abacus.
Scott, P.
1954. 'Migrant Labour in Southern Rhodesia', *Geographical Review*, XLIV, pp. 29–48.
Scotton, C.
1972. *Choosing a Lingua Franca in an African Capital.* Edmonton, Canada: Linguistic Research Inc.
Scudder, T.
1962. *The Ecology of the Gwembe Tonga.* Manchester University Press.
1969. 'Relocation, Agricultural Intensification and Anthropological Research' in D. Brokensha and M. Pearsall (eds.) *The Anthropology of Development in Sub-Saharan Africa.* Kentucky University Press. Monograph No. 10, The Society for Applied Anthropology.
Scudder, T. and Colson, Elizabeth
1971. 'The Kariba Dam Project: Resettlement and Local Initiative' in R. Bernard and P. Pelto (eds.) *Technical Innovation and Cultural Change.* New York: Macmillan.
Serjeantson, Mary S.
1935. *A History of Foreign Words in English.* London: Routledge & Kegan Paul.
Sheffield, J. R. (ed.)
1967. *Education, Employment and Rural Development.* Nairobi: East African Publishing House.
Shorter, A.
1974. *East African Societies.* London: Routledge & Kegan Paul.
Simmons, J. W.
1968. 'Changing Residence in the City: a Review of Intraurban Mobility', *Geographical Review*, Vol. 58, pp. 622–51.

Cumulative Bibliography

Skinner, Elliott
1974. *African Urban Life: The Transformation of Ouagadougou.*
Sofer, Cyril and Rhona
1955. *Jinja Transformed: a Study of a Multi-Racial Township.*
East African Studies 4, East African Institute of Social Research.
Southall, A. W.
1954. 'Alur Migrants' in A. I. Richards (ed.) *Economic Development and Tribal Change.*
1961a (ed.) *Social Change in Modern Africa.* London: Oxford University Press for the International African Institute.
1961b. 'Kinship, Friendship, and the Network of Relations in Kisenyi, Kampala' in A. W. Southall (ed.) *Social Change in Modern Africa*, pp. 217–29.
1961c. 'Population Movement in East Africa' in Barbour and Prothero (ed.) *Essays on African Population.* Routledge & Kegan Paul.
1966. 'The Growth of Urban Society in East Africa' in S. Diamond and F. G. Burke (eds.) *The Transformation of East Africa.* New York: Basic Books, pp. 463–93.
1970. 'The Illusion of Tribe', *Journal of Asian and African Studies*, V, 1–2, pp. 28–50.
1974. 'State Formation in Africa' in *Annual Review of Anthropology* B. J. Siegel (ed.) Annual Reviews Inc. Palo Alto.
1975a. 'National Integration in Uganda' in K. Bentsi-Enchill and D. R. Smock (eds.) *National Integration in Africa.*
1975b. 'From Segmentary Lineage to Ethnic Association—Luo, Luyia and Others' in Maxwell Owusu (ed.) *Essays in Honor of Lucy Mair.* Evanston: Northwestern University Press.
1975c. 'General Amin and The Coup: Great Man or Historical Inevitability?' Journal of Modern African Studies, XIII, I, pp. 85–105.
Southall, A. W.
and P. C. Gutkind. 1957. *Townsmen in the Making: Kampala and Its Suburbs.* East African Studies 9, East African Institute of Social Research.
Southern Rhodesian Government
1962. *Report of the Secretary for Native Affairs and Chief Native Commissioner for the Year 1961.* Salisbury: Government Printer.
Southwold, Martin
1959. Community and State in Buganda. Cambridge University Ph.D.
Spencer, P.
1974. 'Drought and the Commitment to Growth.' *African Affairs*, LXXII, 293.
Ssekamwa, J. C.
1967. 'Witchcraft in Buganda Today.' *Transition*, 30, 31–39.
Stahl, K. M.
1969. 'The Chagga' in P. H. Gulliver (ed.) *Tradition and Transition in East Africa.* London: Routledge & Kegan Paul.

356 *Cumulative Bibliography*

Stren, R.
1972. 'A survey of lower income areas in Mombasa' in J. Hutton (ed.) q.v.

Swartz, Marc J. (ed.)
1968. *Local-Level Politics*. Chicago: Aldine.

Taylor, John
1958. *The Growth of the Church in Buganda: An Attempt at Understanding*. London: S.C.M.

Thistlethwaite, F.
1960. 'Migration from Europe Overseas in the 19th and 20th Centuries', *Rapports du XIe Congrès International des Sciences Historiques*, Stockholm, pp. 34–57.

Timothy, Kristen
1968. Grass-Root Communication: The Evolution of Information Channels in Kigesi, Uganda. University of East Africa, M. A. thesis.

Todaro, M. P.
1969. 'A Model of Labor Migration and Urban Unemployment in Less Developed Countries', *American Economic Review*, 59, pp. 138–48.

Todaro, M. P. and Harris, J. R.
1968. 'Urban Unemployment in East Africa: An Economic Analysis of Policy Alternatives', *East African Economic Review*, December.

Turnbull, C. M.
1962. *The Lonely African*. New York: Simon and Schuster.

Turner, V. W.
1968a. 'Mukanda: The Politics of a Non-Political Ritual' in M. J. Swartz (ed.) *Local-Level Politics*. Chicago: Aldine.
1968b. *The Drums of Affliction*. Oxford University Press for the International African Institute.

Uchendu, V. C.
1968. 'Socio-Economic and Cultural Determinants of Rural Change in East and West Africa', *Food Research Institute Studies*, VIII, 3, pp. 225–42.
1966. 'Anthropology and Agricultural Development in Sub-Saharan Africa' in D. Brokensha and M. Pearsall (eds.) *The Anthropology of Development in Sub-Saharan Africa*, pp. 5–13.
1970. 'The Impact of Changing Agricultural Technology in African Land Tenure', *The Journal of Developing Areas*, IV, 4, pp. 477–86.

Uganda Argus.
21 August 1972. '*All* Asians must go.'
23 August 1972. 'These Asians can stay.'
13 November 1972. 'Asians to work in fields.'

Uganda Protectorate
1957. Introduction to 'The Ankole Landlord and Tenant Law, 1937' in *Land Tenure in Uganda*. Entebbe: Government Printer, pp. 27–30.
1958. Legal Notice 65/1958, The Census Uganda Order, 1958.

Cumulative Bibliography

Uganda Republic
1966. *Work for Progress: Uganda's Second Five-Year Plan.* Entebbe: Government Printer.
1969. Public Lands Act, 1969. (13/1969).
1969. Trade (Licensing) Act, 1969 (14/1969).
1971. *Report on the 1969 Population Census: Volume I. The Population of Administrative Areas.* The Statistics Division, Ministry of Planning and Economic Development, Entebbe: Government Printer.
1972. *Third Five-Year Development Plan 1971/2–1975/6.*

United Nations
1965. *Demographic Dictionary*
1965b. Social Aspects of Housing and Urban Development. (E/CN. 5/392).
1970. *Methods of Measuring Internal Migration.* Manual VI, Population Studies, No. 47, ST/50A/Ser. A/47. New York.

Valkonen, Tapani
1969. 'Individual and Structural Effects in Ecological Research' in Dogan, Mattei and Rokkan, Stein (eds.) *Quantitative Ecological Analysis in the Social Sciences.* Cambridge, Mass.: The M.I.T. Press, pp. 53–68.

van Velsen, J.
1960. 'Labour Migration as a Positive Factor in the Continuity of Tonga Tribal Society', *Economic Development and Cultural Change,* 8, pp. 265–78.
1963. 'Some Methodological Problems in the Study of Labour Migration' in *Urbanization in African Social Change.* Edinburgh: Centre of African Studies, pp. 34–42.

van Velzen, H. U. E. Thoden.
1971. *'Staff, Kulaks and Peasants: A Study of a Political Field.* Mededelingen van het Afrika-Studiecentrum, No. 3, Leiden.

Vincent, J.
1971. *African Élite: The Big Men of a Small Town.* New York: Columbia University Press.

Voice of Uganda
5 January 1973. 'They must be recruited here.'

von Neuman, J. and Morgenstern, O.
1947. *The Theory of Games and Economic Behaviour.* New Jersey:

Wanji, Barri A.
1971. A Preliminary Postgraduate Research Paper on the Nubi in East Africa. Working Paper 115, Department of Sociology, Makerere University, Kampala.

Watson, W.
1958. *Tribal Cohesion in a Money Economy.* Manchester University Press.

Weeks, S. G.
1967. 'Are Hostels Necessary? A Study of Senior Secondary Pupils in Greater Kampala', *Journal of Developing Areas,* I, 3, pp. 357–74.

358 *Cumulative Bibliography*

Weisner, T.
1969. 'One family, Two Households: A Rural-Urban Network Model of Urbanism'. Paper presented at the University of East Africa Social Science Council Conference.

Welbourn, F.
1962. 'Some Aspects of Kiganda Religion', *Uganda Journal*, 26, 2, 171–182.
1965. *Religion and Politics in Uganda: 1952: 1962*. Kampala and Nairobi: East African Publishing House.

Werlin, H. H.
1974. *Governing an African City*. New York & London. Africana Publishing Co.

Wertheim, W. F.
1964. *East-West Parallels*. The Hague: Mouton.

White, C. M. N.
1961. 'Modern Influences upon an African Language Group', *Rhodes-Livingstone Journal*, No. 11, pp. 66–71.

Whiteley, W. H.
1963. 'Loan-words in Kamba: A Preliminary Survey' in *African Language Studies IV*, pp. 128–45.
1967. 'Loanwords in Linguistic Description: A Case Study from Tanzania, East Africa' in L. Rauch and C. T. Scott (eds.) *Approaches in Linguistic Methodology*. Madison: The University of Wisconsin Press.
1969. *Swahili: The Rise of a National Language*. Methuen, London.
(ed.) 1971. *Language Use and Social Change*. OUP for IAI.
(ed.) 1974. *Language in Kenya*. OUP. London and Nairobi.

Wilson, Monica and Mafeje, Archie
1963. *Langa: A Study of Social Groups in an African Township*. Cape Town: Oxford University Press.

Young, C. E.
1971. 'Rural-Urban Terms of Trade', *African Social Research*, No. 12 (December) pp. 91–4.

Yudelman, M.
1964. *Africans on the Land*. London: Oxford University Press.

Zelten, and Witalo, Jackson, P.
1967. 'A Socio-Economic Survey of Kalingalinga', The Research Unit, Department of Community Development, Ministry of Co-operatives, Youth and Social Development, Lusaka (roneo).

Zachariah, K. C.
1962. 'A Note on the Census Survival Ratio Method of Estimating Net Migration.' *Journal of the American Statistical Association*, 57, pp. 175–83.

INDEX

absenteeism, in Rhodesia, 93–112
Acholi, 266
African National Congress, 34, 304n.
agriculture, 18, 20, 22, 23, 102, 116, 166, 170, 193, 196–7, 204–10; *see also* farming, farms
Aliangulu (Sanye), 20
Alur, 160
Amhara, 268
Amin, President, 5
Amin, Samir, 4, 6–7, 9, 10, 19
Apter, David, 216
Aquina, Sister Mary, 115, 119
Arabs, 232–7, 249; *see also* ASIM
Ashanti, 268
Asians, 151, 255, 260, 261; *see also* ASIM
ASIM (Arabs, Somalis, Indians and Mixed ethnic group), 276–87
associations, 148, 273, 289

Babua, 267
Bailey, F. G., 182–3
Banton, M., 213, 214, 281
Barber, W. J., 116
Barth, Frederik, 265n.
Batanyisako, M. N., 162
Bemba, 10, 29, 30, 36, 229–49
Berry, B. J. L., 329
Bisa, 233n.
Blantyre, 16, 33, 41; ecology of social groups in, 308–18
Blau, P., 119
Brandel-Syrier, Mia 269
Brett, E., 7, 18
bridewealth, 11, 14, 15, 122, 162
Bujra, J., 39
Bukuba, 18

Caldwell, J. C., 319
cattle, 11, 170, 193
census data, 126, 128, 129, 300, 301, 321–36

Cewa, 27, 28, 315
Chagga, 20, 22, 36
children, 132, 133, 198, 204, 250–62, 314, 316
Chilivumbo, A. B., 4, 41, 308–18
Chipata Reports, 294n.
Christianity, 28, 31, 215, 216, 224, 225, 270, 315
civil servants, 20
coffee, 18, 20, 160, 167, 168, 193
Cohen, A., 13
Colson, Elizabeth, 273n.
Colson, Elizabeth and Scudder, T., 23, 190–210
Constandse, A. K. and Hofstee, E. W., 161, 162
controllers, in rural Tanzania, 178–89
cotton, 18, 160, 209, 210
crops, 160, 167, 168, 170, 171, 199, 206, 210

Dak, O., 278
dancing, 314
Dar-es-Salaam, 16, 29, 32, 33, 36, 267
diet, 207
diviners, 214, 212–6
Dodoma, 16
Dorobo, 20
Doxiadis Associates, 129, 130
Dumont, René, 180n.

Easton, David, 179
education, 31–2, 100, 203, 250–63, 311
elites, 20, 21, 178–89, 269, 274, 275, 290
English language, 4, 31, 32, 230, 231, 315
Epstein, A. L., 272, 273
ethnic groups, 147–50, 177; linkage between town and country, 265–75; migration in Kisenyi, Kampala, 276–87

360 *Index*

ethnicity, 10, 32–9, 308–18
Europeans, in Blantyre, 310; farms, 11, 14, 98

farmers, farms, 11, 14, 20, 21, 22, 167, 170, 171, 183, 202–3, 309–10
Federation, Central African, 4, 22
Field, M. J., 214
Firth, Raymond, 266
fishermen, fishing, 197, 203
Forde, Daryll, 167–8
Frank, Andre Gunder, 16, 178
French language, 31

'game' analysis, in Tanzania, 183–5
Ganda, 25, 27, 28, 29, 36, 37, 38, 39, 160, 213–27, 267, 268, 274, 276–87, 330–31
Garbett, G. K., 13–15, 113–25
Geita, 19, 166–72, 176
Ghana, migration in, 319–20
Gogo, 20
Gould, W .T. S., 6, 250–62
Grillo, R. D., 26
Grohs, G., 42
Gugler, J., 274
Gulliver, P. H., 155, 172
Gusii, 170, 171
Gutkind, Peter, 216–17
Gwembe Valley, new economic relationships in, 190–210

Halpenny, Philip, 38, 39, 276–87
Hill, K., 319n.
Hirst, M. A., 33, 36, 163, 319–36
home visits, 163
hospitals, 203, 208
houses, housing, 33, 41–4, 117, 132, 148, 151–2, 198, 203–4, 207–8, 298–299, 309–11, 314
households, 129, 149

Ibo, 10, 267
illness, 202
Islam, 28, 29, 213, 215, 216, 225, 281, 291, 315

Jahoda, G., 214
Jinja, 16, 160, 254, 255

Kagwa, A., 217–19
Kalenjin, 266
Kamba, 147

Kampala, 16, 25–30, 33, 36, 40, 160, 161; continuity and change in Kiganda religion, 213–27; distribution of migrants in, 319–36; ethnic migration in Kisenyi, 276–87
Kamwengo, M. M., 299n.
Kapferer, B., 117, 120
Karamojong, 20
Kariba Dam Project, 22, 190–210 *passim*
Keesing, R. M., 119
Kenya Emergency, 151, 152
Kiga, 163
Kigezi, 159, 160, 162
Kikuyu, 27, 36, 37, 39, 147, 148, 151, 152, 153, 267–9, 272, 273
King, N. Q., 227
Kinshasa, 26, 30, 214–15
kinship, 33, 119, 121, 122, 162, 202, 273, 312–17 *passim.*
Kisii, 19, 166–72, 175
'kitchen Kaffir', 30, 245
Korekore, 11, 14, 15, 119–23 *passim*
Kru, 267

La Fontaine, Jean, 26, 28, 214–15
Lamb, G., 21
land, 19, 42, 114, 149, 150, 167–71 *passim*, 175, 176, 315; rent, 310; —squatters in Zambia, 294–307; Tribal Trust Lands, 95–7, 100, 107, 115, 116
Land Apportionment Act, 106, 115
language, 24, 29–31, 127, 228–49
Langworthy, Harry, 233n.
Latin, 230, 231, 237
Latin America, 178, 297
Leach, E. R., 119
Lenje, 30
Leslie, J. A. K., 32, 36, 319
Leys, C., 21
Lilongwe, 16
lingua francas, 29–31
Long, Norman, 182
Lugbara, 266
Luo, 10, 26, 27, 37, 38, 39, 147–53, 160, 161, 162, 267, 269n., 272, 277
Lusaka, 15–16, 22, 25, 29, 30, 33–37, 40–43; migration and urbanization in, 129–44; squatters in, 294–307
Luunda, 233n.
Luyia, 10, 36, 37, 266, 267

Index

361

Mabogunje, Akin L., 289
Maclean, Una, 214
Mafeje, Archie, 271n., 272n.
Mair, Lucy, 219
Mambwe, 10
Manners, A., 19
marriage, 163, 208, 271, 281, 282, 292, 313
Masai, 20
Mayer, Philip, 120, 121, 269, 270, 271, 319
Mazabuka study, 166, 273
Mazulu village, 22, 23, 27, 190–210
Mboya, Tom, 265
Meebelo, Henry S., 232, 233, 237
Middleton, John, 37
migration: 'bright lights' theory, 24, 168; circulatory in Rhodesia, 113–25; distribution in Kampala, 319–36; ethnic in Kisenyi, 276–87; Hosts and Migrants, 267, 268, 273, 281, 286–7; internal context and development, 3–9; labour migration, 93–125; language, 228–49; major migrant areas in Africa, 167–8; models of migratory processes, 9–16; 'push-pull' process, 117–19, 161; reasons for migration, 10–11; residential segregation, 322–4; rural development, 16–24, 165–77; in Uganda, 159–64; and unemployment, 145–58; and urbanization, 126–44
missionaries, missions, 30, 31, 194, 236, 237, 238, 241, 254–5 256
Mitchell, J. C., 7–15 passim, 25, 26, 28, 93–112, 115–20 passim, 145–6, 151–5 passim, 272n.
Mossi, 268
Mpashi, Stephen, 247
Mulingwa, Patrick, 277n.
Mushanga, T. M., 16, 159–64
Music, 314
Musulumba village, 23, 190–210
Muwonge, John, 277n.
Mwanakatwe, J. M., 239

Nairobi, 26–30 passim, 33, 34, 36, 39, 267; migrations and settlement in, 145–55
nationalism, 5–6, 315–16
Nguluwe survey, 294–307 passim
Nguni, 271, 272

Nyakyusa, 272
Nyamwezi, 233n.
Nyanja, 29, 30, 36, 138, 233n., 248
Nyerere, President, 181

Obbo, Christine, 8, 39, 40, 269n., 279n., 282, 288–93
Ohadike, Patrick, 5, 15, 16, 29, 40, 41, 126–44, 232
Okumu, J., 55n.
ox plough, 19, 171

Pandawa, Abel, 305
Parkin, David, 1–44, 145–55, 267, 268n., 278
Parrinder, G., 214
p'Bitek, Okot, 269n.
Pirenne, Henri, 308
Polome, E. G., 31
polygyny, 150
Pondo, 272
population figures, 129, 141, 168, 169, 300–303, 321; density, 99, 159, 160, 161, 167, 325–35
Portuguese, 5, 232, 235, 236–7
Prothero, M., 128

railway, 22, 194–5, 190–210 passim
Ranger, T. O., 215n.
Ravenstein, E. G., 276
'Red-School' division of Xhosa, 120, 121, 269–71, 272
Redfield, R., 289
religion, traditional, 25, 27, 28, 29, 202, 213–27
Rhodesia, 11–12, 13; circulatory migration in, 113–25; rural male absenteeism in, 93–112
Richards, Audrey, 219, 269n.
Richards, A. and Reining, P., 282
Rigby, Peter and Lule, Fred, 25, 213–27
Roberts, Andrew, 233n., 235n., 237
Ruanda, 19, 160, 161, 193
Rundi, 160, 266
Rungwe, 20

Sala, 37
Sali, 37
Salisbury, 25, 26, 27, 33, 121
Samburu, 20
Schapera, I., 273

362 *Index*

schools, 199, 200, 250–62
Scudder, T., 176
Senegal, 6–7
Serjeantson, Mary S., 230
sex ratios, 127–8, 134–5, 142
Shangaan, 272
shops, 206, 207, 291
Skinner, Elliott, 268n.
slums, 277, 289
Somali, *see* ASIM
Sotho, 271, 272
Southall, Aidan, 7, 8, 33, 155, 265–75, 277n., 287
Southall, Aidan and Gutkind, Peter, 215, 277n.
Southwold, M., 219, 282
spirit possession, 222–5
squatters, 42, 43; urban in Zambia, 294–307
status, 178–89 *passim*, 312, 313
Stren, R., 33
Sukuma, 19, 169
Swahili, 29, 30, 31, 32; loan words in Bemba, 232–47
syncretism, 214, 215, 226

Tanzania, 4, 5, 16, 19, 20; controllers in rural Tanzania, 178–89
Taylor, John, 282
tea, 170
Temne, 267, 281
Teso, 18, 19, 166–72
Tikili, E., 298
Tiv, 10
Tonga, 22, 27, 29, 37, 119, 190–210
Toro, 286
towns, 176; ethnic linkage between town and country, 265–75; interaction of town and country, 228–49; types of towns, 33–4, 37; women's careers in, 288–93
trade, 203, 279–80
trade unions, 148, 307
tsetse fly, 168–9, 193
Tswana, 271, 272
Tutsi, 266

Uchendu, Victor C., 5, 6, 16–18, 19, 165–77
Uganda, 5, 6, 16, 18, 19; notes on migration in, 159–64; schools and schoolchildren in, 250–62
unemployment, 6, 9, 145–55, 160, 173–5

Vai, 267
van Doorne, H., 305n.
van Velsen, Jaap, 41, 42, 43, 119, 294–307
van Velzen, Thoden H. U. E., 16, 20, 21, 178–89
Venda, 272
villages, 23, 35, 182, 190–210, 270, 282

Watson, W., 10
Weeks, S. G., 258
Weisner, T., 36, 154n.
Welbourn, F. B., 216, 219
welfare organizations, 161, 267–8
Wertheim, W. F., 186
White, C. M. N., 228–9, 230, 231
witchcraft, 10, 25, 26
women, 192, 200, 201, 208, 275, 278, 315; careers, 288–93; as cheap labour, 8; household heads, 282; migration, 285; as prostitutes, 283, 290; status of, 38–41; work of, 40, 163–4, 204–5, 314, 316
Wood, L. J., 319n.

Xhosa, 120, 121, 269–71

Yao, 27, 28
Yoruba, 267, 268, 274

Zambia, 4, 5, 10, 15; migration and urbanization in, 126–44
Zaramo, 29, 267
Zezuru, 123
Ziba, 283
Znaniecki, 95
Zomba, 16
Zulu, 30